ARMSBEARING AND THE CLERGY
IN THE HISTORY AND CANON LAW
OF WESTERN CHRISTIANITY

ARMSBEARING AND THE CLERGY IN THE HISTORY AND CANON LAW OF WESTERN CHRISTIANITY

Lawrence G. Duggan

THE BOYDELL PRESS

First published 2013
The Boydell Press, Woodbridge
Paperback edition 2019

ISBN 978 1 84383 865 4 hardback
ISBN 978 1 78327 400 0 paperback

The Boydell Press is an imprint of Boydell & Brewer Ltd
PO Box 9, Woodbridge, Suffolk IP12 3DF, UK
and of Boydell & Brewer Inc.
668 Mt Hope Avenue, Rochester, NY 14620–2731, USA
website: www.boydellandbrewer.com

The publisher has no responsibility for the continued existence or accuracy
of URLs for external or third-party internet websites referred to in this book,
and does not guarantee that any content on such websites is,
or will remain, accurate or appropriate

A CIP catalogue record for this book is available
from the British Library

This publication is printed on acid-free paper

TABLE OF CONTENTS

DEVON
coniugi, consciae unanimaeque
optimae quidem
d.d.d.

PREFACE AND ACKNOWLEDGEMENTS

Despite the temptation to play on the opening words of Vergil's *Aeneid* ('Arma virumque cano', 'Of arms and a man I sing') in the title of this book (*Arma clerumque cano*), reason prevailed in the end. While this is a book intended primarily for scholars, I also have in mind more general readers whose interests cover a wide spectrum – church history, war and the military, social history, law, European and U.S. history, the Middle Ages and the modern period, the crusading mentality, theories of the just war and the holy war, and the profound connections between religion and violence in the history of the West. I have therefore translated all non-English sources quoted in the text and relegated the original to the notes, except where philological problems require discussion of the meaning of particular words. I have also cited available translations of source material whenever possible. Furthermore, because so much material has never been translated and because the words of the original texts can often convince and impress a reader far more effectively than the words of the most skilled historian, I have quoted from the sources with greater frequency and at greater length than is perhaps common. Even after working on this subject for many years, I am still sometimes startled by the sources I am reading and the views they express. I have therefore chosen to let the sources speak for themselves as often as possible.

One of the wisest of my readers urged me, in fairness to the subject and the reader, to clarify my own attitude at the outset. Originally this book began as a page or two of another work reevaluating the place of the clergy in late medieval and early modern Europe. What started as a brief attempt to understand and explain how the clergy came to be allowed the use of arms has resulted in this book and more. In the course of doing it, I found not only that I had to carry the story down to the present, but also that my own feelings changed the closer it came to the present: from sympathetic concern with reconstructing what happened in the High Middle Ages to incomprehension at the seeming indifference of some major Christian churches in modern times on the subject of the clergy and violence. I acknowledge that this has at times influenced my diction, but I believe the evidence will support my personal view. More than once I have been reminded of a common Roman interpretation of the letters 'SCV' on Vatican license plates. Officially, they stand for 'Stato della Città Vaticana', but the Romans believe otherwise: 'Si Cristo vedesse' or 'If only Christ could see this!'

I have tried to keep in mind the non-academic reader in several other respects also. On any subject likely to be unfamiliar, I have tried to provide some references in English for further reading. For the sake of scholars I have also attempted to cite pertinent works in other languages as well; but in a book of this sort, touching on so many large topics on many of which a vast literature exists, it is impossible to be exhaustive. The second point here is related to the citation of sources, especially legal sources, which I have sought to keep as simple as possible. Instead of writing in the notes, for example, 'lib. VI, tit. XII, cap. vi, par. 4,' I have rendered this as '6.12.6.4,' proceeding from the largest unit down to the smallest, and always adding the page number of the edition used to eliminate any possible confusion. I have also employed the more simple, modern way of citing the texts of canon law, as is explained in the Abbreviations.

It is a great pleasure to acknowledge my enormous debts to the many people who have given me references, suggestions, and help over the course of several decades. Among them are the late Carlrichard Brühl, Daniel Callahan, John Tracy Ellis, Leopold Genicot, Robert M. Grant, Richard Helmholz, John Keegan, the late Stephan Kuttner, John Lynch, James Van Horn Melton, the late John Moorman, Karl Morrison, James Muldoon, Maurice Sheehan, Robert Somerville, and Robert Trisco. Without their generosity this book would have taken much longer to complete and would never have been as rich as it has become. Several deserve special thanks. Giles Constable, the late Joseph Lynch, James Johnson, James Muldoon, and several unknown referees all read and glossed the entire manuscript with great care, while Robert Stacey and the late Gerald Straka saved me from errors on the English church and nation in Chapter 6. Monsignor Agostino Lauro of the Sacred Congregation for the Clergy in Rome graciously undertook a considerable amount of research in response to two inquiries. Bishop Peter James Lee of the Diocese of Virginia kindly had the diocesan records culled in connection with the case of the Reverend General William Nelson Pendleton. I also twice benefitted from the comments of scholars before whom I informally presented parts of this work: first, my colleagues in the History Department at the University of Delaware who attended the department forum at which I spoke in 1984; and the dozen medievalists gathered at the Institute for Advanced Study in Princeton who heard my talk in November 1987 and throughout that year gave freely of their vast knowledge and experience. In his wise and gentle way, Giles Constable made possible and encouraged the wonderful atmosphere among the medievalists at the Institute, and so to him my debt is enormous. Finally, with the help of a grant from the Honors Program at the University of Delaware, David Lloyd, then an undergraduate at the University, plowed through hundreds of volumes of state historical journals in search of warrior clerics of the U.S. Revolutionary and Civil Wars.

I am indebted to certain institutions as well. My first thanks go to my home institution, the University of Delaware, which has provided a nourishing atmosphere in which to study and to teach. I gratefully thank the Faculty of the School of Historical Studies of the Institute for Advanced Study in Princeton, where we spent an unforgettable year in 1987–88. The Harry Frank Guggenheim Foundation helped subsidize that year with a timely and generous grant. The Alexander von Humboldt Stiftung has for over thirty years generously underwritten my research in Europe, some of which appears here. I hope that these benefactors of learning will be pleased with this result of their trust.

The libraries abound to which I am grateful for the magnificent opportunities they offered for conducting the research necessary for this book. Those of Harvard University, The Catholic University of America, Princeton University, Princeton Theological Seminary, the University of Pennsylvania, and the University of Tübingen stand in the forefront, and the Interlibrary Loan offices of the University of Delaware and the Institute for Advanced Study deserve special commendation. Special thanks are also due to the library of the University of Vienna for sending without charge a xeroxed copy of a rare book unobtainable in this country, and to the Austrian Embassy in Washington for arranging this unexpected largesse.

I am forever indebted to Caroline Palmer of Boydell and Brewer for her boundless patience, and to other members of her staff for their wisdom and experience in moving this book along to completion.

Finally, my deepest thanks go to my family and especially to my wife Devon, who persevered in the hope that there truly was an end to this seemingly endless project. I hope – no, I pray – that this book will repay her investment of time and patience in it.

Lawrence G. Duggan
Newark, Delaware,
Feast of Pope St Leo IX, 2013

ABBREVIATIONS

AC	*The Anglican Canons 1529–1947.* Gerald Bray, ed. Church of England Record Society, 6. Woodbridge, 1998.
Bainton	Roland Bainton, *Christian Attitudes Toward War and Peace* (Nashville, 1960).
Brundage, 'Holy War'	James A. Brundage, 'Holy War and the Medieval Lawyers', in T. P. Murphy, ed., *The Holy War* (Columbus, 1976), pp. 99–140.
CCCM	Corpus Christianorum Continuatio Mediaeualis.
Chambers, *Popes*	D. S. Chambers, *Popes, Cardinals and War. The Military Church in Renaissance and Early Modern Europe.* London-New York, 2006.
CHR	*Catholic Historical Review.*
C&S	*Councils and Synods, with Other Documents Relating to the English Church.* Vol. 1, *A.D. 871–1204.* D. Whitelock, M. Brett, and C. N. L. Brooke, eds. Oxford, 1981. Vol. 2, *1205–1313.* F. M. Powicke and C. R. Cheney, eds. Oxford, 1964.
CG	*Concilia Germaniae.* J. F. Schannat and J. Hartzheim, eds. 11 vols. Cologne, 1759–63. Repr., Aalen, 1970–96.
CIC	*Corpus iuris canonici.* E. Friedberg and E. L. Richter, eds. 2 vols. Leipzig, 1879. Repr., Graz, 1959.
CLCE	*The Canon Law of the Church of England. The Report of the Archbishops' Commission on Canon Law, together with Proposals for a Revised Body of Canons; and a Memorandum 'Lawful Authority' by the Honourable Mr Justice Vaisey.* London, 1947.
Clementines	*Clementines* issued by Pope John XXII (see below).
Code or *Codex*	*Code of Canon Law* of 1917 or 1983 (see below).
DA	*Deutsches Archiv für Erforschung des Mittelalters.*
DDC	*Dictionnaire de droit canonique.* R. Naz, ed. 7 vols. Paris, 1935–65.

DEC	*Decrees of the Ecumenical Councils*, eds G. Alberigo et al., tr. Norman Tanner, S.J., et al. 2 vols. London-Washington, 1990.
Decretales	*Liber decretalium* of Pope Gregory IX (see below).
Decretum	*Decretum* of Gratian (see below).
DMA	*Dictionary of the Middle Ages.* Joseph Strayer, gen. ed. 12 vols. New York, 1982–89.
DNB	*Dictionary of National Biography.* London, 1885–.
DTC	*Dictionnaire de théologie catholique.* A. Vacant et al., eds. 15 vols. Paris, 1903–50.
EHD	*English Historical Documents.* D. C. Douglas, gen. ed. London, 1953–.
EHR	*English Historical Review.*
ELJ	*Ecclesiastical Law Journal.*
Erdmann	Carl Erdmann, *The Origin of the Idea of Crusade*, tr. Marshall Baldwin and Walter Goffart (Princeton, 1977).
Gousset	Thomas Gousset, ed., *Les actes de la province ecclésiastique de Reims.* 4 vols. Reims, 1842–44.
HMPEC	*Historical Magazine of the Protestant Episcopal Church* (since 1986 entitled *Anglican and Episcopal History*).
JEH	*Journal of Ecclesiastical History.*
JMH	*Journal of Medieval History.*
Mansi	G. D. Mansi, *Sacrorum conciliorum nova et amplissima collectio.* Continued by L. Petit and J. B. Martin. 60 vols. Paris, 1899–1927.
MGH	Monumenta Germaniae historica.
MGM	Monographien zur Geschichte des Mittelalters.
NCE	*New Catholic Encyclopedia.* 16 vols. Washington, 1967.
ODCC	*Oxford Dictionary of the Christian Church.* 3rd rev. ed. F. L. Cross and E. A. Livingston. Oxford, 2005.
PL	Patrologia Latina. Ed. J. P. Migne.
Prinz, 'Clergy and War'	Friedrich Prinz, 'King, Clergy and War at the Time of the Carolingians', in Margot King and Wesley Stevens, eds., *Saints, Scholars and Heroes. Studies in Medieval Culture in Honour of Charles W. Jones* (Collegeville, Minn., 1979), 2:301–329.
Prinz, *Klerus*	Friedrich Prinz, *Klerus und Krieg im frühen Mittelalter* (Stuttgart, 1971).
RS	Rerum brittanicarum medii aevi scriptores. 99 vols. London, 1858–1911 (Rolls Series).
SC	*Studia canonica.*
Sext	*Liber sextus* of Pope Boniface VIII (see below).

xiii

SH	*Synodicon Hispanum*. A. Garcia y Garcia, ed. 10 vols. to date. Madrid, 1981–.
TRHS	*Transactions of the Royal Historical Society.*
Wilkins	David Wilkins, *Concilia Magnae Britanniae et Hiberniae A.D. 446–1717.* 4 vols. London, 1737. Repr., Brussels, 1964.
ZRG KA	*Zeitschrift der Savigny-Stiftung für Rechtsgeschichte, Kanonistische Abteilung.*

Canon Law Abbreviations

Between the twelfth century and 1918 the general canon law governing the Roman Catholic Church was the *Corpus iuris canonici* (*CIC*). Its constituent parts consisted of the following: (1) the *Decretum*, a collection compiled by the Bolognese monk Gratian toward the year 1140; (2) the *Decretales* or *Liber extra*, issued by Pope Gregory IX in 1234 (and in the old style abbreviated *X* for 'extra'); (3) the *Sext* or *Liber sextus decretalium* promulgated by Pope Boniface VIII in 1298 (originally abbreviated *VI*, since it was the sixth book); (4) the *Clementines*, originally promulged by Pope Clement V at the Council of Vienne in 1311 and definitively by Pope John XXII in 1317; (5) the *Extravagantes* of Pope John XXII (1316–34); and (6) the *Extravagantes communes* of various decretals or letters of the popes between 1294 and 1484. Only the second, third, and fourth items were, strictly speaking, issued as law by the popes. Gratian's collection was, however, from the outset treated as a comprehensive source collection, even if his positions were often soon modified or rejected. Both *Extravagantes* were routinely published, together with the earlier sources, from 1499 onward and received effective papal approval as genuine fonts of canon law in 1582.

In 1917 all this was replaced by a new *Code* or *Codex* decreed by Pope Pius X and taking effect on Pentecost 1918 (whence the varied references to it as the *Code* of 1917 or 1918). The edition used here is the edition of the *Codex iuris canonici* annotated by Pietro Cardinal Gasparri (Vatican City, 1974), of which an English translation by Edward N. Peters finally appeared in 2001.

This *Codex* was superseded in turn in 1983 by an entirely new *Code*. The text cited here is the *Code of Canon Law. Latin-English Edition*, prepared by the Canon Law Society of America (Washington, 1983).

INTRODUCTION

THE argument of this book is simply that, contrary to what is widely assumed, the clergy in western Christianity (at least in the Roman Catholic and Anglican-Episcopal traditions) have not been categorically forbidden to bear arms since the High Middle Ages (c.1100–1300) and are not today. Readers intrigued enough to go on, but still concerned about the efficient use of their time, are advised to proceed directly to the Conclusion after finishing this Introduction. They are warned, however, that most of the juicy bits lie in between.

Even historians who have worked on some aspect of this subject habitually either assume that clerics who bear arms automatically violate canon or ecclesiastical law, or else they considerably oversimplify the matter. In his *Christian Attitudes Toward War and Peace* Roland Bainton wrote that 'The approval of the Church was never bestowed on those clerics and monastics who had taken defense into their own hands. St Thomas, writing even after the commencement of the crusades, held that the clergy should be excluded from military functions, not so much, however, for ethical as for sacramental reasons.'[1] As we shall see, Bainton has, like so many others, confused Aquinas' opinions as a theologian with the law of the church.[2]

A definitive reference work, *The Oxford Dictionary of the Christian Church*, asserts in an entry on 'war, participation of the clergy in', that 'Since the Middle Ages clerics in major orders have been expressly forbidden to take a direct part in the shedding of blood.'[3] One could reasonably infer from this that this prohibition has been in force only since the Middle Ages, that it applied only to clerics in major orders, and that as long they did not shed blood they might possibly otherwise participate in warfare. Despite these ambiguities, this entry has remained essentially unchanged across four editions between

---

[1] Bainton, p. 109.
[2] See, for example, A. Vanderpol, *Le droit de guerre d'après les théologiens et les canonistes du moyen-age* (Paris, 1911), pp. 193–5, whose highly misleading selection of sources on this question would leave the impression that no respectable medieval canonist or theologian condoned arms-bearing by the clergy in any form.
[3] *ODCC*, 1st ed. (1957), pp. 1438–9; 2nd ed., (1974), p. 1460; 3rd ed. (1997), p. 1720; 3rd ed. rev. (2005), p. 1732.

1957 and 2005 and goes on to note that 'this teaching is embodied' in the Roman Catholic canon law Codes of 1917 and 1983.

Small wonder, then, that in an otherwise illuminating essay on clerical violence in early modern Spain, Henry Kamen starts off on the wrong foot by taking the ecclesiastical prohibition for granted and therefore seeks the explanation elsewhere in the relationships between Spanish society and the Spanish church. Although this 'war and society' approach has in recent decades wonderfully enriched the study of military history, it here goes somewhat awry because it mistakes the relevant ecclesiastical legislation, if understandably so.[4] Similarly, in his *Popes, Cardinals and War*, which provides the most thorough coverage in English of the military engagement of the popes and cardinals of the Middle Ages and the Renaissance, D. S. Chambers conflates the whole spectrum of behavior ranging from personal armsbearing to direction of troops from afar and assumes that none of it was licit in the law of the Church. And a recent military history of the modern papacy does not consider the legal issues at all.[5]

The premises of Bainton, Kamen, and Chambers are, furthermore, incompatible with statements made by other writers. In an essay on military musters of the English clergy during the Hundred Years War, Bruce McNab writes that 'A cleric was strictly forbidden under canon law to bear arms or to shed blood, although one who incurred canonical penalties by defending himself against assault on his person might readily find dispensation'.[6] The implication here seems to be that self-defense, although canonically culpable, was easily, almost automatically, excusable at law, and the insinuation is that that legal system was corrupt. By contrast, Philippe Contamine, who has worked extensively on war in the Middle Ages, asserts that in ecclesiastical law 'even clerics could legitimately resist violence'.[7] In an earlier work on war in the late Middle Ages, however, Contamine fails to clarify whether this principle applies to a cleric's property as well as to his person.[8] Contamine and McNab thus appear to contradict each other as well as Bainton, Kamen, and Chambers.

As for the Anglican-Episcopal tradition, the closest offshoot of the Roman Catholic system in law as in liturgy and doctrine, it is again customarily taken as a given that clergy who in any way take up weapons, for whatever reason, automatically violate the law of the church and are 'deposed' ('defrocked' in lay language). Even an ecclesiastical commission appointed in 1939 to revise

---

[4] Henry Kamen, 'Clerical Violence in a Catholic Society: The Hispanic World 1450–1720', in W. J. Shiels, ed., *The Church and War*, Studies in Church History 20 (Oxford, 1983), pp. 200–16.

[5] David Alvarez, *The Pope's Soldiers. A Military History of the Modern Vatican* (Lawrence, Kan., 2011).

[6] Bruce McNab, 'Obligations of the Church in English Society: Military Arrays of the Clergy, 1369–1418', in William C. Jordan, Bruce McNab, and Teofilo F. Ruiz, eds, *Order and Innovation in the Middle Ages. Essays in Honor of Joseph R. Strayer* (Princeton, 1976), pp. 293–314, at 293.

[7] Philippe Contamine, *War in the Middle Ages*, tr. M. Jones (Oxford, 1984), p. 292.

[8] Philippe Contamine, *Guerre, état et société à la fin du moyen age. Etudes sur les armées des rois de France 1337–1494* (Paris, 1972), pp. 171–4.

the canon law of the Church of England made this erroneous assumption.[9] *The Oxford Dictionary of the Christian Church*, on the other hand, says somewhat ambiguously that 'The C[hurch] of E[ngland] has commonly upheld the medieval discipline, though ecclesiastical penalties have not been imposed on the few clerics who have entered the services and such clerics have been allowed to resume their clerical life when the war has ended.'[10]

There is a perfectly good reason for this confusion, for there exists no adequate historical treatment of this complex subject from the High Middle Ages onward. By comparison, there are several fine studies of the period up to the High Middle Ages, and my enormous debt to them will be obvious to those familiar with these works. I should signal out for particular recognition the work of Stephan Kuttner, Carl Erdmann, Friedrich Prinz, Rosalio Castillo Lara, Ferminio Poggiaspalla, James Brundage, Frederick Russell, and Ernst-Dieter Hehl.[11] They focus, however, on the thinking of canon lawyers, whereas I stress the legislation of the popes and of bishops, which they often unconsciously tend to slight.

Finally, although the cumulative effect of the work of these scholars points to significant changes in the High Middle Ages in the millennium-old ban on clerical armsbearing, neither they nor anyone else has offered an adequate, comprehensive, historical treatment of the question since the thirteenth century, which is the customary *terminus ad quem* for 'high medievalists'.

Thus the author of the skimpy article in the *Dictionnaire du droit canonique* (barely two columns) devotes nearly half that space to Gratian, commits egregious errors, and takes stunning leaps through time.[12] Far more careful is the great history of canon law by Paul Hinschius, which was incomplete at the time of his death in 1898. Nevertheless, in six volumes he devotes but two pages to the issue. Although those pages are astonishingly meaty, they approach the subject indirectly from the standpoint of clerical irregularity and as an historical treatment are confusing.[13] The history of Catholic and Lutheran canon law by Hinschius' contemporary, Emil Ludwig Richter, summarizes the whole tradition by noting that clerics have been forbidden

[9] CLCE, pp. 67–8. For other instances of this assumption, see Nelson Waite Rightmyer, *Maryland's Established Church* (Baltimore, 1956), p. 175; Albert Marrin, *The Last Crusade. The Church of England in the First World War* (Durham, NC, 1974), p. 189; and Chapter 6, below, passim.

[10] ODCC, pp. 1438–9 (1st ed.), 1460 (2nd), 1720 (3rd), and 1732 (3rd rev.).

[11] Stephan Kuttner, *Kanonistische Schuldlehre von Gratian bis auf die Dekretalen Gregors IX.*, Studi e testi 64 (Vatican City, 1935, repr. 1961), esp. 334–79 ('Notwehr'); Erdmann, *Origin*; Rosalio Castillo Lara, *Coaccion eclesiastica y Sacro Romano Imperio. Estudio juridico-historico sobre la potestad coactiva material suprema de la Iglesia* (Turin, 1956); Ferminio Poggiaspalla, 'La Chiesa e la partecipazione dei chierici alla guerra nella legislazione conciliare fino alla Decretali di Gregorio IX', *Ephemerides iuris canonici* 15 (1959):140–53; Prinz, *Klerus und Krieg*; Brundage, 'Holy War'; Frederick Russell, *The Just War in the Middle Ages*, Cambridge Studies in Medieval Life and Thought, 3rd ser. 8 (Cambridge, 1975); Ernst-Dieter Hehl, *Kirche und Krieg im 12. Jahrhundert. Studien zu kanonischem Recht und politischer Wirklichkeit*, MGM 19 (Stuttgart, 1980).

[12] E. Thamiry, 'Armes', in DDC 1: 1047–8.

[13] Paul Hinschius, *Das Kirchenrecht der Katholiken und Protestanten in Deutschland* (Berlin, 1869–97, repr. Graz, 1959), 1:26–7; see also 124–6 and 137–8.

to render military service or bear arms 'except when traveling'.[14] The more recent, five-volume history of canon law by Willibald Plöchl gives less than one page to the issue. More comprehensive than Hinschius' treatment, it is also less meaty, makes at least one significant mistake, provides a better but still insufficient historical treatment, and says nothing about the Roman Catholic *Code* of 1917.[15] The pertinent canon in this *Code* was treated in a 1938 dissertation that is sometimes confusing and inadequate when not downright erroneous.[16] There are two excellent treatments from the late seventeenth and eighteenth centuries by Louis Thomassin and above all by Lucio Ferraris;[17] but, aside from the problem that neither account goes beyond its age, such old works are inaccessible to most people and likely to be read only by more recondite scholars – if the latter are interested in canon law at all, a taste which in the later twentieth century largely went out of favor.[18] Even within the Roman Catholic Church, one gathers, widespread aversion to the 'excessive legalism' of the past has taken deep root in the wake of Vatican II.

The main weight of this study will nonetheless fall on the treatment of clerical armsbearing in ecclesiastical or canon law, and necessarily so. After an opening chapter that surveys actual armsbearing by the clergy from the late Roman Empire to the present day, the second chapter will seek to show that attitudes toward clerical armsbearing on the part of clerics and laymen alike have been far more varied than is usually supposed – hence the title of the chapter, 'Quot homines, tot sententiae'. Such diversity of opinion alone would recommend shifting one's focus to canon law, but there is also the question of justice. Is it not fair to judge such clerics in the first instance by what canon law commands, encourages, allows, or forbids them to do, regardless of what one personally thinks? One may conclude that canon law on this issue was peculiar or wrongheaded, but one should know what that law was if one presumes to judge those who were subject to it. Finally, the attempt to comprehend not only the changes in canon law from the twelfth century onward, but also the reasons for those changes, should lead to a deeper understanding of the evolution of Christianity in the West, the intricate interrelationships between church and society, the profound influence of Roman law, the inner processes of legal change, the unforeseen consequences of the ecclesiastical reform movement of the eleventh and twelfth centuries, and the conditional acceptance of violence in western history by men who

---

[14] Aemilius Ludwig Richter, *Lehrbuch des katholischen und evangelischen Kirchenrechts. Mit besonderer Rücksicht auf deutsche Zustände*, 8th ed. (Leipzig, 1886), p. 368.

[15] Willibald Plöchl, *Geschichte des Kirchenrechts* (Vienna, 1952–68), 3: 168. See below p. 103 n.5.

[16] John Thomas Donovan, *The Clerical Obligations of Canons 138 and 140*, Catholic University of America Canon Law Studies 272 (Washington, 1948), pp. 87–101.

[17] Louis Thomassin, *Ancienne et nouvelle discipline de l'église*, new ed. rev. by M. André (Bar-le-Duc, 1864–7), 7:443, 452–5; Lucio Ferraris, O.F.M., *Bibliotheca canonica iuridica moralis theologica nec non ascetica polemica rubricistica historica*, new ed., 9 vols. (Rome, 1884–99), 1: 407–12. Sometimes this work appears under the title *Prompta bibliotheca*...

[18] Thus Daniel B. Stevick, *Canon Law. A Handbook* (New York, 1965), p. vii: 'Indeed, the study of and regard for canon law seem to have fallen on evil days.'

in the public mind are ordinarily held to be emblematic of peace. This book, then, although centered on law and the church, is not simply about law or the church.

The approach taken here to ecclesiastical law is somewhat different from, and more complicated than, the prevailing one, which is to look to the 'high' tradition of law-making and jurisprudence, often to the simplest statements of the law, and almost always to the commentators on, rather than the promulgators of, those laws. Thus the famous text invariably cited in connection with the clergy and arms is from the first comprehensive official collection of canon law promulgated by a pope, the *Decretales* of Gregory IX (1227–41) of 1234: 'Clerics bearing arms and usurers are excommunicated.'[19] This seems perfectly clear and straightforward. But if one reads the statutes issued by provincial councils and diocesan synods from this time onward, they only occasionally decree anything as uncomplicated as that and in fact usually concede certain telling exceptions to this rule. What does this betoken? Widespread resistance to the universal jurisdiction, legislative and judicial, claimed by the papal monarchy? Not at all, but rather that the legislation at the top was more complex than is usually supposed. For if one considers other relevant passages from the *Decretales*, not to mention other texts – scriptural, patristic, papal, conciliar, and canonistic – adduced or produced a century either side of the *Decretales*, then the "canon law of arms" for the clergy was far from clear, particularly when viewed from the ordinary diocese.

Yet it was precisely at this local level that the average cleric lived and had to be taught before the advent of the seminary in the post-Reformation era. Since most clerics thus received rather little schooling before then, the complexities of law-making and legal thinking at the highest levels had to be reduced to intelligible, crisp formulae at the local level. These were then promulgated at diocesan synods and provincial councils as statutes or constitutions, which from the thirteenth century until well into the early modern period served as the principal means of providing the parochial clergy with rudimentary instruction in theology and law. In fact, Christopher Cheney remarked, 'nowhere does one find that the Church had any other plan for their systematic education.'[20]

For this reason, and out of a general interest in the transmission and reception of laws, this book will therefore devote a great deal of attention to how synods and councils dealt with these problems with respect to clerical arms. Although this is a sphere of legislative and interpretive activity frequently ignored, it is a fruitful one to investigate because it illumines sharply how administrators, especially bishops, had to grapple with the issues which could be endlessly discussed by lawyers and theoreticians and boil the results of these learned discourses down to a few simple sentences. It was those few

---

[19] *Decretales* 3.1.2.
[20] C. R. Cheney, 'Some Aspects of Diocesan Legislation in England during the Thirteenth Century', in his *Medieval Texts and Studies* (Oxford, 1973), p. 187.

simple sentences that the overwhelming majority of the clergy understood to be the law of the church. Scholars reading this book may be intrigued by the tortuous questions raised by clerical armsbearing and by the sometimes even more tortuous answers given by canonists, but one should never forget the 'real life' for which, after all, these laws were drawn up. It is easy but danger-ous to forget this in the academy.

But if the complexity of legislation and discussion in the High Middle Ages has perhaps deterred anyone from undertaking a synthesis on clerical armsbearing, the difficulties attendant on looking to the local level are even more dismaying. First is the staggering number of dioceses. By one count, on the eve of the Reformation there were 266 in Italy alone (excluding the addi-tional 35 in Sicily, Sardinia, and Corsica), and 267 in Germany, France, Iberia, England, and Scotland, not to mention the rest of Latin Christendom.[21] Any investigation, unless sharply restricted chronologically or geographically, is therefore necessarily highly selective.

This is particularly so if one must rely on the available printed texts. For the basic *Corpus iuris canonici* by which the Catholic Church was gov-erned from the High Middle Ages to 1917, we must, with few exceptions, continue to rely on Emil Friedberg's edition of a century ago, which was based on the Roman edition of 1582 and with substantial parts of which Friedberg was himself dissatisfied.[22] Similarly, for local legislation one still cannot do without the great collections put together by Mansi, Schannat and Hartzheim, Wilkins, and many others in the early modern centuries.[23] They all present problems. There are substantial lacunae. One German diocese scarcely represented in Schannat-Hartzheim, much less Mansi, is Speyer, with which I have some acquaintance. Perhaps to rectify this defect, the prince-bishop reigning in 1786 issued a collection of all synodal statutes and other forms of legislation for the clergy enacted between 1397 and 1720; it comprises 534 tightly printed pages.[24] Such use of the printing press became fairly common in most of Europe by the seventeenth century, just as synods were becoming both more regular and more prolix. One catalogue of the statutes of the dioceses of France from the thirteenth through the eight-eenth centuries contains 498 pages, while an inventory of synodal statutes printed in Italy between 1534 and 1878 numbers 1,762 items, and a general bibliography on synods lists over 3,400 entries.[25] All these factors forced the

---

[21] Denys Hay, *The Italian Renaissance in its Historical Background* (Cambridge, 1961), p. 49, n. 3.

[22] One exception is the edition by Jacqueline Tarrant (now Brown) of the *Extrauagantes Iohannis XXII*, Monumenta iuris canonici B/6 (Vatican City, 1983), which contains nothing pertaining to armsbearing.

[23] See E. F. Jacob, "Wilkins's *Concilia* and the Fifteenth Century,' *TRHS* 4th ser., 15 (1932):91–131.

[24] *Collectio processuum synodalium et constitutionum ecclesiasticarum dioecesis Spirensis ab anno 1397 usque ad annum 1720* (Bruchsal, 1786).

[25] André Artonne, Louis Guizard, and Odette Pontal, *Répertoire des statuts synodaux des diocèses de l'ancienne France du XIIIe à la fin du XVIIIe siècle*, 2nd rev. ed. (Paris, 1969); Silvino da Nadro, O.F.M.Cap., *Sinodi diocesani italiani. Catalogo bibliografico degli atti a stampa 1534–1878*, Studi e testi 207 (Vatican City, 1960); J. T. Sawicki, *Bibliographia synodorum particularium*, Monumenta iuris canonici C/2 (Vatican City, 1967).

great compilers to exercise ever greater selectivity in the post-Reformation period.

The problem for the pre-Reformation period is quite different. Survival of the sources begins the list of obstacles. For example, we know that the clergy of the province of Canterbury convened in convocation no fewer than thirteen times during the episcopate of Archbishop Thomas Bourchier (1454–86). Despite the late date, the constitutions of only two of those thirteen convocations are extant.[26] The paucity of materials would be serious enough were it not for the lamentable state of their transmission. What is so often true of England is probably often true of the Continent: 'the precise contents of the statutes as first issued are irrecoverable,'[27] not only because of later modifications in transcription, but also because of their frequent origin in 'pools' of statutes, especially of more distinguished prelates.[28] Different manuscripts, when they survive, can present troublesome variations. Sometimes these matter, sometimes not. The four manuscripts of the council of Clermont of 1095 (at which Pope Urban II launched what later came to be remembered as the First Crusade) differ only in their numbering of the canon on clerical armsbearing, but not on substance, for they all summarily forbid it.[29] But sometimes variations are very vexing indeed, as will be seen in a number of instances. It is only in recent decades that exacting textual criticism has been applied to such texts, first in England, now in Spain and France[30]; and since here quantity has been sacrificed for quality, we must in most cases still make do with older editions. Fortunately, since our focus is on the patterns of legislation on armsbearing and not on its history in any single diocese, we need not worry too much about this problem, for the patterns are very distinctive. On the other hand, the dates supplied by earlier editors are often quite inaccurate and must be treated with great caution. Where modern editors have calculated more carefully or there exists other reason for doubt, I have ordinarily indicated the range of possible dates with a slash, i.e. '1244/9', which means sometime between 1244 and 1249.[31] Thus one sacrifices in this

---

[26] F. R. H. Du Boulay, ed., *Registrum Thome Bourgchier Cantuariensis archiepiscopi A.D. 1454–1486*, Canterbury and York Society 54 (Oxford, 1957), pp. xxix, xxxi.

[27] *C&S* 2: vii. For some Continental examples, see Helmut Maurer, 'Zu den Inskriptionen der Mainzer Provinzialstatuten von 1310', *ZRG KA* 53 (1967):338–46, and Alfred Säbisch, 'Drei angebliche Breslauer Diözesansynoden des 15. Jahrhunderts', *ZRG KA* 50 (1964):272–8.

[28] Besides the introduction to *C&S* 2, see the two essays by Cheney, 'Textual Problems of the English Provincial Canons' and 'Statute-making in the English Church in the Thirteenth Century', in *Medieval Texts and Studies*, pp. 111–37 and 138–57; and for a more general discussion with substantial bibliography, Paul Saenger, 'Silent Reading. Its Impact on Late Medieval Script and Society', *Viator* 13 (1982):380–2.

[29] Robert Somerville, *The Councils of Urban II*, 1, *Decreta Claromontensia*, Annuarium historiae conciliorum, Supplementum 1 (Amsterdam, 1972), pp. 77, 113.

[30] For England, *C&S* and bishops' registers and *acta*; for Spain, *Sinodicon Hispanum*; for France, 'Sources d'histoire medievale' and 'Collection des documents inédits sur l'histoire de France'.

[31] The editors of *C&S* use 'x' rather than a slash for such indeterminate dates, which I find too cumbersome; and for clarity's sake I prefer the slash in such cases to the hyphen, which I take to be inclusive, whether of the length of a life, the dates of rule, or the duration of an assembly (thus the Council of Trent, 1545–63).

case elegance for precision, in another quantity for quality: it is a kind of Heisenberg principle of modern scholarship.

I must here state that I claim no competence as a lawyer in the lawyer's ways of handling legal texts. If I have run aground in my sifting of the texts, I beg the forgiveness of the members of that guild. However, the mind of the legislator is not always pellucidly apparent from his choice of words. Just as one must take care not to treat legal language too cavalierly, so too one must not read too much into it: laws may be vaguely or even badly written.

This is particularly so on the matter of clerical armsbearing, which was almost always a minor item of synodal legislation, at least to judge from the small amount of space accorded to it. Sometimes long stretches of time would pass without any allusion to it at all. Thus not one of the thirteen provincial councils of Tours between 1201 and 1467 mentions it, although they do treat clerical violence, gambling, visiting of taverns, and the like; and in the English church it has not been the subject of explicit legislation since the thirteenth century.[32] One major reason for this is that among clerical vices and failings, armsbearing has been a relatively minor one, usually confined to relatively small numbers of the clergy. One of the few studies of this topic was devoted to violence, brawling, and homicide among the Cistercians. Over the space of seven hundred years, in an order embracing over seven hundred monasteries and thousands of monks and nuns, Anselme Dimier turned up a total of about sixty such cases.[33] Even if (as I believe) Dimier did not cast his nets widely and arrived at an estimate on the low side, that would still not be many.

To look at the matter differently, it has been calculated that over four hundred clergy became aggressively involved in Mexico's struggle against Spain between 1808 and 1820. This figure is astonishing until one sets it against the total number of clergy in Mexico at the time—about 8,000 according to one scholar, 10,000 according to another.[34] In other words, at a time of passionate conflict perhaps five percent of the clergy participated actively in the revolution in Mexico. Similarly, only four or five of the 122 incumbent Anglican clergy in Virginia are recorded as acting as soldiers in the American Revolution.[35] These figures should be compared with the inevitably crude and often partisan guesses as to the percentage of sexually incontinent clergy in any given age, which can run as high as thirty or forty percent and never as low as five. This kind of contrast is startlingly clear in the reports on 530

[32] Joseph Avril, ed., *Les conciles de la province de Tours. Concilia provinciae Turonensis (saec. XIII-XV)* (Paris, 1987); and see Chapter 6 below for England.

[33] Anselme Dimier, 'Violences, rixes et homicides chez les Cisterciens', *Revue des sciences religieuses* 46 (1972):38–57.

[34] On these highly controverted matters, see Karl M. Schmitt, 'The Clergy and the Independence of New Spain', *Hispanic American Historical Review* 34 (1954):289–312, especially 289, 292, 300, 304; and Nancy M. Farriss, *Crown and Clergy in Colonial Mexico 1759–1821. The Crisis of Ecclesiastical Privilege* (London, 1968), pp. 122, 198–201, 254–65. The two estimates are cited by Schmitt (pp. 289, n. 2, and 304). Neither he nor Farriss conjectures on the total number of clergy, although Farriss cites one calculation of 3,112 regular clergy in Mexico in 1810 (p. 122 and n. 2).

[35] G. MacLaren Brydon, 'The Clergy of the Established Church in Virginia and the American Revolution', *Virginia Magazine of History and Biography* 41 (1933):16, 21–2, 239–40, 242–3, 301–3.

clergy in the diocese of Eichstätt visited in 1480.[36] The odd thing – the very odd thing, in fact – is that Catholic Church has never accommodated its rules to the sexual behavior of the clergy, whereas it gradually ameliorated its regulations on armsbearing for a far smaller segment of the clerical population. These modifications therefore did not come about as a simple capitulation to 'reality'.

One choice already intimated is not as arbitrary and parochial as it may seem, and that is that with one major exception this study will be confined to the legal tradition of the Roman Catholic Church. Certain facts should be remembered. Until the sixteenth century – the first 75% of Christian history – the Roman Catholic Church was the only official church in the West. Today it is still by far the largest Christian denomination and is one of the two largest religions in the world. In addition, the Roman Catholic system of ecclesiastical law is the oldest, most highly developed, and most influential in western Christianity, and it continued to influence Protestant churches long after the Reformation.[37] It is also the most centralized and easiest to examine, although not nearly as easy as many people think.

The Protestant churches, by comparison, are nearly impossible to study. Ever since the abandonment of the principle of *cuius regio, eius religio* in the eighteenth and nineteenth centuries, the 'Protestant' principle of the right of the individual to interpret Holy Writ has accelerated the fragmentation and proliferation of Protestant denominations. As a result, there are hundreds of denominations, each with its own traditions and institutions.[38] Every form of Protestantism, furthermore, has come to define itself partly in terms of reaction against the Roman Church, especially against what is generally perceived as its centralism and legalism. Thus there is a decided tendency to leave much to the decision of local congregations and to individuals, both of which hamper a legal historian searching for general, explicit, binding norms.[39] A final barrier is this: to one extent or another, most forms of Protestantism, again largely in reaction against Rome, retained little if any conception of a sacral priesthood sharply distinguished from the laity. The overall tone of that reaction was captured in the Presbyterians' *First Book of Discipline* printed in 1621, but essentially authored by John Knox sixty years earlier:

> The Papisticall Priests have neither power nor authority to minister the sacraments of Christ Jesus, because that in their mouth is not the sermon of exhortation; and therefore to them must strait inhibition be made notwithstanding any usurpation they have had in the time of blindnesse. It is neither the clipping of their crownes,

36 Peter Lang, 'Würfel, Wein und Wettersegen. Klerus und Gläubige im Bistum Eichstätt am Vorabend der Reformation', in Volker Press and Dieter Stievermann, eds, *Martin Luther. Probleme seiner Zeit* (Stuttgart, 1986), pp. 219–43, especially 222–27.

37 See Wilhelm Maurer, 'Reste des Kanonischen Rechtes im Frühprotestantismus', *ZRG KA* 51 (1965):190–253, and R. H. Helmholz, ed., *Canon Law in Protestant Lands. Comparative Studies in Continental and Anglo-American Legal History* (Berlin, 1992).

38 See Craig Atwood, *Handbook of Denominations in the United States*, 13th ed. (Nashville, 2010).

39 See Robert L. Schenck, ed., *Constitutions of American Denominations*, 3 vols. (Buffalo, 1984).

the greasing of their fingers, nor the blowing of the dumb dogges called the Bishops, neither the laying on of their hands that maketh Ministers of Christ Jesus. But the Spirit of God inwardly first moving the hearts to seeke Christs glorie, and the profite of his Kirk, and thereafter the nomination of the people, the examination of the learned, and publick admission (as before is said) make men lawfull ministers of the Word and Sacraments.[40]

Luther's vigorous reassertion and reinterpretation of the priesthood of all believers has thus not been helpful to legal or legally minded historians interested in 'the clergy'. Ministers in many churches are frequently only temporary and, even when permanent, in many respects indistinguishable from the laity. How can one possibly study them? For all these reasons, the Protestant churches are excluded from this study. The first two chapters will mention in passing various Protestant ministers who have borne arms in recent centuries, but no judgments will be offered as to their culpability within their own ecclesiastical tradition. Roland Bainton may well be right in holding that Lutheranism remained true to the ancient prohibition, but I remain unconvinced.[41]

The one exception will be the Church in and of England, but for reasons of space not the more than twenty-five other branches of the Anglican Communion.[42] Both of these churches, besides being of interest to readers on both sides of the Atlantic, have produced some extraordinary clerical warriors. Although the Anglican Communion is rightly thought to have remained closest to Rome of all the 'Protestant' traditions, it has also attempted to incorporate the best of both worlds. In the long run, both the episcopate and the sacramental priesthood have survived, if not without some dicey moments and some eclipse of power. In its search for comprehensiveness and its intention to stay focused on essentials, the Anglican Communion has developed a distinctive approach to theology and law.[43] In his 'Foreword' to the final report of the commission for the revision of the canon law of the Church of England, the chairman, Archbishop Cyril Garbett of York, put it this way in 1947:

On the other hand, we have definitely rejected an attempt to form a complete code of Canon Law. This would have meant a task requiring many years of intensive research and study; and, moreover, a complete and exhaustive code such as is possessed by the Roman Catholic Church would be incompatible both with the spirit of English law and with the genius of the Church of England, which has always disliked excessive formulation.[44]

---

[40] *The First Book of Discipline. With Introduction and Commentary by James K. Cameron* (Edinburgh, 1972), 'The Ninth Head, Concerning the Policie of the Kirk', pp. 206–7. On the text of *The First Book*, see pp. 75–7.

[41] Bainton, p. 189, and the literature he cites there.

[42] The relevant canon law of the Episcopal Church of the United States will be treated in a separate article.

[43] For a general conspectus, see Norman Doe, *Canon Law in the Anglican Communion. A Worldwide Perspective* (Oxford, 1998).

[44] *CLCE*, pp. v–vi.

This is canon law, but informed by a love-hate relationship with Rome. More recently, Gerald Bray put it more moderately: 'the break with Rome gave Anglican law a life of its own which helps us to define it as a distinct, if not really as a separate, branch of western canon law in general'.[45] Its consequences we shall see later.

Although the retention of sacral priesthood by Rome and Canterbury is one criterion marking the limits of this study, the term 'clergy' is more elusive than one might suppose. For both churches it can be, like the terms 'order' and 'orders', construed strictly and loosely. Technically, a cleric is someone who is ordained in or to an order of sacred ministry and so is 'in orders'. Until the Reformation there was a consensus that there were at least seven orders, four minor (porter, lector, exorcist, and acolyte, in ascending order) and three major or holy (subdeacon, deacon, and priest). Until the High Middle Ages, however, the subdiaconate was a minor order and was elevated to major status only by the thirteenth century. Furthermore, some thinkers argued for other orders (especially gravedigger), many wondered whether the office of bishop constituted a separate order, and most asserted the necessity of tonsure for admission to orders while simultaneously denying that tonsure itself was an order. Each of these orders orginally had specific responsibilities. An essential distinction was that those in minor orders could marry and revert to lay status, whereas those in major orders were theoretically bound permanently by celibacy and their other vows, since priesthood, in the Roman view, is forever according to the order of Melchisedech (see Heb. 5.10). Most of the minor orders save acolyte, however, fell into desuetude by the High Middle Ages and, despite a half-hearted attempt to revive them by the Council of Trent in 1563, continued to deteriorate until their formal suppression, together with the subdiaconate, and the resurrection of the permanent married diaconate between 1967 and 1972.[46] Finally, as is well known, in the Roman Catholic Church women cannot be ordained and hence cannot be clerics.

In common parlance, the term 'clergy' also embraces nuns, monks, brothers, and others professing some form of approved religious life as 'religious' in an 'order' or following a particular rule as 'regulars' (from the Latin *regula* for 'rule'). None of these religious need in fact be ordained and is therefore necessarily a cleric, and monasticism in fact began as a movement of laymen, not clerics. All through the Middle Ages laypeople could be members of, or attached to, religious houses as *conversi* or 'converts' from the world to 'religion'. Many monks have been ordained as clerics, but Roman Catholic nuns

---

[45] Gerald Bray, ed., *The Anglican Canons 1529-1947*, Church of England Record Society 6 (Woodbridge-Rochester, NY, 1998), p. xv.

[46] For a succinct discussion, rich in bibliography, see the article by René Metz in *DMA* 3:440-6, who considers the episcopate a separate eighth order. For a fuller treatment, see the studies by Roger Reynolds collected in his *Clerical Orders in the Early Middle Ages. Duties and Ordination* (Aldershot, 1999). For recent changes, see Felician Foy and Rose Avato, eds, *1995 Catholic Almanac* (Huntington, Indiana, 1994), pp. 227-9.

are by definition excluded from ordination. These perplexities continue in the revised *Code of Canon Law* of 1983, which speaks of 'Religious Institutes of Consecrated Life,' 'Secular Institutes of Consecrated Life,' and 'Societies of Apostolic Life.' The world may regard such persons as clerics, but the Roman Church has not done so either in the Middle Ages or today. Its legislation has habitually treated 'clergy' in a category separate from 'religious'. Thus canon law explicitly forbids the holding of secular political office to clerics, but not to religious.

Similarly, in the Middle Ages synods frequently legislated separately for the 'clergy' and for 'religious', and distinct problems are associated with each. 'Clergy' is normally the most precise term used, which leaves one in the dark as to whether the statute in question equally bound those in minor and major orders, the unbeneficed as well as the beneficed, not to mention the merely tonsured. Since regulations concerning armsbearing usually appear in these sections on 'Clergy' in both medieval and modern legislation, one may ask whether they apply to religious. Such men and women were subject to the rule and statutes of their orders and their houses, but were they also bound by the legislation of the diocese in which they found themselves, especially if they were ordained clerics or if they stepped outside the precincts of their houses into the diocese beyond? This is rarely clear. This legal conundrum was exacerbated from the High Middle Ages onward by the legal exemption of many religious orders from the authority of the local bishop, originally an instrument of reform which metamorphosed into an abuse sorely needing reformation by the time of the Council of Trent. Endless wrangling emerged from such tangled issues.[47]

As for the Anglican Church, the Reformation in England cleared away many of these difficulties concerning the secular and the regular clergy by suppressing the religious orders entirely and by reducing the orders of the clergy to the three original ones of bishop, priest, and deacon. The revival of religious orders since the nineteenth century has complicated both the public picture of the Anglican clergy and their status at canon law, although still not as much as in the Roman Catholic Church. On the other hand, so many varieties of opinion and practice are tolerated within the Anglican Communion, which lacks any one central way of resolving controversies, that it is best with the Anglican Communion, as with the Roman Church, to use the word 'clergy', complete with all its potential ambiguities, as it is used in the sources unless otherwise specified.

Finally, a word about 'armsbearing', a seemingly straightforward word required by the constraints of modern title pages and justified by the terse Latin phrase habitually used in canonical legislation, *arma portare*. What do these words mean?

First, what are 'arms'? Swords, spears, bows and arrows, pistols, guns—

---

[47] For reasons of economy, the legislation of the medieval and early modern Catholic religious orders on armsbearing will be treated in a separate monograph.

these are manufactured, offensive, and lethal. But what of small paring knives and similar instruments which can be used in deadly fashion but were not fashioned for such purposes? What of natural objects like stones and stout sticks which can used defensively or offensively? What of the knives so necessary for quotidian life and carried by most people down into the eighteenth and nineteenth centuries? Were these considered *arma* in ecclesiastical legislation?

A difficulty of a different order revolves around translation of foreign words for various arms, particularly Latin words as these words are used again and again over the course of hundreds of years. Even without the problems of translation, weapons are simply not that easy to pin down: 'there is no definition of the sword, that is, none that differentiates it from all other weapons. The reason is simple – the series of knife, sword, espadon, and glaive is an unbroken one, and there is no point that can be agreed upon as that at which a division should always be made.'[48] Bearing this caveat in mind, I have dealt with the frequently recurring Latin terms as follows. *Cultellus* is a generic word for 'knife' and I have so translated it throughout; but without further specification about length, width, blade (double-edged or single?), and the like, there is no way of knowing whether what a tenth-century Benedictine monk in Tuscany regarded as a *cultellus* corresponded very closely to what a sixteenth-century German Dominican called by the same name. *Ensis* is even more problematical, for although it was often used interchangeably with *gladius* in classical Latin, it is not often so used in medieval Latin. I have tended to translate *ensis* as 'dagger', but cautiously so. *Gladius* is thoroughly vexing. Until rather late in writing this book I had rendered this word as "sword." Then I encountered two independent fourteenth-century instances, together with two seventeenth-century derivative usages, in which *gladius* was carefully defined as the equivalent of *cultellus*. Although these cases are few and late and may possibly reflect classical influence (since the *gladius* of the Roman army was a short 'sword'), they vitiate certainty about the exact meaning of this word and therefore of *ensis* as well. In doubtful cases I have therefore supplied the Latin original with my tentative translation.

Portare means 'to bear' or 'to carry'. Once the ancient ban began to be modified in the High Middle Ages, questions inevitably came to be asked about what exactly that meant. By the later thirteenth and fourteenth centuries cautious legislators found it wise to forbid clergy to 'have' (*habere*) or 'retain' (*retinere*) arms. Questions still arose. Even if one did not have or keep arms oneself, was it licit to use arms, especially for purely defensive purposes or under extraordinary circumstances? If one could defend oneself with arms, could one also defend another, ecclesiastical property, the *patria*, or some just or holy cause? Could a cleric act on his own initiative, or did he

---

[48] George Cameron Stone, *A Glossary of the Construction, Decoration and Use of Arms and Armor in All Countries and in All Times* (New York, 1934), p. 591; pp. 595–6 list different kinds of, and names for, 'swords'.

need to obtain leave from a superior? And what kind of usage of arms was permitted under such circumstances? Was minimal response always called for? What is the importance of intention? If one kills or wounds another or sheds his blood, is a cleric always and everywhere automatically rendered 'irregular' and incapable of exercising his sacred office or of promotion to another order until dispensed by higher authority? Beyond these questions concerning the personal 'bearing' of arms lay others. May a cleric, even if he himself may not take up arms, lead others in a defensive, just, or righteous war or action? If he may not lead them, may he at least exhort them and urge them on to victory in the name of this cause?

'Bearing arms', then, far from being a simple term, covers a considerable spectrum of activities ranging from aggressive slashing with the most deadly weapons down through command of troops to sermons and speeches calculated to urge them on. There are many valid, important distinctions to be drawn here. Yet in the minds of many people such distinctions seem to be irrelevant, particularly with respect to command of troops or any kind of engagement in military activities. Although according to the celebrated accounts of Erasmus and Guicciardini Pope Julius II commanded troops, directed siege operations, and entered Rome arrayed in armor, he did not, strictly speaking, 'bear arms' on any of these occasions. Yet Julius might as well have slaughtered women and children with a scimitar, to judge from the prodigious sense of moral outrage which both writers so eloquently expressed. In the later seventeenth century, Archbishop John Williams of York and Bishop Joshua Trelawny of Bristol would be vilified by contemporary satirists for doing even less. Yet, although canon law has traditionally denounced indecorous dress for the clergy, it has never, strictly speaking, forbidden the armor which the pope and the archbishop may or may not have worn; and there is no reason why a scrupulous chaplain to whom the idea of carrying any weapon would be repugnant may not today wear a bulletproof vest into battle. A cuirass is no more a weapon than a bulletproof vest is. To Erasmus and the other critics, of course, the armor was but a symbol of a more fundamental and objectionable clerical militancy and involvement in things incompatible with clerical status; but in terms of canon law they stood on even less sure ground here than they did on arms.

As recorders of accurate historical information such critics may not be particularly reliable, although presumably Erasmus and Guicciardini reported the worst there was to tell. Unfortunately, we ordinarily know in most cases very little, if anything, about how a cleric conducted himself in action – whether he merely brought troops to the field, commanded troops only from a distance, defended himself only when attacked, used any weapons at all, and, if he did, wielded them as defensively and minimally as possible. If Chapter 1, a survey of such distinctive clerics over a sweep of 1,500 years from the late Roman Empire to the present, seems thin on details much of the time, that is because it seeks to stick as faithfully as possible to the sources, which are only rarely eyewitness accounts. Such problems have rarely troubled the people whose views on these warrior clerics are examined in Chapter 2. Their attitudes, if not safe guides to historically determinable truth, are nevertheless valuable as indicators of *a* mentality of a given era, since deciding whose voice is representative of an age is very tricky business indeed. We can put such considerations aside, however, and try to listen dispassionately to these voices from the past, especially those that say what we do not wish or expect to hear.

These problems with the historical record are nicely illustrated in the case of a warrior cleric only slightly less famous than Pope Julius II. Around 1050, when he was about fourteen, Odo received from his half-brother William, duke of Normandy, the see of Bayeux, which Odo then held until his death in 1097. The first edition of *The Oxford Dictionary of the Christian Church* dutifully records what everyone by now 'knows' was Odo's role in the conquest of England: 'He fought in person at the Battle of Hastings (14 Oct. 1066), armed with a mace so that as a cleric he might not shed blood.'[49] There exists not a single shred of evidence for this charming fabrication. Its source seems to have been the nineteenth-century English historian Edward Freeman, who provided a memorable description of Odo's behavior, but no source for it.[50] One of the most nearly contemporary and reliable accounts, that of William of Poitiers, explicitly denies that Odo bore arms, although he was much feared by warriors because of his sagacity on military matters.[51] As Odo's chaplain, William was not disinterested, nor was he present at the battle; but he was no more partisan than Freeman and, unlike Freeman, 'clearly derived his information from survivors' in the considered opinion of a distinguished scholar.[52] Just as no written evidence supports Freeman, neither does the Bayeux Tapestry, although if Odo was its patron he ironically perhaps planted a seed there which flowered so wondrously in Freeman's mind eight hundred years later. For one scene in the tapestry depicts Odo with this description: 'Hic Odo ep[iscopu]s baculu[m] tenens confortat pueros'. Depending on how one construes these words, this means: 'Here Bishop Odo, holding a staff [stick, baton], encourages [urges on] the young men'. Whether or not Odo was being given credit here for rallying the faltering troops, he is not shown wielding an ordinary weapon or inflicting wounds. Even if *baculum* is best rendered not as 'staff' but as 'mace' (and its similarity to what Duke William visibly holds has often been noted), it is far more probable that Odo bore it as a sign of his authority and, it has been argued, of his unique relationship to the duke, the only other person carrying one, rather than that Odo used it to inflict wounds without drawing blood. But *baculus* was also the word ordinarily used for a bishop's staff, which Odo might simply have

---

49 ODCC, p. 976 (1st ed., 1957). The three later editions between 1974 and 2005 merely state that he was present at the battle.
50 Edward A. Freeman, *The History of the Norman Conquest of England* (Oxford, 1870–79), 3:464.
51 'Gesta Willelmi ducis Normannorum,' in *Scriptores rerum gestarum Willelmi conquestoris*, ed. J. A. Giles, Caxton Society 3 (London, 1845; repr., New York, 1967), pp. 149–50: 'Arma neque movit unquam, neque voluit moveri: valde tamen timendus armatis. Bellum namque utilissimo consilio, cum necessitas postularet, juvabat, quantum potuit religione salva'.
52 Frank Stenton, ed., *The Bayeux Tapestry* (New York, 1956), p. 21.

been holding in that capacity. Nevertheless, despite all these points and the complete absence of any proof, the story persists because people, even good historians, believe what they wish and wish to believe it.[53]

Then there is the problem of the legal status of a cleric who has taken up arms, especially if this has occurred as part of a larger pattern of behavior tantamount to rejection of clerical life. The thirteenth-century Cistercian writer Caesarius of Heisterbach devoted one of the chapters of his *Dialogue on Miracles* to the story 'Of the apostate monk, who being mortally wounded in fighting, in the contrition of his confession, chose for himself 2,000 years in Purgatory.'[54] On his own deathbed admission, this monk had taken up with robbers and had killed people, and so Caesarius regarded him as 'apostate'. Although it seems to have been the monk's intention to reject his habit, he probably could not do so unilaterally from a legal point of view (depending on the vows he had taken and at what age); and in many other cases the intention is obscure or indeterminable. Are such 'clerics' any longer clerics? They, the church, their order, and the world at large may not have agreed on the answer.

'Armsbearing by the clergy,' then, ineluctably conjures up a series of questions and issues in different realms, including historical perception and historical memory, and so imposing rigid limits on the scope of this study is neither desirable nor possible. Nevertheless, two clearly related but separate issues, hunting and violence, will not ordinarily be treated except for comparative or explanatory purposes. Thus intriguing if repulsive characters like the Reverend Samuel Marsden (1764–1838), 'The Flogging Parson' of New South Wales, will not figure here unless they somehow 'bore arms' or were directly involved in warfare of some kind.[55] Besides, violence in principle has always been forbidden the clergy, and so has hunting, or at least noisy hunting in modern times (*venatio clamosa* or *strepitosa*).[56] Armsbearing, on the other hand, came to be allowed under restricted circumstances from the twelfth century onward for nearly all the clergy, regular as well as secular, and the principal focus of this study will remain the laws that two of the central Christian churches have chosen to make for their own clergy during the last nine hundred years.

---

[53] Even the best treatments of Odo available do not go far enough in destroying this myth: see David Bates, 'The Character and Career of Odo, Bishop of Bayeux (1049/50–1097)', *Speculum* 50 (1975):1–20, at 6; and David Bernstein, *The Mystery of the Bayeux Tapestry* (London, 1986), p. 32. The older discussion of the sources of the battle, Wilhelm Spatz's *Die Schlacht von Hastings* (1896; repr., Vaduz, 1965), pp. 54–5, dismisses with contempt another scholar's suggestion that 'Odo confortat pueros' means exactly what it says: 'Der Bischof bemühte sich, mutlos gewordene Trossknechte wieder zur Vernunft zu bringen. - Odo hatte doch sicherlich in der Schlacht selbst etwas besseres zu thun!' Most recently, the otherwise very thorough and judicious book by Richard Huscroft, *The Norman Conquest. A New Introduction* (Harlow, 2009), does not address this question at all.

[54] Caesarius of Heisterbach, *The Dialogue on Miracles*, tr. H. von E. Scott and C. C. Swinton Bland, 2 vols. (London, 1929), 2.2, 1:64.

[55] See Robert Hughes, *The Fatal Shore* (New York, 1987), pp. 187–92.

[56] See Augustine Thompson, O.P., 'The Afterlife of an Error. Hunting in the Decretalists (1190–1348),' *SC* 33 (1999):151–68.

The heart of this book lies in the following chapters on the ecclesiastical laws governing clerical armsbearing. Here a problem of which I have been quite aware is a seeming contentment on my part with a simple recitation of the relevant statutes, canons, and regulations without much consideration of the background or context of those enactments. Even if this book could accommodate that wish, the published sources in the great majority of cases either are wanting or simply will not tell us what we wish to know. Some archival records would undoubtedly be helpful here and there, but identifying which of those sources might be fruitful is largely a matter of educated guesswork. The singular exception here are the published *acta* of the Pontifical Commission which produced the revised *Code of Canon Law* of 1983, which, we will see, are astonishingly revealing.

In 1965 a professor of canon law wrote that 'the study of and the regard for canon law seem to have fallen on evil days.'[57] Like Harvey Cox and his prognostications in *The Secular City*, he could not have been more wrong. This book is appearing at a time of almost unprecedented worldwide interest in the law of both the Roman Catholic and Anglican Churches. The sexual abuse scandals in the Roman Catholic Church, most openly exposed in the United States but hardly confined to it, have raised many questions about a legal system which seems to treat pedophile priests and the bishops responsible for them so charitably, while in the Anglican tradition the election and consecration of an openly gay bishop in the United States and the blessing of gay unions in Canada in 2003 have threatened to fracture the fragile Anglican Communion and perplexed and frightened many people within and without it. This unexpected popular curiosity comes in the wake of a scholarly resurgence of interest in canon law as well. The revised *Code* of Catholic canon law of 1983 has prompted the production of a spate of commentaries by the canon law societies of many countries (including two in the United States in 1985 and 2000), which in turn seems to have helped inspire in the United Kingdom the formation of The Ecclesiastical Law Society in 1987, which publishes the *Ecclesiastical Law Journal*; the establishment of a master's degree in canon law at the University of Cardiff, the first such program at a British university since the abolition of the study and teaching of canon law in the realm in 1534; a flowering of new introductions to and comparative studies in canon law;[58] and a series of texts and studies in the English canonical tradition brought out by the publisher of this book.

---

[57] Stevick, *Canon Law*, p. vii.
[58] James A. Coriden, *An Introduction to Canon Law* (London, 1990, and New York-Mahwah, 1991); T. Briden and B. Hanson, eds., *Moore's Introduction to English Canon Law* (3rd ed., London, 1992); Richard Helmholz, ed., *Canon Law in Protestant Lands*, Comparative Studies in Continental and Anglo-American Legal History 2 (Berlin, 1992); Mark Hill, *Ecclesiastical Law* (London, 1995); Norman Doe, *The Legal Framework of the Church of England* (Oxford, 1996); Rhidian Jones, *The Canon Law of the Roman Catholic Church and the Church of England. A Handbook* (Edinburgh, 2000); Mark Hill, ed., *Faithful Discipleship. Clergy Discipline in Anglican and Roman Canon Law* (Cardiff-Rome, 2001).

CHAPTER 1

JULIUS EXCLUSUS?

First of all, what monstrous new fashion is this, to wear the dress of a priest on top, while underneath it you're all bristling and clanking with blood-stained armor?

THUS St Peter begins his indictment in the *Julius Exclusus* of the late Pope Julius II (1503–13) for his engagement in war, particularly his campaigns to impose effective rule in the Lands of St Peter. Peter lodges many other charges as well, but this above all: that Julius, his putative successor, has waged war and befouled his priestly raiment. For this reason he is to be barred from heaven forever. The author of this Senecan parody, first published anonymously in 1517, was long thought to have been Desiderius Erasmus (c.1466–1536), with whose Latin style and pacifist views the *Julius* seems to be entirely consonant.[1] (Erasmus always disavowed the authorship, which the English humanist and cleric Richard Pace always claimed and for which Pace has recently begun to receive the recognition he deserved;[2] the fact that Erasmus was thought for nearly five-hundred years to be the author is the historically crucial point.) As one of the most distinguished and influential of Renaissance humanists, Erasmus has ever since informed the attitudes of educated westerners.[3] Regardless of his genius as a patron of the arts, Julius' reputation has never recovered from this literary bill of attainder, and it helps explain why Julius was one of the last warrior popes. But was Erasmus or Pace right to condemn him for bearing arms? Was Julius *exclusus* in two senses – set apart from his fellow clerics here on earth, and likely to be excluded from the company of heaven?

---

[1] 'Julius Excluded from Heaven: A Dialogue', tr. M. J. Heath, in *Collected Works of Erasmus*, 27, ed. A. H. T. Levi (Toronto, 1986):155–97. The quotation appears on p. 169. On the consensus on Erasmus' authorship, see pp. 159–60.

[2] The 1996 Cambridge Ph.D. dissertation of Catherine Mary Curtis, 'Richard Pace on Pedagogy, Counsel and State', arguing for his authorship, remains unpublished, but it has begun to win acceptance in the literature, e.g. Diarmaid MacCulloch, *The Reformation* (New York, 2004), pp. 101–2, and Chambers, *Popes*, pp. 132–33. Richard Pace (c.1482–1536) had opportunity to observe Julius II while serving Christopher Bainbridge (1462/4–1514), archbishop of York (1508–14), cardinal (1511–4), and ambassador of Henry VIII to the pope from 1509 to 1514. Pace later became secretary to the King and dean of St Paul's, Exeter, and Salisbury in succession.

[3] Thus Michael Howard began his Trevelyan Lectures on *War and the Liberal Conscience* (London, 1978) with Erasmus (pp. 13–16).

Origins of Warrior Clergy in the Late Roman Empire

Certainly Julius stood solidly within a clerical tradition that reached back more than a thousand years. As the Roman Empire disintegrated from the fourth and fifth centuries onward, bishops by default and by delegation gradually filled the vacuum left by the collapse of the army and the disintegration of the administration.[4] In the West in particular bishops assumed more and more the new office of 'defender of the city' (defensor civitatis), even though this post was not originally intended for them.[5] Men like Hilary of Arles (†449), Nicetius of Trier (†566), Sagittarius of Gap (†585), and his brother Salonius of Embrun fortified, governed, and protected their city-states.[6] The disappearance of most towns in the West not governed by bishops attests the significance of their work. The agglomeration of this power in their hands in turn attracted not only the late Roman aristocracy, who were born to rule and now increasingly had to turn to the church for posts in the cursus honorum, but also to the Germanic nobility, who were born to fight as well as to rule and so accelerated the militarization of the episcopate in the West.

How rapidly this occurred is a matter of disagreement. Friedrich Prinz, reacting to old charges (often made by French historians) that the Teutons destroyed the Roman Empire, sees an early militarization of the episcopate resulting from the internal disintegration of the Empire rather than from the barbarization caused by the Germanic tribes which moved into it.[7] Other German scholars have followed Prinz's lead by stressing the legal delegation of authority to bishops by the later emperors.[8] Patrick Geary, synthesizing a great deal of recent work, describes a more gradual process taking place over the course of three centuries in which late Roman bishops, highly educated and often holy, tended mainly to fortify their cities. These then gave way by the seventh century to bishops less learned, less holy, and more likely to be skilled in arms, a process reaching its nadir in the frankly political warrior bishops of the early eighth century.[9] All these historians agree, however, that the episcopate was markedly more militaristic by the seventh century than it had been before.

---

[4]   J. H. W. G. Liebeschuetz, Barbarians and Bishops. Army, Church, and State in the Age of Arcadius and Chrysostom (Oxford, 1990), pp. 231–5, provides a helpful explanation of this phenomenon. See also Mark Whittow, 'Ruling the Late Roman and Early Byzantine City: A Continuous History', Past and Present 129 (Nov. 1990):3–29.

[5]   See The Institutes of Justinian, tr. J. B. Moyle, 5th ed. (Oxford, 1913), 1.20.5, p. 26.

[6]   A good survey in English is Prinz, 'King, Clergy and War', who summarizes here much of his earlier work. See also Martin Heinzelmann, 'Bischof und Herrschaft vom spätantiken Gallien bis zu den karolingischen Hausmeiern', in Friedrich Prinz, ed., Herrschaft und Kirche. Beiträge zur Entstehung und Wirkungsweise episkopaler und monastischer Organisationsformen, MGM 33 (Stuttgart, 1988), pp. 23–82 (with rich bibliography in n. 1).

[7]   Friedrich Prinz, 'Die bischöfliche Stadtherrschaft im Frankenreich vom 5. bis zum 7. Jahrhundert', Historische Zeitschrift 217 (1973):1–35, and, more generally, Klerus und Krieg.

[8]   Heinzelmann, 'Bischof und Herrschaft', and Reinhold Kaiser, 'Königtum und Bischofsherrschaft im frühmittelalterlichen Neustrien', in Prinz, ed., Herrschaft und Kirche, pp. 83–108.

[9]   Patrick Geary, Before France and Germany (New York, 1987), pp. 33–35, 123–35, 176, 210–14.

The History of the Franks by Gregory, bishop of Tours (†594), tends to cor-roborate this view. In his account, Sagittarius of Gap and Salonius of Embrun stand out sharply as the only bishops who engage in arms in any way, while other bishops continue to rely on other methods, including prayer.[10] In Gregory's view, in fact, even Roman emperors could achieve more this way. Theodosius I (379–95) 'put all his hope and all his trust in the mercy of God. He held many peoples in check, more by vigils and prayer than by the sword, and so he strengthened the Roman state and was able to enter the city of Constantinople as a conqueror.'[11] Whether one construes this passage as naive, hopeful, or desperate, it demonstrates Gregory's commitment as a bishop to the power of prayer and, as an historian, to the necessity of teaching this lesson to future generations.

The future lay with those rulers and bishops more committed to action, and the bellwether was Gregory of Tours' contemporary, Gregory I, bishop of Rome (590–604), later remembered as 'the Great', who would have appreci-ated the spiritual wisdom often ascribed to Ignatius of Loyola: 'Pray as if all depended on God; act as if all depended on you.' From the beginning of his pontificate he maintained close contact with the military commanders of the region of Rome, not only exhorting them to glory, but sometimes acting as the nodal point of their campaigns and occasionally giving them precise tacti-cal directives, including attacking the Lombards from the rear and plundering their settlements. In 598/99 he also sharply reproved Archbishop Januarius of Cagliari (in Sardinia) for his fecklessness and urged him to fortify his see and other cities, organize the watch, and take other steps to repulse the enemy.[12] Given the great influence Gregory's words exerted later in so many dimensions of life and thought in the history of the West (as in the famous defense of art as the 'book of the illiterate'), one has to wonder how much of an example he provided to future bishops in the realm of warfare.[13] Certainly he does not appear to have considered his decisiveness problematical.

Whatever Pope Gregory's possible influence, in the Frankish kingdom the parvenu Carolingians who overthrew the Merovingian dynasty in the mid-eighth century faced an already powerful episcopate accustomed to warfare. Charles Martel (†747), Pepin (†768), and Charlemagne (†814) moved suc-cessfully to coopt these bishops and to integrate them into the royal system of power. Although the Carolingians scarcely began the militarization of the

---

[10] Gregory of Tours, *The History of the Franks*, tr. L. Thorpe (Harmondsworth, 1974), pp. 116–17, 237, 285–87, 291, 369, 421.

[11] Ibid., p. 92.

[12] Georg Jenal, 'Gregor der Grosse und die Stadt Rom (590–604)', in Prinz, ed., *Herrschaft und Kirche*, pp. 108–45, especially 125–32, 137–38; Chambers, *Popes*, p. 5.

[13] On Gregory's influence, see Lawrence G. Duggan, 'Was Art Really the "Book of the Illiterate"?', *Word & Image* 5 (1989):227–51, reprinted (together with 'Reflections on "Was Art Really the 'Book of the Illiterate'?"') in *Reading Images and Texts. Medieval Images and Texts as Forms of Communication*, eds Marielle Hageman and Marco Mostert, Utrecht Studies in Medieval Literacy 8 (Turnhout, 2005), pp. 64–119; and idem, '"For Force Is Not of God?" Compulsion and Conversion from Yahweh to Charlemagne', in James Muldoon, ed., *The Varieties of Religious Conversion in the Middle Ages* (Gainesville, 1997), pp. 49–62.

Frankish episcopate, as used to be thought, they did make military obligations the general rule for the bishops and abbots of their lands. Even if these
prelates did not themselves use weapons, they were expected to supply and
ordinarily to lead large contingents of troops in the service of the king.[14]

The Iberian peninsula in the early Middle Ages witnessed a different course
of development. In this less exposed part of the Empire the Visigoths had
settled in the early fifth century after expelling the Vandals. While Frankish
royal power decayed under the later Merovingians, the reverse occurred in
Spain, so much so that by the seventh century 'It was the kings, not the
bishops, who governed Spain and with it the Spanish Church.'[15] The crown
nevertheless experienced considerable difficulties raising troops during emer-
gencies because of, in the words of E. A. Thompson, 'the reluctance of the
rich to defend Spain.'[16] When King Wamba (672–80) faced this problem in
dealing with a revolt shortly after his election, he responded by issuing in
November 673 'the great army law' requiring all his subjects, under pain of
drastic penalties, to obey the royal summons to the host to repel any invasion.
The bishops and the clergy were not exempted.[17] In fact,

> anyone who thus, through delay, fear, malice, or lukewarmness, fails to exert
> himself, with all his power, against our enemies for national defense, if he be a
> priest, or belong to a sacerdotal order, and does not have the means to satisfy the
> damages incurred by the invasion of said enemy, he shall be exiled to such place as
> the king may select.[18]

The vigorous protests of the clergy notwithstanding, Wamba's successor
Erwig in 681 renewed the law and denied any concession to the clergy. Thus
by royal decree designed to provide for the adequate defense of the realm,
the entire Spanish clergy, not merely the episcopate, could be mobilized for
the common good. It would have an abiding effect on the history of Spain
and its clergy.

The Second Wave of Invasions and Their Effects

Elsewhere, the militarization of the clergy proceeded even more rapidly in
the later ninth, tenth, and early eleventh centuries not because of the growth
of government and of rulers' reliance on the church, but because of the
frightening threats to order posed by the 'second wave of invasions' from the
Saracens, the Magyars, and above all the Vikings. Churchmen took up arms,

---

[14] Prinz, 'King, Clergy and War', passim.
[15] E. A. Thompson, *The Goths in Spain* (Oxford, 1969), p. 282.
[16] Ibid., p. 264.
[17] See ibid., pp. 228, 262–63, and Joseph O'Callaghan, *A History of Medieval Spain* (Ithaca, 1975), p.
      50.
[18] *The Visigothic Code*, tr. S. P. Scott (Boston, 1910), 9.2.8, pp. 325–26. Large parts of this Code
      were incorporated into Las Siete Partidas in the thirteenth century, and King Charles III in 1788
      declared that it had not been repealed as a whole by subsequent statutes (ibid., pp. xl–xli).

sometimes in obedience to royal command, sometimes in self-defense against both the invaders and the local nobility when they sought to bring the church under their own control. Violence became even more normal, and so did clerical participation in it. The bishops of Rome again and again took up arms in defense of the Eternal City – Leo IV and John VIII in the ninth century, John X and John XII in the tenth, Benedict VIII in 1012–14 (whom a great church historian compared to Julius II), and Leo IX in 1053.[19] D. S. Chambers believes that it is 'arguable that the papal resistance was largely responsible for saving the mainland of Italy from the Muslim domination that befell Sicily and much of Spain.'[20] Leo IX's biographer Wibert tells us that when a deacon in Toul, Leo was as expert in military matters as if they were his sole profession. His skill, however, did not prevail in battle against the Normans, who took him prisoner. He appears to have scrupulously refrained from personally bearing arms, but otherwise to have had no reservations about his participation in warfare.[21]

Prelates everywhere in Europe were similarly drawn in during this chaotic period. Since then the Germans in particular have suffered from 'an image problem' in this respect. Some astonishing facts and figures suggest that it is a well-deserved reputation, such as the death of ten bishops in battle between 886 and 908 alone; but the Germans have ironically contributed to this dubious distinction by writing about this subject far more than anyone else has and, less directly, by arguing that a unique symbiotic relationship existed between the German monarchy and the church (the 'imperial church system' or *Reichskirchensystem*). There were plenty of warriors and war leaders in the German hierarchy, but several of them were also central figures in the movement to reform the church: Adalbero of Metz (929–62), St Bruno of Cologne (953–65), Wazo of Liège (called Judas Maccabeus by his biographer), and Bruno of Toul, the future Leo IX.[22]

By comparison, one must piece together similar pictures of clerical warriors in other parts of Europe. In Italy, for instance, the bishops of Troia and Acerenza were killed fighting on the Byzantine side against the Normans at Montemaggiore in 1047, and the bishop of Cassano in 1059 led Calabrian resistance to the Normans.[23]

As on the Continent, necessity encouraged the development of military obligations incumbent on Anglo-Saxon prelates in the ninth and tenth

---

[19] Johannes Haller, *Das Papsttum. Idee und Wirklichkeit*, rev. ed. (Munich, 1965), 2:133–91; Philippe Contamine, *War in the Middle Ages*, tr. M. Jones (Oxford, 1984), pp. 268–70; Chambers, *Popes*, pp. 3–11. The comparison between Benedict VIII and Julius II was drawn by Albert Hauck, *Kirchengeschichte Deutschlands*, 8th ed. (1922; repr., Berlin, 1954), 3:519–20.

[20] Chambers, *Popes*, p. 5.

[21] Erdmann, *Origin*, p. 118.

[22] A very helpful introduction to the considerable literature on this subject is by Benjamin Arnold, 'German Bishops and Their Military Retinues in the Medieval Empire', *German History* 7 (1989):161–83 (especially 163 n. 11), who also carries the story into the High Middle Ages.

[23] G. A. Loud, 'The Church, Warfare and Miliary Obligation in Norman Italy', in W. J. Shiels, ed., *The Church and War*, Studies in Church History 20 (Oxford, 1983), p. 34, and G. A. Loud, *Church and Society in the Norman Principality of Capua* (Oxford, 1985), p. 157.

centuries.[24] The *Anglo-Saxon Chronicle* lists bishops and abbots as commanders or participants in military campaigns in 825, 836, 845, 871, 903, and 992, and in which no fewer than three were killed.[25] Despite the continuing Norse threat, Frank Barlow's *English Church 1000–1066* suggests a relatively quiescent time for eleventh-century prelates, although he does note that under Edward the Confessor the bishops of Worcester and Hereford commanded armies on the Welsh march and that several abbots were at Hastings, having personally conducted their thegns to the battlefield.[26] If one probes other sources, however, one finds that Bishop Eadnoth of Dorchester and Abbot Wulfsige of Ramsay fell at the battle of Ashingdon in 1016; that the will of Bishop Theodred of London (c.950) bequeathed his two best swords and shields; that the will of Bishop Alfwold of Crediton (c.1000) disposed of a large amount of military equipment, including a great ship; and that around the same time Archbishop Aelfric of Canterbury legated to the king his best ship, sixty helmets, and sixty coats of mail.[27] While these prelates need not have personally used these weapons, they did come from a class to whom the arts of war were no less alien than to their confreres on the Continent.

One of the central questions of English history concerns the degree of continuity between Anglo-Saxon and Norman England. On the subject of warrior prelates the answer is clear: there was no break for some time. As duke of Normandy, William had already created as bishop of Bayeux his fourteen-year-old half-brother Odo, who, as we have seen, fought at Hastings with a padded mace.[28] He also later avenged the murder of Bishop Walcher of Durham and his clergy by the Northumbrians in 1080.[29] Nearly as famous as Odo was Bishop Geoffrey of Coutances (1049–93), who at Hastings acted as chaplain-in-chief but soon became more active.[30] When the West Saxons rebelled in 1080, 'the men of Winchester, London, and Salisbury, under the leadership of Geoffrey bishop of Coutances', according to the monastic chronicler Orderic Vitalis, 'marched against them, killed some, captured and mutilated others, and put the rest to flight.'[31] In 1075 Geoffrey and Odo were some of the prelates among the 'generals' of Archbishop Lanfranc who protected the realm against rebellious barons in the absence of the king. And on the occasion of that revolt and another in 1088, St Wulfstan, bishop of Worcester, organized and led the defense of his city.[32]

---

[24] See Nicholas Brooks, 'The Development of Military Obligations in 8th and 9th Century England', in P. Clemoes and K. Hughes, eds, *England Before the Conquest. Studies in Primary Sources Presented to Dorothy Whitelock* (Cambridge, 1971), pp. 69–84.

[25] *EHD*, 1:171–73, 178, 191, 213, 227.

[26] Frank Barlow, *The English Church 1000–1066* (London, 1979), pp. 98, 170–71.

[27] *C&S* 1:77, 239, 383–86.

[28] See above, p. 15.

[29] Frank Stenton, *Anglo-Saxon England*, 3rd ed. (Oxford, 1971), pp. 613–14.

[30] See John Le Patourel, 'Geoffrey of Montbray, Bishop of Coutances, 1049–93', *EHR* 59 (1944):129–61.

[31] *The Ecclesiastical History of Orderic Vitalis*, ed. and tr. M. Chibnall (Oxford, 1969–78), 2:229.

[32] See below, p. 63.

A Break in the High Middle Ages?

The eleventh and twelfth centuries witnessed a stunning reversal in the fortunes of Europe. The invaders were repulsed, and westerners took the offensive as warriors, traders, missionaries, and travelers. With the growth of the crusading movement, the revival of long-distance commerce and towns, the preoccupation with order in the legal and intellectual spheres, the beginnings of universities, and the ecclesiastical reform movement, one might have expected much greater peace and much less clerical violence in Europe in the High Middle Ages. And so it seemed to Orderic Vitalis, writing around 1127, who saw the turning-point in the great reform council convened at Rheims in 1049 by Pope Leo IX, where 'the pope utterly prohibited priests from bearing arms or taking wives. From that time the fatal custom began to wither away little by little. The priests were ready enough to give up bearing arms, but even now they are loath to part with their mistresses or to live chaste lives.'[33] Similarly, a modern commentator on the *Song of Roland* believes that Archbishop Turpin, of whom that epic presents the most vivid portrait of any sword-wielding cleric in western literature, was rendered anachronistic by the reform movement.[34]

But in fact he was not, nor did the clerical warrior disappear. Orderic himself notices that on at least two occasions the bishops of France eagerly responded to King Louis VI's need for help. In 1108 the king sought to 'put an end to the oppressions of bandits and rebels. As a result the bishops set up the communities of the people in France, so that the priests might accompany the king to battle or siege, carrying banners and leading all their parishioners.'[35] In 1119, having been defeated at Bremule and threatened by a Norman insurrection, the king ordered the bishops to muster 'an army of the whole community': 'They readily obeyed him, and pronounced excommunication on the priests of their dioceses with their parishioners, unless they hurried to take part in the king's campaign at the appointed time, and crushed the rebel Normans with all their forces.'[36]

Whatever doubts gnawed at these clergy could have been dispelled by the example given at the top by the popes themselves. Gregory VII contemplated leading, as *dux et pontifex*, a crusade of sorts in 1074 to come to the aid of the Byzantines, but nothing came of it.[37] Ironically, although the great reform movement resulted in Europe at large in the emergence of an effective papal monarchy, at home it led to catastrophic losses of territory which forced the popes to take to arms to maintain what they had as well as to recoup what

---

[33] *Ecclesiastical History*, 3:121–23.
[34] Dorothy Sayers, in the Introduction to her translation of *The Song of Roland* (Harmondsworth, 1957), pp. 18–19.
[35] *Ecclesiastical History*, 6:157.
[36] Ibid., 6:243–5.
[37] H. E. J. Cowdrey, 'Pope Gregory VII's "Crusading" Plans of 1074', in his *Popes, Monks and Crusaders* (London, 1984), no. X, 27–40; Chambers, *Popes*, p. 9.

they had lost. Between 1121 and 1229, for example, the popes were more or less constantly at war with the counts of Ceccano and their allies. Beyond them there always lay the Norman threat.[38] Like Leo IX in 1053, Innocent II in 1139 was captured in an abortive campaign against the Normans and later commanded an equally unsuccessful assault on the town of Tivoli.[39] Adrian IV was captured by the Normans at Benevento in 1156.[40] A republican revolt in Rome in the 1140s elicited strong papal countermeasures, although the exact degree of pontifical participation is disputed. According to one account, but only one, Pope Lucius III was killed leading his soldiers in their attack on the Capitol in 1145.[41] According to some sources, Eugenius III three years later led the army's attempt to reestablish a foothold in Rome, but John of Salisbury says that the pope had handed command of the army to Cardinal Guy, nicknamed 'The Maiden' (*Puella*).[42] At least one modern secondary account nevertheless says that both popes led their armies and that Lucius was killed in battle.[43]

Other prelates in southern Italy were also ineluctably drawn into warfare. Like the popes, the abbots of Monte Cassino had to fight for their possessions. Abbot Girardus in 1115 devastated the area around Sessa Arunca in the course of his feud with Rangarda of Gaeta. His successor Oderisius was denounced by Pope Honorius II before an assembly of laymen in 1125 for acting more like a soldier than an abbot and for poor economic administration, even though it had been at the command of Pope Calixtus II that Oderisius in 1123–24 had besieged and captured Castel Pico, which furthermore lay not in the Lands of St Peter or of Monte Cassino, but of the Normans! In 1126 Honorius, who as bishop of Ostia had had poor relations with Oderisius, deposed his enemy after Oderisius failed to answer a triple summons.[44] Elsewhere, the bishop of S. Agata dei Goti led part of Robert of Capua's army operating against King Roger II of Sicily and was present at the battle of Nocera in 1132.[45]

In preaching the 'First Crusade' in 1095, Pope Urban II made clear his will with respect to clerical participation: 'we do not want those who have abandoned the world and have vowed themselves to spiritual warfare either to bear arms or to go on this journey; we go so far as to forbid them to do so.'[46]

---

[38] This generally unappreciated dimension of papal policy is emphasized by Hartmut Hoffmann, 'Petrus Diaconus, die Herren von Tusculum und der Sturz Oderisius' II. von Monte Cassino', *DA* 27 (1971):1–109, especially 85–86, 88.

[39] See below, p. 63.

[40] Chambers, *Popes*, p. 11.

[41] G. W. Greenaway, *Arnold of Brescia* (Cambridge, 1931), p. 107. The source, Godfrey of Viterbo, also qualified his report by saying 'as we have heard' (*sicut tunc audivimus*).

[42] John of Salisbury, *Historia pontificalis*, ed. and tr. M. Chibnall (corrected ed., Oxford, 1986), p. 60.

[43] The 'Introduction' by Elizabeth Kennan to Bernard of Clairvaux, *Five Books on Consideration. Advice to a Pope*, tr. J. Anderson and E. Kennan (Kalamazoo, 1976), pp. 10–11.

[44] Hoffmann, 'Petrus Diaconus', pp. 75–91; Herbert Bloch, *Monte Cassino in the Middle Ages* (Cambridge, Mass., 1986), pp. 960–62.

[45] Loud, *Church and Society in Capua*, p. 157.

[46] Quoted in Jonathan Riley-Smith, *The First Crusade and the Idea of Crusading* (Philadelphia, 1986), p. 26.

Although he primarily had monks in mind here, he also forbade priests and other clerics to depart without leave from their bishops and without providing for their parishes. These words evidently produced the desired effect on the First Crusade, for the only cleric who is indisputably attested as bearing arms – a Provençal priest – was sufficiently conspicuous to come to the attention of the Byzantine princess Anna Komnene in Constantinople.[47]

The later crusades originated in an altered climate of opinion and ineluctably attracted different kinds of clerics, moved by deeply felt religious impulses to take the cross, dim prospects at home, an appetite for adventure or violence, or simple obedience to their lords – and all intensified by the emergence of the military-religious orders which St Bernard of Clairvaux stoutly defended against all critics. On the Third Crusade, for example, Bishop Hubert Walter of Salisbury accompanied the archbishop of Canterbury and 500 soldiers in a fruitless attack on Saladin's troops in November 1190. Hubert Walter appeared again on the battlefield in the Holy Land at least twice and won King Richard's admiration for his abilities. Elected Archbishop of Canterbury in 1193, he governed England during Richard's long absence and fielded troops against the Welsh in 1198. His formidable contemporary Samson, abbot of Bury St Edmunds, together with other abbots appeared armed (*armati*) at the siege of Windsor in 1193.[48]

While English prelates often warred in obedience to the king, the no less aggressive clergy of England were inclined instead to violate the king's laws. The Austin canon William of Newburgh reports that in 1163 Henry II was informed that more than a hundred homicides had been committed by clerics in England since his accession in 1154.[49] Even allowing for the usual unreliability of medieval numbers and perhaps for a desire to please the king's ear, this is a startling figure which illuminates the passion behind the Constitutions of Clarendon enacted a year later.

Whether French clerics were more quiescent at home or abroad is doubtful. Let the information provided by one famous source suffice here. Jean de Joinville (†1317) recorded in his *Life* of King St Louis IX the story of his chaplain, Jean de Voisey, who on foot and with only a spear routed eight Saracens. 'From that time onwards my priest was well known in the camp, and people pointed him out to one another and say: "Look! There's my Lord of Joinville's priest, who routed eight Saracens."'[50] Joinville also recounts that the patriarch of Jerusalem had excommunicated Count Walter of Brienne for refusing to surrender a tower he held at Jaffa called the Patriarch's Tower. Walter requested at least provisional absolution until his return from an expedition with the army. The patriarch refused.

---

[47] Ibid., pp. 82 and 187 n. 178, on the lack of evidence that Bishop Adhemar of Le Puy bore arms. On Anna Komnene, see below, pp. 94–5.

[48] See below, pp. 65–6, 67, for references and further discussion of these two men.

[49] *EHD* 2:331.

[50] Jean de Joinville, 'The Life of St Louis', in Villehardouin and Joinville, *Chronicles of the Crusades*, tr. Caroline Smith (Harmondsworth, 2008), p. 211.

The count of Brienne had with him a certain valiant cleric who was the bishop of Ramla and had performed many fine knightly deeds alongside the count, and he said to him: 'My lord, don't let it trouble your conscience that the patriarch does not absolve you, since he's in the wrong and you're in the right. I absolve you in the name of the Father, and of the Son, and of the Holy Spirit. Now let's get at them!'[51]

Joinville's extraordinary tale of a Parisian cleric who killed three assailants, to be discussed in the next chapter, suggests that the scale of clerical violence in Europe had perhaps not abated in the thirteenth century. At the great battle of Bouvines in 1214 the effective commander of the French army was Garin, an old Hospitaller and bishop-elect of Senlis (†1227). Whether he actually bore arms is unclear, but on the left flank there rode the bishop of Beauvais, Philip of Dreux, who with a club apparently knocked off his horse William Longsword, the leader of the mercenary troops of King John of England. Peter des Roches, bishop of Winchester (1205–38), led one of the four divisions of the royal army at the second battle of Lincoln in 1217, and in papal service in 1235 he shared command of the army that crushed the Romans at Viterbo. One of Charles of Anjou's field officers at Benevento in 1266 was the bishop of Auxerre.[52] And at Campaldino in 1289, the commander of the men of Arezzo who fell with them was their bishop, Guglielmino Ubertini.[53] There are many more such individual examples.

Greater insight into clerical life in the thirteenth century can be gained by examining at some length the ecclesiastical careers of three members of one of the more ambitious aristocratic families in Europe. Count Thomas of Savoy (c.1178–1233) sired at least eight sons, the five youngest of whom were destined for the clergy and held benefices by the time their father died. The first, William, proved his abilities in the arts of both war and peace as bishop-elect of Valence from 1225 onward. After the marriage of his niece Eleanor of Provence to King Henry III of England in 1236, he became the king's most influential counselor. Despite the king's backing, however, the monks of Winchester refused to elect him bishop, precipitating a dispute which lasted well beyond William's death in 1239.[54]

Both more successful in England and more controversial was his younger brother Boniface. Born around 1207, in 1232 he became bishop of Bellay and the prior of the Cluniac house of Nantua nearby, both of which he successfully defended against the lords of Thoire-Villars. Elected archbishop of Canterbury in 1241, he continued, according to the English monastic chronicler Matthew Paris, periodically to return to the Continent to fight for the

51 Ibid., p. 278.
52 Charles Oman, *A History of the Art of War in the Middle Ages* (London, 1924), 1:408, 466, 469, 470, 474, 484.
53 *Dino Campagni's Chronicle of Florence*, tr. D. Bornstein (Philadelphia, 1986), 1.10, pp. 12–3. Herbert Oerter, 'Campaldino, 1289', *Speculum* 43 (1968):429–50, does not mention that the bishop was killed.
54 Eugene Cox, *The Eagles of Savoy. The House of Savoy in Thirteenth-Century Europe* (Princeton, 1974), pp. 15, 34–51, 59–61, 67–68, 70–80, 152–53, 270–71, 290.

pope and, in 1256, to participate in a campaign to liberate his brother Thomas, then besieged in Turin. While the sources are unhelpful in disclosing the nature and extent of Boniface's soldierly engagement in all these battles, it is indisputable that Matthew Paris hated foreigners and especially Boniface. It was therefore with particular glee that in his *Chronica majora* Matthew Paris told of Boniface's visitation of the priory of St Bartholomew in London in 1250. The archbishop encountered resistance and, as he pummeled the obstreperous subprior, his robes suddenly parted, revealing to the horror of all a breastplate underneath.[55]

The veracity of this story is highly doubtful. Matthew Paris notoriously hated both foreigners and Franciscans. Present at the scene at St Bartholomew's was Adam Marsh, a young, highly respected Franciscan. His report to the Franciscan minister in England is sympathetic to Boniface and records no violence, and in a letter to Bishop Robert Grosseteste of Lincoln Marsh he noted that many scurrilous stories about Boniface were being widely circulated. More to the point, it has recently been noticed that in his *Historia Anglorum* Matthew Paris qualified the story with the phrase *ut dicitur* ('as it is said') and later pasted a slip of paper over the whole incident.[56] In any event, his insinuation that such bellicose prelates were foreign to England was belied by St Wulfstan, Hubert Walter, Samson, and many others to come.

The third and youngest of these brothers of the house of Savoy was Philippe (†1285). More like William than Boniface, he both refused to take holy orders and held Valence as bishop-elect (1241–67) and Vienne as dean of the cathedral chapter. Just as William had been pivotal in the Rhone valley in the struggle between Pope Gregory IX and Emperor Frederick II, Philippe was central in the continuation of that conflict between the later popes and Frederick and his successors. In 1245, in fact, Pope Innocent IV had persuaded the gentle incumbent archbishop of Lyons to resign and give way to the vigorous young Savoyard. As a martial prelate Philippe served the papacy well and was suitably rewarded with benefices. His consistent refusal to receive major orders, however, eventually occasioned some scruples at the papal court, especially after he had outlived his original usefulness. In 1264 Clement IV offered him the choice between ordination or resignation of all his benefices and offices. In the presence of the cardinals, in a speech undoubtedly not verbatim yet probably accurate, Philippe announced to the pope:

> Holy Father, if you will grant me these benefices in simple tonsure, I will continue to serve you and maintain the rights of the church with my own person, as I have done in the past. If not, then you can take your benefices and do whatever you want

---

[55] Ibid., pp. 17–19, 110, 139 and n. 11, 175–79, 382–92; *Chronicles of Matthew Paris. Monastic Life in the Thirteenth Century*, ed. and tr. R. Vaughan (New York, 1984), pp. 220–21. On Matthew's prejudices, see ibid., pp. 7–10.

[56] *Monumenta Franciscana*, ed. J. S. Brewer, RS 4 (London, 1858), pp. 163, 327–9, nos. 53 and 182; Leland Wilshire, 'Boniface of Savoy, Carthusian and Archbishop of Canterbury 1207–1270', *Analecta Cartusiana* 31 (1977):42–3, who offers additional reasons undermining the credibility of the story. On Matthew's prejudices, see Vaughan's introduction to the *Chronicles*, pp. 7–10.

with them, for with the help of God, our house has the wherewithal to sustain us without my being a bishop.

Philippe then threw his garments to the floor and left, celebrated the abandonment of his ecclesiastical career, married and sired children to continue his family, and died in 1285.[57]

The Late Middle Ages

Far from disappearing in the thirteenth century, as is sometimes alleged, the fighting cleric became even more prominent in the fourteenth century and, to a lesser degree, the fifteenth. Although relations between clergy and laity were perhaps more peaceful than they had been in the High Middle Ages, the level of ordinary and organized warfare in Europe rose appreciably because of the curtailment of outward expansion, economic stagnation and competition, and crises of political succession nearly everywhere. And nearly everywhere clerics were present at the fighting.

As is so often the case, the tone was set at the top in Rome. Although fewer popes seem to have appeared at or near the battlefield than earlier, those who did were particularly dramatic. Pius II (1458–64), a distinguished humanist, authored the only autobiography ever written by a pope, which he significantly named his *Commentaries* after Julius Caesar's. Aside from customary papal involvement in the defense of the patrimony of St Peter and naming three bombards after himself and his parents, Pius was determined personally to lead a crusade against the Turk, and in fact died in Ancona just before embarking. In 1464 Pius was finally realizing the dream of Gregory VII in 1074, which no pope in the interim had sought to do.[58] And then there was the most celebrated warrior pope of all, Julius II (1503–13), who aside from his personal temperament found it difficult to find competent generals.[59]

Most popes in the late Middle Ages, however, relied heavily on cardinal-legates to command their armies. In fact, remarks D. S. Chambers, 'in the early thirteenth century we enter the great age of the warrior-cardinal, which lasted for the next three hundred years.'[60] Among the dozens of them was Gil Albornoz (1310–67), a Castilian and archbishop of Toledo, who had been at the battle of Taifa (1340) and the siege of Algeciras (1344), and was sent in 1353 to pacify the Papal States. He fought for fourteen years to do so, built no fewer than eight strong fortresses, and proceeded to make Ancona a naval base where Pius II later gathered his crusading fleet.[61] So common did this

---

[57] Cox, *Eagles of Savoy*, pp. 61, 66, 141, 144–5, 150–52, 258–9, 346–63; the address at the Curia is given on p. 357.
[58] Chambers, *Popes*, pp. 53–74.
[59] Ibid., pp. 110–33. See also Christine Shaw, *Julius II, the Warrior Pope* (Oxford-Cambridge, Mass., 1993).
[60] Chambers, *Popes*, p. 18.
[61] Ibid., pp. 28–32. For the many other cardinals, see ibid., pp. 17–52, 75–109.

kind of military activity become that in his treatise of 1510 on the cardinalate (*De cardinalatu*) the humanist Paolo Cortesi gave no fewer than nine reasons for which cardinals should be ever ready to go to war, be prepared to defend themselves, and maintain both a bodyguard and an armory.[62]

Meanwhile, far to the north the renewal of sharp conflict between the English and the Scots in the late thirteenth century resuscitated the obligation of the northern bishops to defend the frontier. Back in 1138 the Scots had suffered defeat at the hands of an army raised at Durham by Archbishop Thurston of York who, like his French counterparts, directed every parish priest to enlist troops.[63] Both secular and ecclesiastical authorities, however, combined to discourage this practice at the conclusion of the civil wars of King Stephen's reign (1135–54).[64] Edward I (1272–1302) revived the custom and relied heavily on a good king's man, Anthony Bek, bishop of Durham from 1283 till his death 1311. He commanded the left wing at Falkirk in 1298 and at other times stood at the ready. In November 1299, the king asked him to assemble five or six thousand of the best infantry of the bishopric at Berwick within a month. The substantial forces at Bek's disposal sometimes tempted him beyond his strength. He offered to Pope Boniface VIII to take 300 knights to Palestine and serve there for three years at his own expense, an offer which the pope accepted. At home, Bek decided to resolve some old quarrels with the monks of Durham by investing the cathedral and its precincts with several hundred soldiers in August 1300, culminating in the battering down of the gates of the cloister while the monks celebrated High Mass on Sunday.[65]

The remilitarization of the English hierarchy, particularly in the north, proceeded apace. Archbishop William Melton of York headed the shire levy at Mytton (1320), and Archbishop William Zouche, assisted by the bishop of Carlisle, repelled the greatest Scottish invasion of the century at Neville's Cross in 1346. At least two English bishops were not satisfied by these conflicts at home. Thomas Hatfield, bishop of Durham (1345–81), having fought at Crécy and on the Scots border since 1356, in 1372 offered his services as a kind of *condottiere* to Pope Gregory XI, but the king ignored a papal entreaty and denied Hatfield permission to leave the kingdom. Henry Despenser, bishop of Norwich (1370–1406), zestfully crushed the peasants in the great uprising of 1381 and then embarked on a crusade to Flanders on behalf of Pope Urban VI in 1383. In 1390 he obtained a papal dispensation for having killed several people on his expedition to the Continent.[66]

[62] Ibid., pp. 108–9, 131.
[63] Donald Nicholl, *Thurstan, Archbishop of York (1114–1140)* (York, 1964), pp. 218–28; and see below, p. 64.
[64] Michael Powicke, *Military Obligation in Medieval England* (Oxford, 1962), p. 52.
[65] R. K. Richardson, 'The Bishopric of Durham under Anthony Bek, 1283–1311', *Archaeologia Aeliana* 3rd ser. 9 (1913):89–229, especially 138, 156–9, 180; Gaillard T. Lapsley, *The County Palatine of Durham* (Cambridge, Mass., 1924), pp. 301–10; C. M. Fraser, *A History of Antony Bek, Bishop of Durham, 1283–1311* (Oxford, 1957), pp. 9–10, 15, 25, 52, 66–7, 123–52, 164–5, 231.
[66] Oman, *History*, 1:526, 580; J. R. L. Highfield, 'The English Hierarchy in the Reign of Edward III', *TRHS* 5th ser. 6 (1956):135–8; Margaret Aston, 'The Impeachment of Bishop Despenser', *Bulletin*

The Scots, too, had their share of clerical warriors. The bishop of Glasgow, Robert Wiseheart (1272–1316), evidently was too successful against the English, for Edward II in 1308 vigorously denounced him to the pope for his scandalous conduct.[67] Later, at Otterburn in 1388, the chaplain of the Earl of Douglas, William of North Berwick, so distinguished himself in the fighting that he won everlasting fame in Froissart's *Chronicles*.[68] As late as 1513, Bishop Alexander of St Andrews (1509–13), bastard son of King James IV, fell with his father at Flodden and gained immortality from the pen of Erasmus himself.[69]

Although Edouard Perroy, the great historian of the Hundred Years War, dismissed Bishop Henry Despenser as 'this peculiar prelate',[70] he and Bishop Hatfield had a few French counterparts. Among the many prisoners taken at Crécy were the bishop of Noyon and the archdeacon of Paris, while at Poiters the archbishop of Sens was captured and the bishop of Chalons was killed.[71] After the latter battle Pope Innocent VI wrote to the kings of England and France and denounced clerical participation in the war – in vain, it seems, for the English clergy continued to be impressed into military service as local militia by royal writs of array between 1369 and 1418.[72] Many French clergy were engaged as well in the later campaigns of the war, although less so in the fifteenth century than in the fourteenth.[73]

Pope Innocent VI's efforts to discourage clerical resort to arms suffered a setback in the election of one of his successors. The cardinals who withdrew their obedience from Pope Urban VI in 1378 had no known qualms about electing as Clement VII Robert, cardinal of Geneva and kinsman of the king of France, who twenty months before had ordered the slaughter of the unarmed population of Cesena, an act which horrified the archbishop of Prague and much later St Antoninus of Florence, but which Robert never felt obliged to defend or excuse.[74]

Bellicose bishops were not wanting elsewhere on the Continent. In Italy the foundations of Visconti power in Milan were laid principally by two archbishops from the family, Ottone (1263–95) and Giovanni (1349–54).[75]

of the Institute for Historical Research 38 (1965):127–48. On reactions to Despenser, see below, pp. 72–3, 190–6.

[67] Wilkins 2:308.

[68] See below, pp. 73–4.

[69] G. Donaldson and R. S. Morpeth, comps, *Who's Who in Scottish History* (New York, 1973), p. 46; and see below, pp. 81–2.

[70] Edouard Perroy, *The Hundred Years War*, tr. W. B. Wells (New York, 1965), p. 183.

[71] Oman, *History*, 1:146, 175.

[72] Bruce McNab, 'Obligations of the Church in English Society: Military Arrays of the Clergy, 1369–1418', in W. C. Jordan, B. McNab and T. Ruiz, eds., *Order and Innovation in the Middle Ages. Essays in Honor of Joseph A. Strayer* (Princeton, 1976), pp. 293–314.

[73] Philippe Contamine, *Guerre, état et société à la fin du moyen âge* (Paris, 1972), pp. 171–4.

[74] Walter Ullman, *The Origins of the Great Schism* (1948; repr., New York, 1967), pp. 162–3. Ullman's description of Antoninus as 'one of the chief reporters of the scenes' is impossible, since Antoninus was born only in 1389.

[75] D. M. Bueno de Mesquita, *Giangaleazzo Visconti, Duke of Milan (1351–1402)* (Cambridge, 1941), pp. 3, 6–7.

In ever-turbulent Genoa, the leader of the Fregoso family after 1459 was Archbishop Paolo (1453–98), who thrice seized the dogeship, was named cardinal in 1480 and head of the papal forces to drive the Turks from Otranto, and at times of exile was a roving soldier.[76] German prelates retained the martial reputation they had earned long before, but the Spaniards proved their equal in the later Middle Ages. Maintaining a tradition going back to the seventh century, King Alfonso the Wise of Castile (1252–84) specified the military obligations of the clergy in his celebrated law collection, *Las Siete Partidas* (1256). Exempting both the higher and lower clergy from military service against Christians, he required that in wars with enemies of the faith lower clergy be prepared for wall duty, while prelates and other clerics holding lands of the crown were to render personal service.[77] Spanish bishops sometimes exceeded royal expectations. It was said, for instance, that the archbishop of Santiago could raise 300 men-at-arms and 3,000 foot soldiers.[78] The power of such potentially overmighty subjects inspired in Ferdinand and Isabella a firm determination to subordinate the church to royal authority, but they otherwise did little to defuse episcopal militancy. Married in 1469 and fighting with the aristocracy a civil war that lasted another six years, the royal couple in 1473 convened a council of the Spanish church at Toledo, the primatial see, which at some length condemned what it called the absurd and dishonorable practice of the clergy's serving in the military entourage of any secular lord – except those of the king and of other royal persons.[79]

It would be a mistake to think of most, or even many, of these late medieval prelates as ignorant or corrupt. Thomas Hatfield was admittedly one of the few uneducated bishops created during the reign of Edward III, but Zouche and Despenser were university-trained lawyers.[80] Robert of Geneva was by no one's standard a model of piety; but two other cardinals, one German, the other Spanish, cannot be easily dismissed as either corrupt or 'political', for neither their contemporaries nor later scholars have ever laid such charges against them. Nicholas of Cusa (1404–64) was one of the most original thinkers of the fifteenth century as well as an ecclesiastical reformer, if not an especially successful one. As bishop of Brixen in 1460 he directed his troops against those of the count of the Tyrol in a vain effort, precisely parallel to that of Pope Julius II fifty years later, to reassert the rights of his church.[81]

Julius' contemporary, Francisco Ximenez de Cisneros (1436–1517), was to our modern eyes a coincidence of opposites, as Cusa might have phrased it: a cardinal who refused to put aside his simple Franciscan habit despite papal

[76] Jacques Heers, *Genes au XVe siècle* (Paris, 1961), pp. 160, 306, 533, 603–4; C. Avery, gen. ed., *The New Century Italian Renaissance Encyclopedia* (New York, 1972), p. 416.
[77] *Las Siete Partidas*, tr. S. P. Scott (Chicago, 1931), 1.6.52, p. 107.
[78] J. N. Hillgarth, *The Spanish Kingdoms 1250–1516* (Oxford, 1976–8), 2:93–5.
[79] Mansi 32:394.
[80] Highfield, 'English Hierarchy', pp. 126–7, 131–2.
[81] Wilhelm Baum, *Nikolaus Cusanus in Tirol* (Bozen, 1983), pp. 352–3, 366, 380, 385–6, 388.

remonstration, a passionate promoter of the latest biblical scholarship and of the forced conversion of Jews and Moslems, and a zealous reformer of the church and warrior against the Moslems. He personally financed a number of campaigns against Islam in North Africa. He organized, financed, and directed the siege of Oran in May 1509. According to his humanist biographer, he addressed the troops there with these words while seated on a mule (the traditional animal for strict clerics, for horses symbolized pride) and wearing a sword at his side.

> Where can the priests of God find a better place than on the battlefield, fighting for their country and religion? Many of my noble predecessors in the see of Toledo have given me an example, and have died a glorious death on the field of battle.[82]

The wielding of arms was hardly confined to prelates in the later Middle Ages. On occasion this appears to have been relatively harmless. The most fabled of these lower clergy became widely known, although for many other things besides his expertise at arms. Ferdinand of Cordova (1420–after 1500) made his debut in Paris in 1446, an event recorded by another cleric. Master of the liberal arts and of medicine, doctor of both laws and of theology, he was also a distinguished musician, painter, illuminator, and disputant.

> Besides this, there was no one to touch him when it came to fighting. He could wield a two-handed sword so amazingly skillfully that no one could be compared to him. When he saw his opponent he never failed to leap forward upon him, twenty or twenty-four paces in a single bound ... Also he speaks most expert Latin, also Greek, Hebrew, Chaldee, Arabic, and all other languages. And he is an armed knight.[83]

One other 'fabulous' member of the lower clergy deserves mention. The 'Friar Tuck' in the Robin Hood legends appears in the 1470s, not too long after his probable model had made his mark. Robert Stafford, however, was no friar, but rather chaplain of Lindfield in Sussex, where he is attested in documents between 1417 and 1429 as the leader of a band of armed malefactors who hunted and robbed in Sussex and Surrey, hunted without license, and so harassed the royal foresters and warreners that they could not conduct the king's business.[84] Whether or not all their activities were directed against the crown, justly or unjustly, Stafford and his men came to be memorialized by the people for their efforts on behalf of justice. And even if Friar Tuck was originally no friar, it is revealing that the popular imagination had no qualms about venerating a cleric fighting for the right.

---

[82] Karl von Hefele, *The Life of Cardinal Ximenez*, tr. Dalton (London, 1860), pp. 406–14; the quotation appears on p. 414.
[83] *A Parisian Journal 1405–1449*, tr. J. Shirley (Oxford, 1968), pp. 361–2.
[84] J. C. Holt, *Robin Hood* (London, 1982), pp. 58–9, 179; *DMA* 10:435–7.

The Early Modern Period

The Moslem threat to Europe from the east and the south infused new life into the tradition of clerical warriors. It inspired the foundation of at least two new military-religious orders, the Order of St George established, by Emperor Ferdinand III in 1478, and the Order of St Stephen, created in 1562 by the Grand Duke of Tuscany to repel the Barbary pirates. More than 500 Knights Hospitaller died at Rhodes in 1522, another 300 at Malta in 1565.[85] At the fateful battle of Mohács in August 1526, one of the two commanding generals was Pal Tomori (1475–1526), a nobleman and experienced frontier fighter who later became a Franciscan and then archbishop of Kalocsa (1523). One other archbishop and nine bishops were present at the battle; both archbishops and six bishops were killed. We do not know whether the prelates were armed or how they conducted themselves during the fighting.[86]

The religious passions fired by the Reformation and the Counter-Reformation also fed the old tradition. Of the thirty or so clerics at the battle of Kappel in 1531, more than a score died. Whether most were armed or not is unknown, but at least one chaplain who fell wore helmet and armor and wielded a sword – Ulrich Zwingli, the Reformer of Zurich.[87] Whether Thomas Müntzer himself bore arms is doubtful, but he certainly incited others to violence in the name of the Gospel and was executed in 1525 for his part in the Peasants War.[88] English fears of Spain later in the century were so great than the plan for the defense of the realm drawn up in 1569 required the clergy along with regular officials of the crown to provide and maintain a harquebusier.[89] Anticipation of the Armada in 1588 moved the privy council to require one of its members, Archbishop John Whitgift of Canterbury (1583–1604), as he in turn wrote,

> in very earnest sorte to move all the bishopes, within my province, with what convenient spede may be, effectuallie to deal with those of their cathedral churches, and othr beneficed men in their dioceses, but especially such as be of better habilitie, for the furnishing of themselves with lawnses, light horses, petronells on horsebacke, muskets, calivers, picks, holberts, billes, or bowe and arrowes, as in regard of their several abilities shal be thought most convenient . . . [M]ove such ecclesiastical persons of your diocese to be readie with free and voluntarie provision of men, horse and furniture, as your lordships shall think good to allotte . . .[90]

[85] Charles Oman, *A History of the Art of War in the Sixteenth Century* (1937; repr., New York, 1979), pp. 635, 646, 648, 716; Jonathan Riley-Smith, *The Crusades. A Short History* (Yale, 1987), p. 251.

[86] Lászlo Alföldi, 'The Battle of Mohács, 1526', in János Bak and Béla Király, eds, *From Hunyadi to Rákóczi. War and Society in Late Medieval and Early Modern Hungary* (New York, 1982), pp. 189–201.

[87] G. R. Potter, *Zwingli* (Cambridge, 1976), pp. 413–4.

[88] For a survey of the vast literature on Müntzer, see Tom Scott, 'From Polemic to Sobriety: Thomas Müntzer in Recent Research,' *JEH* 39 (1988):557–72.

[89] Edward Cardwell, ed., *Documentary Annals of the Reformed Church of England* (Oxford, 1844), 1:347–9; Lindsay Boynton, *The Elizabethan Militia 1558–1638* (London, 1967), pp. 60–61.

[90] Wilkins 4:336.

Even though Whitgift emphasized the voluntary character of this levy, he also mustered a series of strong arguments in its support:

> ... being members of one and the selfsame common-weale, and imbarked in the like common dangers with others, if not more in respect of our calings and publick profession of religion, wherby we are also bound to go before others, as well in worde as in good example; we are therefore to remember and advisedly to weight with our selves, what dutifull forwardnes against these extraordinary imminent dangers of very congruence is expected at our handes, for the defence of our gracious soveraigne, ourselves, our families and countrie; ... a good means also to stoppe the mouthes of such as do think those temporal blessinges, which God hath in mercy bestowed upon us, to be too much, and therefore spare not in grudging manner to saye, that themselves are forced to their great charges to fight for us, whiles we lie quietly at home, without providing any munition in thse publick perills.[91]

Despite some demurrals, the clergy provided 560 cavalry, and a second Spanish scare in 1599 yielded another 430 horsemen.[92]

Even if Julius II was the last military pope, he was hardly the last of the warrior bishops, who had their last great age in the seventeenth century. German prince-bishops donned armor to uphold the Reich, the church, and their territories during the Thirty Years War and later. The most celebrated of them, Christoph Bernhard von Galen, bishop of Münster from 1650 to 1678, was also a genuine reformer in the spirit of the Counter-Reformation.[93] The Spanish army in the Thirty Years War was led for several years by the Cardinal Infanta, Ferdinand, brother of Philip IV, until his death in 1641.[94] In France, Cardinal Richelieu had no reservations about posting prelates to military commands. To Henri d'Escoubleau de Sordis (1593–1645), bishop of Maillezais (1623–29) and archbishop of Bordeaux (1629–45), he entrusted the artillery at the siege of La Rochelle (1628) and later the fleets of France as his 'deputy on the sweet and bitter waters' as admiral. Louis de Nogaret (1593–1639), Cardinal de La Valette, served Richelieu faithfully as a general until his death. He, Sordis, Richelieu, and the archbishops of Paris and Narbonne were inducted in 1633 as ecclesiastical commanders of the military Order of the Holy Spirit.[95] Not to be outdone was the house of Savoy, which complemented its thirteenth-century contributions in the person of Cardinal Maurice. Information about the inspiration given to the lower clergy by such prelates is hard to come by, but well worth searching out. At the siege of Dole

[91] Ibid. On Whitgift, see Vivienne Sanders, 'John Whitgift: Primate, Privy Councillor and Propaganist', *Anglican and Episcopal History* 56 (1987):385–403, especially 399–403.
[92] C. G. Cruickshank, *Elizabeth's Army*, 2nd ed. (Oxford, 1966), pp. 30–2.
[93] See below, p. 83.
[94] Alfred van der Essen, *Le Cardinal-Infant et la politique européene de l'Espagne 1609–1641*, 1 (Brussels, 1944):45–8, 84, 89; Georges Pagès, *The Thirty Years War* (New York, 1970), pp. 169, 172, 194.
[95] *Nouvelle biographie générale* (Paris, 1853–66), 29:968–9 and 44:257–60; Robin Briggs, *Early Modern France 1560–1715* (Oxford, 1977), pp. 169–70.

in 1636, for example, Carmelites and Dominicans heaped up earth while a Capuchin loaded cannon.[96] French *curés* were sometimes in the lead of agrarian revolts in the seventeenth century, particularly in 1636, 1637, and 1639.[97]

In early modern Spain clerical involvement in wars and upheavals loomed even larger than in France. The tremendous Comuneros movement in 1520–21 represented a much earlier and less diffuse threat to the government, with more conspicuous participation by the clergy, than did the rebellions of seventeenth-century France. Although most of these participants appear to have been from the lower and regular clergy, especially the Franciscans and Dominicans, at least one prelate carved out a distinctive place for himself. Antonio de Acuña, bishop of Zamora (1507–22), in 1520 went to battle for the movement at the head of 300 clergy armed at his command. Not surprisingly, when captured he was garroted on the express orders of Charles I (Emperor Charles V).[98] Nowhere else in Europe were bishops able to raise up such legions of armed clergy. Although armsbearing by the clergy was totally banned in the diocese of Burgos in 1565 and the archdiocese of Seville in 1645, these decrees were not about to extirpate centuries of habitual behavior.[99] Thus during the War of the Spanish Succession (1702–13), the French ambassador in Madrid reported to Louis XIV in 1706 that the bishop of Calahorra had armed and marched 1,500 of his clergy to the defense of the frontier and that the bishop of Murcia had conducted 1,300 troops to the relief of Alicante.[100] Even discounting for exaggeration, these are impressive figures, especially if the bishop of Calahorra mustered even 1,000 *armed clergy*, let alone 1,500. At that rate, this would have been the greatest clerical army in western history.

Stuart England

Clerical participation in the English civil wars of the seventeenth century has yet to be carefully investigated, which is curious when one considers certain eccentric facts. The Quakers issued their first official declaration of absolute pacifism only in January 1661 – after the Restoration. Before then many Quakers had been soldiers, including prominent leaders like James Nayler, John Whitehead, and George Fox the Younger, while as late as 1660 Fox was asked whether members could serve in the army.[101] Nevertheless, the study of the manifold connections between religion and the civil wars has fallen on

[96] André Corvisier, *Armies and Societies in Europe, 1494–1789*, tr. A. Siddell (Bloomington, 1979), p. 8.

[97] Perez Zagorin, *Rebels and Rulers, 1500–1660* (Cambridge, 1982), 1:183, 223, and 2:11.

[98] Henry Kamen, 'Clerical Violence in a Catholic Society: The Hispanic World 1450–1720', in Shiels, *Church and War*, pp. 201–16 at 201–2; Zagorin, *Rebels and Rulers*, 1:266–7.

[99] Kamen, 'Clerical Violence', pp. 211–12.

[100] Ibid., pp. 202–3; idem, *The War of Succession in Spain 1700–15* (Bloomington, 1969), pp. 264–5, 276–7, 307–8.

[101] Christopher Hill, *The World Turned Upside Down* (New York, 1972), pp. 194–5.

hard times in the last century until a very recent revival. C. H. Firth notes that 'Many clergymen driven from their livings became chaplains to regiments or commanders in the Royalist army', but he provides not a single example.[102] At the other end of the spectrum are *obiter dicta* like those of H. M. Gwatkin in his discussion of the late Stuart episcopate: 'Dolben and Lake and Mews and Compton had fought in the wars,' and 'Williams of York and Wright of Lichfield, who bore arms for the king, could scarcely complain.'[103]

Close reading of the appropriate entries in the *Dictionary of National Biography* rather undermines such remarks, for Dolben, Lake, Mews, and Compton were all ordained only after they had served in the civil war.[104] To be sure, Robert Wright (1560–1643) was already bishop of Chichester (1632) upon the outbreak of hostilities in 1640, but he died in 1643 during the siege of his episcopal residence of Eccleshall Hall, the defense of which lay not with Wright, but a certain Dr Bird.[105] Gwatkin is partly correct about Archbishop John Williams of York (1642–52), who was wounded as he directed the siege of Conwy Castle in November 1646. The castle belonged to the archbishop, however, so it is misleading to assert that Williams fought for the king, particularly since this is the sole military action in which Williams' direct involvement is recorded.[106]

It seems, nevertheless, undeniable that both Peter Mews and Henry Compton 'took up arms' in some way during the troubles of the 1680s. In 1685 Mews, recently elevated to Winchester, was apparently present at the battle of Sedgemoor, but what part he played, if any, is not at all clear. One scholar says he suffered another serious wound while directing the royal artillery. Another implies that it was only when the king's guns fell silent for want of horses and drivers that Bishop Mews brought up his coach horses and harnessed them to the guns to draw them into battle; and yet another devotes twenty-six pages to a dissection of the battle without mentioning Mews.[107] No doubt exists, however, that during the Glorious Revolution of 1688 Bishop Compton of London brandished sword and pistol at the head of the contingent guarding Princess Anne as it marched into Oxford.[108] In the first half of the eighteenth century prelates on the northern frontier had yet again to

---

[102] C. H. Firth, *Cromwell's Army* (1902; repr., 1962), pp. 311–12.

[103] H. M. Gwatkin, *Church and State in England to the Death of Queen Anne* (London, 1917), pp. 381, 322. Mews is also misleadingly portrayed in Norman Sykes, *Church and State in England in the XVIIIth Century* (1934; repr., Hamden, Conn., 1962), pp. 14–5.

[104] *DNB* 4:899–903, 5:1094–7, 11:416–7 and 443, 13:314–6.

[105] Ibid., 21:1038–9.

[106] Ibid., 21:414–20; B. Dew Roberts, *Mitre and Musket. John Williams. Lord Keeper, Archbishop of York, 1582–1652* (Oxford, 1938), pp. vii, 191–212, 244–54.

[107] Sykes, *Church and State*, p. 15; W. McDonald Wigfield, *The Monmouth Rebellion* (Totowa, N.J., 1980), pp. 64, 68; Robin Clifton, *The Last Popular Rebellion. The Western Uprising of 1685* (London, 1984), pp. 199–225.

[108] Edward Carpenter, *The Protestant Bishop. Being the Life of Henry Compton, 1632–1713, Bishop of London* (London, 1956), pp. 134–9; Lawrence Brown, 'Henry Compton, 1632–1713, Bishop of London 1675–1713, Pioneer Leader in the Expansion of the Anglican Communion', *HMPEC* 25 (1956):29; and see below, pp. 85–6.

be watchful, this time against Scottish and Jacobite threats. Bishop William Nicholson of Carlisle and Archbishop Thomas Herring of York were put on full military alert in 1702 and 1745, respectively, and organized local defenses accordingly.[109] Chapter 6 will provide more details about the inclination to arms of the English clergy in general.

The Early Modern Lower Clergy

Prelates who served in official wars were far more likely to be recorded than the lower clergy, especially if the latter revolted against the established order or aided other rebels. Unknown but sufficiently disturbing numbers of clerics bore arms, pillaged, and captured other clerics in the rebellion against King Henry III of England (1260–64) to prompt the convening of a *parlementum* of bishops and barons in London in October 1264.[110] It does not appear that John Ball actually bore weapons in inciting the Peasants' Revolt in 1381, nor is it clear how many of the clerics executed for their part in the German Peasants' War of 1525–26 were armed combatants. In Spain, as has been seen already, hundreds of regular and secular clergy are reported to have marched with the Comuneros in 1520–21 and again in Valencia in 1705 and Aragon in 1706. Gun-toting priests were involved in numerous peasant revolts in seventeenth-century France, but again figures are hard to come by.

Small wonder, then, that in the eyes of many public authorities in late medieval and early modern Europe the lower clergy were often regarded as part of the potentially dangerous rabble. The government of Hungary took this position explicitly in a law of 1514 after the suppression of a peasant revolt. The law forbade the carrying of arms by the rebellious elements in society, which it defined as the unbeneficed clergy, students, and peasants.[111] Churchmen often shared this view. From the High Middle Ages onwards diocesan synods routinely denounced wandering clergy and prohibited the clergy from going to taverns (except when traveling), not only because of the scandal given to the laity, but also, as a synod of Ely expressed it bluntly sometime between 1239 and 1256, because of the heinous crimes that might occur – 'adultery, homicide, and the like.'[112] While such decrees reveal nothing of the magnitude of the problem, they do strongly imply that clerical violence and rowdiness were a matter for genuine and fairly constant concern.

It was presumably partly for that reason that secular authorities had for a long time in many places sought to harness those energies for good causes, above all the service of the state. Although this policy perhaps fed the

[109] Sykes, *Church and State*, pp. 72–7.
[110] *C&S* 2:696–7; and see below, pp. 189–90.
[111] András Borosy, 'The *Militia Portalis* in Hungary before 1526,' in Bak and Király, eds., *From Hunyadi to Rákóczi*, p. 71.
[112] *C&S* 2:519, c. 17.

problem of clerical violence, those clerics who have so chosen to direct their predilection to violence have ordinarily received the approval of others and of society at large. Many instances have been recounted thus far, and many more will be in the chapters to come. Let two suffice here. Henry Teonge (1621/23–90), although holder of two rectorates in England, was driven by financial exigency in the 1670s to seek a chaplaincy in the Royal Navy. He served on three ships and traveled widely. In his *Diary* he tells us that he routinely made cartridges for the captain's gun, 'for my staff gun, and some for muskets also.'[113] When traveling in the environs of Antioch, out of fear 'I made my sword and pistol ready, and made a halt for Captain Harman, who I knew was but a little behind me.'[114] Teonge was ready to use these weapons in obedience to command (as will seen later), and the inventory of his estate compiled in 1690 listed two guns.[115] Little wonder, then, that weapons in the hands of other clerics did not bother him, even if it was in fun:

> . . . we had a friar with us, who, having been drinking wine, was grown a little valiant, and he had got a musket in his hand, a collar of bandoleers about him; and to see him stand in his white coat, bald pate, his musket in his hand, and the Twelve Apostles rattling about him, was a sight which caused much laughter.[116]

The second diary was written several decades later not by a clergyman, but a layman. Dudley Rider chronicled in detail the events of the Jacobite rebellion of 1715–16 as an observer. The clergy in general he regarded as potential mischief-makers of the worst sort, even if they did not resort to arms: 'It is certain the clergy in the country have been the greatest instrument in raising this spirit of rebellion through the nation and that have done by the most false and malicious stories.'[117] Yet Rider's treatment of a cleric loyal to the crown who took to arms is quite different. These are his words in two separate passages about 'General' James Wood (1672–1759), Nonconformist minister at Atherton, Lancashire.

> However went to meeting. Heard Mr. Wood, a dissenting parson of a congregation 14 miles from Preston. He himself gathered together 300 men chiefly of his own congregation to assist the King's forces against the rebels at Preston and were posted at Ribble Bridge. To bed at 10.
>
> Went to the Fountain, where several young persons, among whom were Mr. Wood, whom they call 'General' because he brought under his command 300 men for the King against the revels at Preston, and Mr. Winter, a young man that preaches where Mrs. Crisp goes in the country. He told us Mr. Wood, having a congregation that loved him extremely and who would follow him anywhere, he brought them to associate together when the rebels first were upon their march

---

[113] *The Diary of Henry Teonge, Chaplain on Board H.M.'s Ships Assistance, Bristol, and Royal Oak 1675–1679*, ed. G. Manwaring (London, 1927), p. 226.
[114] Ibid., p. 168.
[115] Ibid., p. 11.
[116] Ibid., p. 243. The 'white habit' suggests that he may have been a Carmelite.
[117] *The Diary of Dudley Rider 1715–1716*, ed. W. Mathews (London, 1939), p. 152.

southwards and then led them out armed partly with swords and pistols and guns and partly with scythes fixed to the ends of straight sticks.[118]

The Eighteenth Century

It was only in the eighteenth century that clerical participation in warfare and violence conspicuously receded in Europe. Several factors promoted this development. Although this century was more peaceful than its predecessor, changes in the character of armies proved far more decisive. For the cumulative effect of the emergence of professional standing armies wearing distinctive attire and marching in disciplined ranks was to exclude non-soldiers, all those who did not fit into this new kind of order, including clerics. The old custom, reaching back to the early Middle Ages, of summoning all the free men to the host fell out of use, while the modern idea of systematic conscription of all eligible young men to be refashioned into soldiers was still to come.

The church gradually disengaged itself from entanglements in the world in new, specific ways in the seventeenth and eighteenth centuries, as witness the deepening disapproval attached to holding of secular political office by the clergy and the complete extinction of the ancient maledictory powers of the clergy. However consciously and willingly the church, or churchmen, withdrew from violence and warfare at this time, the creation of the seminary in the wake of the Reformation turned out to be the crucial step in the slow domestication, professionalization, and pacification of the clergy on the Continent. The clergy were to be the 'professional' men of peace and live accordingly.

The North American Colonies

Yet in one place in western civilization the past and the future – the past of refractory and righteous people and of harsh conditions of life, the future of passions unleashed by political ideas – met in the eighteenth century: in the colonies of North America. Sometimes such conditions wore away the veneer of civilization in men trained under very different circumstances. The Jesuits in Europe were accused of many failings and vices, but I am not aware of armsbearing as one of those charges. Outside Europe it was sometimes otherwise. In the early eighteenth century in Latin America government reports repeatedly accused Jesuits of aiding their Indians with arms in every way, an allegation resurrected in the film *The Mission*.[119] More specifically, when English raiders killed Father Sebastian Râle, S.J., in Maine in 1724, they later

---

[118] Ibid., pp. 231, 234.
[119] See Pablo Pastells, S.J., and F. Mateos, S.J., *Historia de la Compañia de Jésus en la provincia de Paraguay* . . . (Madrid, 1912–49), 6:61, 65, 66, 270–71, 278–9, 352–4, 364–7, 371, 430, 432.

remembered that he had tried to defend himself with a weapon, although the French account holds that Râle died as he advanced alone attempting to protect his Abenaki Indians.[120]

Are such charges plausible? In view of the evidence from seventeenth-century China, the answer may well be yes. The Ming and Manchu emperors wanted the Jesuits working to spread Christianity there to supply them with western knowledge of arms manufacture, and the Jesuits obliged.[121] One of them was Johann Adam Schall von Bell (1592–1661), successor of Matteo Ricci at the Ming court. In 1644, as the Manchus swept into Peking, prompting the Ming emperor to commit suicide, Schall sought to protect his property against looters and recorded this in his memoirs:

> I knew that the Chinese were not very brave, but I knew not yet where their rage might lead, nor what had caused this unusual tumult. So I grasped a Japanese sword (*arrepto acinace japonico*) and posted myself at the great door before the main hall, ready to bear or break the charge. All then happened as I had hoped. For those who were on the roof, seeing me thus armed and determined, and adorned besides with a beard which would have been sufficient for all of them, began to apologize, shouting that they were looking for robbers and since there were clearly none in the house, they would withdraw immediately.[122]

What is remarkable about this passage is that Schall, who like any other auto-biographer had reason and opportunity to ignore or gloss over anything of which he could or should have been ashamed, saw no reason to hide his seizing a sword to defend his goods. This makes it all the more possible that Sebastian Râle might have tried to defend his beloved Indians.

If conditions in long-civilized China could elicit such responses, how much more likely that the untamed and cruel spaces of North America were likely to do so, especially for missionaries with a propensity toward violence that was increasingly circumscribed in Europe. Bennet Allen was such a case. Born around 1737, M.A. of Oxford, and ordained priest in 1767, he acquired an unsavory reputation in London society and decided in 1766 to go to Maryland to accept a living from Lord Baltimore. In 1768 he barely avoided a duel, only to assault someone else with his cane. He returned to England in 1775, there to kill in a duel in Hyde Park the half-brother of the man he had throttled in Maryland in 1768.[123]

As early as 1690, the leader of a rebellion against the governor of Maryland was an Anglican priest, John Coode.[124] In North Carolina, a Baptist minister,

---

[120]   The best treatment is in *Dictionary of Canadian Biography* (Toronto-Quebec, 1966-), 2:544.

[121]   See John K. Fairbank, Edwin O. Reischauer, and Albert M. Craig, *East Asia. The Modern Transformation* (Boston-Tokyo, 1964), p. 42; Immanuel C. Y. Hsü, *The Rise of Modern China*, 3rd ed. (Oxford, 1983), pp. 103–4; Jonathan Spence, *To Change China* (Boston, 1969), pp. 14–5.

[122]   *Lettres et memoires d'Adam Schall, S.J.*, ed. Henri Bernard, S.J. (Tientsin, 1942), p. 135. I have used here the translation in Spence, *To Change China*, pp. 15–6.

[123]   Josephine Fisher, 'Bennet Allen, Fighting Parson', *Maryland Historical Magazine* 38 (1943): 299–322 and 39 (1944):49–72.

[124]   Nelson Rightmyer, *Maryland's Established Church* (Baltimore, 1956), pp. 11, 173–6.

John Gano, declined a captain's commission during a war with the Cherokee Indians around 1760,[125] and it is not known whether the Reverend Adam Smith, rector of Botecourt Parish in Botecourt County, Virginia, served as chaplain or combatant with the Virginia militia in the expeditions against the Cherokees in 1776–77.[126] But another Virginia minister, Charles Cummings of Holsten, did fight Indians and during the Revolution entered his church with gun and ammunition, which he laid aside just before beginning services.[127]

If Cummings was not typical in his response to the Revolution, neither was he unusual. For the American Revolution aroused such profound feelings that even pacifists could forget themselves, as witness the formal disownment by the Quakers of more than 1,700 of their members who had actively engaged in the conflict.[128] The Revolution thus easily resurrected old patterns of behavior among the conventional Christian clergy with their ambivalent attitudes toward war and violence, especially if they were being roughly treated or shot at. On occasion they defiantly courted trouble. The boldest Tory among the Anglican clergy of Connecticut, the Reverend John Beech (or Beach) of Newtown and Redding, refused to close his churches or to desist from praying publicly for the king. Whether or not he died of a bullet fired at him while he was delivering a sermon in March 1782, he had been shot at least once before and threatened on another occasion.[129] Another Connecticut clergyman, Judah Champion, the Congregational minister of Litchfield, countered the arrival of British cavalry with a civilized malediction:

> Oh Lord, we view with terror and dismay, the approach of the enemies of thy holy religion; wilt thou send storm and tempest, and scatter them to the uttermost parts of the earth; but, peradventure, should any escape thy vengeance, collect them together, Oh Lord, as in the hollows of thy hand, and let thy lightnings play upon them.[130]

Such sublimation of their bellicose energies did not suffice for some clergy who did take up arms. Again, as with the English civil wars of the seventeenth century, the facts are often unclear, and some historians seriously misrepresent them. For example, in his *Nationalism and Religion in America 1774–1789*, Edward Humphrey says that among the Episcopal clergy who bore arms were three bishops – John Croes of New Jersey, Samuel Provoost of New York, and Robert Smith of South Carolina.[131] This is impossible, since

[125] Joel T. Headley, *The Chaplains and Clergy of the Revolution* (New York, 1864), p. 254.
[126] G. MacLaren Brydon, 'The Clergy of the Established Church in Virginia and the Revolution', *Virginia Magazine of History and Biography* 41 (1933):301.
[127] Headley, *Chaplains and Clergy*, pp. 273–5.
[128] Arthur McKeel, *The Relation of the Quakers to the American Revolution* (Washington, 1979), p. 335.
[129] Epaphroditus Peck, *The Loyalists of Connecticut* (New York, 1934), pp. 11–12; Charles Mampoteng, 'The New England Anglican Clergy in the American Revolution', *HMPEC* 9 (1940):290.
[130] Quoted in Alice Baldwin, *The Clergy of Connecticut in Revolutionary Days* (Yale, 1936), p. 24.
[131] Edward F. Humphrey, *Nationalism and Religion in America, 1774–1789* (Boston, 1924), p. 44. This error is then repeated in Lester Joyce, *Church and Clergy in the American Revolution* (New York, 1966), p. 59.

the 'Episcopal' Church did not yet exist, there were no bishops in the colonies before 1784, and Croes was ordained deacon only in 1790, priest in 1792, and bishop in 1815.[132] Provoost was during the Revolution a priest whose revolutionary sympathies so antagonized Loyalists that he resigned from Trinity Church in New York in 1771 and was recalled only in 1784. What he did during the intervening thirteen years is a matter of highly contradictory assertions among scholars, some averring that he served in the militia, others that he declined a chaplaincy and remained in seclusion in Duchess County, New York, throughout the conflict.[133] About Robert Smith, however, there is no doubt. Although not elected the first bishop of South Carolina until 1795, he was rector of St Philip's Church in Charleston from 1759. Upon the out-break of war, he was appointed chaplain-general of the Southern department of the Continental Army. During the siege of Charleston in 1780, however, he acted as a soldier; and he was thereafter so active in the American cause that Cornwallis placed his name at the head of the list of those rebels whose estates were sequestered in September 1780.[134]

While Smith was evidently only gradually, and perhaps reluctantly, drawn into the status of combatant on behalf of the rebels, another Anglican clergy-man, much more hotheaded and passionate in the king's cause, rushed into the fray well before the outbreak of open hostilities. The Reverend Jonathan Boucher was rector of Queen Anne's Parish in Prince George's Country, Maryland, in the early 1770s. So outspoken a royalist was he that, on his own proud admission, in response to threats

for more than six months I preached, when I did preach, with a pair of loaded pistols lying on the cushion; having given notice that if any man, or body of men, could possibly be so lost to all sense of decency and propriety as to attempt really to do what had been long threatened, that is, to drag me out of my own pulpit, I should think myself justified before God and man in repelling violence by violence.[135]

When Mr Osborne Sprigg tried to prevent Boucher from preaching by occu-pying the church with 200 armed men, Boucher persisted and

so at the proper time, with my sermon in one hand and a loaded pistol in the other, like Nehemiah, I prepared to ascend the steps of the pulpit, when behold, one of my friends (Mr. David Crawford of Upper Marlborough) having got behind me, threw his arms around mine and held me fast. He assured me on his honour he had both

---

[132]   William Stevens Perry, *The Bishops of the American Church Past and Present* (New York, 1897), p. 37; Walter Stowe, 'John Croes (1762–1832), First Bishop of New Jersey (1815–1832)', *HMPEC* 35 (1966):221–30.

[133]   Perry, *Bishops*, p. 9; *Dictionary of American Biography* (New York, 1927–), 8:249–50; *HMPEC* 16/1 (March 1947) ('250th Anniversary Number, The Parish of Trinity Church in the City of New York'):28–9, 32–3.

[134]   Albert Thomas, 'Robert Smith (1732–1801), First Bishop of South Carolina (1795–1801)', *HMPEC* 15 (1946):15–29.

[135]   *Reminiscences of an American Loyalist 1738–1789, Being the Autobiography of the Rev.d Jonathan Boucher, Rector of Annapolis in Maryland and afterwards Vicar of Epsom, Surrey, England*, ed. Jonathan Boucher (Boston, 1925), p. 113.

seen and heard the most positive orders given to twenty men picked out for the purpose to fire on me the moment I got into the pulpit . . . It occurred to me . . . that there was but one way to save my life. This was by seizing Sprigg, as I immediately did, by the colar, and with my cocked pistol in the other hand, assuring him that if any violence was offered to me I would instantly blow his brains out, as I most certainly would have done. I then told him that if he pleased he might conduct me to my horse, and I would leave them. This he did.[136]

In September 1775 Boucher left for England, never to return, later received a rectory in Surrey, and in the 1790s published an account of his travails.[137]

Of all denominations, the Congregational clergy of Connecticut took the most active role in preaching to troops, organizing them, and leading them into battle. While Judah Champion contented himself with no-nonsense oraisons to the Lord, other ministers inclined toward a more vigorous course of action even before the outbreak of revolt. When news arrived in September 1774 of troubles in Boston, the Reverends Jonathan Todd of East Guilford, Benjamin Boardman of Middle Haddam, and Eleazar May of Haddam each marched in readiness at the head of upwards of a hundred of their townsmen. Benjamin Trumbull, minister in North Haven from 1760 till his death in 1820, captained a company of sixty volunteers, and in November 1779 he joined a small force trying to delay the British advance on New Haven. This motley crew had assembled under the Reverend Naphthali Daggett, professor at Yale and its acting president in 1776–77. Daggett kept shooting at the British long after his men had fled and refused to lay down his weapons even when captured.[138]

While it appears that none of the Anglican clergy of Connecticut took up arms, four and possibly five of the 122 incumbent Anglican clergy in Virginia did (where theirs was the established church).[139] As has already been noted of Adam Smith, it is unknown whether he worked solely as a chaplain or as a soldier as well. The other four priests became officers: General John Peter Muhlenberg (1746–1807), Colonel Charles Myron Thruston (1738/54–1812), Colonel Isaac Avery, and Captain James Madison (1749–1812). Of all the clergy of the Revolutionary era, Muhlenberg probably enjoys the greatest fame, although it rests on some serious misconceptions. Although he came of a strong Pennsylvania Lutheran background and had desired Lutheran ordination, his failure to persuade his elders of his worthiness led him to England and ordination as an Anglican priest by the bishop of London in 1771. In that year he was appointed rector of Beckford Parish, Dunmore City, Virginia, which he held for the next four years. Thus, although Lutherans (including

---

[136]   Ibid., pp. 121–2; and see pp. 106–7 for another instance of Boucher's feistiness.

[137]   On the considerable literature on Boucher, see the articles in *HMPEC* 36 (1967) and 42 (1978) and in *Journal of American History* 58 (1972).

[138]   Headley, *Chaplains and Clergy*, pp. 199–204, 234–7; *Dictionary of American Biography* 3:28 and 10:7–8; Baldwin, *Clergy of Connecticut*, pp. 154–67.

[139]   What follows in this paragraph is drawn from Brydon, 'Clergy in Virginia', pp. 16, 21–2, 239–40, 242–3, 301–3.

Roland Bainton) like to claim him as one of their own, he had in fact not only become an Anglican, but an Anglican priest to boot.[140] In January 1776, having accepted a commission as colonel and evidently considering it incompatible with his status as clergyman, he resigned his office in the church. This much is indisputable; but there is apparently no contemporary evidence for the appealing story retold again and again.[141] Bainton's version runs this way:

> John Peter Gabriel Muhlenberg in his farewell to his congregation in January, 1776, declared: 'In the language of Holy Writ, there is a time for all things. There is a time to preach and a time to fight; now is the time to fight.' After the benediction he removed his vestment and stood in the uniform of a Virginia colonel. He never went back to his vestment; one or the other it must be. This the Lutherans still felt.[142]

Muhlenberg's other three Anglican colleagues from Virginia chose differently. Thruston, a graduate of William and Mary, was, like Muhlenberg, ordained in England and a rector at the onset of hostilities. He raised a company of soldiers, rose from captain to colonel, was badly wounded at Trenton, lost an arm at Amboy in March 1777, and resigned his commission in January 1779, having won the epithets 'warrior parson' and 'warrior parson of the Shenandoah'.[143] Of Isaac Avery, ordained and licensed in 1769, no record of parochial incumbency exists. He was posted colonel of the county militia in April 1779 and County Lieutenant in December 1778, an office he filled until May 1781. Of these Virginia priests, it was James Madison, a cousin of the later President of the United States, who achieved the lowest rank in the military hierarchy and the highest in the ecclesiastical. Ordained in England in 1775, he was elected President of William and Mary College in 1777 and retained this post until 1812. On 11 August he was commissioned captain of the militia of students at William and Mary and saw active service during the war. On 19 September 1790 he was consecrated the first Episcopal bishop of Virginia.[144]

Some Presbyterian clergy fought as well, though the truth here is no easier to ascertain than in the case of the Episcopalians. James Caldwell (1734–81), pastor of the congregation of Elizabethtown, New Jersey, like some of his confreres found himself in a vortex he may never have anticipated. At first simply a chaplain, he soon began to spy; and when the British reacted by setting a price upon his head, he went about armed at the ready and is even supposed to have positioned his pistols at his side while he preached. But whether he actively used weapons is nowhere openly asserted, while at the

---

[140] The best treatment is by Thomas Rightmyer, 'The Holy Orders of Peter Muhlenberg', *HMPEC* 30 (1961):183–97.

[141] See David Holmes, 'The Episcopal Church and the American Revolution', *HMPEC* 37 (1978):281, n. 42.

[142] Bainton, *Christian Attitudes*, p. 189.

[143] Besides the material in Brydon, see also the entry in *Appleton's Cyclopaedia of American Biography*, eds J. Wilson and J. Fiske (New York, 1886–9), 6:107.

[144] Besides Brydon, see *Dictionary of American Biography* 6:182–3.

battle of Springfield in 1780 all he appears to have done was supply the troops with prayer books from which they could tear paper for wadding for their guns. He is nevertheless remembered as the 'Soldier Parson' and 'Fighting Parson'.[145] An earlier Presbyterian 'Fighting Parson' before the Revolution was John Elder of Lancaster County, Pennsylvania, leader of the Paxton Rangers, a force he raised in the fall of 1763. According to his son, he regularly carried a musket, even into his pulpit; but one of the many myths which have grown up about him is that he held a commission as a colonel.[146] Tradition has it that the zeal of the Reverend John Harris, minister at Ninety-Six in South Carolina, surpassed that of Jonathan Boucher, for he preached not only with a gun in his pulpit, but with a powder-horn about his neck as well.[147]

With respect to other Presbyterian clergy we are on surer footing. James Hall (1744–1826) of North Carolina acted as both captain and chaplain of his parish company of cavalry, although he declined General Thomas Greene's offer of a brigadier-generalship because it would have removed him from his flock. David Caldwell led a volunteer company as captain, Thomas Read took arms with fifty neighbors and parishioners, and James Lyon offered to lead an expedition to Nova Scotia. Samuel Doak was originally only a chaplain; but when his services were interrupted by a rider announcing the murder of a whole family by Indians, Doak grabbed a gun and at the head of his congregation pursued the Indians.[148]

The U. S. Civil War

Evidently no clergy assumed arms during the War of 1812, which is not surprising in view of the fact that it was neither a civil war nor one in which the very existence of the nation was imperiled.[149] It was quite otherwise with the U. S. Civil War, although the subject of clerical combatants in this conflict has not been nearly as well studied as for the Revolutionary War. Many scholars who touch on the issue speak in general terms about clerical warriors, but only occasionally offer specific figures.[150] The obstacles to research

145   Cf. Headley, *Chaplains*, pp. 217–32; Everard Kempshall, *Caldwell and the Revolution* (Elizabeth, 1880), pp. 41–3; Henry Ford, 'A Revolutionary Hero: James Caldwell', *Journal of the Presbyterian Historical Society* 6 (1911):260–6; Leonard Kramer, 'Muskets in the Pulpit: 1776–1783', ibid. 32 (1954):43–4, who notes the difficulty of establishing the truth about the activities of clergymen in war (p. 42 n. 117).

146   Charles Anderson, 'Presbyterian Personalities', *Journal of the Presbyterian Historical Society* 23 (1945):48–54, especially 49–50.

147   Claude Van Tyne, 'Influence of the Clergy and of Religion and of Sectarian Forces on the American Revolution', *American Historical Review* 19 (1913–4):57; Kramer, 'Muskets', p. 46. Durward Stokes, 'The Presbyterian Clergy in South Carolina and the American Revolution', *South Carolina Historical Magazine* 71 (1970):281, merely remarks cryptically that 'The Presbyterian clergymen were neither afraid nor reluctant to accept military duty when it was feasible.'

148   Headley, *Chaplains*, pp. 245–9; Kramer, 'Muskets', p. 46.

149   William Gribbin kindly confirmed the impression I had derived from his *Churches Militant. The War of 1812 and American Religion* (Yale, 1973) and other works.

150   Typical is R. L. Stanton, *The Church and the Rebellion* (New York, 1864), pp. 174–5, who under

are admittedly considerable. Aside from the prevailing lack of interest in the clergy and church history among modern historians, there is the simple problem of numbers – millions of men in the Civil War, as opposed to thousands in the Revolution. One would also not ordinarily expect that the occasional chaplain who picked up a gun in the heat of battle would be recorded, but the observation of one historian investigating the corps of chaplains of the Army of Northern Virginia suggests that the problem is even more complex: 'Ministers who served in the ranks as soldiers, but who on occasion would preach to the troops, are usually referred to as chaplains, even though they were not commissioned.'[151] A final factor distorting the evidence centers on the voluntary character of the military service of the clergy. In the North the refusal of the Federal government automatically to exempt the clergy from combatant service, much less from conscription, presumably accounts for most of the numbers there, whereas the Confederacy exempted the ordained clergy throughout the war despite its acute shortage of manpower. Southern clergy who had already enlisted as soldiers, however, were forbidden as of 1863 to become chaplains.[152]

Yet the few exact figures uncovered thus far point to an extraordinarily enthusiastic and voluntary response of the Southern clergy rather than of the Northern. In 1912 William Sweet published his *Methodist Episcopal Church and the Civil War*. He acknowledged that the following numbers must be handled gingerly, for they are both incomplete and incommensurable. In 1862 'it was reported' that no fewer than sixty-three Methodist preachers held commissions in the Union Army (four colonels, two lieutenant-colonels, one major, thirty-six captains, and twenty others). From the spotty records of the Confederate Army Sweet culled no fewer than 141 Methodist preachers who served as officers or soldiers. He concluded that 'It is very probably true that there were at least as many Methodist preachers in the Southern armies serving as soldiers (non-chaplains) as in the Union armies.'[153] Interestingly, neither the 1860 nor the 1884 edition of *The Doctrine and Discipline of the Methodist Episcopal Church* alluded in any way to armsbearing in the 'Rules for a Preacher's Conduct.'[154]

---

the rubric 'Leading Clergymen in the Rebel Army' lists four by name and then adds that 'many other ministers of distinction have had military commands in the rebel armies.' Even more vague is Lewis Vander Velde, *The Presbyterian Churches and the Federal Union 1861–1869* (Cambridge, Mass., 1932), p. 432.

151   W. Harrison Daniel, 'Chaplains in the Army of Northern Virginia. A List Compiled in 1864 and 1865 by Robert L. Dabney', *Virginia Magazine of History and Biography* 71 (1963):328, who remarks that 'The Confederate chaplain is one of the more elusive figures of the Civil War period' (p. 327).

152   Eugene Murdock, *One Million Men. The Civil War Draft in the North* (Madison, 1971), pp. 24, 207–17; Gardiner Shattuck, Jr, *A Shield and Hiding Place. The Religious Life of the Civil War Armies* (Macon, Ga., 1987), pp. 67–71.

153   William Warren Sweet, *The Methodist Episcopal Church and the Civil War* (Cincinnati, 1912), pp. 94, 224–5; the quotation is on p. 225.

154   Pp. 60–3 in the 1860 edition, pp. 77–9 in the 1884, which simply repeated the rules of 1860. Both editions were published in New York under this title.

To some historians these days, numbers like these constitute the real meat of history ('hard data'), all other forms of evidence being merely 'anecdotal' or 'impressionistic'. More traditional historians value the latter precisely because they are concrete, personal, and human. There need be no war between these views, for all historians should learn, through a disciplined exercise of the imagination, to exploit all kinds of evidence in different ways to illumine the many facets of the past. To supplement Sweet's figures for Methodist ministers I have discovered upwards of a half-dozen stories, although they rectify with vividness what they lack in quantity. The most colorful of these Methodist Episcopal clerics was his 'Radical Reverence', John H. Cox. Born in 1833, ordained in 1856, he joined a Unionist 'Prairie Home Guard' in northeast Missouri in June 1861 as private and within a few days was promoted to sergeant. He fought and ministered spiritually to his men. At the request of old friends and parishioners, he assumed the captaincy of Company H of the 21st Missouri Infantry. Finding that he disliked command, he tendered his resignation. His colonel refused it and offered instead the chaplaincy, which Cox accepted. After the war he pursued careers in both politics and the church and died in 1902.[155]

Another Methodist preacher, Darbey Ball of Virginia, showed a similar flexibility about his own behavior in a letter written to President Jefferson Davis on 5 February 1862. Although he drafted the letter to denounce Bishop Edward R. Ames, he revealed in passing, and without embarrassment, his easy passage from clergyman to soldier:

> I am myself a Methodist preacher and have been for nineteen years. I have been a member of the Baltimore Conference stationed for some years past in Baltimore and Washington cities. I was in charge of a congregation in Baltimore when our present troubles burst forth upon us. I resigned my congregation in June and came to my native Virginia to do whatever I might for her and the south. I was immediately called into the activities of the present struggle, – first as a lieutenant in a company of mounted riflemen . . . [and now] my present position upon General J. E. B. Stuart's staff as major and chief of staff to his brigade.[156]

There can be no doubt about the readiness to shoot of another Methodist preacher, Augustus B. Longstreet, former President of the University of Mississippi. As the Yankees approached the school at Oxford in 1863,

> I got ready to give them a little fighting on my own plan. With Jim's [General James Longstreet's] gun and fourteen buckshot in each barrel. But just as I was about to start the Yankees skedaddled. If I had drawn a bead upon them with 'the drop sight and double wabble' I should have been good for at least four at a crack. I shouldn't have been like young soldiers shooting every which way, and at every distance, but I should have tolled them on to within 70 yards when I would have let them have

---

[155] Leslie Anders, 'His "Radical Reverence" John H. Cox', *Missouri Historical Review* 65 (1971):139–58.
[156] The letter appears as 'Appendix C' in Sweet, *Methodist Episcopal Church*, pp. 208–10.

the first 14 and at 50 the other 14 taking them ranging, and dear me how I would have spread them.[157]

A flair for the histrionic capped the zeal of a German Methodist preacher prepared to 'die a true patriot and a soldier of the cross, a gun in hand and Christ within my heart' in the defense of Galveston. And a preacher in Florida defended his joining the army in an open letter to fellow clerics declaring his preference for 'annihilation to subjugation.'[158]

Given this kind of enthusiasm among the Methodist Episcopal clergy (despite the disapproval of at least three bishops[159]), it is perhaps not surprising that the only conspicuous example on the Federal side of active clerical engagement occurred in this denomination. The man responsible for the creation of the 'Preacher Regiment', officially known as the Seventy-Third Regiment of Illinois Infantry Volunteers, was the Rev. James Frazier Jaquess (1819–?), who was President of Quincy College at the declaration of war. Starting as chaplain to the Sixth Illinois Cavalry, he felt increasingly dissatisfied with his position and after the disaster at Shiloh requested the privilege of raising and commanding a 'Methodist Regiment'. It soon attracted a number of ministers, who in turn drummed up so many soldiers (mostly from walks of life having to do with church or school) that two overflow regiments had to be formed. Although most of the men were lay, many of the officers were clergy.[160] A letter which made the 'Methodist Preacher Regiment' nationally known was published in the Cincinnati *Commercial* in September 1862 by the adjutant's clerk, Henry Castle. In the letter he listed the officers in command. The colonel (Jaquess), lieutenant-colonel, the major, six of the ten captains, and six or seven of the twenty lieutenants were 'licensed Methodist preachers. Being thus officered,' Castle concluded, 'you may rest assured we are a good set of boys.'[161]

No study comparable to Sweet's has been done for any other church, at least with reference to the subject of this book. Some Baptist chaplains engaged in battle, one of the more illustrious of whom was the Reverend I. T. Tichenor of the 17th Alabama Regiment. He killed a Federal colonel, a major, and four privates.[162] One Georgia regiment alone had fourteen ministers (twelve of them missionary Baptist), but whether they fought in any way is unknown.[163] A correspondent of the Louisville *Courier* praised another

---

157   Quoted in Willard Wight, 'The Churches and the Confederate Cause', *Civil War History* 6 (1960):370–1.

158   Ibid., pp. 370–1.

159   Ibid., p. 371: 'Bishops Andrew, Early, and Pierce of the Methodist church not only disapproved of ministers accepting combat assignments but wondered if there was not "a mixture of vain-glory or love of earthly fame moving them in their course"'.

160   W. H. Newlin et al., *A History of the Seventy-Third Regiment of Illinois Infantry Volunteers* (n.p., 1890), pp. 20–1, 534–62.

161   Ibid., p. 645. The colonel of one of the spinoff regiments was the Rev. Jesse Moore (ibid., pp. 20–1).

162   Sidney Romero, 'The Confederate Chaplain', *Civil War History* 1 (1955):134.

163   J. William Jones, *Christ in the Camp; or, Religion in Lee's Army* (Richmond, 1887), p. 32, does not indicate whether these ministers fought; but John Shepard, Jr., 'Religion in the Army of

Baptist minister without reservation, but without sufficient clarity from the historian's viewpoint:

> Our fighting chaplain, Rev. H. A. Tupper, of the ninth Georgia, a chaplain at the Confederate army and a Baptist minister at home, a lover and defender of civil and religious liberty everywhere, preached us a very able discourse from the advice of Eli to Joshua: 'Be ye men of good courage.' It was no war philippic, but an earnest, heartfelt, Christian discourse.[164]

One Baptist preacher who ultimately did fight without reserve, rose very high, and left a brief autobiography was Brigadier-General Mark Perrin Lowrey (1828–85) of Mississippi. After serving in the Mexican War he became a Baptist minister, turning his back on all other callings. When in the fall of 1861 Mississippi called for 10,000 men for 60 days, his neighbors raised a company and elected him captain, ultimately persuading him to accept the temporary post. The fall of Fort Donelson in February 1862 precipitated a fateful crisis in his soul.

> All felt that every man who could bear arms should rise up and stand between his home and the enemy, and he who would not do so was deemed unworthy to be called a Mississippian. Churches felt they had no use for pastors then – fighting men were in demand. I was restless, and my blood was hot within me. The thought of sitting still until the enemy would overrun my home and family was more than I could bear. The result is soon told: I raised and organized the Thirty-second Mississippi regiment in a little less time than any other regiment was ever raised and organized in north Mississippi.[165]

General Lowrey then goes on to tell of his many engagements in action, in one of which he was wounded, and of his resignation in March 1865 for three reasons, none of which was a sense of incompatibility with his position as a minister of the Gospel.

Another preacher from Mississippi who left an autobiography was Thomas W. Caskey (1816–96), a 'Campbellite' or member of what later were called the Disciples of Christ. Although Caskey rejected the whole concept of ordination or the laying on of hands, he dedicated his life to preaching the Gospel and so is usually entitled 'Reverend'. During the Civil War his congregation expressed its desire that 'I should vacate my pulpit except on Sundays, and take the field.'[166] He became a chaplain and devoted himself mostly, but not entirely, to the appropriate duties. The following testimony may be unique in the annals of Christian witness:

Northern Virginia', *North Carolina Historical Review* 25 (1948):342, citing this page in Jones, says that 'In one Georgia regiment there were fourteen ministers in combat service.' Shepard recounts several instances of armsbearing clergy, but without indicating their denominations (pp. 352–3).

[164] Quoted in Jones, *Christ in the Camp*, p. 35
[165] General M. P. Lowrey, 'An Autobiography [September 1867]', *Southern Historical Society Papers* 16 (1888):365–76 at 368.
[166] Thomas W. Caskey, *Caskey's Last Book. Containing an Autobiographical Sketch of His Ministerial Life, with Essays and Sermons*, ed. B. J. Manire (Nashville, 1896), p. 29.

Apart from singing, praying and preaching on Sundays, and our nightly prayer meeting, taking care of the sick, comforting as far as I could the dying, and burying the dead, I would get pugnacious. The old Adam would overcome the new. I would shoulder a gun, and go in with company A into the fight. I do not think I killed any one or broke any arms but I tried to break as many legs as I could. Had all done as I did, I do not think there would have been many killed, but the number of artificial legs would have been greatly multiplied. I never could see any sense, common or uncommon, or humanity either, in killing a man or in breaking his arm. If you kill him, he is left on the field to take care of himself. If you break his arm, he can walk off unaided. If you break his leg, it takes two men to pack him off, and they take care not to pack themselves back till the fight is ended. I commend this mode of fighting to all who wish to amuse themselves by shooting each other.[167]

Lest one conclude that Caskey had completely forgotten his pastoral calling, another story should cause us to pause. Upon the resignation of a major after a battle in which Caskey had threatened to shoot some men in retreat, the regiment offered him the post 'for what they called an act of heroic bravery on the field of battle.' Caskey declined on the grounds that he already held an office higher than any he could receive: 'I would not exchange it for the crown of a king, nor for the presidency of a republic. I was called "the fighting parson", from that time till the close of the war.'[168] In so relishing the epithet 'fighting parson', Caskey dispels any possible doubt about whether he declined the officer's commission out of a sense of incompatibility with his calling as a preacher of true Christianity.

Information about combatant Presbyterian clergy in the Civil War is also anecdotal. One chaplain drawn into fighting was the Reverend James Sinclair of the 5th North Carolina. At the first battle of Manassas he acted as lieutenant-colonel, led several charges, and was offered by General James Longstreet a sword and a position on his staff.[169] The Rev. Willis L. Miller captained the Thomasville (N.C.) Rifles,[170] while the Rev. Thomas Markham of Lafayette Presbyterian Church in New Orleans more modestly enlisted as a private in the Confederate Guards.[171] A third was Dabney Carr Harrison, chaplain at the University of Virginia. After his brother and three other relatives were killed early in the war, he raised a company and became its captain. He fell at Fort Donelson while leading his men and waving his sword.[172] His cousin, Randolph McKim, an Episcopal priest and chaplain who did not use arms, later described Harrison's death in an oddly dispassionate way: 'my Uncle Peyton's son, Dabney Harrison, was killed, gallantly leading his company. He was a Presbyterian minister, but felt the call to defend his State from the invader, and, doffing his ministerial

---

167 Ibid., p. 34. For some incidents in which Caskey practiced what he preached, see pp. 38–40.
168 Ibid., p. 40.
169 Ibid., p. 134.
170 Jones, *Christ in the Camp*, p. 24.
171 Sidney Romero, 'Louisiana Clergy and the Confederate Army', *Louisiana History* 2 (1961):284–6.
172 Jones, *Christ in the Camp*, pp. 122–9.

office, raised a company in his own congregation and was elected its captain.'[173]

McKim's ambivalence makes sense in the context from which he came. The church from which the Methodists had dissented in the eighteenth century was the one for which the most abundant and arresting anecdotal material on clerical combat in the Civil War is recorded – the Episcopal Church, whose clergy had also distinctively given of themselves during the Revolutionary War. No one has yet compiled for the Episcopal clergy tabulations comparable to Sweet's for the Methodists, but much can be gleaned from articles and studies. As usual, one must exercise care in accepting what one reads. Thus the dedication of Bishop Joseph Cheshire's *Church in the Confederate States* (1912) to 'Edwin Augustus Osborne, Archdeacon of Charlotte, Sometime Colonel of the Fourth N. C. Regiment, C.S.A.' might cause a reader to suppose that Osborne had been simultaneously officer and priest, but the text reveals that he was ordained only in 1877.[174]

Nevertheless, the untroubled movement back and forth between ministerial and military capacities among Methodist ministers was a common pattern among Episcopal priests as well. Bishop Cheshire wrote, for instance, of the Rev. William Meredith of Virginia that he was a faithful chaplain, 'only it was said that he always forgot he was a chaplain during the battle, and took his place in the fighting line until the battle was over, when he would resume his ministrations to the wounded and dying.'[175]

How many other instances of this sort occurred will require much more research directed precisely to this issue. One article on the Episcopal diocese of Mississippi mentions three priests who enlisted in the Confederate Army, one of whom was a lieutenant-colonel, but it offers no further information on the roles they played.[176] Articles on the dioceses of Texas and Virginia say nothing about combatant clergy except for one famous example, William Nelson Pendleton of Virginia.[177]

The stories of Pendleton and of an even more illustrious Episcopal clergyman have a significance which exceeds ordinary anecdotal value. Both were graduates of West Point who had chosen the ministry for their careers, and both were asked upon the outbreak of war to offer themselves to the Confederacy. Leonidas Polk (1806–64) had become the first Episcopal bishop of Louisiana in 1841. Offered a brigadier-generalship by Jefferson Davis, he accepted after slight demur. After several years of field service he was killed in action at the battle of Pine Mountain in June 1864. Pendleton (1809–83)

---

[173] Randolph McKim, *A Soldier's Recollections* (New York, 1910), p. 69.
[174] Joseph Cheshire, *The Church in the Confederate States* (New York, 1912), Dedication and p. 77.
[175] Ibid., p. 86.
[176] Nash Burger, 'The Diocese of Mississippi and the Confederacy,' *HMPEC* 9 (1940):52–77, at 69.
[177] DuBose Murphy, 'The Protestant Episcopal Church in Texas During the Civil War', *HMPEC* 1 (1932):90–101; G. MacLaren Brydon, 'The Diocese of Virginia in the Southern Confederacy',' *HMPEC* 17 (1948):384–410, especially 399–400.

was rector of Latimer Parish in Lexington, Virginia. At West Point he had specialized in artillery. In the spring of 1861 he was called upon to train Washington College students in infantry tactics and then to command the Rockbridge Artillery. Initially declining this offer, he reluctantly acceded and found himself gradually sucked into the maws of war. His was no ordinary accomplishment, however, for he achieved the rank of brigadier-general and the post of Chief of Artillery of the Army of Northern Virginia. More on Polk, Pendleton, and other combatant Episcopal clergy will appear in the Conclusion, where their position in the Episcopal church will be considered.

Although I have discovered almost no evidence of combatant activity by Roman Catholic or Lutheran clergy in the Civil War, suffice it to say in conclusion that, at least on the Confederate side, general clerical enthusiasm for the war and for an active part in it was grave enough to warrant consideration by the Chaplains' Association in its meeting of 25 April 1863. The minutes record this discussion:

> The subject of the proper position of chaplains in battle was then taken up. Much conversation was had on this topic. Many chaplains stated what had been their habits. Some had gone regularly into battle with a musket. The opinion of many prominent officers was stated; and the general conclusion was as follows: No absolute rule can be laid down. A chaplain shall be wherever duty calls him, irrespective of danger. But ordinarily it is thought wrong for him to take a musket. Some shall be in charge of ambulances, some at the field infirmaries and some at the point where the litter-bearers meet the ambulances, and where many die. The chaplain should ascertain *the opinion of his regiment* on this subject.[178]

Several things need to be remembered in evaluating this document. It was drawn up by the chaplains, not just the combatant clergy; it was not an official statement; and it represents an attempt to reach consensus after the presumably free airing of differences of opinion. Nevertheless, the chaplains aimed at a consensus rather than remain content with the expression of denominational differences; they decided that no absolute rule obtained; and, most tellingly, although they thought it 'ordinarily ... wrong for him to take a musket', they recommended that when in doubt a chaplain should consult the men of his regiment, but apparently not his church or its officials.

The Last Two Centuries

For reasons already listed in connection with the U. S. Civil War, it is hard to assemble solid figures or information on clerical armsbearing in the last two centuries. Yet the scraps of published evidence do point to continued, if possibly diminished, clerical resort to arms and participation in warfare.

The best documented country seems to be Spain, where openly antagonistic

---

[178]   Quoted in Jones, *Christ in the Camp*, p. 522 (emphasis in the original).

policies toward the clergy on the part of secular authorities have again and again elicited fervent responses. Members of the religious orders in particular engaged in the wars of liberation against Napoleon between 1808 and 1813, especially after the suppression of monasteries was ordered in August 1809. The Franciscans were conspicuous but not alone. The prior of the Carmelites in Logrono urged his men to become 'religious warriors' ready to die 'on the battlefield of a Holy Crusade.'[179] Some Capuchins of Andalusia did die for the cause, and in 1910 the head of this province wrote a book celebrating their dual martyrdom.[180] The royalist uprising of 1822–23 witnessed 'massive clerical participation in armed opposition' to the liberal government; more than a hundred priests fell in the assault on Cervera in Catalonia.[181] Friars and monks 'joined' in the first Carlist uprising of 1834.[182] The second Carlist rebellion of 1872 attracted several northern *curas*, the most fearsome of whom, Manuel de Santa Cruz, pastor of Hernialde and guerrilla leader, is said to have read his breviary daily as scrupulously as he coldly ordered the execution of upwards of twenty prisoners without benefit of confession.[183]

While the clergy of Spain rose against Napoleon in the first decade of the nineteenth century, the clergy of Mexico were rising against Spanish rule. The discussion in the Introduction of scholars' estimates as to the nature and degree of this militant clerical participation suggests that even the lower, conservative figures are very impressive.[184] Whether the level of clerical 'armsbearing' in the revolts elsewhere in nineteenth-century Latin America was comparable to that in Mexico is unclear, but it existed and deserves more study.[185] In the revolutions of 1817 and 1824 in Brazil, the Carmelites alone were so involved that no fewer than eleven were executed after the revolutions were over.[186] In Venezuela the ecclesiastical court at Mérida on 23 May 1817 suspended twenty priests for their service in the revolution, classifying most of them as 'insurgents'. The bishop of Mérida, Lasso de la Vega, had led his parishioners in the royalist cause, while Father Andrés Torrellas also fought on the same side. Many more priests fought as revolutionaries, one of whom, José Félix Blanco, became a general.[187]

Priests took an active part in native insurrections in the Philippines against

---

[179] William J. Callahan, *Church, Politics and Society in Spain, 1750–1874* (Cambridge, Mass., 1984), pp. 88–9.

[180] See below, pp. 87–8.

[181] Callahan, *Church, Politics, and Society*, pp. 124–6, who implies that the hundred priests who died at Cervera actually bore arms.

[182] Ibid., pp. 149–50, where no instance of armed involvement is given.

[183] Ibid., p. 267. There is much additional material in Carro Celada Esteban, *Curas guerrilleros en España* (Madrid, 1971), which unfortunately lacks notes.

[184] See above, p. 8.

[185] Much information can be gleaned from Enrique Dussel, gen. ed., *Historia general de la iglesia en America Latina*, 7 vols. to date (Salamanca, 1981–).

[186] Joachim Smet, O.Carm., *The Carmelites. A History of the Brothers of Our Lady of Mount Carmel* (Darien, Ill., 1975–85), 4:73–5.

[187] Mary Watters, *A History of the Church in Venezuela, 1810–1930* (Chapel Hill, 1933), pp. 66–7.

Spain and then the United States between 1896 and 1902. Although Father Maximo Viron believed he could under no circumstances take up arms, other priests disagreed. Esteban Daes organized several battalions of *sandatahanes* or bolo-equipped infantry. Gregorio Crisostomo committed himself whole-heartedly to the people of Malabon, 'just like the least soldier, defending a trench, mingling with the masses, or helping one of the wounded.' Elsewhere, especially in Nueva Segovia, priests not only encouraged but also often commanded fighting men. Gregorio Aglipay, for example, led guerrillas for eighteen months.[188]

Revolutions and wars in Europe outside of Spain also sometimes swept the clergy up into their furor, if hardly on the same scale. In the dioceses of Milan and Como some Catholic priests took up arms in the revolution of 1848.[189] The struggles to liberate Bosnia and Herzegovina from Turkish rule in 1875–76 drew into the conflict Franciscans as well as Roman Catholic and Orthodox secular priests.[190] In World War I, a postwar Vatican decree reveals that some clergy who had started as chaplains came to take up arms and that some of them had incurred irregularity by killing or wounding others.[191] These clergy required dispensations, and to that end sixteen bishops of France (out of about 100), twenty bishops of Italy (out of about 320), and the heads of three religious congregations requested from Rome the faculty to grant the necessary dispensations.[192] Beyond these skimpy numbers few other reliable figures seem to be available or, I strongly suspect, determinable, although memoirs and diaries can doubtless yield many tidbits of anecdotal evidence.

The numbers are slightly better for the Anglican clergy in the First World War. Here nearly 400 of the 1,274 students enrolled in the theological colleges of England in 1914 promptly enlisted after the declaration of war.[193] These young men were of course not ordained and so were not clergy. Almost all the priests who did volunteer did so for non-combatant duty, but a distinct minority signed on as combatants. The bishop of Bristol reported that of the 310 clergy in his diocese in August 1914, 71 had been commissioned as chaplains, four were working in Church Army Huts, and four were combatants. He noted these statistics in May 1918, at which time another 41 priests were immediately available for military service. Of these 41, four took combatant

188 John Schumacher, S.J., *Revolutionary Clergy. The Filipino Clergy and the Nationalist Movement, 1850–1903* (Quezon City, 1981), pp. 114–5, 120–1, 124–6, 157–62, 164–70, 187, 211–2. The quotation appears on p. 125 and is from the newspaper *La República Filipina*.
189 Mansi 43:437.
190 Vicko Kapitanovic, O.F.M., 'Die Stellung der Franziskaner zur Gewaltanwendung im Freiheitskampf in Bosnien und Hercegowina, 1875', *Archivum Franciscanum historicum* 76 (1983):357, 359.
191 *Acta Apostolicae Sedis* 10 (1918):481–6 and 11 (1919):177–8.
192 I am deeply grateful to Monsignor Agostino Lauro of the Sacred Congregation of the Clergy at the Vatican for doing this research and providing me with these results.
193 Albert Marrin, *The Last Crusade. The Church of England in the First World War* (Durham, N.C., 1974), pp. 16, 187–8.

status.[194] An unknown number of Anglican clergy volunteered for combat duty during World War II.[195]

To be sure, when patriotic feeling did not inspire clerical enlistment during World War I, massive social pressure often did. In addition, some Anglican clergy were abashed that they, unlike their Roman Catholic and Dissenting colleagues, were ordinarily not allowed to be in the front lines with the troops. As Chapter 6 will reveal, Parliament debated on numerous occasions during the war clerical exemption from conscription and actually abolished it for six days in April 1918. Even, then, however, the clergy were bound only to non-combatant duty. Anglican priests who volunteered to fight thus did so freely.

The same was not necessarily true elsewhere. Conscription of the clergy was hardly new or modern. Throughout the Middle Ages the upper clergy were habitually obliged as barons to raise and lead troops, and sometimes the lower clergy were impressed as well. By contrast, in modern history Caesar in his claims has exempted the higher clergy (presumably since fellow members of the governing classes should not have to risk their lives, their liberty, and their sacred pensions on the battlefield), but not the lower clergy. The Catholic clergy of Austria and Germany fretted nervously about their exemption in 1848,[196] and during the U. S. Civil War the Roman Catholic and Episcopal churches protested, often in vain, against the refusal of the Federal government to exempt the clergy.[197] The most vigorous anticlerical policies have been pursued in France. In the Concordat of 1803 Napoleon acceded to Pius VII's plea for exemption of the Italian clergy, but in France it has been otherwise.[198] A law of 1889 obliged seminarians to do a year's military service, and during World War I the government drafted nearly 33,000 Catholic priests for combat duty. Of these, 4,608 were killed, most of them as front-line soldiers.[199] Furthermore, John Keegan informed me, these priests were systematically discouraged, sometimes even forbidden, to exercise their sacerdotal functions.

Fear of conscription and social pressure have caused some modern clergy to take up arms, but these factors do not suffice to explain why clergy have willingly taken up arms when non-combat service would ordinarily have assuaged their neighbors and their governments. Even in the worst of wars, it is never necessary for all eligible males to serve; and of those who serve in a modern army, only a minority are actually combat soldiers. Yet patriotism can run as deep in the clergy as in the laity, from whose ranks after all the clergy are recruited and, since the High Middle Ages, almost always at an age

---

[194] G. K. A. Bell, *Randall Davidson. Archbishop of Canterbury*, 3rd ed. (Oxford, 1952), p. 890, n. 1.
[195] The record-keeping section of the Royal Army is regrettably unable to provide such figures.
[196] See Mansi 43:75, 372, and 47:442–3.
[197] See Murdock, *One Million Men*, pp. 214–7, and above, p. 47.
[198] Mansi 41:986, art. 18, which is to be compared with arts. 6–7 of the Concordat of 1801 with the French Republic (ibid., 41:499).
[199] John McManners, *Church and State in France, 1870–1914* (London, 1972), pp. xviii, xx, xxii; Alan Wilkinson, *The Church of England and the First World War* (London, 1978), p. 42.

level when their values are already well formed. Most important perhaps is the thirst for justice, which may be more characteristic of the clerical profession than of any other, a thirst which can move clerics to oppose regimes as well as defend them, by force of arms if necessary.

But events do not always proceed as we might expect. Given the persistent pattern of clerical militancy in Spanish history, whether for or against the government, it is surprising how little of this evidently occurred during the Spanish Civil War in the 1930s, when 'the greatest clerical bloodletting in the entire history of the Christian Church' occurred.[200] During one six-month period in 1936 (July–December), 6,832 'clergy' were killed, nearly twelve per cent of the total clerical establishment of 60,000 and about twenty-five per cent of those behind Republican lines.[201] Yet little documented clerical armsbearing apparently took place in response. One study that devotes more space to this issue than most treatments of the Spanish Civil War gives only four specific instances of armed clergy in action.[202] In 1937 the bishops of Spain issued a collective letter voicing their concern about the excessively 'active' outlook of many priests in the conflict, and they denounced to the pope Basque priests in particular for their political activity and armsbearing.[203] Even allowing here for hierarchical hysteria, there may be some truth to the charge, which ought to be investigated.

As for the Second World War and the many wars since then, I have heard much but been able to corroborate little. Although I have been unable fully to document any of these stories, Chapter 5 will make it plain why Roman Catholic chaplains could legally carry weapons in a perfectly ordinary way. One Catholic priest who probably did not bear arms but who, like Pope Julius II, was in a position of command was Thierry d'Argenlieu, superior of the Carmelites in France before World War II. He joined the Free French Forces and became Admiral and Commander-in-Chief of the Free French Navy. His address to his crews on D-Day is recorded in the movie *The Longest Day*. Anglican clergy also served as combatants in that war, as the committee appointed to reform the canon law of the Church of England remarked in 1947, but without providing any details.[204]

Finally, as of this writing one hears and reads reports of priests bearing arms, not in reaction to brutal anticlericalism, nor in the dangerous circumstances of a declared war, but rather in revolutions conducted in the name of justice and on behalf of the oppressed in the Philippines, Latin America,

---

[200] Jose Sanchez, *The Spanish Civil War as a Religious Tragedy* (Notre Dame, Ind., 1987), p. 8.

[201] Ibid., pp. 8–10. Sanchez here relies on the detailed calculations of Antonio Montero Moreno.

[202] Ibid., pp. 107–8.

[203] Hugh Thomas, *The Spanish Civil War*, rev. ed. (New York, 1977), p. 697; Pierre Broué and Emile Témime, *The Revolution and the Civil War in Spain*, tr. T. White (MIT Press, 1970), pp. 433–4, who assert the following without providing details or references: 'There is no doubt that, since the beginning of the war, the majority of the priests had taken sides, often in an active and even violent manner, in favor of the rebellion.'

[204] CLCE, pp. 67–8.

and elsewhere.[205] It is possible that the clerical warrior, a constant if variable feature of western Christian history since the late Roman Empire, may be about to stage a comeback.

---

[205] At Medellin, Colombia, in August 1968 more than 900 priests subscribed to a document which sharply distinguished between the unjust violence of the oppressors and the just violence of the oppressed: *Between Honesty and Hope. Documents from and about the Church in Latin America. Issued at Lima by the Peruvian Bishops' Commission for Social Action*, tr. John Drury (Maryknoll, 1970), p. 84.

CHAPTER 2

QUOT HOMINES, TOT SENTENTIAE

As a master of rhetoric, capable of simultaneously entertaining and instructing, Erasmus again and again advanced most persuasively his views on the clergy and warfare. We must not allow his skill or own prejudices to mislead us. We must avoid the trap of making too much of Erasmus, of inferring that his is *the* Renaissance attitude toward the clergy and arms, just as it would be wrong to conclude that the *Canterbury Tales* faithfully mirrors the state of the English clergy at the dawn of the fifteenth century, or that Thomas Aquinas presents *the* medieval position on the armed cleric. In Aquinas' age, as in Erasmus', there were many different opinions on most subjects, and this one was no exception. Throughout the ages, for every condemnation of clerical armsbearing, one can usually find an encomium, and not necessarily one penned by a sycophant. In fact, a great many of them come from other clerics. What follows is not meant to be a representative or balanced selection, but simply an indication that many people, including clerics, disagreed with Erasmus.

The division of opinion appeared quite early. Bishop Theodoret of Cyrrhus (†466) recounted with approval the story of Bishop James of Nisibis (c.325–c.350), who was 'at once bishop, guardian, and commander in chief' of this city on the Persian frontier which King Sapor had been besieging for seventy days. When Bishop James was implored to curse the Persians, 'he discharged no other curse than to ask that mosquitoes and gnats might be sent forth upon them, so that by means of these tiny animals they might learn the might of the Protector of the Romans.' Clouds of these insects soon filled the trunks, nostrils, and ears of the elephants and horses, driving them to unseat their riders and causing complete disarray among the fleeing Persians. 'So the wretched prince', concludes Theodoret, 'learned by a slight and kindly chastisement the power of the God who protects the pious.'[1]

More to the point at hand, Synesius, bishop of Ptolemais (c.410–c.414), praised the priests of Axomis for organizing and leading the local peasantry against the barbarians. He singled out a deacon, Faustus, who, though unarmed, marched at the head of his troops. Upon encountering the enemy,

---

[1] Theodoret, *Ecclesiastical History*, 2.26, tr. B. Jackson (1892; repr., Grand Rapids, 1979), pp. 91–2.

Faustus grabbed a stone and struck a barbarian violently on the head, inspiring his men to plunge into battle. Synesius, who before becoming a bishop had performed similar feats, had only admiration for these brave men: 'I would willingly give a victor's wreath to all those who participated in the engagement.'[2]

Like Synesius, St Germanus, bishop of Auxerre from 418 to 448, had a military background; unlike Synesius, Germanus' conversion was complete, according to his monastic biographer, Constantius. 'He deserted the earthly militia to be enrolled in the heavenly.'[3] With one small exception, Germanus thereafter consistently relied on prayer as his arms. Once, while he and other bishops were conducting missionary work in Britain, the Britons appealed to them for aid against an imminent attack of Saxons and Picts. The bishops promptly came—'to have such apostles for leaders was to have Christ Himself fighting in the camp.' The bishops preached, baptized large numbers of soldiers, and built a church. 'The soldiers paraded still wet from baptism, faith was fervid, the aid of weapons was little thought of, and all looked for help from heaven.'[4] What Constantius then records is surprising in light of his own attitudes. As the enemy approached and the Britons picked up their weapons, Germanus assumed command and began disposing the troops. As the enemy neared,

> Germanus rapidly circulated an order that all should repeat in unison the call he would give as a battle-cry. Then, while the enemy were still secure in the belief that their approach was unexpected, the bishops three times chanted the Alleluia. All, as one man, repeated it and the shout they raised rang through the air and was repeated many times in the confined space between the mountains.

The enemy fled in terror. 'Thus the British army looked on at its revenge without striking a blow, idle spectators of the victory achieved. The booty strewn everywhere was collected; the pious soldiery obtained the spoils of a victory from heaven. The bishops were elated at the rout of the enemy without bloodshed and a victory gained by faith and not by force.'[5] Would Germanus have fallen back on the familiar weapons of war had need arisen? Perhaps, although he and Constantius placed their hope in the efficacy of prayer and were always proved right.

With similar confidence in the power of prayer, Gregory, bishop of Tours, at the end of the sixth century scorned his episcopal colleagues, the brothers Sagittarius of Gap and Salonius of Embrun, for their bellicosity: 'Instead of seeking protection in the heavenly Cross, they were armed with the helmet

---

[2] *The Letters of Synesius of Cyrene*, tr. A. Fitzgerald (Oxford, 1926), pp. 212–3, no. 122. On Synesius, see J.H.W.G. Liebeschuetz, *Barbarians and Bishops. Army, Church and State in the Age of Arcadius and Chrysostom* (Oxford, 1990), pp. 228–35.

[3] Constantius of Lyons, 'The Life of St Germanus of Auxerre', in Sulpicius Severus et al., *The Western Fathers. Being the Lives of Martin of Tours, Ambrose, Augustine of Hippo, Honoratus of Arles, and Germanus of Auxerre*, tr. F. R. Hoare (New York, 1954), p. 287.

[4] Ibid., p. 300.

[5] Ibid., p. 301.

and breastplate of this secular world and, what is more, they are said to have killed many men with their own hands.'[6]

But at about the same time Venantius Fortunatus, Latin poet and bishop of Poitiers (†c.610), praised Nicetius of Trier as a good pastor for building castles and other defenses, and later the biographer of Bishop Desiderius of Cahors (630–54) similarly lauded Desiderius for his attention to fortifications.[7] Most striking of all is the praise of the anonymous biographer of a real warrior, St Arnulf (c.580–before 655), bishop of Metz and progenitor of the Carolingian dynasty: 'For who is able to recount the greatness in fighting and the power in arms of this man, especially since he often drove back the war machines of enemy peoples at the point of his sword?'[8]

By the eighth century the militarization of the Frankish episcopate had proceeded at the expense of holiness, provoking a sharp reaction in St Boniface, the Anglo-Saxon 'Apostle to the Germans.' In 742 he reported to Pope Zacharias on his work among the Franks: 'And certain bishops are to be found among them who, although they deny that they are fornicators or adulterers, are drunkards and shiftless men, given to hunting and to fighting in the army like soldiers and by their own hands shedding blood, whether of heathens or Christians.'[9] Determined to restore right order, five years later Boniface was able to write to Archbishop Cuthbert of Canterbury that his reforming synods had 'forbidden the servants of God to wear showy or martial dress or to carry arms.'[10]

Nevertheless, although Charlemagne did much else to reform the church and promote Christianity, he, even more relentlessly than his grandfather and father, insisted that military service be rendered by the bishops and abbots of his realms in obedience to his will. When Archbishop Arno of Salzburg complained about these demands, Charlemagne's principal adviser, the Anglo-Saxon monk Alcuin, somewhat lamely cited scriptural injunctions to obey earthly rulers, above all a ruler so wise and so devoted to religion.[11] Opinion polarized even further in the later ninth century as the Carolingian empire disintegrated. Pope Nicholas I (858–67), the most forceful pope of the century, was such a rigorist that he denounced bishops for mounting watches against pirates, but other popes in that chaotic era themselves took up the sword in the defense of Rome. In the tenth century, criticism by contemporaries of St Bruno the Great of Cologne evoked from his biographer, Ruotger, eloquent praise of Bruno's

---

6 Gregory of Tours, *The History of the Franks*, tr. Lewis Thorpe (Harmondsworth, 1974), 4.42, p. 237.

7 MGH *Scriptores rerum Merovingicarum* 4, ed. B. Krusch (Hannover-Leipzig, 1902, repr. 1977), c. 17, pp. 575–6.

8 Ibid., 2:433, c. 4: 'Nam virtutem belligerandi seu potentiam illius deinceps in armis quis enarrare queat, praesertim cum saepe phalangas adversarum gentium suo abigisset mucrone?'

9 *The Letters of Saint Boniface*, tr. Ephraim Emerton (New York, 1940, repr. 1976), p. 80.

10 Ibid., p. 137.

11 MGH *Epistolae* 4 (*Epistolae Karolini aevi* 2), ed. E. Dümmler (Hannover, 1895, repr. 1974), no. 265, pp. 422–4.

successful pursuit of peace by inspiring fear and terror (*timor et terror*) in his enemies.[12]

Opinion divided even more strongly in the later eleventh century as the two fiery issues, increasingly intertwined, of sacred war and of reform of both church and Christian society came to dominate public life and discussion.[13] The prior of Conques and his fellow clerics who battled evildoers with weapons won execration from Fulbert of Chartres (†1029), praise from Bernard of Angers, but mixed reactions from others.[14] So, too, did Pope Leo IX for his conduct in 1053. One bishop lauded 'his pious deeds of war', while Peter Damien and others took the opposite stance.[15] Although Gregory VII did not personally take up arms or lead an expedition, and although technically he condemned ecclesiastical armsbearing, his extremism and intransigence in the cause of righteousness pitted people against each other as no pope had ever done, and he greatly accelerated (if he did not actually initiate) the tendency on both sides of reform issues to resort to force. His partisans, such as Anselm of Lucca and Bonizo of Sutri, advocated clerical recourse to arms under certain circumstances, while his opponents vehemently censured the Gregorians for causing so much bloodshed. The anonymous monk of Hersfeld blasted Gregorian bishops such as Hartwig of Magdeburg, Burkhard of Halberstadt, and Gebhard of Salzburg as generals reveling in blood, not true pastors of souls.[16]

In the twelfth century the conduct of Odo of Bayeux and Geoffrey of Coutances neither surprised nor offended Orderic Vitalis, whose indignation was aroused far more readily by sexual offenses.

What shall I say of Odo, bishop of Bayeux, who was an earl palatine dreaded by Englishmen everywhere, and able to dispense justice like a second king? He had authority greater than all earls and other magnates in the kingdom, and gained much ancient treasure ... In this man, it seems to me, vices were mingled with virtues, but he was more given to worldly affairs than to spiritual contemplation. Holy monasteries had good cause to complain that Odo was doing great harm to them, and violently and unjustly robbing them of the ancient endowments given them by pious Englishmen. Then there was Geoffrey bishop of Coutances, of noble Norman stock, who had fought in the battle of Senlac as well as offering up prayers, and had led his knights in various other battles between English and invaders.[17]

---

[12] *Ruotgeri vita Brunonis archiepiscopi Coloniensis*, ed. Irene Ott, in MGH *Scriptores rerum Germanicarum* N.S. 10 (Cologne, 1958), especially cc. 30 and 41, pp. 31 and 43–4. See the discussion in Prinz, *Klerus*, pp. 175–96.
[13] The following paragraph draws heavily upon Erdmann, pp. 35–94.
[14] Ibid., pp. 77–80.
[15] Ibid., pp. 118–9, 123–4.
[16] Ibid., pp. 241–61.
[17] *The Ecclesiastical History of Orderic Vitalis*, ed. and tr. Marjorie Chibnall, 5 vols. (Oxford, 1969–78), 2:264–7. On Orderic, see eadem, *The World of Orderic Vitalis* (Oxford, 1984), and Christopher Holdsworth, 'Orderic, Traditional Monk and the New Monasticism', in D. Greenway, C. Holdsworth, and J. Sayers, eds, *Tradition and Change. Essays in Honour of Marjorie Chibnall* (Cambridge, 1985), pp. 21–34.

Later, Orderic softened in his attitude toward Odo even more: 'He was a man of eloquence and statesmanship, bountiful and most active in worldly business. He held men of religion in great respect, readily defended his clergy by words and arms, and enriched his church in every way with gifts of precious ornaments ... [He] did both good and evil during the fifty years and more that he ruled over the see. Sometimes the spirit triumphed in him to good ends, but on other occasions the flesh overcame the spirit with evil consequences. Yielding to the weakness of the flesh he had a son.'[18]

As for Geoffrey of Coutances, the author of the best modern study of his life and deeds concludes that his military activity scandalized not his contemporaries, but only the Victorian historian E. A. Freeman.[19]

Another bishop who joined Odo and Geoffrey in opposing the revolts of 1074 and 1088 was Wulfstan of Worcester, the only Anglo-Saxon bishop to survive the Conqueror's purge of the episcopate. His charity and piety were so legendary as to merit his canonization by Pope Innocent III in 1203. Wulfstan's response to the troubles of 1088 was painted in grand strokes by another twelfth-century monk, Florence of Worcester:

> Having heard about these developments, a man of great piety and dovelike simplicity, beloved of God and of the people he ruled in all things, faithful in every way to the king as his earthly lord, the revered father Wulfstan, bishop of Worcester, is troubled by great disgust but, renewed by the mercy of God, now prepares himself like another Moses to stand firm vigorously for his people and his city.[20]

Twelfth- and Thirteenth-Century Attitudes

Orderic Vitalis and Florence of Worcester wrote in the twelfth century about prelates of the eleventh. By the time they were composing their histories, no one could any longer be considered representative of the attitude of his age toward clerical armsbearing, for the simple reason that every possible attitude on the spectrum from encomium to execration was now expressed. Seemingly neutral reportage of course continued, which can be difficult to interpret. For example, three different Italian accounts of Pope Innocent's II's futile campaigns against King Roger of Sicily in 1138–39 appear to be so dispassionate that one would be hard put to judge whether the authors were practicing great discretion, preferred to 'let the facts speak for themselves', or simply had a remarkably blasé attitude toward such papal behavior.[21]

---

[18] Ibid., 4:114–7.
[19] John Le Patourel, 'Geoffrey of Montbray, Bishop of Coutances', *EHR* 59 (1944):129, 155–7.
[20] Florence of Worcester, *Chronicon*, ed. Benjamin Thorpe (London, 1848; repr., Vaduz, 1964), 2:24–5; see also 2:11 for Wulfstan's part in the suppression of the earlier baronial revolt of 1075. Interestingly, nothing about these events is mentioned in William of Malmesbury, *Vita Wulfstani*, ed. R. R. Darlington, Camden Society, 3rd ser. 40 (London, 1928), which was a reworking of the Old English life by Coleman (c.1075–1113).
[21] MGH *Scriptores* 19, ed. G. H. Pertz (Hannover, 1866; repr., New York-Stuttgart, 1963): 283

Sometimes narratives could be manifestly sympathetic without engaging in outright praise. Archbishop Thurstan of York received such treatment from at least one clerical chronicler for his part in the battle of the Standard against the Scots in 1338, while Richard, prior of the Augustinian house of Hexham from 1135 to 1139, without blush praised Thurstan for rallying the barons, assuring them that the defense of holy Church and their country was a most just and pious cause, and mustering his parishioners behind his cross-bearing priests. Ailred, abbot of the Cistercian monastery of Rievaulx, was somewhat more cautious in his account of the battle. His lack of warmth sprang not from criticism of Thurstan, however, but rather from a desire to stress the role of Walter de Espec in the battle. Given this kind of motivation, Ailred's account is surprisingly uncritical:

> And Thurstan also, archbishop of York, published an episcopal edict throughout his whole diocese that all who could proceed to the wars should hasten to the nobles from each of his parishes, preceded by the priests with cross and banners and relics of saints, to defend the church of Christ against the barbarians.[22]

Interestingly, over three hundred years later another Cistercian, Thomas de Burton, abbot of Meaux from 1396 to 1399, in assembling the chronicle of his monastery, borrowed Ailred's version of Thurstan's speech and then mentioned in passing that Thurstan was unable to be present at the battle because of his age and illness.[23]

On the other hand, Pope Eugenius III's vain attempt to retake Rome in 1149 elicited a frank reproach from Gerhoh of Reichersberg (1093–1169), one of the more zealous reformers of the German church. While visiting the papal court on one of his numerous embassies on behalf of his priory, Gerhoh listened to the pope complain about the enormous costs of the campaign in relation to such paltry gains. Gerhoh then replied:

> Granted that that wretched peace was bought for such a great price, it was nevertheless better than a year of fighting, because when the Roman Pontiff prepares himself to conduct war with mercenaries, it seems to me like Peter drawing an iron sword. But when it does not go well for him who is fighting or about to fight, I seem to hear Christ saying to Peter, 'Put up your sword in its sheath.'

Just to insure that the lesson was not lost on future popes, Gerhoh carefully recounted this story in a letter to Eugenius' successor, Alexander III.[24]

(Annales Ceccanenses), 309 (Annales Casinenses), 420–24 (annals of Romuald II, archbishop of Salerno from 1153 to 1181).

[22] The two accounts are printed in *Chronicles of the Reigns of Stephen, Henry II., and Richard I.*, 3, ed. Richard Howlett, RS 82/3 (London, 1886): 160–1, 182; and partial translations are given in Alan O. Anderson, *Scottish Annals from English Chroniclers, A.D. 500 to 1286* (London, 1908), pp. 191–2. Donald Nicholl, *Thurstan, Archbishop of York (1114–1140)* (York, 1964), contains a long account of the events surrounding the battle with many excerpts from the sources.

[23] *Chronica monasterii de Melsa*, ed. E. A. Bond, RS 43 (London, 1866–68), 1:121: 'Et cum ipse archiepiscopus senio et morbi causa pugnae non potuit interesse . . .'

[24] The Latin text (also in PL 193:568–9) is reproduced in G. W. Greenaway, *Arnold of Brescia* (Cambridge, 1931), p. 125, n. 3.

More tactful and, on the whole, more successful as a mentor was Gerhoh's contemporary and Eugenius' teacher, Bernard of Clairvaux (1090–1153). In the *Five Books on Consideration* written for his protégé, Bernard in one place counseled him to sheathe his sword and in another extolled Eugenius' predecessors who had gone out and conquered the world not with swords, but with 'the firey word and the mighty wind, powerful arms from God.'[25] Elsewhere, in a letter to the bishop and clergy of Troyes, Bernard clearly states that 'It is not lawful for the clergy to fight with the arms of soldiers, nor for a subdeacon to marry.'[26]

Yet, like Scripture and Augustine, Bernard can seem to contradict himself. Aside from his eloquent advocacy of the crusades – which of themselves had nothing to do with clerical armsbearing – Bernard also authored the constitutions of the Knights Templar and sang their praises as incorporating the best features of the monastic and the military life. Similar sentiments can be found in Bernard's contemporaries Peter the Venerable, abbot of Cluny, Guigo, grand abbot of the Carthusians, and Pope Innocent II.[27] Far better known are two great contemporary works of literature, *The Song of Roland* and *The Cid*, with their praises of two warrior prelates, Archbishop Turpin and Bishop Don Jerome.

The battlefield activities of Hubert Walter, bishop of Salisbury and then archbishop of Canterbury, were taken up by the celebrated Welsh cleric and courtier Gerald of Wales. In a letter to the archbishop, Gerald praised his recent successful campaign against the Welsh in 1198 in the language of the liturgy.

Blessed be God who has 'taught your hands to war and your fingers to fight' [Ps. 144.1]. Blessed be God who by the hand of His anointed has given you such a glorious victory over your enemies. And blessed be His Holy Name who was ordained that this realm should be ruled by law and pacified by arms through the unwearied labour of His Pontiff and Primate, strong both in spiritual and worldly warfare, fighting with either sword, and by his marvellous skill moulding himself to meet the vicissitudes of these times.[28]

Is this praise or parody? Although it has been interpreted as criticism,[29] from any another contemporary this could easily be read as genuine praise. And although Gerald was understandably enraged at the commander of this invasion of his native land, he was not above praising Hubert Walter elsewhere.[30]

---

[25] Bernard of Clairvaux, *Five Books on Consideration. Advice to a Pope*, tr. John D. Anderson and Elizabeth T. Kennan (Kalamazoo, 1976), 3.1 and 4.7, pp. 79–80 and 117–8; see also 1.7, p. 36n

[26] *The Letters of St Bernard of Clairvaux*, tr. Bruno James (Chicago, 1953; repr., New York, 1980), no. 262, p. 342.

[27] See the texts gathered and discussed by Ernst-Dieter Hehl, *Kirche und Krieg im 12. Jahrhundert*, Monographien zur Geschichte des Mittelalters 19 (Stuttgart, 1980), pp. 117–20.

[28] *The Autobiography of Gerald of Wales*, ed. and tr. H. E. Butler (London, 1937), p. 131.

[29] C. R. Cheney, *Hubert Walter* (London, 1967), p. 99.

[30] In his *Retractationes*, as noted by Giles Constable, 'An Unpublished Letter by Abbot Hugh II of

Another problem is that within a few pages of the same letter Gerald reveals his knowledge of the legal principle in Roman and canon law of the right to repel violence with violence, even though he chooses to make bitter fun of it.[31] Finally, even though Gerald did directly denounce Hubert Walter as an iniquitous warrior to Pope Innocent III,[32] his motives were hardly unimpeachable. Gerald traveled in the 1190s in the entourage of Prince John while Hubert governed as regent, and Hubert had also blocked Gerald's election to the see of St David's in his native land.[33] So while Gerald's hatred of Hubert as a Welshman and as a courtier was entirely comprehensible, his intensely personal engagement with Hubert raises questions about the extent to which Gerald's condemnation was genuine and also represented the values of his age.

There is much evidence to suggest that on this matter Gerald was not typical and not even just. After a careful examination of the evidence, Christopher Cheney concluded that 'Archbishop Hubert was scrupulous not to bear arms in defiance of the canons.'[34] Hubert's contemporaries faulted him for many shortcomings, but not for that, and on the whole they lauded his achievements as archbishop and regent.[35] Hubert's deeds as a crusader were characterized, for example, by the anonymous chronicler of Richard the Lion-Heart's crusade as those of 'a man whose excellence is fulfilled as a knight in arms, as a leader in the camp, and as a pastor among the clergy.'[36] In England he enjoyed good repute among, and the support of, the Cistercians and especially the Premonstratensian canons.[37]

To be sure, at least one of Hubert's advocates was not disinterested. Hugh, abbot of Reading from 1186 to 1199, then became abbot of Cluny and thus one of the more powerful men of his day. In 1194 his monks of Reading had assisted Hubert Walter in the military operations against Marlborough Castle, then held by John's men, and so it comes as no surprise that in a letter to Pope Celestine III in 1197 Abbot Hugh celebrated Archbishop Hubert Walter as the protector of the oppressed, the poor, and widows, and as one who knew how to wield both swords wisely so as to provide peace and promote the honor of God.[38]

Reading concerning Archbishop Hubert Walter', in his *Cluniac Studies*, Collected Studies 109 (London, 1980), 12, p. 27. n. 66.

[31] *Autobiography*, p. 139: 'Since therefore Law and Justice permit men to repel violence with violence ... blessed be God, who by the inspired vigour and virtue of one man freed the country thus mightily ...'

[32] Ibid., pp. 176, 180–81, 214–8, 272–3.

[33] See Cheney, *Hubert Walter*, pp. 81, 130–33, 165, 178, 189–90; Robert Bartlett, *Gerald of Wales* (Oxford, 1982), pp. 49–54, 65, 68.

[34] Cheney, *Hubert Walter*, p. 99.

[35] For a review, see ibid., pp. 177–81.

[36] Quoted in Charles R. Young, *Hubert Walter, Lord of Canterbury and Lord of England* (Durham, N.C., 1968), pp. 34–5.

[37] Constable, 'An Unpublished Letter' (n. 30 above), pp. 17–20.

[38] Constable, 'An Unpublished Letter', pp. 23, 29–31: 'Ecclesiarum specialis tutor effectus, oppressorum adiutor, pius protector pauperum, pupillorum pater, defensor uiduarum. ... De quo nunc illud cunctis predicitur mirabile, quod utrumque gladium in Anglia, uidelicet regis et ecclesie, tanta tam decenti moderatur temperie, ut ad honorem dei ecclesia plena tranquillitate uigeat,

One of their contemporaries was Abbot Samson, who ruled the monastery of Bury St Edmunds from 1182 to 1211. He was well named and memorable, earning a somewhat romanticized place in Carlyle's *Past and Present* (1843). The more accurate and contemporary guide to Samson's life was by his chaplain Jocelin, monk of Brakelond, who recorded Samson's role in the siege of Windsor in 1193 in this way:

> And after doing this he went to the siege of Windsor, at which, with certain other abbots of England, he carried arms, having his own standard and leading a number of knights at great expense, *though shining rather in counsel than in prowess*. But we cloister monks judged that such conduct was hazardous, for we feared that in consequence some future abbot might perchance be constrained to go forth in person on some warlike expedition.[39]

The italicized words, which might reveal so much about Samson's conduct and Jocelin's attitude, are vexatious, for they are set off by one editor as if this were a quotation (the source of which he does not identify) and by another editor labeled an incomplete construction.[40] In any event, Jocelin does not criticize Samson for being *armatus*, but only for having set a bad precedent which could create heavy obligations for future abbots.

Jocelin's views were complemented by those of another English monk, Richard of Devizes, monk of St Swithun's in Winchester, in his chronicle of the crusade of King Richard between 1189 and 1192. Far from criticizing Hubert Walter and other ecclesiastical soldiers, he had utter contempt for one prelate for reneging on his vow to go on crusade.

> Walter, archbishop of Rouen, was, as is common among the secular clergy, cowardly and timid. Having saluted Jerusalem from afar, unasked he laid aside his anger against Saladin. He gave the king, who was going to fight in his stead, everything he had brought with him for the expedition. He also laid aside the Cross. Forgetting all shame, he gave as his excuse a devotion that even the most wretched of mothers would bear with distrust. He alleged (that is to say) that the shepherds of the Church should preach rather than fight and that it was not fitting for a bishop to bear any other arms than those of the virtues. The king, however, to whom the sight of his money was more necessary than the presence of his person, approved his excuses, as if overcome by his exceedingly lively logic.[41]

---

et regia potestas multis pridem ut diximus iniuriis lacessita, in pristinum decorem iam plenius conualescat' (pp. 30–1).

[39] *The Chronicle of Jocelin of Brakelond Concerning the Acts of Samson, Abbot of the Monastery of St Edmund*, ed. and tr. H. E. Butler, Nelson's Medieval Texts (London, 1949), pp. 54–5: 'Post quod factum iuit ad obsidionem de Windleshor, ubi armatus cum quibusdam aliis abbatibus Anglie, uexillum proprium habens, et plures milites ducens ad multas expensas, plus ibi consilio quam probitate nitens. Nos uero claustrales tale factum periculosum iudicauimus, timentes consequentiam, ne forte futurus abbas cogatur in propria persona ire in expedicionem bellicam.'

[40] By Butler in the first instance, by Thomas Arnold in the second (*The Memorials of St Edmund's Abbey*, RS 96 [1890–96], 1:259 n).

[41] *The Chronicle of Richard of Devizes of the Time of King Richard the First*, ed. and tr. John T. Appleby (London, 1963), pp. 27–8.

Richard of Devizes' experience of bishops was evidently such that he found Archbishop Walter's excuse a miserable lie.

The case of a later archbishop of Canterbury, Boniface of Savoy, is somewhat different from that of Hubert Walter. The story recounted in the last chapter that he savagely thrashed the subprior of St Bartholomew's, London, appears in the *Chronica majora* of Matthew Paris, who hated not only foreigners, but also the Franciscans whom Boniface favored. A young, highly respected Franciscan, Adam Marsh, was present at the scene at St Bartholomew's. His report to the bishop of London is clearly sympathetic to Boniface and records no such violence, and elsewhere Marsh noted that many scurrilous stories about Boniface were widely circulated. However politic Marsh may have been, is it likely that someone who enjoyed the favor of Grosseteste would have supported such a brute as Matthew Paris depicts? Or is it more likely that Paris, given his notorious prejudices, heard what he wanted to hear and then some?

Matthew Paris' contempt for 'foreigners' might well have been confirmed had he been able to read Joinville's *Life* of King St Louis IX. Joinville the layman takes obvious pleasure in the admiration of the crusading army for the courage of 'his priest', Jean de Voysey, in battle.[42] This is self-interested pride, but it must also be set off against Joinville's own disinterested respect for the warrior bishop of Ramleh.[43] All of this Matthew Paris could have written off as owing to the corruption of the French, of foreigners generally, or of the laity. What he could not so easily have dismissed are the striking attitudes of Joinville's lord and patron, Louis IX, known as the most just ruler of his age, canonized within thirty years of his death, and intensely reform-minded about both the ecclesiastical and the secular realms. How would King Louis react to a violent cleric, not in the Levant where the right of self-defense was taken for granted, but in France itself, where Louis sought to establish order and discourage recourse to violence? Joinville tells an arresting tale of a cleric who in the environs of Paris went well beyond the bounds of simple self-defense. The provost (mayor) of Paris reported to the king that three of his sergeants had been going about robbing people. They met this cleric and took all his clothes.

> 'The clerk, with nothing on but his shirt, went back to his lodgings, snatched up his crossbow, and got a child to carry his sword. As soon as he caught sight of the thieves, he shouted after them, saying he would kill them. He got his crossbow ready and shot at them, piercing one of them through the heart. The two others took to their heels; but the clerk seized hold of the sword the child was carrying and followed after them . . . [he] struck at [one of them] with his sword, cutting right through his leg . . . Then he went after the other man, who tried to get into a strange house where the people were still awake; but the clerk struck him a blow with his sword right through the middle of his head and split it open down to the teeth, as

---

[42] Jean de Joinville, 'The Life of St Louis,' in Joinville and Villehardouin, *Chronicles of the Crusades*, tr. Caroline Smith (Harmondsworth, 2008), p. 210.

[43] Ibid., p. 298.

your Majesty can see. The clerk', continued the provost, 'told what he had done to the neighbors in the street, and then came and gave himself up as your Majesty's prisoner. And now I have brought him to you, to do with what you will. Here he is.'

'Young man', said the king, 'your courage has lost you the chance of becoming a priest; but because of your courage I will take you into my service, and you shall go with me oversea. I am doing this not only for your sake, but also because I wish my people to understand that I will never uphold them in any of their misdeeds.' When the people who had gathered there heard this, they called on our Saviour, praying Him to intercede with God, so that He would grant the king a long and happy life and bring him back to them in joy and health.[44]

The king was familiar enough with canon law to know that the cleric was now barred from ordination as a priest. His own response, taking the young man into his own service, may seem lenient enough when considered on its own terms, but seems disturbingly so when measured against some of Louis' other attitudes as recorded by Joinville. With respect to attacks on Christianity, for example, he advised that 'a layman, whenever he hears the Christian religion abused, should not attempt to defend its tenets, except with his sword, and that he should thrust into the scoundrel's belly, and as far as it will enter.'[45] Nor did Louis have any truck with blasphemy of any kind:

The king had so deep a love for our Lord and His sweet Mother that he punished most severely all those who had been convicted of speaking of them irreverently or of using their names in some wicked oath. Thus I saw him order a goldsmith of Caesarea to be bound to a ladder, with pig's gut and other viscera round his neck, in such a quantity that they reached up to his nose. I have also heard that, since I came back from oversea, he had the lips and nose of a citizen of Paris seared for a similar offence; but this I did not see for myself.[46]

It is well to conclude this consideration of attitudes toward armsbearing by clergy in the High Middle Ages by turning to three German clerics, the first of whom reveals why German bishops continued to suffer from their iniquitous reputation into the thirteenth century and beyond. Caesarius of Heisterbach (c.1180–1240) entered the Cistercian monastery of Heisterbach, near Bonn, around 1199. For the edification of novices he wrote around 1223 a twelve-book work entitled *Dialogue on Miracles*, an enormously rich font of material on many facets of medieval life. One chapter begins this way:

A few years ago this terrible saying was uttered against bishops by a clerk in Paris: 'I can believe a great deal', he said, 'but there is one thing I can never believe, namely, that any bishop in Germany can ever be saved!'

Novice: Why should he condemn the bishops in Germany rather than those of France, England, Lombardy or Tuscany?

Monk: Because all the bishops in Germany have both swords committed to

44 Ibid., p. 193.
45 Ibid., p. 175.
46 Ibid., p. 336.

them; I mean the temporal power as well as the spiritual; and since they hold the power of life and death, and make wars, they are compelled to be more anxious about the pay of their soldiers than the welfare of the souls committed to their charge. Nevertheless we find among the bishops of Cologne, who were both Pontiffs and temporal Princes, some who were also saints; for instance, the blessed Bruno, S. Heribert and S. Hanno.[47]

Caesarius' response by way of the monk is defensive. Although he points out the warrior-saints of the see of Cologne, he denies neither the charge against German prelates nor the conviction that for that reason they are damned. These observations about Caesarius's sentiments are confirmed by other stories – of the apostate monk mentioned in the Introduction who had taken up with robbers and killed people, of the warrior bishop Leopold of Worms, and of the parish priest near Cologne who for fear carried a sword one night and was terrorized by Satan as a result.[48] Caesarius's disapproval seems perfectly clear except for one story, with considerable potential, of a nobleman who refused to confess to a bishop a murder he had committed for love of justice, and to whom God miraculously gave the Eucharist even though the bishop had refused to communicate him.[49] Even though the lesson is not directly applicable to clerics, God clearly loves the triumph of justice so much that He is willing to dispense from His own divinely instituted arrangements for the regular dispensing of His saving grace.

Whatever Caesarius's position on clerics and arms – after all he resided in relative peacefulness in a Rhineland abbey – it was, understandably, not necessarily shared by his clerical colleagues to the more violent east where the Germanic peoples were vigorously engaged in Christianizing and civilizing the Slavic peoples. *The Chronicle of the Slavs* by Helmold may or may not be typical. Born sometime between 1118 and 1125 in Westphalia, Helmold took the monk's habit in Saxony and by 1163 was pastor of the church at Bosau, where he wrote his *Chronicle* between 1167 and 1172 and died sometime in the 1170s. His attitude toward Gerlav the priest might well have scandalized Caesarius: 'I shall tell of an event worth remembering by posterity.' In the region of Sussel three thousand Slavs were besieging a small fort held by about four hundred Frisians. When some of the Frisians wanted to accept the Slavs' offer to spare them if they surrendered, 'a most steadfast priest' exhorted the Frisians 'to plunge into their vitals your swords . . . and be avengers of your blood.'

> And as he spoke these words he showed them his plucky spirit. He threw open the portals and with only one man hurled back the enemy wedge, slaying a prodigious number of Slavs with his own hand. He did not slacken in the fight even after one eye had been stricken out and he had been wounded in the abdomen; he displayed

---

[47] Caesarius of Heisterbach, *The Dialogue on Miracles*, tr. H. von E. Scott and C. C. Swinton Bland, 2 vols. (London, 1929), 2.27, 1:110–1.

[48] Ibid., 2.2, 2.9, and 5.55, at 1:64–7, 80–1, and 388–9.

[49] Ibid., 9.38, 2:140–2.

divine strength both of soul and of body. Those most noted sons of Sarvia, or the Maccabees, did not fight more valiantly of old than the priest Gerlav and the handful of men in the stronghold Sussel.[50]

More matter-of-fact is the later chronicle by Henry of Livonia, who was born in Saxony around 1188, emigrated to Livonia around 1205, became a member of the household of Bishop Albert of Riga (1198–1229?), and was still alive as a parish priest in 1259. Usually without much comment he relates the martyrdom of priests who make no effort to defend themselves,[51] the command of armies by Bishop Albert and other prelates,[52] and clerics' rushing to arms when attacked. When the Kurs appeared before Riga, 'the citizens, the Brothers of the Militia, and the *ballistarii* [operators of large, wheeled crossbows], few though they were, together with the clerics and the women, all had recourse to arms, and having sounded the bell which was rung only in time of war, they assembled the people.'[53] When the Oeselians, who were ravaging the province of Metsepole, approached the village of Legedore, Godfrey the priest not only aroused the neighboring parishes to fight the Oeselians; he also 'belted on his weapons for war and put on his breastplate, like a giant, desiring to save his sheep from the jaws of the wolves.'[54] Henry's allusions here to passages from Maccabees, Matthew, and John suggest warm approval, an inference confirmed when Henry elsewhere tells us without reluctance of two separate incidents when he took up arms himself. Once, while baptizing in Wierland, he hears people shouting that 'a great host of pagans was coming against us. We immediately put down the holy chrism and the other holy articles, therefore, and hurried to the ministry of shields and swords.'[55] Although this turned out to be a false alarm, on the occasion of an Oeselian attack Henry reveals what he was prepared to do with his weapons: 'When we had heard that it was the enemy of Christ's name, we hurried toward them and after the ninth hour we caught four of them who were burning a village. After killing them and taking their horses, we hurried after the others.'[56]

The Later Middle Ages

Bishop Antony Bek of Durham may be dismissed by modern historians as 'the warrior bishop',[57] but many of his contemporaries had a higher regard

---

[50] *The Chronicle of the Slavs by Helmold, Priest of Bosau*, tr. F. J. Tschan, Columbia University Records of Civilization 21 (New York, 1935), pp. 178–9.

[51] *The Chronicle of Henry of Livonia*, tr. James A. Brundage (Madison, 1961), pp. 70–2, 119, 140–1, 175–6. On Henry's life, see pp. 11–16.

[52] Ibid., pp. 73–4.

[53] Ibid., p. 97.

[54] Ibid., p. 165.

[55] Ibid., p. 179.

[56] Ibid., p. 184.

[57] This phrase appears in John E. Morris, *The Welsh Wars of Edward I* (Oxford, 1941, repr. 1968), p. 261.

for him, particularly his magnanimity. One poet went so far as to call him 'the most valiant clerk in Christendom.'[58] Pope Clement V created him Patriarch of Jerusalem in 1306, the only Englishman ever to receive that honor.[59] On his death in 1311 he became the first bishop of Durham since St Cuthbert (†687) to be interred in the cathedral.[60] Such contemporary criticism of his military activities as existed was not as harsh as one might have expected. When Bek had trouble keeping his men under control at Falkirk and upbraided them, one knight shot back: 'It is not for you, sir bishop, to teach us now of fighting, rather you should be busy at Mass.'[61] Sharp replies like this, responses to a scolding, are perhaps better considered expressions of annoyance rather than moral judgments. Had the knight been truly offended by Bek's 'unclerical' behavior, he would probably have spoken more forcefully and bitterly. As for Bek's siege of Durham cathedral in 1300, the author of this anonymous poem indicts the monks almost as severely as he does Bek:

> Alas to Durham's monks there came
> Harsh violence and bitter shame,
> In cloister flourished evil men:
> The very saints were shaken then.
> All decent order overthrown,
> Christ's glorious tunic slashed and torn,
> The prior defeated and deposed,
> The brethren grieving and amazed,
> The sheep of Christ torn from the fold,
> By jaws of wolves and dogs were mauled.
> Durham's bishop thus upheld
> By wicked men, wished to enforce
> A visitation on the house.
> But his violent plan was foiled . . .
> In vain [the prior] quibbled, for my lord
> Put the matter to the sword.
> From boyhood Bishop Anthony
> Had learned to fight most readily,
> And in violence trusted more
> Than in the texts of canon law . . .
> At this the monks were terrified
> Lest to the secular world outside
> The secrets of their order be
> Known and debated publicly.[62]

However much we may be repulsed by Henry Despenser, the crusading bishop of Norwich crushing peasants at home and townsmen in the Low

---

[58] C. M. Fraser, *A History of Antony Bek, Bishop of Durham, 1283–1311* (Oxford, 1957), pp. 230–2.
[59] Ibid., pp. 164–5.
[60] Ibid., pp. 228–9.
[61] Quoted in ibid., pp. 75–6.
[62] *The Chronicle of Bury St Edmunds 1212–1301*, ed. and tr. Antonia Grandsden (London-Edinburgh, 1964), pp. 161–3.

Countries in the 1380s, at least three of his English clerical contemporaries applauded his vigor. The first was the monk of Leicester who continued the chronicle of Henry Knighton on the rebellion of 1381:

> Likewise at Peterborough the neighbors and tenants of the abbot rose against him and proposed to kill him—which they would have done without redress had God not laid his restraining hand upon them at the last moment. For help came in the shape of lord Henry le Spenser, bishop of Norwich, who, through the agency of divine mercy, arrived with a strong force. He prevented the malefactors from carrying out their aims and scattered the mob, paying them back as they deserved. Sparing no one, he sent some to death and others to prison ... Just as they had spared no one from their own furious vengeance, so now the bishop's eye spared none of them—he repaid them in like kind and measure for measure. Because they had come to destroy the church and churchmen I dare to say that they deserved to perish at the hands of an ecclesiastic. For the bishop gladly stretched his avenging hand over them and did not scruple to give them final absolution for their sins with his sword. So was fulfilled the saying of the prophet: 'You will rule them with iron rods, and break them like a potter's vessel' (Ps. 2.9) This vigorous bishop took similar measures at various places in the counties of Cambridge and Huntingdon: wherever he heard of rebels, he immediately went to meet and disperse them, crushing their arrogance at its root.[63]

A second Benedictine monk, the anonymous author of a chronicle produced at St Mary's Abbey in York, waxed slightly less rapturous in his version of Bishop Henry's campaign to crush and 'behead for their wicked deeds' these rebels who had raged 'like beasts' out of 'malice' and 'mischief.' If Henry is here not openly praised, neither is he in any way censured.[64] The third clerical witness is the archbishop of Canterbury, William Courtenay (1381–96), who in 1383 solicited the bishops of the province for contributions to offset the costs incurred by Bishop Despenser in his disastrous Continental venture. The archbishop's letter spoke warmly of Bishop Henry's courage and zeal for God, church, and country: 'conducting himself vigorously amidst the dangers of war, and aided with the help of divine favor, he triumphed brilliantly over the enemy on different occasions from the beginning of his campaign.'[65]

Similarly, the priest and chronicler Jean Froissart sang with undisguised pleasure of the bravery at Otterburn in 1388 of the chaplain of the Earl of Douglas, William of North Berwick. Father William

> was not there as a priest but as worthy man-at-arms, for he had followed [the earl] all night through the thick of battle with an axe in his hand. This doughty warrior was laying about him near the Earl, keeping the English back with the great blows he dealt them with his axe, for which service the Scots were truly grateful. It earned him

---

63 Quoted in R. B. Dobson, ed. and tr., *The Peasants' Revolt of 1381* (London, 1970), p. 238.

64 *The Anonimalle Chronicle, 1333 to 1381*, ed. V. H. Galbraith (Manchester, 1970), p. 151.

65 Wilkins 3:177–8: 'zelo legis Dei, et ecclesie, ac regni Angliae fervore successus' and 'periculosis bellorum eventibus strenue se exponens, et assistenti sibi divini favoris clementia, in initio sui progressus in diversis locis de inimicis laudabiliter triumphavit.'

great renown and in the same year he became archdeacon and canon of Aberdeen. It is a fact that he was a tall, finely built man—and brave, too, to do what he did.[66]

Even John Wycliffe, usually fairly straightforward, not to say extreme, in his views, on this issue appears to be somewhat confusing. On the one hand, he preached that fighting priests cannot discharge the duties of their office; on the other hand, he blasted clerical owners of property for not fighting for their countries, including invading other lands.[67] One of Wycliffe's major biographers finds it 'impossible' to square these assertions.[68] That is not necessarily so, for in the second case Wycliffe was considering clerical possessioners, who for that reason owed services to the nation. That would seem strange, were it not for Wycliffe's firm conviction that the church must be disendowed so that the clergy be not misled by concerns temporal. By suggesting that the clergy saw that they had rights but not responsibilities by virtue of their ownership of property, Wycliffe reinforced his argument for disendowment. Furthermore, in his treatise *On the Office of the King* (*De officio regis*) he went out of his way to reject Roman law as a legitimate foundation for the law of arms, which should have the Bible as its sole source.[69]

A rather different late medieval cleric who has enjoyed no less of a reputation than Wycliffe for religious probity was the Augustinian canon Thomas Hamerken from Kempen in the diocese of Cologne, better known as Thomas à Kempis (1383–1471), to whom *The Imitation of Christ* continues to be credited. Thomas lived for sixty-three years in the monastery of Mount St Agnes in the diocese of Utrecht. Under the aegis of Bishop Frederick von Blankenhem (1393–1423) the 'Modern Devotion', embracing both the Brethren of the Common Life and affiliated monasteries like Mount St Agnes, had flourished and spread. But Bishop Frederick had done much more, and when he died at about the age of eighty Thomas à Kempis sang his praises this way:

> He ruled the diocese of Utrecht strenuously and in honourable wise during thirty years, for the grace of God Almighty succoured him: his power was increased by many victories, and he gave the Church peace, his country safety, and his people tranquillity before his death. This is he that was a potentate of renown, a pillar of the priesthood, a guiding star to Clerks, a father to the Religious, a friend to all devout persons, a defender of the orphan, an avenger upon the unjust.
>
> This is he that was the glory of rulers, the delight of subjects, that upheld dignity among the aged, and uprightness amongst the young; he was a pinnacle of learning, the ornament of the wise; he gave weapons to the warriors and a shield to them that strove; he inspired terror in his foes, and courage in his people . . . And because the Bishop feared God, honoured Holy Church, and loved and defended all that served

---

[66] Jean Froissart, *Chronicles*, tr. Geoffrey Brereton (Harmondsworth, 1968), p. 344.
[67] *Johannis Wyclif sermonum*, ed. J. Loserth (London, 1887–90), 2:374–75; 3:98, 101, 103; 4:47, 143, 210–11.
[68] Herbert B. Workman, *John Wyclif. A Study of the English Medieval Church* (Oxford, 1926), 2:303.
[69] *Iohannis Wyclif Tractatus de officio regis*, eds Alfred Pollard and Charles Sayle, Wyclif's Latin Works 8 (London, 1887), c. 7, especially pp. 193–4.

the Lord, therefore the Majesty on High protected him from the enemies that were round about, making rebellious nations subject to him, especially those Frisians who had invaded his territories.[70]

Would Thomas a Kempis have said something similar but a few decades later about Popes Alexander VI and Julius II, who, it could be persuasively argued, also sought to pacify their domains and repulse the foreigners who had invaded their territories? Perhaps, but one does have to admit that by the start of the sixteenth century that most mysterious and irrational of things, the 'climate of opinion', was becoming profoundly antagonistic to such prelatical behavior. Few popes suffer from greater malodor than these two.

Even then a prelate of sufficient distinction might escape criticism. Cardinal Ximenes has attracted almost no adverse commentary for his militancy. Unlike the popes who were nominally his masters, he is remembered almost exclusively in a positive light as a reformer and as a patron of the latest biblical scholarship. This is probably owing in good part to his being 'offstage' in Iberia and not at the papal court, where he could be seen by all. In Spain Ximenes has enjoyed a very good press. The main source for all later biographers was written by Alvaro Gomez de Castro (†1580), who wrote at the behest of the University of Alcala, which Ximenes had founded and where Gomez was professor. It is he who records the speech given by Ximenes at the siege of Oran in 1509 and quoted in Chapter 1. 'Records' is a misleading word inasmuch as Gomez as a typical humanist historian felt free to put plausible speeches in the mouth of the Cardinal. It is for that reason all the more significant that Gomez invented a speech which did not embarrass him, his readers, or the memory of Ximenes. Another source that has recently come to light and on which Gomez drew was written c.1519 by a Franciscan who had at least some contact with the Cardinal. Although the author ascribes no speeches to his subject, he speaks with decided warmth of this crusade on behalf of the faith.[71] Even Prescott, no lover of things Catholic, recounts the campaign and the incident with admiration, although he cannot resist observing dryly that had Ximenes 'lived in the age of the crusades, he would indubitably have headed one of those expeditions himself; for the spirit of the soldier burned strong and bright under his monastic weeds.'[72] But, then, Ximenes was warring against non-Christians, whereas the popes were not.

[70] Thomas à Kempis, *The Chronicle of the Canons Regular of Mount St Agnes*, tr. J. P. Arthur (London, 1906), pp. 63–5; see also p. 172.
[71] Lynn H. Nelson and Arnold H. Weiss, 'An Early Life of Francisco Jimenez de Cisneros', *Franciscan Studies* 42 (1982): 156–65, at 162–3.
[72] William H. Prescott, *History of the Reign of Ferdinand and Isabella the Catholic*, ed. J. F. Kirk (Philadelphia, 1872), 2.21, 3:313.

Julius II in Contemporary Opinion

Shortly before the *Julius exclusus* appeared, another reformer was ostensibly praising Julius II to his face. In one of the opening addresses of the Fifth Lateran Council (1512–17), Giles of Viterbo, the General of Luther's order of Augustinian friars, congratulated the pope on the outcome of his wars in the Papal States, but then somewhat later elaborated on St Ambrose by remarking that 'Our arms, however, are piety, religion, probity, supplications, prayers, the cuirass of faith, and the arms of light.'[73] Giles' skillful exercise in praise and blame perhaps perplexed his hearers and certainly has modern scholars, who have seen entirely different messages in his words.[74] Although the implied censure is more likely to linger in the memory because of its later placement, and although Giles' Augustinian background almost insures that this is the correct interpretation, the fact is that he did publicly congratulate Julius on his triumphs.[75]

Whatever his true meaning, Giles of Viterbo scarcely represented the attitudes of all of his contemporaries toward Julius II, who, whether he personally bore arms on the battlefield or not, certainly did command troops and had long been celebrated for his prodigious temper. Vasari's life of Michelangelo records some of the better known of Julius' rages at the papal court, in which he lashed out in violence or threats of violence against anyone who crossed him. Despite Burckhardt's brilliant defense of Julius grounded in his astute recognition that Julius had no choice but to be 'anvil or hammer',[76] despite the marshaling of favorable contemporary reactions to Julius' expeditions and policies by Pastor and others,[77] it is unquestionable that no pope or prelate has ever excited such indignation and opposition for his personal engagement in warfare. Certainly none has stimulated such famous and masterful denunciators.

None of them is better remembered than Erasmus, and with reason. For some time before the publication of the *Julius exclusus*, Erasmus had been excoriating Julius by name in letters to Cardinal Raffaele Riario, Pope Leo X, and others.[78] His numerous and brilliant invectives against war, particularly

---

[73] Mansi 32:669–76; the relevant passages are on pp. 673–4.

[74] Cf. Peter Partner, *Renaissance Rome 1550–1559* (Berkeley-Los Angeles, 1976), pp. 209–10, and John W. O'Malley, S.J., *Giles of Viterbo on Church and Reform* (Leiden, 1968), pp. 127–9.

[75] On the rhetorical context within which Giles' oration should be considered, see John W. O'Malley, S.J., *Praise and Blame in Renaissance Rome. Rhetoric, Doctrine, and Reform in the Sacred Orators of the Papal Court, c.1450–1521* (Durham, N.C., 1979).

[76] Jacob Burckhardt, *The Civilization of the Renaissance in Italy*, 1.10, tr. S. G. C. Middlemore (Harper Torchbook, 1958), 1:134: 'That he should himself lead his forces to battle was for him an unavoidable necessity, and certainly did him nothing but good at a time when a man in Italy was forced to be either hammer or anvil, and when personality was a greater power than the most indisputable right.' It is particularly ironic that the Swiss Protestant Burckhardt should be Julius' stoutest and most eloquent advocate.

[77] See Ludwig Pastor, *History of the Popes from the Close of the Middle Ages*, tr. F. I. Antrobus (St. Louis-London, 1901), 6:450–1; Loren Partridge and Randolph Starn, *A Renaissance Likeness. Art and Culture in Raphael's Julius II* (Berkeley-Los Angeles, 1980), p. 47.

[78] *The Correspondence of Erasmus*, 3, ed. J. K. McConica (Toronto, 1976): 89, 102–4, nos. 333 and 335.

among Christians, hammered home his message with incomparable persua-
siveness and proved that the pen—at least the deftly wielded pen—is mightier
than the sword. Even today, nearly five hundred years after its composition,
the best of his pacifist declamations, *Dulce bellum inexpertis* ('War is sweet
to those who know it not'), cannot fail to touch even the most hawkish of
hearts.[79]

It helped Erasmus' campaign that he did not lack for distinguished
company. The greatest historian of the sixteenth century, Francesco
Guicciardini (1483–1540), no less a master of rhetoric than Erasmus, and with
personal experience based on his activities as a papal general and governor,
drew astute sketches of Julius in his *History of Italy* in which he delineated
both the bad and the good, especially the 'unusual loftiness of his spirit.'
Guicciardini's lengthy description of the siege of Mirandola in 1511 deserves
special comment because, even though he in no way depicts Julius as armed
or armored, Guicciardini nevertheless calls this 'an unexpected occur-
rence, something unheard of throughout the centuries', that 'Julius was not
restrained by the consideration of how unworthy it was for the majesty of so
high a position, that the Roman pontiff should lead armies in person against
Christian towns.' Everyone at the Curia, Guicciardini says, was 'astonished',
but no amount of criticism could stop Julius.[80] Guicciardini later finishes off
his treatment of Julius with a rhetorical tour-de-force which only Erasmus
could have matched.

> A Prince of inestimable spirit and resolution, but impetuous and given to bound-
> less schemes, and if these traits did not hurl him to his ruin, he was sustained
> more by the feeling of reverence felt toward the Church, the disagreement among
> princes and the conditions of the times, than by moderation and prudence – worthy
> undoubtedly of the highest glory had he been a secular prince, or if that same care
> and purpose which he had used to exalt the Church to temporal greatness by the
> arts of war had been employed to exalt it in spiritual matters by the arts of peace.
> Nevertheless his memory is honored and esteemed more than any of his prede-
> cessors, especially by those who (having lost the true significance of things, and
> confusing distinctions and failing to weigh them rightly) consider that the main
> purpose of pontiffs is to extend, by arms and the blood of Christians, the power of
> the Apostolic See, rather than to labor by the good example of their lives, and by
> correcting and curing corrupt manners, for the salvation of those souls for whom
> they boast that Christ established them as his vicars on earth.[81]

---

[79] Margaret Mann Phillips, *The 'Adages' of Erasmus. A Study with Translations* (Cambridge, 1964),
pp. 308–53.

[80] Francesco Guicciardini, *The History of Italy*, tr. and ed. Sidney Alexander (London, 1969), Book
9, pp. 212–5; the quotations appear on p. 212.

[81] Ibid., Book 11, p. 273. Guicciardini recorded his contempt for his papal masters in this well-
known passage from his *Maxims and Reflections (Ricordi)*, tr. Mario Domandi (Philadelphia,
1965), p. 48: 'I know of no one who loathes the ambition, the avarice, and the sensuality of the
clergy more than I – both because each of these vices is hateful in itself and because each and all
are hardly suited to those who profess to live a life dependent upon God. Furthermore, they are
such contradictory vices that they cannot coexist in a subject unless he be very unusual indeed.'
'In spite of all this, the positions I have held under several popes have forced me, for my own

Perhaps Guicciardini exaggerated in suggesting that everyone at the papal court was astonished by Julius' conduct,[82] but the only man there who equaled Julius' *terribilità* was no less bitter than Guicciardini – Michelangelo, whom Julius bullied into creating some of his most enduring works of beauty.

Michelangelo did not necessarily see it that way and had his revenge. The first of these two sonnets evidently embraces more people than Julius:

> They make a sword or helmet from a chalice,
> And sell the blood of Christ here by the load.
> And cross and thorn become a shield, a blade,
> And even Christ is being stripped of patience.
>
> He should not come again into this province
> Up to the very stars his blood would spread,
> Now that in Rome his skin is being sold,
> And they have closed the way to every goodness.
>
> If ever I wished that riches were cut off
> What's happening here has changed all that in me;
> The Cloak can do as Gorgon did in Atlas.
>
> Yet if high Heaven favors poverty,
> But other goals cut off our other life,
> What is there in our state that can restore us?[83]

But that Julius is certainly one of these is shown by another sonnet dedicated to Julius himself.

> If any proverb's true, my Lord,
> This is the one, that those who can, don't wish.
> You have believed what's fabulous and false,
> And let truth's enemy have your reward.
>
> I am your faithful servant, as of old;
> I am to you as the sun's rays are his.
> My time does not disturb you or distress,
> I've pleased you the less the more that I have labored.

good, to further their interests. Were it not for that, I should have loved Martin Luther as much as myself—not so that I might be free of the laws based on Christian religion as it is generally interpreted and understood; but to see this bunch of rascals get their just deserts, that is, to be either without vices or without authority.'

82 Although Julius' biographer Christine Shaw says that none of the cardinals criticized his decision to go to Bologna, she also correctly notes that 'For a cardinal to lead or accompany a military expedition was commonplace, virtually normal practice. For a pope to do so was unheard of' (*Julius II. The Warrior Pope* [Oxford-Cambridge, Mass., 1993], p. 149. On the truth of the other charges against Julius, see pp. 209, 268–71, and 273–4.

83 *Complete Poems and Selected Letters of Michelangelo*, tr. Creighton Gilbert (New York, 1963), Poem 10, p. 8.

At first I hoped your height would let me rise;
The just balance and the powerful sword,
Not echo's voice, are fitted to our want.

But virtue's what the Heavens must despise,
Setting it on the earth, seeing they would
Give us a dry tree to pluck our fruit.[84]

The fourth member of this distinguished company of scourgers, Martin Luther, requires separate treatment.

Luther and Clerical Armsbearing

Whereas Erasmus, Guicciardini, and Michelangelo trained their guns primarily on Julius II and condemned him largely on moral grounds, Luther excoriated all clerics engaged in secular affairs on the basis of both Scripture and canon law, particularly in his tract of 1529, 'On the War Against the Turk.' Luther singles out not only 'the wicked iron-eater' and 'half-devil' Julius, but also Pope Clement VII (1523–34), 'who people think is almost a god of war.' For it is 'not right for the pope, who wants to be a Christian, and the highest and best Christian preacher at that, to lead a church army, or army of Christians. For the Church ought not strive or fight with the sword.'[85] Luther goes further and ascribes the disastrous crusade of Varna (1444) and the catastrophe at Mohács (1526) to the bishops whose presence on the battlefield provoked God's just wrath.

> If I were emperor, king, or prince in a campaign against the Turk, I would exhort my bishops and priests to stay at home and mind the duties of their office, praying, fasting, saying mass, preaching, and caring for the poor, as not only Holy Scripture, but their own canon law teaches and requires ... It would be less harmful to have three devils in the army than one disobedient, apostate bishop, who had forgotten his office and assumed that of another. For there can be no good fortune with such people around, who go against God and their own law.[86]

Catholic bishops were not the only pollutants in Luther's view. For the ex-priest Thomas Müntzer, a former disciple gone mad, Luther reserved a special curse.

> What was Müntzer seeking in our own times, but to become a new Turkish emperor? He was possessed by the spirit of lies and therefore there was no holding him back; he had to take on the other work of the devil, take the sword and murder and rob, as the spirit of murder drove him, and he created a rebellion and such misery.[87]

---

[84] Ibid., Poem 6, p. 6.
[85] 'On War Against the Turk', tr. C. Jacobs, in *Works of Martin Luther* (Philadelphia, 1915–43), 5:84–5.
[86] Ibid., 5:86.
[87] Ibid., 5:97.

Two years after Luther wrote this sweeping tract, the death of another ex-priest on the battlefield, Ulrich Zwingli, elicited a now predictable, terse verdict from Luther: 'all who take the sword die by the sword', and 'God has now punished twice, first under Müntzer, now under Zwingli.'

Luther's revulsion had several sources. Aside from his reading of Scripture, which is what Luther scholars would emphasize, there was the contemporary climate of educated opinion molded largely by reaction against Julius II. On this subject Luther and Erasmus agreed, regardless of their other disagreements. There was, however, probably a third factor informing Luther's attitude toward arms and the clergy, and that was the long-standing, even unique, refusal of his own Augustinian order to allow armsbearing in any way.[88]

Zwingli in the Judgment of His Contemporaries

The brilliance and appeal of the condemnations of Julius II by so many luminaries, and of Luther's indictment of all clerical armsbearing, should not mislead us into thinking that these were responses typical of the sixteenth century, harbingers of a new age of enlightenment on matters of war and peace and of proper clerical conduct. To get an immediate sense that things do not change that quickly and that the sixteenth century was as complex as any other, we have only to turn to Luther's nemesis, Ulrich Zwingli. Fortunately, a century ago Ludwig Erichson compiled the most complete dossier ever assembled of contemporary reactions to a clerical warrior.[89] As the news spread quickly of Zwingli's violent death at Kappel in 1531, people divided largely, but not entirely, along confessional lines. Luther's severe condemnation ranged him with the Catholics, who found little to admire in such a so-called 'Reformer'.[90] Among Protestants, clerical and lay, greater diversity reigned. Geryon Sailer, physician and city councillor of Augsburg, noted the hypocrisy of Protestant attacks on the militant papacy while using force to spread a particular view of the Gospel.[91] To Martin Bucer, the former Dominican who had become the leader of the Reform in Strasbourg, letters flowed in from everywhere, asking how one should interpret Zwingli's end. His answers tended to be cautious and apologetic at best. To Zwingli's widow he confessed that it was a deserved punishment from God, and to Ambrosius Blarer, reformer of Esslingen, he admitted that while he thought it possible that a bishop could go to battle in obedience to God's will, he doubted that Zwingli had received such a command.[92]

---

[88] See my *Legislation of the Medieval and Early Modern Religious Orders on Clerical Armsbearing*, forthcoming.

[89] [Ludwig] A[lfred] Erichson, *Zwingli's Tod und dessen Beurtheilung durch Zeitgenossen* (Strasbourg, 1883).

[90] Only summarily treated in ibid., pp. 10–12.

[91] Ibid., pp. 19–20.

[92] Ibid., pp. 8–9, 18.

Other reformers, convinced of the righteousness of the Protestant cause, saw the matter differently. Bullinger, Zwingli's successor in Zurich, understandably regarded Zwingli as the good shepherd who had died not only for and among his sheep, but also in obedience to the magistrates.[93] Oecolampadius of Basel echoed Bullinger's sentiment that Zwingli had given of himself as a good pastor and burgher.[94] Others went further. The Augsburg preacher Michael Keller declared that Zwingli's death, 'indeed the very manner of his death', would prove to be of very great advantage. 'He has served the fatherland not merely with his teaching and his whole life, he has offered his body and shed his blood for it as well. His death will yield even more splendid results than his life.'[95] Others eulogized Zwingli as a Christian hero. Katharina Zell, wife of one of the other reformers of Strasbourg, characterized Zwingli as such (Christenheld), while Leo Judae, who published Zwingli's translation of the Psalms in 1532, in the preface held up Zwingli as the model hero who for the sake of justice and the truth does not avoid death, but rather meets it wholeheartedly.[96]

Here was a dilemma in the western tradition: for those to whom the principle 'necessity knows no law' was unacceptable, 'the pursuit of justice knows no bounds' may have been all too attractive. How much had really changed since the Gregorian zeal for justice in the eleventh century?

Other Sixteenth-Century Attitudes

The tendency to excuse or forgive clerical armsbearing can be found in Erasmus himself, if for different reasons. Given the depth of his feeling on the subject, it may seem odd that Erasmus could compose an extended eulogy of a fallen clerical combatant. Yet that is precisely what he wrote in the adage *Spartam nactus es, hanc orna* ('You have obtained Sparta, now adorn it'), published in the 1515 edition of his *Adages*, in which he immortalized the 'boy archbishop' of St Andrews, Alexander, who had been killed two years before on Flodden Field with his father, King James IV of Scotland.

> Killed with this bravest of fathers, was a son worthy of him – Alexander, Archbishop of St Andrews, a young man, indeed only twenty; in whom you would have found no quality lacking for perfect manhood. He was exceedingly handsome, tall and stately as a hero, with a mind which was even-tempered but keen in the acquisition of all kinds of knowledge. [I know this] for I lived with him once in the town of Siena; he was having lessons from me at that time in rhetoric and Greek . . . Tell

---

[93] Ibid., pp. 13–6.
[94] Ibid., pp. 21–2.
[95] Ibid., p. 8: 'Aber ich weiss, dass sein Sterben, ja gerade die Art seines Todes, uns und Allen zum Besten dienen wird. Nicht blos mit seiner Lehre und seinem ganzen Leben hat er dem Vaterland gedient, sondern indem er auch für dasselbe seinen Leib daran gesetzt und sein Blut verspritzt hat. Sein Tod wird noch herrlichere Früchte bringen als sein Leben' (Erichson's modernized German).
[96] Ibid., pp. 9, 17.

me, what had you to do with Mars, the stupidest of all the poets' gods, you who were consecrated to the Muses, nay, to Christ? Your youth, your beauty, your gentle nature, your honest mind – what had they to do with the flourish of trumpets, the bombards, the sword? Why should a scholar be in the front line, or a bishop under arms? You were influenced, it seems, by exceedingly filial devotion and while you were strongly showing your love for your father, you fell miserably slain by his side.[97]

For a beloved former student and disciple, even Erasmus, like the pope, could dispense when he wished.

Another sign of the complexity of opinion in the sixteenth century is the great Portuguese epic, *The Lusiads* (1572), by Luis Vaz de Camoens (1524–80). In Canto 8, Paulo da Gama, brother of Vasco, is explaining to Catual of Calicut the meaning of the events depicted on the ship's banners. Two scenes commemorate priests who, he says, had fought gloriously against the Moslems during the Reconquista and won eternal life.

Here is a priest brandishing a sword against Arronches, which he captures in revenge for Luria, that had earlier fallen into Moslem hands; he is the Prior Teotonio . . .

And here comes another fighting churchman, exchanging his golden crozier for a lance of steel. See how resolute he is in the midst of doubters over joining issue with the daring Moslem. And look at the sign from Heaven that is vouchsafed him and that enables him to infuse new spirit into his small troop . . .[98]

Yet Camoens ends the final canto with this exhortation to young King Sebastian of Portugal:

Favour all men in their several professions, in accordance with the talent they show for them. Let those who are vowed to religion engage regularly in prayers for your regime and seek with penance and fasting to hold vice in check. Ambition let them renounce as but an empty wind, for the good and true religious does not pursue futile glory or riches.[99]

Is this meant as a reproach of clerical armsbearing, or is it rather a general counsel to the king to insure that the clergy tend to their proper business? However one interprets these passages, there remains a palpable but elusive difference in tone between this epic and epics like the *Song of Roland* and *The Cid* of the High Middle Ages.

Certainly one detects no equivocation in Archbishop Whitgift's appeal to the clergy of the province of Canterbury to come to the aid of the nation in 1588, even allowing for the fact that as a member of the privy council Whitgift was only carrying out orders. Among the clergy of England and of Europe in general in the sixteenth century there was a considerable range of views on the propriety of clerical armsbearing, with a much greater acceptance of,

[97] Phillips, '*Adages' of Erasmus*, pp. 105–7.
[98] Luis Vaz de Camoens, *The Lusiads*, tr. W. Atkinson (Harmondsworth, 1952), pp. 181–2.
[99] Ibid., Canto 10, p. 248.

and often enthusiasm for, it than one might expect.[100] Nor was it primarily the laity who were scandalized by such clerical propensities. The lines of enthusiasm and opposition do not fall out so conveniently. Michelangelo and Guicciardini were laymen, Erasmus and Luther clerics. And it was the essentially lay governments of England and Spain that during much of their history have required clerical military service.

The Seventeenth Century

In many ways the seventeenth century is more giving and interesting than the sixteenth on the complex issues related to the clergy and arms. Thus the Cardinal Infanta of Spain laid aside his cardinatial scarlet and wore armor, but not for the reason one might suspect. When he was appointed governor of the Netherlands, Archduchess Isabella asked him to avoid his clerical clothing as much as possible, since cardinals as governors in the Low Countries enjoyed no high repute.[101] Her suggestion sprang from sensible political considerations, not a sense of the incongruence of the situation, since it was clear from the outset that he was to command troops.

The status of the clerical warrior was also illumined when the Cardinal General Duc de La Valette died in 1639. Pope Urban VIII refused to permit the usual display of cardinatial honors at his funeral—ostensibly because La Valette had fought with heretics against Catholics, officially because popes did not preside at the funerals of cardinals who had not died in Rome, certainly because the Spanish would have taken offense, but in any event not because La Valette had disgraced himself by his warlike behavior.[102]

The most celebrated warrior cleric of the century was Christoph Bernhard von Galen, prince-bishop of Münster from 1650 to 1678. Until the publication of a revisionist study in 1978, the evaluation of von Galen had been nearly uniform for three hundred years and epitomized in such epithets as 'soldier in soutane', 'Bommenbernd', 'priest in armor', and 'Kanonenbischof'. As late as 1958 he appeared as 'Bommen-Berend' in the 'Groningen Symphony' commissioned by the Dutch government from Hendrik de Vries.[103] Not even Julius II has been so consistently pilloried into modern times or been so wanting for defenders. The popes, however, von Galen's ultimate superiors and judges, supported and encouraged his activity.[104]

---

[100] See the studies by John Hale, 'Incitement to Violence? English Divines on the Theme of War, 1578 to 1631', in his *Renaissance War Studies* (London, 1983), pp. 487–517; and *War and Society in Renaissance Europe 1450–1620* (Leicester, 1985), pp. 35–7.

[101] C. V. Wedgwood, *The Thirty Years War* (Garden City, 1961), p. 334.

[102] D. P. O'Connell, *Richelieu* (Cleveland-New York, 1968), p. 398.

[103] See Manfred Becker-Huberti, *Die tridentinische Reform im Bistum Münster unter Fürstbischof Christoph Bernhard von Galen 1650 bis 1678*, Westfalia Sacra 6 (Münster, 1978), pp. 1–5.

[104] See my 'The Last Warrior Bishop? Christoph Bernhard von Galen, Prince-Bishop of Münster, 1650–1678, and His Relations with the Holy See,' forthcoming.

Stuart England

The root meaning in Latin of 'fame' is 'rumor', and the disparity between fame and fact is sometimes enormous. The problem of reputation with respect to armsbearing is nicely illustrated in the case of four English prelates of the seventeenth century. The first is Archbishop John Williams of York, who was involved in the siege of Conwy Castle in 1646. Clarendon says that Williams 'took a commission from the rebels to take a castle of the King's, in which there was a garrison, and which he did take by a long siege [and was wounded]; because he might thereby, and by being himself governor there, the better enjoy the profits of his own estate which lay thereabouts.'[105] Ignoring here the distortions in Clarendon's account, one may note here simply that Clarendon indicted Williams not for conduct unbecoming a clergyman in besieging a castle, but for advancing his private interest at the expense of his obedience to the king. At the other end of the scale are contemporary depictions of Williams which exaggerated his military activity by showing him equipped with the latest weapons and armor. The one source makes almost nothing of his 'bearing arms' in the broad sense, the other sources rather too much: *quot homines, tot sententiae.*

Bishop Peter Mews escaped contemporary comment entirely despite his possible command of the royal artillery at Sedgmoor in 1685. Only much later did Ranke observed in passing, and without any perceptible note of disapproval, that

> Strangely enough, the first to offer an energetic resistance was a bishop, who, as one of his predecessors had formerly done in the struggle against Wat Tyler, has arisen to defend Church and state in arms: I mean Dr. Peter Mew, not long before made Bishop of Winchester. He had hastened from the Parliament, which James [II] prorogued on the 2nd of July, to the field of battle. Here he noticed that the royal artillery was at a great distance from the decisive spot; he brought up two cannon with his own horses, and these offered the first check to the advance of the enemy.[106]

By comparison, a prelate who did much less earned much greater opprobrium. Sir Jonathan Trelawny (1650–1721), baronet and bishop of Bristol, Exeter, and Winchester, came of a family of military men, succeeded to the baronetcy in 1680 on the death of his elder brother, and was vice-admiral of the Cornwall coast from 1682 to 1693. In this capacity he signed all the commissions summoning the militia during Monmouth's Rebellion in 1685, and again in 1691 he provided for the defense of Exeter against a landing by the French fleet. For this he was memorialized as 'fighting Joshua' in the 'Tribe of Levi' (1691): 'a spiritual dragoon/ Glutted with blood, a really Christian

---

[105] Edward, Earl of Clarendon, *The History of the Rebellion and Civil Wars in England Begun in the Year 1641*, ed. W. Macray, 6 vols. (Oxford, 1888, repr., 1958, 1969), 4.137, 1:470.

[106] Leopold von Ranke, *A History of England Principally in the Seventeenth Century* (Oxford, 1875), 4:257.

Turk,/ Scarcely outdone by Jeffreys or by Kirke.' The author of this doggerel was not singling out Trelawny for his indecorousness, but as one of the seven bishops who had opposed James II's Declaration of Indulgence in 1688 and suffered imprisonment in the Tower for a month as a result. Politics made Trelawny the target of this absurd caricature, and 'fighting Joshua' has stuck ever since.[107]

According to Jonathan Swift, it was also politics that determined the making of the even more unsavory reputation of Henry Compton, bishop of London, for his flamboyant yet basically innocuous behavior at Oxford in 1688. Macaulay painted the enduring picture:

> Compton wholly laid aside, for the time, his sacerdotal character. Danger and conflict had rekindled in him all the military ardour which he had felt twenty-eight years before, when he rode in the Life Guards. He preceded the Princess's [Anne's] carriage in a buff coat and jackboots, with a sword at his side and pistols in his holsters. Long before she reached Nottingham, she was surrounded by a body guard of gentlemen who volunteered to escort her. They invited the bishop to act as their colonel; and he consented with an alacrity which gave great scandal to rigid Churchmen, and did not much raise his character even in the opinion of Whigs.[108]

Macaulay rightly refers in his notes to many contemporary lampoons, but on balance one should also note the reactions of some of Compton's fellow ecclesiastics. Bishop Gilbert Burnet fumed less than Macaulay: 'And in a little while a small army was formed about [Princess Anne], who chose to be commanded by the bishop of London; of which he too easily accepted.' Dean Swift's gloss on Burnet was calculatedly unforgettable: 'And why should he not?'[109] Swift put his finger on the problem with Compton and the cause of this intramural bickering in his laconic reply to Burnet's summation of Compton: 'But with these good qualities Compton was a weak man, wilful, and strangely wedded to a party.' Swift's gloss: 'He means to the church.'[110]

In his funeral eulogy of Compton in 1713 his chaplain Thomas Gooch alluded to these larger issues:

> Pursued and persecuted, as if, with him alone, the Reformation was to stand or fall ... He never desponded or despair'd; but thought it then a proper time to resume his care and charge, and to guard our present Sovereign against any attempts on her religion, or her liberty ...
>
> He rescued our present Sovereign; he hid her (as it were) till Popish Tyranny

---

107 *DNB* 19:1106–09; M. G. Smith, *Fighting Joshua. A Study of the Career of Sir Jonathan Trelawny, bart. 1650–1721, Bishop of Bristol, Exeter and Winchester* (Redruth, 1985), pp. 8–12, 20; Agnes Strickland, *Lives of the Seven Bishops ...* (London, 1866), pp. 373, 384, who believes the worst of Trelawny.

108 Thomas Babington Macaulay, *The History of England from the Accession of James the Second*, ed. C. H. Firth, 6 vols (London, 1914), ch. 9, pp. 1164–6.

109 Ibid., 3:318, note 'r'; and *The Prose Works of Jonathan Swift*, ed. H. Davis (Oxford, 1939–68), 5:289.

110 Ibid., 5:277.

was overpast. For this too, how invidiously, nay how contradictorily, has he been treated? He has been envied and arraigned for the self-same thing: as if he had done both too much and too little.[111]

Yet it is significant that Swift and Gooch did not openly defend Compton's flamboyant behavior, even though it led to no harm. Their guardedness, taken together with the flood of rebukes of Williams and Compton in England and of von Galen on the Continent, suggest that by the later seventeenth century the climate of literate or educated opinion had tipped against clerics in arms, just as in the eighteenth century it turned in Catholic states against prince-bishops and prince-abbots. There is a curious irony in this tide of criticism which, originating in a secular and anticlerical spirit, sought to bring the clergy back to the observance of their own original canons forbidding them involvement in secular things.

If, however, one considers some other evidence, it might be wise in the previous paragraph to stress the words 'literate or educated opinion' and to change 'clergy and 'clerics' to 'bishops' or 'prelates', for in the eyes of many people ordinary clerics only enhanced their status by their agility at arms. Thus in the 1650s John Weale, purser of H.M.S. *Jersey*, wrote to Hugh Peters, Oliver Cromwell's chaplain, in search of a good chaplain for his ship. If possible, he reported, the captain preferred to have again his old chaplain, Dan Pell:

> Sir, did your Hon. know but the worth of that gent in but half the measure I did, he would be as precious in your sight . . . Take him as a scholar, take him as godly man, an exemplary good liver, take him as occasion be, as well with sword in hand as the word in his mouth, if I should but endeavor to set him forth as we say, in his proper colours, my paper would shorter be full.[112]

Nor did Henry Teonge raise any eyebrows several decades later with his armsbearing during four years' service on three ships of the Royal Navy. In fact, on one occasion

> Aftr 9 at night, a lusty ship coming up with us gave us a sudden alarm; everyone that could snatched up a musket. I went to the top of the poop with my staff-gun, and stood by our Lieutenant Monck, who hailed the ship and commanded them to come on board us. They refusing, as we thought, he bade me fire at them, which I did: then they immediately lowered their top-sail[113]

Teonge, incidentally, was a B.A. of Cambridge (1643), an educated man.

---

[111] Thomas Gooch, *A Sermon Preached . . . July, 26.1713. On Occasion of the much-lamented Death of the . . . late Lord Bishop of London* (London, 1713), pp. 11–12, quoted in part in Carpenter, *The Protestant Bishop*, p. 139.

[112] Quoted in Waldo Smith, *The Navy and Its Chaplains in the Days of Sail* (Toronto, 1961), p. 20.

[113] *The Diary of Henry Teonge . . .* , ed. G. Manwaring (London, 1927), p. 242; and see above, p. 39.

Modern Times

Historical developments, however, rarely run in straight lines, and this is no exception. For if the tide had for some time been running against militaristic clergy (or at least bishops), and if in the eighteenth century clergy so inclined maintained a low profile, since then nationalism, the rise of political ideology, and a growing revolutionary zeal to set the world right have all worked in different but convergent ways to rekindle an old but scarcely extinct clerical fieriness which would also enjoy widespread lay support, and not only from governments. In the next two chapters more clergymen and laypeople, especially from the last two centuries, will speak for themselves. For the moment, let four disparate clerical voices from the last century bear their witness.

The first is that of Ludwig Erichson, director of the Protestant Theological House of Studies in Strasbourg in the 1880s and compiler of the most detailed report ever done on contemporary response to a clerical warrior. Whatever his feelings at the outset of his study, Erichson came to align himself with those who had viewed Zwingli as a Christian hero, 'a victim of his zeal for the Gospel,' 'a martyr for his ecclesiastical office,' 'the shepherd amidst his flock.' Those who insist on regarding Zwingli's death as a divine judgment, Erichson continued, can find support only in the Old Testament, 'an historical outlook as little Christian as it is modern, which one would find at most in Catholic circles. A remnant of this Jewish spirit has unfortunately survived in our age. We are still not yet free from that partisan spirit which approves of hardness and injustice toward those who think differently.'[114]

In 1910 the provincial of the Capuchins in Andalusia, Ambrosio de Valencia, published a study of the participation of the members of his order in Andalusia in the war of independence against Napoleon between 1808 and 1812. Given the relentless hostility of the French Revolutionaries toward the church, it was understandably hard to distinguish then between politics and religion and to resist thinking of resistance as a holy war. Even so, the evidence which de Valencia adduces and his treatment of it a hundred years later are striking. He cites at length a letter sent in March 1809 to all the Capuchins of the province by their superior, Serfin de Hardales, exhorting them to do everything, 'excluding the shedding of blood', to repel this 'barbarous people' come to destroy 'our country and our pure and sacrosanct religion.' But by the end of the letter he was carried away, proclaiming this a time 'for courage and arms' in which it is better to die than to tolerate such destroyers.[115] A substantial number of Capuchins chose to act, some as guerrillas,[116] others more openly; and of them Father de Valencia approved entirely in 1910. In reaction to French savagery, Father Julian de Delica 'took

---

[114] Erichson, *Zwingli's Tod* (n. 89 above), pp. 1, 42–43. Erichson expressed similar sentiments in his more widely available *Zur 400 jährigen Geburtsfeier Zwingli's* (Strasbourg, 1884), p. 31.

[115] Ambrosio de Valencia, O.F.M.Cap., *Los Capuchinos de Andalucia en la guerra de la independencia* (Seville, 1910), pp. 80–7.

[116] Ibid., pp. 95ff., 139–47.

up arms, like another Maccabeus, to fight against the enemies of his faith
... not to gain honors, but only to defend religion and country.'[117] At the
siege of Cadiz in 1810–11 a number of Capuchins took part (no fewer than
five are named as soldiers), and those who died were 'martyrs for religion
and country.'[118] In 1813 more than a hundred others died 'defending their
country.'[119] Nowhere in this long narrative does Father de Valencia display
the slightest trace of censure.

Some might dismiss this fervor as 'typically Spanish' or 'typically Catholic.'
Enthusiasm takes many forms, however, especially for righteous causes.
While few people would now defend militant popes like Julius II, many would
champion clerics ready to fight for their country in its hour of need. The
last great warrior bishop, Leonidas Polk, who fell at Pine Mountain in 1864,
received this treatment as recently as 1912 from a fellow Episcopal bishop
(and Southerner). After announcing that 'I shall not attempt any discussion
of Bishop Polk's case', Bishop Joseph Cheshire went on to say that

> So far as his character and the purity and disinterestedness of his motives are
> concerned, he needs no defense. In general it is admitted that the obligation of
> the Ordination Vow seems to shut a clergyman off *from any secular calling*, from
> that of a soldier as from every other. Personally, however, I have no hesitation in
> saying that I regard the hard, unselfish, perilous, self-sacrificing life of a soldier in
> the camp and in the field, in time of war, as far less inconsistent with lofty spir-
> itual attainments, and with the adequate illustration of the very highest qualities of
> the Christian and priestly character, than indulgence in selfish ease, and personal
> comfort, and all the relaxations of an easy fortune, which few of us fail to practice
> when we have opportunity. Let it be admitted that the common mind and con-
> science of the Church have realized in experience that to bear arms is inconsistent
> with the priestly character. Be it so! But let the Christian mind and conscience go
> on and realize that many other things, which it has not come to reprobate, are still
> more deadly to the spiritual life and power of the clergy.[120]

At the end of the twentieth century such zeal in the cause of the nation-
state has come into some disfavor, often only to be replaced by anger on
behalf of the oppressed. Listen to Gordon Rupp, distinguished historian of
the Reformation, on Thomas Münter, the fanatical reformer executed for his
leadership of the Peasants War in Saxony. He whom Luther the Augustinian
friar had excoriated in 1529, along with Julius II and Zwingli, received in 1969
rather more sympathetic treatment from Rupp the Methodist minister:

> Without capitulating to Marxist dialectic, or a regime which in the 20th century
> would exploit Thomas Müntzer's memory to support the view that theirs is the
> true, Christian revolution – views which none the less are not to be dismissed out

[117] Ibid., pp. 96–9.
[118] Ibid., pp. 137–8.
[119] Ibid., pp. 146–7.
[120] Joseph Blount Cheshire, *The Church in the Confederate States* (New York, 1912), p. 48. Cheshire
was bishop of North Carolina from 1893 to 1932.

of hand – recognizing the evident element of tragic fanaticism, and the theological weaknesses of Müntzer's great argument, at least this is true, that in him we come nearer than in any other Reformer to contact with the smothered undercurrent of medieval pain and injustice. Now voices were cut off and silent, in the time of savage reprisal. They would not be heard again for a long time, but they would one day return, angry, one-sided, anticlerical and anti-Christian, to knock at the gates of a Christian world; and to them a Christian Church, by reason of its own failures of nerve, of justice and of compassion, cannot return an unqualified No.[121]

Mutatis mutandis, Roman Catholic Liberation theologians would probably vigorously agree.

---

[121]   E. Gordon Rupp, *Patterns of Reformation* (Philadelphia, 1969), p. 247.

CHAPTER 3

THE CANON LAW OF THE ROMAN CATHOLIC CHURCH ON CLERICAL ARMSBEARING (I): TO THE TWELFTH CENTURY

THE diverse opinions of Synesius, Orderic Vitalis, Gerald of Wales, Richard of Devizes, Jean Froissart, the monk of Leicester, Thomas à Kempis, Giles of Viterbo, Erasmus, John Whitgift, Macaulay, Ludwig Erichson, Ambrosio de Valencia, and Gordon Rupp on militant clerics are, in the end, *personal* opinions, no matter how eloquently expressed. While it is useful to know what Aquinas, Erasmus, and other writers thought about the great issues of their day, it is not enough to know what they thought, especially since so many others did not agree with them. It is much fairer to judge the clergy, at least in the first instance, by what the Church expects of them as expressed in its laws. Although it is widely assumed, even by ecclesiastical historians, that Roman Catholic canon law has always simply forbidden the clergy to bear arms under any circumstances, this has not been true since the twelfth and thirteenth centuries and is not true today. This chapter and the next will examine at several levels the evolution of the canonical 'law of arms' for the clergy through the High Middle Ages. It is an investigation not of what theologians and others believed the clergy ought to do, but rather of what ecclesiastical laws permitted, required, or forbade them to do.

After a survey of the history of the prohibition in the first thousand years of Christianity, the main weight of the next chapter will fall on the period of the twelfth and thirteenth centuries for two reasons. First, the major breakthroughs in the ancient prohibition occurred in the High Middle Ages. Second, the subject of the clergy and arms in law and in practice has been intensively and well studied up to the early thirteenth century, and my great debt to other scholars will be evident from the notes. Many medievalists, however, particularly church historians, in practice do not go beyond the Fourth Lateran Council of 1215, and this caesura between the twelfth and thirteenth centuries has affected the study of clerical armsbearing.[1] The farther away from the twelfth century one moves, the less the subject has been studied.

---

[1] The only one who really goes beyond the *Decretales* of 1234 is Castillo Lara, *Coaccion eclesiastica*, especially pp. 36–46, 74–82; but even he does not go beyond the thirteenth century.

Early Christianity

The *loci sacri* for the prohibition are many. In the Sermon on the Mount Jesus exhorted his hearers, 'Do not resist one who is evil. But if any one strikes you on the right cheek, turn to him the other also,' and 'Love your enemies and pray for those who persecute you' (Mt. 5.39, 44). At his betrayal he rebuked one of his followers for cutting off an ear of the slave of the High Priest: 'Put your sword back into its place; for all who take the sword will perish by the sword' (Mt. 26.52; Jn 18.11). On the cross he begged his Father to forgive his executioners (Lk. 23.24). St Peter said of Christ that 'When he was reviled, he did not revile in return; when he suffered, he did not threaten; but he trusted to him who judges justly' (1 Pet. 2.23). St Paul reminded Christians not to seek revenge and repay evil with evil (Rm. 12.17–19), while bishops in particular were to be 'not violent but gentle,' not 'quarrelsome but kindly to everyone' (1 Tim. 3.3; 2 Tim.2.24–5).

Yet difficulties arose from very early on. Was pacifism or non-violence at the core of Jesus' message? Or were other themes such as repentance, forgiveness, love, and compassion more central? To judge from the responses of Christians in the first few centuries, one would have to conclude the latter. Troubled as to whether to construe the words of Christ as *law*, from his own words ('If thou wilt be perfect . . .') and from Paul's (1 Cor. 7) they developed a distinction between precepts or mandates, binding on all and necessary for salvation, and 'counsels' offered to those willing and able to seek the higher way of perfection.[2] Gradually they came to single out three such counsels which later formed the foundation of monastic vows and of religious life – poverty, chastity, and obedience – all in imitation of Christ. Significantly, none of these counsels centers on non-violence.[3] Finally, complex modes of biblical interpretation also evolved. With reference to violence, an important threshold was crossed when St Augustine (354–430), noticing that Christ himself did not turn the other cheek and taking a cue from Paul's stress on internal disposition as opposed to mere externals ('circumcision of the heart'), argued that turning the other cheek pertained to the heart rather than to outward behavior.[4] Other commentators also pointed out that Jesus announced that he came to bring not peace but a sword (Mt. 10.34) and that he violently overturned the tables of the moneychangers in the Temple.[5]

Paul, who in the history of Christianity has perhaps been quoted more frequently than Christ, further complicated matters by his frequent use of

---

[2] The few treatments of this crucial subject are brief essays in the *Encyclopedia of Religion and Ethics*, ed. James Hastings (1914; repr., New York, 1961), 4:203–5, and *The New Schaff-Herzog Encyclopedia of Religious Knowledge* (New York, 1908–14), 3:245–6. In the first four centuries the distinction was used by Hermas, Cyprian, Origen, Methodius, Ambrose, Jerome, and Augustine.

[3] See *DTC* 3:1176–82; *Encyclopaedia of Religion and Ethics*, 4:203–5; *Dizionario degli istituti di perfezione* (Rome, 1974–2003), 2:1630–1685, especially 1634–1661.

[4] See Louis J. Swift, ed., *The Early Fathers on War and Military Service* (Wilmington, Del., 1983), pp. 124–6.

[5] See ibid., pp. 17–31, for a brief introduction.

military imagery to describe how Christians ought to behave: 'the weapons of our warfare are not worldly but have divine power to destroy strongholds' (2 Cor. 10.3–4); 'Stand therefore, having girded your loins with truth, and having put on the breastplate of righteousness . . . taking the shield of faith . . . and the helmet of salvation, and the sword of the spirit, which is the word of God' (Eph. 6.14–7); and 'Share in suffering as a good soldier of Christ Jesus. No soldier on service gets entangled in civilian pursuits' (2 Tim. 2.3–4).[6]

Early Christians adopted this view of themselves as fighting the good fight in and against a hostile world, and it developed into one of the principal leitmotifs of Christian imagery, thinking, and language until fairly recently. Although such imagery has consciously sought to distinguish sharply the ends and methods of Christian fighting from those of the secular world, it has also unwittingly kept 'fighting' at the forefront of language and therefore thought. It cleaves a fine line and always embodies the potential for going awry. By comparison, the image of the 'spiritual athlete' battling inner rather than external demons has been much less prominent, at least in western Christian history. In fact, Katherine Allen Smith has recently argued,

> Over the course of the first millennium, monastic exegetes made spiritual (or spir-
> itualized) warfare central to the historical narrative of Christianity. Their work also
> ensured that the concept of spiritual battle informed the daily lives of individual
> monks, who, in the guise of *milites Christi*, fashioned the Psalms into missiles to
> hurl at demons and wrested the souls of lay benefactors away from the devil.[7]

Nevertheless, in the first three centuries the Christian church held to a strongly pacifistic position. Some leading thinkers like Origen argued forcefully that killing under any circumstances was wrong for a Christian, but it is clear that they were conducting a debate within the Christian community. More to the point, among the few surviving laws of a Christian church in this period are the 'Apostolic Traditions' of the Roman Church ascribed to Hippolytus in the early third century. In a long list of occupations viewed as incompatible with Christianity, that of the soldier received special attention:

> A soldier of the civil authority must be taught not to kill men and to refuse to take
> an oath; if he is unwilling to comply, he must be rejected. A military commander or
> civic magistrate that wears the purple must resign or be rejected. If a catechumen or

---

[6] On the interpretive possibilities of these early texts, see the very good Introduction in ibid., pp. 17–31, and Brundage, 'Holy War,' pp. 101 and 126, nn. 11–12.

[7] Katherine Allen Smith, *War and the Making of Medieval Monastic Culture*, Studies in the History of Medieval Religion 37 (Woodbridge, 2011), p. 197, which now fills a long-standing gap in the literature since Adolf Harnack gathered a great deal of material in his *Militia Christi. The Christian Religion and the Military in the First Three Centuries*, tr. David Gracie (Philadelphia, 1981), pp. 27–64, and which also illumines the kind of overly defensive stance to be found, for example, in Eug. Manning, 'La signification de "militare-militia-miles" dans la regle de Saint Benoit,' *Revue bénédictine* 72 (1962): 135–8, who believes that the six occurrences of these words in St Benedict's Rule refer to 'service,' 'obedience,' or 'manner of life.'

a believer seeks to become a soldier, they must be rejected, for they have despised God.[8]

Although one of the principal Christian objections to holding posts in the Roman army or civil service was the obligation to offer sacrifice to the gods of Rome, homicide was clearly also regarded as abhorrent, if not quite as sinful as idolatry.

The Awful Revolution

All this changed when the Christians finally achieved their ambition: the conversion of the Roman Empire. Beginning around 312 with Constantine, the emperors tolerated and favored Christianity, then at the urging of bishops like Ambrose moved more aggressively against its rivals, and finally decreed in 416 that only Christians could serve in the Roman army. Christianity was now the sole official religion of the Empire.

The consequences were momentous for both, but especially for Christianity. It was no longer a religion which one consciously chose and for admission to which one had to demonstrate high moral standards. Those who became Christians also brought their own cultural heritage with them, including Greco-Roman or Germanic ideas about the conduct of war. Finally, the fate of Christianity and Rome were now bound up with each other in perilous times in which the Empire was being overrun. The inevitable occurred: Christians came to fill the army, and churchmen came to view the whole situation in a new light. For the western tradition, Ambrose (c.339–397) and Augustine (354–430) were to be decisive in fusing the classical and Christian traditions on war and peace. By distinguishing between the public and private realms, by stressing the danger to the Christian empire posed by pagans without, by reiterating the importance of intention (peace and love, not the infliction of harm), and by drawing on ideas in Aristotle and particularly Cicero on the proper conduct of war, they successfully fused the two traditions. Using Christian principles in part, Ambrose went so far as to deny the right in Roman and natural law of the private individual to defend himself against attack *and* to assert the moral obligation of the individual to come to the defense of others and of the empire.[9] It was an elegant reconciliation of Roman public duty and the prohibition on private armsbearing, on the one hand, and, on the other, of Christ's injunction to turn the other cheek and his great counsel to be prepared to lay down one's life for another (Jn. 15.13). The tenets of Christianity now dovetailed with the requirements of both internal peacekeeping and of patriotism.

All this applied only to the laity, however, and more than any other thinker

---

[8] *The Apostolic Tradition of Hippolytus*, tr. and ed. B. Easton (1934, repr., New York, 1962), 2.16, p. 42. On this text, see *ODCC*, p. 92.

[9] See Swift, pp. 96–102.

Ambrose insisted again and again that the arms of a cleric are 'tears and prayers.'[10] He reflected, and to some extent shaped, a growing consensus that what had previously been a strong moral imperative for all Christians was now to be a legal requirement for the clergy and monks, who were now the 'real Christians' in the sense that they made a conscious choice to follow the higher, harder way in the imitation of Christ. The legislation of the church began to reflect this new position. The so-called 'Apostolic Canons,' imputed to the Apostles but actually of later fourth-century Syrian origin, authoritatively summed it up. Of the eighty-five canons, two dealt with different aspects of the problem. Number 28 addressed clerical resort to violence: 'We command that a bishop, or presbyter, or deacon who strikes the faithful that offend, or the unbelievers who do wickedly, and thinks to terrify them by such means, be deprived, for our Lord has nowhere taught us such things.' The second (83) condemned military service: 'Let a bishop, or presbyter, or deacon, who goes to the army, and desires to retain both the Roman government and the sacerdotal administration, be deprived. For "the things of Caesar belong to Caesar, and the things of God to God" (Mt. 22.21).'[11] Pope Innocent I (402–417) insisted on even greater stringency in a letter to a bishop of Rouen: 'Similarly, if anyone after the forgiveness of his sins has worn the belt of secular military service, he should not ever be admitted to the clergy.'[12] The ecumenical council of Chalcedon in 451 forbade clergy or monks to take up military service or any secular office on pain of anathematization.[13]

Byzantine historians agree that the Eastern Church maintained the position of the Apostolic Canons all through its history and consistently punished with suspension or deposition those clerics who violated it. They were not a few in number, especially on the frontiers of an empire which spent much of its long existence fighting for its life. Bishops and priests understandably rallied to the cause when their cities or regions were endangered, but Eastern canon law evidently did not accommodate itself to their situation and feelings.[14] In her history of the reign of her father Emperor Alexius I (1081–1118), Princess Anna Komnene was generally repulsed by the violence and cruelty of the Franks on the First Crusade, but she was shocked by the report of 'a

---

[10] Ibid., pp. 108–110.

[11] 'The Ecclesiastical Canons of the Same Holy Apostles,' in *Ante-Nicene Christian Library. Translations of the Writings of the Fathers down to A.D. 325*, eds Alexander Roberts and James Donaldson (Edinburgh, 1867–72), 17:257–69, at 260 and 268. On the Apostolic Canons, which constituted part of the larger Apostolic Constitutions, see *ODCC*, s.v. Although the Apostolic Canons in their entirety were assumed into the legal tradition of the Eastern Church, they were not in the Latin West in the early Middle Ages, which received only fifty of the eighty-five canons. Number 28 was one of them, but number 83 was not.

[12] Mansi 3:1033: 'Item, si quis post remissionem peccatorum cingulum militiae saecularis habuerit, ad clericatum omnino admitti non debet.'

[13] *DEC*, p. 90, c. 7.

[14] Hans-Georg Beck, *Nomos, Kanon und Staatsraison in Byzanz* (Vienna, 1981), pp. 21–5, 35–8. On the problem of what constituted Byzantine canon law, which was never codified, see ibid., pp. 5–8. See also J. M. Hussey, *The Orthodox Church in the Byzantine Empire* (Oxford, 1986), pp. 304–10, 326–7, 334.

certain Latin priest who happened to be standing in the stern [of a ship who] saw what had occurred and shot several times with his bow at Marianus.' She added this gloss: 'Thus the race is no less devoted to religion than to war. This Latin, then, more man of action than priest, wore priestly garb and at the same time handled an oar and ready for naval action or war on land fought sea and men alike. Our rules, as I have just said, derive from Aaron, Moses and our first high priest.'[15] Although the cult of military saints and a positive attitude toward 'holy' war appeared much earlier in the East than in the West,[16] the Eastern Church evidently never relaxed its prohibition on clerical armsbearing, no matter how often it was breached.

The Latin Church in the early Middle Ages also condemned clerical participation in the military. The fourth council of Toledo, attended by sixty-two bishops in 633, decided that in accordance with the ancient canons no one could be ordained priest who had been found guilty of heresy, various grave crimes, or voluntary military service even while a layman.[17] Furthermore, clerics who took up arms in any civil disturbance were to be sentenced to penitential service in a monastery as well as deposition from their order.[18] A council of eight bishops at Lerida in 833 pondered the problem of clerics who were caught up in sieges. Nevertheless, it was decided, they were to avoid shedding any blood, even the enemy's, on pain of two years' loss of office, exclusion from communion, and expiatory penitential rites to be determined by appropriate authority.[19]

In Anglo-Saxon England, Egbert, first archbishop of York (735–66), drew up a long compilation of 'Excerpts from the Sayings and Canons of the Holy Fathers,' of which one of Roman provenance stipulated that since clergy were forbidden to use arms or go to war, those who died in war or fighting should be denied both prayers and offerings, but not Christian burial. This applied in particular to priests and deacons, who were to trust in God rather than in arms.[20] Was the omission of bishops here inadvertent?

---

[15] *The Alexiad of Anna Komnene*, tr. E. R. A. Sewter, rev. Peter Frankopan (Harmondsworth, 2009), 10.8, p. 283. The quotation is a misquotation from Col. 2.21 ('Touch not, *taste* not, handle not'). Extrapolating from this one incident recorded by this single Byzantine source, Sir Steven Runciman wrote that 'The Byzantines were deeply shocked to see in the Crusader armies so many priests who bore arms and went into battle. This outraged Eastern sentiment, which was horrified that men dedicated to God should take part in warfare' (*The Eastern Schism* [Oxford, 1955], p. 105; see also p. 83).

[16] Erdmann, pp. 6 and 38.

[17] Mansi 10:624–5, c. 19: '. . . qui non promoveantur ad sacerdotium ex regulis canonum necessario credimus inferendum, id est, qui in aliquo crimine detecti sunt, qui scelera aliqua per publicam poenitentiam admissise confessi sunt, qui in haeresim lapsi sunt, . . . vel laici sunt, qui saeculari militiae dediti sunt . . . 'This decree should be compared with that of the first council of Toledo in 438, c. 2 (Mansi 3:997–8).

[18] Ibid., 10:630, c. 45.

[19] Ibid., 8:612, c. 1.

[20] Wilkins 1:112 c. 155: 'Clericus quoque non debet armis uti, nec ad bellum procedere; quia canones docent ut quicunque clericus in bello aut in rixa mortuus fuerit, neque oblatione neque oratione postuletur pro eo; sepultura tamen non privetur. Apostolus quoque dicit: 'Nemo militans Deo implicet se negotiis secularibus:' unde non est liber a laqueis diaboli, qui se militiae mundanae voluerit implicare. Et ideo omnimodis dicendum est presbiteris et diaconibus, ut arma non

In the lands of the Franks arms were also forbidden, even if the penalties threatened were not as dire. The council of Mâcon in 583 lumped armsbearing together with the wearing of military and indecorous clothing and specified thirty days on bread and water for all offenders.[21] About a hundred years later (663/75) a council at Bordeaux threatened canonical punishment for clergy found guilty in the future of bearing arms or lances or wearing secular clothing.[22] And about the same time (673/5) another council meeting at Losne simply forbade bishops and clerics to bear arms 'in the secular manner.'[23]

The early Middle Ages nevertheless witnessed two departures of a sort from the general prohibition for the clergy. The first was not exactly a deviation, for it involved the use of small knives for domestic use. St Benedict of Nursia (c.480–543), founder of Monte Cassino and author of the most important rule for religious in the history of the West, took knives for granted. In Chapter 22 of his *Rule*, entitled 'How Monks are to Sleep,' he wisely provided as follows: 'Let them sleep clothed and girt with girdles or cords, but not with their belts, so that they may not have knives at their sides while they are sleeping and be cut by them in their sleep.'[24] In Chapter 55 he stipulated that 'in order that this evil of private ownership may be rooted out entirely, let the abbot provide all things that are necessary: that is, cowl, tunic, stockings, shoes, belt, knife, pen, needle, handkerchief, and tablets, so that all pretext of need be taken away.'[25] Hundreds of years later, the customs of the reformed canons regular of Springersbach (founded in the diocese of Trier in 1107) stipulated carefully that although no one in the entourage of an abbot is to bear arms, upon rising everyone shall gird himself with his knife and that a canon packed off to prison was to be deprived of knife, food, and drink.[26] As for diocesan clergy, knives, too, were doubtless for the most part taken for granted, although the evidence is less copious than before the late Middle Ages.[27]

The second departure was more serious if also more debatable. After careful study of the Frankish legislation of the eighth and ninth centuries, Friedrich Prinz concludes that even before they wrested the Frankish throne from the long-lived Merovingian dynasty in 751, the rapidly rising Carolingian house

---

portent, sed magis confidant in defensione Dei, quam in armis.'

[21] MGH *Concilia*, 1, *Concilia aevi merovingici*, ed. F. Maassen (Hannover, 1893, new ed. 1956), pp. 156–7, c. 5.

[22] Ibid., c. 1, p. 215: 'Ut abitum concessum clerici religiose habitare debeant et nec lanceas nec alia arma nec vestimenta secularia habere nec portare debeant, sed secundum quod scriptum est: "Non in gladium suum possidebunt terram et brachium eorum non liberabit eos, set dextera tua et brachium tuum et inluminatio vultus tui", statutum est, ut, qui post hanc definitionem hoc agere aut adtemtare presumserit, canonica feriatur sententia.'

[23] Ibid., c. 2, p. 218: 'Nullus episcoporum seu clericorum arma more seculario ferre praesumat.'

[24] *The Rule of Saint Benedict*, ed. and tr. Justin McCann (London, 1952), c. 22, p. 71.

[25] Ibid., p. 127.

[26] *Consuetudines canonicorum regularium Springersbacenses-Rodenses*, ed. S. Weinfurter, CCCM 48 (Turnhout, 1978), pp. 18, 48, 161, cc. 6, 16, 46.

[27] The wearing of knives by the secular clergy is, for example, simply taken for granted in several of the cases cited in the title on homicide in the *Decretales* of 1234 (5.12.8, 9, and 12 [*CIC* 2:796–8]).

was determined not only to bring the traditionally formidable prelates of the realm under their sway, but also to legitimize their activities. Instead of trying to disarm bishops and prelates, Prinz argues, the Carolingians brought them within the ranks of the royal armies and accommodated ecclesiastical law accordingly. Charles Martel's two sons took important steps in this direction. In April 742 Carloman convened a Concilium Germanicum, over which St Boniface presided. Although it interdicted to the clergy the use of weapons, it specifically permitted chaplains to accompany the troops and one or two bishops to accompany the leaders of campaigns. The comparable council held in Pepin's part of the kingdom met at Soissons in 744. It decreed only that *abbates legitimi* (i.e. ordained abbots, not lay abbots) were not to go to war. The suspicion that bishops were deliberately passed over in silence and that ordained abbots themselves could still go along on campaigns as non-combatants is confirmed by the legislation of Pepin's son Charlemagne (768–814). The *Admonitio generalis* of 789, the special capitulary for the *missi dominici* in 802, and some of the later legislation of his successors all forbade priests and deacons to bear arms; they say nothing about bishops or abbots. That this was calculated preterition, Prinz believes, is made quite clear by comparison with parallel legislation on hunting, in which bishops and abbots continued to be explicitly forbidden to engage. The ecclesiastical laws of the Carolingian empire thus *ex silentio* exempted prelates from the traditional canonical ban on arms. Whether the initiative came from the crown or the clergy cannot be determined, although it is reasonable to suspect the complicity of both. In any case, the implied modification in law was not purely ecclesiastical in origin or form.[28]

Nor was it long-lived, for a reaction set in after the death of Charlemagne. The decrees issued by the synods of Meaux and Paris of June 845 and February 846, respectively, forbade *arma militaria* to 'whoever are seen to be of the clergy' on pain of degradation.[29] A council at Ticino in 876 forbade all in holy orders to carry arms in military expeditions,[30] and another at Metz in 888 interdicted all armsbearing to all clerics.[31] Pope Nicholas I (858–67), the most forceful pope of the century, went so far as to forbid bishops to mount watch against pirates lest they become too involved in secular matters. And although one of Nicholas' successors, Pope John VIII (872–82), appealed to Charles the Bald and his bishops for aid against the Saracens (implying that the bishops could legitimately render him military aid), it was Nicholas' letter and attitudes, rather than Pope John's, that would later be remembered in the twelfth century.[32]

---

[28] Prinz, 'King, Clergy and War at the Time of the Carolingians,' *passim.*
[29] MGH *Concilia*, 3, *Concilia aevi karolini DCCCXLIII-DCCCLIX*, ed. Wilfried Hartmann (Hannover, 1984), c. 37, p. 102.
[30] Mansi 17A:327, c. 13.
[31] Ibid., 18A:79, c. 6.
[32] See Frederick H. Russell, *The Just War in the Middle Ages* (Cambridge, 1975), pp. 32–4. Nicholas' letter was incorporated into Gratian's *Decretum* (C. 23, q. 8, c. 19), but John's was not.

In fact, if anything the attitude of the western Church toward violence and especially killing in battle grew harsher in the post-Carolingian period, probably in part as a reaction against its ubiquity, possibly also because of the formalistic nature of Germanic thinking and early medieval theology which usually focused on the formal act itself rather than on intention. It was also an age which believed deeply in miracles and the power of prayer to bring them about, including the deflection of violence. Finally, it was a great era of missionary activity, first to the Germanic peoples who had settled in the Roman Empire, then to the Germanic peoples of Scandinavia and to the Slavic peoples in the east. The laurel of martyrdom was still prized and gained. Viewed in retrospect, the story of the death of St Boniface at the hands of the Frisians in 754 as told by Willibald is deeply significant. When his followers rushed to arms at the appearance of the Frisians, Boniface bade the laymen as well as the clergy in his entourage not to defend themselves; and they obeyed, suffering martyrdom with Boniface and the clerics.[33] One wonders whether the example of Boniface and his followers informed not only the ideals of the next few centuries, for laymen as well as for monks and 'clerics,' but practice as well.

Although there is much conflicting evidence on the views of churchmen toward arms and warfare in the ninth, tenth, and eleventh centuries, two related incidents document the Church's continuing hostility to any shedding of blood, even by laymen, even in battle. In 923 the obligation to perform penance was imposed on all the troops of King Charles the Simple and Count Robert of Paris who had participated in the battle of Soissons in June. And after the Battle of Hastings (probably 1067) all who had killed, wounded, or simply participated in the battle were obliged to atone according to a tariff of penances evidently prescribed by the Norman bishops and approved by the papal legate, Bishop Ermenfrid of Sion.[34] This is the last known such incident embodying such penitential rigor in western history.

The Reform Movement of the Eleventh Century and Clerical Armsbearing

It can be argued that one century in particular was the most fateful in the history of western Christianity in the period between the fourth century, when Christianity gradually became the sole official religion of the Roman Empire and ceased to be a voluntary sect, and the sixteenth, when the Protestant Re-formations permanently shattered the already tenuous official unity of Latin Christendom. That century was the eleventh, when various reform movements, reaching back into the tenth century and often looking to the See of Rome for leadership, found papal leadership assumed with unexpected

---

[33] *The Anglo-Saxon Missionaries in Germany*, tr. and ed. C. H. Talbot (New York, 1954), pp. 56-7.
[34] H. E. J. Cowdrey, 'Bishop Ermenfrid of Sion and the Penitential Ordinance following the Battle of Hastings,' *JEH* 20 (1969):225-42; *C&S* 1:581-4.

vigor by Pope Leo IX (1049–54). Often misleadingly called the 'Gregorian reform movement' (after Gregory VII, the most famous and extreme of these popes) or the 'Investiture Struggle' (after one of its most contentious issues), and often embracing sharply differing views about aims and methods, the movement at least sought to achieve the 'liberty' of the Church from secular domination and entanglements in secular society and, concretely, to focus on the abolition of simony, clerical concubinage, and lay investiture and the achievement of 'free' ecclesiastical elections of bishops and other prelates by the clergy alone. One major result, ironically, was a monumental struggle over jurisdiction and the dispensation of justice – sometimes called 'the crisis of Church and State' – from which the papacy emerged as a central monarchy of Europe for the next four hundred years. Whether the reformers of the mid-eleventh century foresaw or intended such consequences is highly doubtful.

While it has occasionally been noted that the reformers condemned armsbearing by the clergy, the frequency with which they did so has never been remarked. Indeed, in the whole history of Christianity there exists no parallel to the intensity with which councils and synods repeatedly did so in the second half of the eleventh century – and often with the explicit support of the papacy. Leo IX launched this campaign at the council of Rheims in 1049, although this was evidently the only one of his nine councils where this issue was acted upon.[35] Nevertheless, it was an important precedent soon widely imitated. During the next thirty years, no fewer than eleven councils or synods followed the example set at Rheims in 1049 in condemning clerical armsbearing; and of these eleven a pope presided over one (Rome in 1059) and papal legates over another six (indicated with an asterisk): Coyanza in 1050, Narbonne in 1054*, Compostella in 1056, Rome in 1059, Tours in 1060*, Normandy around 1067*, Gerona in 1068*, Windsor in 1070, Rouen in 1074, Gerona in 1078*, and Poitiers in 1078*.[36] In short, in thirty years twelve major councils, eight of them under direct papal sponsorship, condemned arms for the clergy. Silence apparently followed for sixteen years, after which Pope Urban II at the council of Clermont in 1095 renewed the prohibition.[37] And according to Orderic Vitalis, the decrees of Clermont were repeated by Pope Calixtus II at Rheims in 1119.[38]

The texts of all these canons differ in many ways, if not in substance. Of

---

[35] Uta-Renate Blumenthal, 'Ein neuer Text für das Reimser Konzil Leos IX. (1049)?' *DA* 32 (1976):23–48, at 29. The texts of Leo's other councils are printed in Mansi 19:721–812.

[36] In chronological order, Mansi 19:787 (Coyanza, c. 3), 850 (Narbonne, c. 15), 856 (Compostella, c. 2), 915 (Rome, c. 10), 927 (Tours, c. 7) (also PL 142:1412), 1071 (Gerona, c. 5); Cowdrey, 'Bishop Ermenfrid' (n. 34 above); *C&S* 1:581; Mansi 20:399 (Rouen, c. 12), 518–9 (Gerona, c. 6), 499 (Poitiers, c. 20).

[37] Robert Somerville, *The Councils of Urban II*, 1, *Decreta Claromontensia*, Annuarium historiae conciliorum, Supplementum 1 (Amsterdam, 1972), pp. 77, 113.

[38] *The Ecclesiastical History of Orderic Vitalis*, ed. and tr. M. Chibnall (Oxford, 1969–78), 6:262–3, although this prohibition does not appear among the six canons later explicitly listed as promulgated by this council (ibid., 6:274–77).

the initial decree at Rheims in 1049 two versions survive: 'Clerics are not to bear arms' and 'No one of the clergy is to carry weapons or serve in the secular military forces.'[39] The council of Coyanza in 1050, held for the diocese of Oviedo under the presidency of King Ferdinand I of Castile, forbade *arma belli* to priests and deacons – perhaps a deliberate omission of bishops, especially in view of the royal presence?[40] For clerics bearing arms the Roman synod under Pope Nicholas II in 1059 decreed deposition for 'as long as they have borne arms,' while the legatine councils of Tours the following year threatened loss of benefice and the fellowship of clerics, at Poitiers in 1078 declared excommunication for such offenders, and at Gerona the year before added denial of Christian burial to excommunication.[41] Finally, at least one of these councils was indirectly motivated by a concern to promote the Peace and Truce of God movements, which consistently took clergy under their protection only to the extent that they did not carry arms. At Narbonne in 1054, ten bishops, meeting under a papal legate, not only repeated this provision (c. 15), but also declared without reserve that it was a sin for any Christian to kill another Christian, 'because he who kills a Christian undoubtedly sheds the blood of Christ' (c. 1).[42]

These complexities of formulation suggest complexity in motivation on the part of the reformers. To some extent they wished to enforce the Peace and Truce of God movements by dissuading clerical violators of the peace by a combination of positive and negative incentives, offering the protection of the law for compliance and threatening severe penalties for failure to do so. But were the reformers also seeking to dissuade clerics who bore arms to *promote* these movements? Although some evidence supports this hypothesis, some reformers may well have been equivocal on this issue. It has also been suggested that the reformers had primarily in mind the bishops and abbots who commanded troops in obedience to the will of secular princes.[43] Finally, the reformers themselves overwhelmingly thought that they were trying to restore the ancient canons, which in this instance they certainly were. Aside from the fact that the sources will disclose very little of the thinking of so many different reformers over a substantial swath of time,

---

[39] Blumenthal, 'Reimser Konzil,' p. 29: 'Clerici arma non ferant' (c. 2 in the V text) and 'Ne quis clericorum arma gestaret aut mundanae militiae deserviat' (c. 6 in the H text, which is that printed in Mansi 19:742).

[40] Mansi 19:787, c. 3: 'Presbyteri vero & diacones, qui ministerio funguntur ecclesiae, arma belli non deferant . . .'

[41] Mansi 19:913, c. 10 ('De clericis arma ferentibus hoc decernimus, ut quamdiu arma tulerint a proprio gradu decidant'), 927, c. 7 ('Quicumque autem clericorum deinceps in armis militaverint; & beneficium, & consortium clericorum amittant'); 20:499, c. 20 ('Clerici arma portantes, & usuarii excommunicentur'), and 518–9, c. 6 ('Decrevit enim, ut clerici arma ferentes, nisi dimiserint arma, sint alieni a Corpore & sanguine Domini, & ab ingressu totius ecclesiae, & Christianorum sepultura, & omni communione ecclesiastica; nunquam amplius in Christi Ecclesia ad majores honores sive gradus, si rebelles institerint, sublimandi').

[42] Ibid., 19:827, c. 1 and 830, c. 15 . For provisions similar to the latter, see ibid., 19:1041 and 1073 (for 1065 and 1068, respectively).

[43] Monika Minninger, *Von Clermont zum Wormser Konkordat. Die Auseinandersetzungen um den Lehnsnexus zu König und Episkopat* (Cologne-Vienna, 1978), pp. 63–4.

there is also the simple fact that all these motives do not necessarily conflict and could coexist simultaneously. What is absolutely crucial to see here is that, whatever the formulation, whatever the motivation, all these repeated denunciations of clerical armsbearing dovetailed in substance, represented an unambiguous consensus among the reformers, and allowed no exception to the ban whatever.

Yet three hundred years later, between 1360 and 1383, a professor of canon and civil law at Bologna was able to set the following questions in a treatise on war, reprisals, and duels:

Whether clerics may participate in war?

Whether those who die in war are saved?

Whether it is lawful to wage corporeal war on behalf of the property and possessions of the Church?

Whether bishops may go to war without the license of the Pope?

Whether prelates, for the temporalities which they hold from the Emperor, may go to war?

Whether prelates, by reason of temporal jurisdiction, may declare war?

Whether the prelate, for the injury of a subject, may declare war?

Whether clerics may declare a war of self-defense?

Whether, although a cleric may defend himself even by killing another, he may do this in a church?

Whether a cleric, attacked in the act of celebration of the Mass, may defend himself, and kill his assailant, and so continue to celebrate the office?

Whether a monk may defend himself without the license of his abbot?

To all of these questions Giovanni da Legnano (c.1320–83), basing his responses on the principles and texts of canon law as it had evolved in the High Middle Ages, was able to give at least a qualified 'Yes' in every case.[44] What, then, had happened in the realm of ecclesiastical law since the eleventh-century reformers had vigorously reaffirmed the ancient ban while launching their revolution three hundred years earlier?

---

[44] Giovanni da Legnano, *Tractatus de bello, de represaliis et de duello*, tr. F. W. Kelsey, ed. T. E. Holland, Classics of International Law (Oxford, 1917), pp. 264–5, 273–5, 281–4, 286–7.

CHAPTER 4

THE CANON LAW OF THE ROMAN CATHOLIC CHURCH (II): 'REVOLUTION IN LAW', c.1120–1317

THE title of this chapter alludes to a stimulating book published in 1983, *Law and Revolution. The Formation of the Western Legal Tradition*. In it Harold J. Berman, a distinguished historian of law, argued that the origins of a distinctive, systematic western legal tradition can be traced to the papal revolution of the High Middle Ages and in particular to the emergence of the canon law of the Roman Catholic Church. Despite some criticism, on the whole it justly earned high praise.[1] Although the book is concerned with the nature and implications of canon law in general rather than with specific issues, on the matter of the clergy and armsbearing Berman's title happens to be perfectly apposite, for during these two centuries the law of the Church on this subject was profoundly altered, and never since then has the Church returned to the earlier prohibition.

The Breakthrough

We can pinpoint quite precisely when the revolution in law regarding clerical armsbearing began: in the Holy Land in the years 1119–1120. After the spectacular initial conquests of the 'First Crusaders' (Edessa and Antioch in 1098, Jerusalem in 1099), their successors, particularly King Baldwin I of Jerusalem (1100–1118), went on to take Acre in 1104, Tripoli in 1109, and Sidon and Beirut in 1110 – the entire Palestinian coastline, in fact, save for Ascalon and Tyre. Huge gaps remained, however. The attempt to take the pivotal city of Aleppo in 1103 resulted in the destruction of an entire army, and passage through the countryside from one city to another always remained danger-ous. Both problems came to the fore in 1119. Around Easter a large group of about 700 pilgrims was attacked in the barren region between Jerusalem and the Jordan; 300 were killed and 60 captured.[2] And on 27 June Prince Roger of Antioch and his army perished on the 'Field of Blood' (*ager sanguinis*) in

---

[1] Charles J. Reid, Jr, 'The Papacy, Theology, and Revolution: A Response to Joseph L. Soria's Critique of Harold J. Berman's *Law and Revolution*,' *SC* 29 (1995): 433–80.

[2] Malcolm Barber, *The New Knighthood. A History of the Order of the Temple* (Cambridge, 1994), pp. 9–10.

his vain effort to attack Aleppo.[3] The city of Antioch stood defenseless. The Patriarch, Bernard, ordered that clergy, monks, and laymen guard the walls of the city. An eyewitness, Walter the Chancellor, attests that it was Bernard, 'with his armed clergy and knights,' who protected the city until the arrival of King Baldwin II of Jerusalem.[4]

Six months later, on 16 January 1120, King Baldwin II and the Patriarch of Jerusalem, Warmund (or Gormund) of Picquigny, convened at Nablus a council of the great men of the realm, ecclesiastical and secular, to enact legislation touching a variety of issues in twenty-five *capitula*. Number 20 boldly decreed that 'If a cleric bears arms for the sake of defense, he is not to be held at fault.' Furthermore, a cleric who abandoned tonsure to become a knight, but who then repented and confessed before the first day of Lent, would be allowed to resume his clerical status according to the judgment of the patriarch (and also of the king after that date).[5] This was legislation without precedent. Was this meant to justify *ex post facto* the earlier behavior of the patriarch of Antioch and his clergy? Possibly, although the patriarch of Jerusalem had no jurisdiction over Antioch.[6] It is far more likely that Warmund meant this provision to apply to his own clergy should similar dangers arise – and both the prologue to the canons of Nablus and a nearly contemporaneous letter he sent to Archbishop Diego of Compostella reveal how frightened Warmund was of a Saracen world closing in from all sides.[7]

What happened to this revolutionary enactment at Nablus? Unfortunately, these *capitula* are the only surviving legislation from the first kingdom of Jerusalem (1100–87). William of Tyre, writing between 1174 and 1180, did not list or even summarize these canons, noting that they were easily accessible

[3] Thomas Asbridge, 'The Significance and Causes of the Battle of the Field of Blood,' *JMH* 23 (1997): 301–16.

[4] Galterius Cancellarius, *Bella Antiochena*, ed. Heinrich Hagenmeyer (Innsbruck, 1896), 2.8.6–8, pp. 95–96: 'statuitque, ut, ubi totius ciuitatis inferior patebat debilitas, ibi tentoria sua protectioni Christianitatis necessaria ponerentur et ut singulae turres, quotquot essent, monachis et cleris mixtim cum laicis pro posse et quantitate Christicolarum eminus munirentur . . . nocte et die cum armato suo clero et militibus, more pugnatorum portas moenia et turres murosque circumcirca et ipsorum custodes uicissim uisitare, consolari et incitare.'

[5] Benjamin Kedar, 'On the Origins of the Earliest Laws of Frankish Jerusalem: The Canons of the Council of Nablus, 1120,' *Speculum* 74 (1999):334, c. 20: 'Si clericus causa defenssionis [sic] arma detulerit, culpa non teneatur. Si autem milicie aut alicujus curi<a>litatis causa coronam dimiserit, usque ad praedictum terminum ecclesiae id confessus coronam reddat et deinceps secundum patriarche praeceptum se habeat. Si autem amplius celauerit, pro regis et patriarche consilio se contineat' (a slightly corrected version of the text in Mansi 21:265). On this meeting, see also Hans Eberhard Mayer, 'The Concordat of Nablus,' *JEH* 33 (1982): 531–43. Although the significance of this council in allowing armsbearing by the clergy for very the first time was recognized by Willibald Plöchl, he misidentified it as the council of Naples rather than Nablus: *Geschichte des Kirchenrechts* (Vienna-Munich, 1952–68), 3:168.

[6] On the status of the patriarchs, see Yael Katzir, 'The Patriarch of Jerusalem, Primate of the Latin Kingdom,' in Peter W. Edbury, ed., *Crusade and Settlement. Papers Read at the First Conference of the Society for the Study of the Crusades and the Latin East and Presented to R. C. Smail* (Cardiff, 1985), pp. 169–75.

[7] Kedar, 'Laws,' p. 331 and n. 98. The significance of these years and events is underscored by Jonathan Phillips, *Defenders of the Holy Land. Relations Between the Latin East and the West, 1119–1187* (Oxford, 1996), pp. 2–5.

in the archives of many churches, from which one may reasonably infer that they continued to be in force.[8] As for the later history of the kingdom, there are statutes issued in 1253 and 1254 at Jaffa and Acre by the papal legate Odo of Châteauroux, but none of these says anything about clerical armsbearing.[9] This same Odo, incidentally, also promulgated statutes at synods at Nicosia in Cyprus in 1249 and 1254. These also have nothing concerning clerical armsbearing, but the extensive surviving legislation of the Latin Church of Cyprus between 1196 and 1373 may help a bit to fill the gap left in the records of the crusading East. In 1313 the synod of Nicosia, again under the presidency of a papal legate, stipulated that 'no cleric shall dare to carry any arms at night, nor in the day, unless such a situation emerges that he could do it licitly without fault.'[10] This is the only germane bit of legislation from Latin Cyprus, which suggests that there was no line of continuity between Nablus and later synods 'beyond the sea' on this point; and by the time it was acted on in 1313, it was under the aegis of a papal legate and reflected the significant changes that had already taken place in western canon law.

Patriarch Warmund did, however, sponsor another, related initiative in 1120 which unquestionably set a new course: the inception of the Templars. William of Tyre assigned this event to 1118, a date generally accepted until fairly recently, when Rudolf Hiestand argued convincingly that in fact it must have occurred sometime between 14 January and 13 September 1120 – and thus possibly at the council of Nablus itself.[11] In any event, the French knights Hugh of Payns, Godfrey of Saint-Omer, and their companions pledged to live 'in the manner of regular canons' (not monks, as is still widely misunderstood) and accordingly took vows of poverty, chastity, and obedience. They did so at the hands of Patriarch Warmund, who with his fellow bishops also enjoined upon these consecrated knights, for the remission of their sins, the principal task of keeping roads and highways safe for pilgrims against thieves and highwaymen.[12] That would presumably involve the use of weapons by

---

[8] William of Tyre, *Chronicon*, ed. R. B. C. Huygens, CCCM 63–63A (Turnhout, 1986), 12.13, p. 563, who speaks with seeming disparagement of these statutes '*quasi* vim legis obtinentia' (emphasis added), which is incorrectly translated into English in *A History of Deeds Done Beyond the Sea*, trans. E. A. Babcock and A. C. Krey (1941; repr., New York, 1976), 1:535, as 'twenty-five articles with the force of law.'

[9] Mansi 26:317–8, 343–7; Benjamin Kedar, 'Ecclesiastical Legislation in the Kingdom of Jerusalem: The Statutes of Jaffa (1253) and Acre (1254),' in Edbury, ed., *Crusade and Settlement*, pp. 225–30.

[10] *The Synodicum Nicosiense and Other Documents of the Latin Church of Cyprus, 1196–1373*, ed. and trans. Christopher Schabel, Texts and Studies in the History of Cyprus 39 (Nicosia, 2001), pp. 214–15, c. 13: 'Item, quod nullus clericus arma quaelibet de nocte portare audeat nec de die, nisi talis casus mergeret quod hoc licite posset facere sine culpa. Quicumque autem fuerit contrarium, privetur armis omnibus per praelatum ad quem hoc pertinet, et ultra hoc, prout de jure fuerit, puniatur. "Arma quidem nostrae militiae non sunt carnalia," dicit Apostolus, sed potius spiritualia, quibus debemus nos defendere ab hostibus ecclesiae et fidei et totum populum Christianum.' The papal legate was Peter of Pleine-Chassaigne, bishop of Rodez.

[11] Rudolf Hiestand, 'Kardinalbischof Matthäus von Albano, das Konzil von Troyes und die Entstehung des Templerordens', *Zeitschrift für Kirchengeschichte* 99 (1988):317–19; Barber, *New Knighthood*, pp. 6–9.

[12] William of Tyre, *Chronicon*, 12.7, pp. 553–4 (Eng. trans., 1:524–5): 'Eodem anno [1118] quidam nobiles viri de equestri ordine, deo devoti, religiosi et timentes deum, in manu domini patriarche

these men endeavoring to live like regular canons. Now if this solemn dedication did take place at the council of Nablus, is it possible that one reason for the passage of canon 20 was to cover this unprecedented and hence dubious situation?[13]

For it was indeed highly anomalous. Although William of Tyre entitled this chapter of his chronicle 'The Military Order of the Temple is established at Jerusalem' (*Ordo militie Templi Ierosolimis instituitur*), his usage was anachronistic. This company received formal recognition and initial statutes only at the council of Troyes in January 1129 (not 1128, as Hiestand again showed[14]), and from the papacy only ten years after that in the privilege *Omne datum optimum* of 1139. According it the status of an 'order' (*religio et ueneranda institutio*) in the Church universal, Pope Innocent II cited John 15:13 ('No one has greater love than he who lays down his life for his friends') in underscoring the task of these *milites Templi* in protecting their brothers against pagan incursions, defending the church, and attacking the enemies of Christ.[15] Two additional bulls, *Milites Templi* (1144) and *Militia Dei* (1145), completed the establishment of this new way of religious life.[16]

It also set a pattern. A variety of hospitals and 'hospital congregations' had grown up in the Latin East, some well before the First Crusade.[17] One of them, the Knights Hospitaller of St John of Jerusalem, achieved special prominence and came to be 'militarized' in the kingdom of Jerusalem in the 1130s and '40s even more rapidly than the Templars.[18] Fighting came to be viewed increasingly as a charitable activity; Pope Eugene III in 1152 spoke of the Hospitallers as 'fighting in the service of the poor.'[19] Nevertheless, some popes were anxious about these developments, especially Alexander III (1159–

Christi servicio se mancipantes, more canonicorum regularium in castitate et obedientia et sine proprio velle perpetuo vivere professi sunt … Prima autem eorum professio, quodque eis a domino patriarcha et reliquis episcopis in remissionem peccatorum iniunctum est, ut vias et itinera maxime ad salutem peregrinorum contra latronum et incursantium insidias pro viribus conservarent.'

13   Although Hiestand and Barber admit the distinct possibility that Hugh and his companions were so recognized at Nablus, neither they nor anyone else, to my knowledge, has suggested this connection with canon 20.

14   Hiestand, 'Kardinalbischof,' pp. 295–325-.

15   *Papsturkunden für Templer und Johanniter. N.F.*, ed. Rudolf Hiestand, Vorarbeiten zum Oriens Pontificus 2, Abh. d. Akad. d. Wiss. in Göttingen, phil.-hist. Kl. 3. F. 135 (Göttingen, 1984), pp. 96–103, at 96: 'Accedit ad hoc, quod tanquam ueri Israelite atque instructissimi diuini prelii bellatores uere karitatis flamma succensi dictum euuangelicum operibus adimpletis, quo dicitur: "maiorem hac dilectionem nemo habet, quam ut animam suam ponat quis pro amicis suis." Vnde etiam iuxta summi pastoris uocem animas uestras pro fratribus ponere eosque ab incursibus paganorum defensare minime formidatis et cum nomine censeamini milites Templi, constituti estis a domino catholice ecclesie defensores et inimicorum Christi impugnatores.'

16   See Barber, *New Knighthood*, pp. 56–59, for summary and discussion.

17   See Jean Richard, 'Hospitals and Hospital Congregations in the Latin Kingdom in the Early Days of the Frankish Conquest,' in his *Croisés, missionaires et voyageurs. Les perspectives orientales du monde latin médiéval*, Variorum Reprints CS 192 (London, 1982), II, 89–100.

18   See Barber, *New Knighthood*, pp. 34–35; Jonathan Riley-Smith, *The Knights of St. John in Jerusalem and Cyprus c.1050–1300* (London, 1967), pp. 52–59.

19   *Cartulaire général de l'ordre des Hospitaliers de St-Jean de Jerusalem (1100–1300)*, ed. J. Delaville Le Roulx (Paris, 1894–1906), 1:163, no. 212: 'fratribus in servitio pauperum militantibus.'

81). Sometime between 1168 and 1170 he reminded the Hospitallers that their principal obligation was to the poor and that bearing arms contravened both the original intentions and the customs of the order.[20] Around ten years later (1178/80) Alexander again sought to recall them to their original purpose and to forbid them the bearing of arms 'except perhaps when the standard of the Holy Cross is carried for the defense of the kingdom or for the siege of some pagan city.' This exceptive clause is remarkable in allowing armsbearing not only in a defensive situation, but for more aggressive purposes as well. The pope went on to specify that the costs of armsbearing should not impinge on expenditures for the poor.[21] Within a decade Alexander had come this far in his acceptance of changes that had seemed inexorable on the eastern frontier of Latin Christendom. Or were they inevitable? If so, they were not limited to the regions of the Crusades. For, as we shall see, it was also Alexander III who accepted as a principle of natural law, applicable to all including the clergy, the right to repel force with force – in short, the natural right of self-defense.

But before Pope Alexander III there was Patriarch Warmund of Jerusalem, who in 1120 was at the center of both the legislation of the council of Nablus and the inception of the Templars. Although on both occasions he acted not alone but in concert with the king, bishops, and barons of the realm, neither of these momentous events would have occurred without his consent. Who was this crucial figure? Regrettably, we know nothing about him before he became patriarch in 1118 except that he was from Picquigny in the diocese of Amiens.[22] As patriarch he was the effective regent during King Baldwin II's captivity between 1122 and 1124, and he negotiated the treaty with Venice to undertake the siege of Tyre in 1124. He also served with the king in the

---

[20] Ibid., 4:249–50, no. 391*ter*: 'ut alimentis et curis pauperum et aliis pietatis operibus, sicut predecessores eorum consueverunt, modis omnibus intendant, et armis militaribus preter consuetudinem et primam eorum institutionem depositis, metam a patribus eorum prefixam nullatenus transgredi attentent, ipsisque comminatur quod, si aliter presumpserint, id incorrectum et impunitum minime omittetur.'

[21] Ibid., 1:360–61, no. 527: 'prudentiam tuam monemus, mandantes atque precipientes ut predecessores tui bone memorie Raimundi sanctos mores et bonas consuetudines observare pro viribus satagas, et ut sollicitiorem curam pauperum habeas, et competencius Christi caritas valeat ordinari, ab armis ferendis juxta consuetudinem predicti Raimundi omnino quiescas, nisi forte tunc cum vexillum sancte Crucis aut pro defensione regni aut pro obsidione alicujus civitatis paganorum delatum fuerit; pro quibus subsidium necessarium esset armorum, quia congruum est et consonum rationi ut, sicut domus Hospitalis ad susceptionem et refectionem pauperum est instituta, ita quoque per tuam instantem sollicitudinem in hoc debeat conservari, presertim cum magis per caritatem et misericordiam erga pauperes exhibitam quam per fortitudinem armorum credatur posse defendi. Hoc autem tam a te quam a successoribus tuis teneri jubemus, ne sub armorum obtentu cura pauperum aliquatenus minuatur.'

[22] Bernard Hamilton, *The Latin Church in the Crusader States. The Secular Church* (London, 1980), p. 64, which Jonathan Riley-Smith has recently confirmed for me. He has no entry for Warmund in his *First Crusaders, 1095–1131* (Cambridge, 1997), nor is there any in the three principal French dictionaries of national biography. The most recent and exhaustive treatment is by Klaus-Peter Kirsten, *Die lateinischen Patriarchen von Jerusalem. Von der Eroberung der Heiligen Stadt durch die Kreuzfahrer 1099 bis zum Ende der Kreuzfahrerstaaten 1291*, Berliner Historische Studien 35 (Berlin, 2002), pp. 201–222.

campaign against Damascus, led the troops at Tyre, and contracted a fatal illness while directing another siege operation in 1128; but the sources, Fulcher of Chartres and William of Tyre, give no indication that he personally bore arms.[23] Although one modern historian regards him as essentially a worldly administrator,[24] William of Tyre thought that he was 'a straightforward, God-fearing man' and that 'During the days of this man and, indeed, through his merits, as most people believed, the Lord deigned to accomplish many splendid works for the consolation and increase of the kingdom.'[25] Warmund deserves more research, especially in western European sources.[26]

How is it that the daring changes initiated by Warmund in Jerusalem around 1120 came to prevail, despite criticism and foot-dragging, in the law and institutions of the western Church by about 1180?

The Larger Context of Legal Change

Before considering these crucial changes in the law of the Church, which actually took place over a period of less than two hundred years between the early twelfth and early fourteenth centuries, it is important to examine some relevant facets of the extra-legal world which encouraged, allowed, or perhaps even forced such profound modifications of the old law. For although any legal system moves according to its own weighty logic and rules, it never operates in a void divorced from the surrounding world of politics and society, thought and action, particularly at times of great change in both realms. Furthermore, the changes in the extra-legal context largely preceded those in the law of the Church, which is another reason for starting there first. It is impossible here to do more than sketch out just a few

---

[23] Fulcher of Chartres, *A History of the Expedition to Jerusalem, 1095–1127*, trans. F. R. Ryan (Knoxville, 1969), 3.4 and 3.28–36, pp. 228, 255–70; William of Tyre, *Chronicon*, 13.6 and 25, pp. 593 and 619 (Eng. trans., 2:10 and 39).

[24] Hamilton, *Latin Church*, pp. 64–67.

[25] William of Tyre, *History*, 12.6, 1:524 (*Chronicon*, p. 553: 'vir simplex ac timens deum ... Huius diebus et meritis etiam, ut creditur, multa magnifice ad regni consolationem et incrementum operari dignatus est dominus.')

[26] See Giles Constable, 'Medieval Charters as a Source for the History of the Crusades,' in his *Crusaders and Crusading in the Twelfth Century* (Farnham-Burlington, Vt, 2008), pp. 93–116. One might point out that Godfrey of Saint-Omer, one of the founders of the Templars, was, like Warmund, from Picardy, while the other founder, Hugh of Payns, was from Champagne, as was King Baldwin II, formerly lord of Le Bourcq east of Rheims (who presumably appointed Gormund as patriarch and gave the Templars property). And sandwiched between these two areas was Nogent-sous-Coucy, whose abbot, Guibert, had famously written before 1110 that 'God has instituted in our time holy wars, so that the order of knights and the crowd running in their wake ... might find a new way of gaining salvation. And so they are not forced to abandon secular affairs completely by choosing the monastic life or any religious profession, as used to be the custom, but can attain in some measure God's grace while pursuing their own careers, with the liberty and in the dress to which they are accustomed' (trans. in Riley-Smith, *First Crusaders*, p. 69, a rendering preferable to that in Guibert of Nogent, *The Deeds of God Through the Franks*, trans. Robert Levine [Woodbridge, 1997], p. 28). How interconnected were these men, and how much did they shape the newly emerging climate of opinion?

of the germane topics and their implications. Although many scholars have paved the way here, much remains to be done, as will be suggested by various speculations and unanswered questions. For the sake of comprehension, the topics for consideration, all bridging the worlds of thought and action, will be grouped under four broad rubrics: the crusades; the structure of the clerical order; the unprecedented emphasis on intention in theology and law; and the unintended, even ironic consequences of the ecclesiastical reform movement itself.

The *Crusades* come to mind most readily as a possible factor. As they are popularly conceived nowadays, these were holy wars conducted aggressively on several fronts by knights dedicated to Christ against the enemies of Christianity in the twelfth and thirteenth centuries, a complex of ideals which was later corrupted, especially by the popes, who came by the thirteenth century to launch crusades against their own enemies in Europe itself, especially the Cathars and secular rulers like the Emperor Frederick II. This supposedly embarrassing chapter of western history was recollected relatively recently when Pope John Paul II was exhorted from many quarters to apologize for the crusades during his tour of the eastern Mediterranean world in the tracks of St Paul during the spring of 2001.

It was Carl Erdmann, more than any other scholar, who in 1935 exploded many of these misconceptions by suggesting that the idea of the crusade developed rapidly in the eleventh century, directed against not only the external enemies of Christendom but internal ones as well. Many other scholars since then have gone to gone on to underscore these points and also to argue that the crusades were generally viewed as just wars, essentially defensive in character, for the recovery of lost, formerly Christian territory and that the knights who fought in them were, in law, only armed pilgrims dedicated to the imitation of Christ by taking up the cross and following Him.[27] What all these observations point to is the conclusion that the crusades were not as aberrant, revolutionary, or aggressive as they had previously been thought to be.

Erdmann also explored at great length the genesis of the crusades, going back as far as the ideas of St Augustine and Pope Gregory the Great and the practices of the early Carolingian rulers in integrating the spheres of religion and war. Erdmann laid particular stress, however, on the ninth and tenth centuries, when the heirs of Charlemagne fought with each other while Europe was swept by new waves of invaders from the north, east, and south. Historians have debated whether these invasions were more damaging than

---

[27] See, for example, James Brundage, *Medieval Canon Law and the Crusader* (Madison-London, 1969); John Gilchrist, 'The Papacy and War Against the Saracens,' *International History Review* 10 (1988): 174–97; Jonathan Riley-Smith, ed., *The Oxford Illustrated History of the Crusades* (Oxford-New York, 1997) and *First Crusaders*, pp. 23–52; Christopher Tyerman, *The Invention of the Crusades* (Toronto-Buffalo, 1998); and the bibliographically rich 'Introduction' to Edward Peters, ed., *The First Crusade. The Chronicle of Fulcher of Chartres and Other Source Materials*, 2nd ed. (Philadelphia, 1998), pp. 1–24.

the earlier incursions of the Germanic tribes into the western Roman Empire, and occasionally doubts are raised about the later attacks because most of the chroniclers were monks or clerics, whose perspective was presumably skewed because their institutions enjoyed 'most favored target' status among the Norse, Saracen, and Magyar invaders.

From the vantage point of this study, one must conclude that the damage wrought in the ninth and tenth centuries was very severe indeed, although it was not all material damage. While these wars were not constant, war became a grinding fact of life for two hundred years or more. Unlike Charlemagne's successful wars of conquest, these were either internecine or defensive, often fought against aggressive non-Christians, a fact which could easily have lent them a religious, even sacred, quality. In any event, the blessing of weapons and of warriors became common by the tenth century, for on them depended the defense of the West and of Latin Christendom.[28] The sacralization of the soldier's calling had begun – significantly, the only other vocation to be so consecrated by the Latin Church after priesthood and kingship.

The clergy, especially bishops and abbots, were easily drawn into the realm of war, sometimes in obedience to royal command, sometimes in defense of the possessions entrusted to them, sometimes in aggressive moves against the lands of others. The bishops of Rome were no exception, and in fact often regarded their wars against their enemies as in some measure holy.[29] This engagement precipitated occasional commentary and debate, much of it focused on Archbishop Bruno of Cologne, the brother of the Emperor Otto I.[30] But war also inevitably works corrupting and distorting effects, as the experiences of the United States in Vietnam and of Israel on the West Bank reveal. As one reads through the letters of Gerbert of Aurillac – tutor to Emperor Otto II, abbot of Bobbio, archbishop of Ravenna, then Pope Sylvester II (999–1002) – one notices his wearied acceptance of his military duties as an inexorable fact of life. Try as he might to avoid it, he was again and again sucked back into the maw of war. In 988, as he awaited the arrival of an archbishop in Rheims, he wrote that 'we are exerting ourselves, and what the shortness of time did not permit us to accomplish we have assigned to this breathing spell and are preparing gifts at the same time as [equipping] troops. Yes! troops! For you know among whom we live and how we are harassed by the monstrous treachery of certain persons, and what kind

---

[28] What Erdmann sees as a development of the tenth century Karl Leyser pushes back into the ninth: see his 'Early Medieval Canon Law and the Beginnings of Knighthood,' in Lutz Fenske, Werner Rosener, and Thomas Zotz, eds, *Institutionen, Kultur und Gesellschaft im Mittelalter. Festschrift für Josef Fleckenstein zu seinem 65. Geburtstag* (Sigmaringen, 1984), pp. 549–66, who draws upon G. Althoff, 'Nunc fiant Christi milites, qui dudum extiterunt raptores. Zur Entstehung vom Rittertum und Ritterethos,' *Saeculum* 32 (1981):317–33.

[29] See Gilchrist, 'Papacy and War Against the Saracens.'

[30] See Prinz, *Klerus und Krieg*, pp. 175–96; Patrick Corbet, *Les saints ottoniens*, Beihefte der Francia 15 (Sigmaringen, 1986), pp. 51–8; Odilo Engels, 'Der Reichsbischof in ottonischer und frühsalischer Zeit,' in Irene Crusius, ed., *Beiträge zu Geschichte und Struktur der mittelalterlichen Germania Sacra* (Göttingen, 1989), pp. 135–75.

of a so-called truce interrupted the siege of the city of Laon, which must be renewed on October 18th.'[31]

Perhaps the most striking piece of evidence of the transforming power of habitual warfare in the tenth century comes from the life of St Gerald of Aurillac (†909), whose life was recorded by St Odo, the second abbot of Cluny (†942). Although Gerald remained a layman and a knight, he always sought to imitate Christ and obey His injunctions. When he had to fight, he ordered his men to use the backs of their swords and to reverse their spears. Miraculously, they always won.

> When therefore they saw that he triumphed by a new kind of fighting which was mingled with piety, they changed their scorn to admiration, and sure of victory they readily fulfilled his commands ... For Christ, as it is written, was at his side [Ps. 117.6], who seeing the desire of his heart, saw that for love of Him he was so well-disposed that he had no wish to assail the persons of the enemy, but only to check their audacity. Let no one be worried because a just man sometimes made use of fighting, which seems incompatible with religion ... For some of the Fathers, and of these the most holy and most patient, when the cause of justice demanded, valiantly took up arms against their adversaries, as Abraham, who destroyed a great multitude of the enemy to rescue his nephew, and King David who sent his forces even against his own son. Gerald did not fight invading the property of others, but defending his own, or rather his people's rights ... It was lawful, therefore, for a layman to carry the sword in battle that he might protect defenceless people, as the harmless flock from evening wolves according to the saying of Scripture [Acts 20.29], and that he might restrain by arms or by the law those whom ecclesiastical censure was not able to subdue ... Hereafter, let him who by his example shall take up arms against his enemies, seek also by his example not his own but the common good.[32]

Although obviously St Odo is not condoning in any way clerical resort to arms, there is otherwise here a remarkable foreshadowing of many of the themes which will come to the fore in the eleventh and twelfth centuries – of the rightness, even the necessity, of violence rightly directed and rightly restrained, and of the special glory of the warrior who wields his weapons in accordance with these norms. There is here, too, a new admiration of the military calling which earlier clerics might well have judged excessive and dangerous.[33]

By the early eleventh century Cluny itself had come to be widely regarded as entirely too wedded to the military ethos. Bishop Adelbero of Laon satirized the Cluniacs in a poem, dedicated to King Robert, in which he depicts a Cluniac monk elaborately arrayed as a soldier of the abbot of Cluny, 'King'

---

[31] *The Letters of Gerbert with His Papal Privileges as Sylvester II*, tr. Harriet Pratt Lattin, Records of Civilization Sources and Studies 60 (New York, 1961), no. 143, pp. 173–4. For Gerbert's complex attitudes, see also nos. 12, 31, 51, 63, 102, 185, and 201.

[32] *St Odo of Cluny*, ed. and tr. Gerard Sitwell, O.S.B. (London-New York, 1958), pp. 90–180, at 100–1.

[33] For a different view of Odo, see H. E. J. Cowdrey, 'Cluny and the First Crusade,' *Revue bénédictine* 83 (1973):295.

Odilo (abbot from 994 to 1049). Satires of course exaggerate rather than reflect reality, and Adelbero admitted as much some lines later.[34] There is no question, however, about the views of a monk who spent five years at Cluny during Odilo's abbacy (1030–35). The status of Raoul (Radolfus) Glaber (c.985–c.1047) as a representative 'Cluniac monk' is therefore problematical. In any case, in his *Histories* he recorded that in Spain the attacks of Moslems were so overwhelming that 'the monks of that area were compelled to take up arms . . . During these long wars many religious in the Christian armies were killed; they had longed to fight for love of their brothers, not for any vain glory of renown and pomp.' Although Raoul approves of their actions, he also stresses that they acted with the right intention, love of neighbor rather than desire for personal glory. Later he recounts a story in which monks who had fallen in battle needed special intercession to gain Christ's pardon – and got it.[35]

Within a few decades the danger to western Europe was coming less from the invaders from without than from the protectors within, the mounted warriors, who increasingly used their power to consolidate and extend their dominions. To restrain them, the Peace and Truce of God movements developed in Aquitaine from the last quarter of the tenth century and spread out from there. Bishops gathered to threaten excommunication and other punishments for those who attacked defenseless persons or fought on Sundays or holy days or during Lent.[36] Ironically, as Erdmann perceived, a significant implication of the imposition of such limits on warfare was that the conduct of war within those limits was, or at least could be, legitimate. The bishops themselves proceeded to prove that by summoning up 'peace militias' to enforce the provisions of the Peace and Truce of God.[37] There was not necessarily anything unusual about this, for, as Erdmann observed, 'Until recently, every organization of peace has simultaneously been an organization of war, since mankind hitherto has not wished to believe in a peace that was not guaranteed by the possibility of war.'[38] Still, the fact that bishops were now organizing violence to create peace as a religious duty represented a momentous change, for here was a core element in the idea of 'holy war.' Furthermore, an important stage was reached here in the neutralization of war as a moral or theological problem and its transformation into a primarily legal question, a process which would be furthered by the canonists in the twelfth century. Finally, righteous war was here being waged by Christians against other Christians who were not even heretics.

[34] Robert Coolidge, 'Adalbero, Bishop of Laon,' *Studies in Medieval and Renaissance History* 2 (1965):71–77.
[35] Rodulfus Glaber, *The Five Books of the Histories*, ed. and tr. John France (Oxford, 1989), 2.18, p. 83, and 3.15, pp. 119–21. See John France, 'War and Christendom in the Thought of Rodulfus Glaber,' *Studia monastica* 30 (1988):105–119.
[36] See the essays in Thomas Head and Richard Landes, eds, *The Peace of God. Social Violence and Religious Response in France Around the Year 1000* (Ithaca, 1992).
[37] Erdmann, *Origin*, pp. 57–94.
[38] Ibid., pp. 62–3.

It was in the eleventh century, then, that the ideas of 'holy' or, more precisely, 'righteous' war and of the 'soldier of Christ' began to emerge. Erdmann's subtle tracing of how and when that happened is worth close reading and has occasioned some controversy which cannot detain us here, since it does not bear directly on our theme.[39] Three points, however, should be made. First, although the exact place of Pope Gregory VII (1073–85) in this evolution of ideas and practices is and always will be hotly debated, there can be no doubt that his pontificate marks a decisive stage in that development.[40] For he was consumed not only by a fiery thirst for what he conceived of as justice, but also by a belief in the use of force to pursue that vision. That force was to be exercised by laymen, but at the direction of churchmen. A slightly ambiguous articulation of that position came in a letter to the bishops and barons of Brittany at a synod in November 1079 assembled for the reform of penitential practice:

> ... if anyone ... shall take up arms except in defense of his own rights or those of his lord or of a friend or of the poor, or in defense of churches and with the advice of men of religion who know how to counsel wisely in view of their eternal welfare ...[41]

The problem lies in deciding whether Gregory meant to say or imply that arms should be wielded *only* upon the advice of men of religion or not. This was certainly the case at the Roman synod exactly a year before, which had decreed that a soldier could not perform the true penance necessary for salvation 'unless he puts down his arms and does not take them up again except with the counsel of religious bishops to defend justice.'[42] On the other hand, the Lenten synod of Rome in 1080 simply condemned those who bore arms in contravention of justice (*contra iustitiam*).[43] In other words, as with Augustine and Luther, Gregory's passion, as is so often the case with such passionate men, carried him into seeming contradictions. Nevertheless, although it has been convincingly argued that Gregory's extremism left no lasting footprints in the canon law of the Latin Church,[44] I think that

---

[39] See, for example, besides the introduction and annotations to the 1977 English translation of Erdmann, the essays by H. E. J. Cowdrey, 'The Genesis of the Crusades: the Springs of Western Ideas of the Holy War' and 'The Origin of the Idea of Crusade' in his *Popes, Monks and Crusaders* (London, 1984); J. T. Gilchrist, 'The Erdmann Thesis and the Canon Law, 1083–1141,' in *Crusade and Settlement. Papers Read at the First Conference of the Society for the Study of the Crusades and the Latin East and Presented to R. C. Smail*, ed. P. W. Edbury (Cardiff, 1985), pp. 37–45; and Jonathan Riley-Smith, *The First Crusade and the Idea of Crusading* (Philadelphia, 1985).

[40] For a highly useful survey of hundreds of books and articles on Gregory, see I. S. Robinson, 'Pope Gregory VII (1073–1085),' *JEH* 36 (1985):439–83; and H. E. J. Cowdrey, *Pope Gregory VII, 1073–1085* (Oxford, 1998).

[41] I have followed here the translation given in *The Correspondence of Pope Gregory VII. Selected Letters from the Registrum*, tr. Ephraim Emerton (New York, 1932), pp. 147–8.

[42] Ibid., 6.6., p. 404: 'recognoscat se veram penitentiam non posse peragere, per quam ad eternam vitam valeat pervenire, nisi arma deponat ulteriusque non ferat nisi consilio religiosorum episcoporum pro defendenda iustitia.' This passage is not translated in the *Correspondence*.

[43] *Register*, 7.14a.5, p. 482.

[44] John Gilchrist, 'The Reception of Pope Gregory VII into the Canon Law,' *ZRG KA* 69 (1973):35–82 and 76 (1980):192–239.

Gregory's vigorous advocacy of the use of force in the pursuit of justice left an abiding imprint on the western Christian tradition and that Christians, and perhaps especially the clergy, have rarely looked back since then to the time before him. On this issue, however reluctant they may be to admit it, Gregory VII permanently moved western Christianity away from its former position.

The second point is partly related to the first, for Gregory's passion for justice was such as to obscure any distinction between the 'just' and the 'holy.' He may not have been atypical in this respect, for a distinguished historian of the crusades has questioned whether the customary distinction drawn between 'holy' and 'just' wars is valid before the sixteenth century.[45] Even if learned men in the High Middle Ages maintained such a clear distinction (and it is not clear whether they did), in the day-to-day thinking of most people, such fine distinctions did not really exist. In short, in the eleventh and early twelfth centuries the atmosphere was such that a war that was conceived to be just – and, as Erasmus later pointed out, who ever doubted the justice of his own cause? – could be very easily understood to be 'holy,' especially if one thinks not in terms of a simplistic binary choice between 'just' and 'holy,' but rather of a continuum from 'just' to 'righteous' to 'holy.' If this catena of observations and inferences is even in part true, then it was very easy under the circumstances for 'warfare,' at whatever level, to have strongly religious or sacral overtones for its participants.

The third point about Gregory concerns his position on the clergy and arms, although it is admittedly a kind of argument *ex silentio*. It may or may not be telling that of the great spate of condemnations of such behavior by major councils, often directed by popes or their legates, between 1049 and 1095, only one dates from his entire twelve-year pontificate, that of Poitiers of 1079. Furthermore, although in one letter Gregory condemned clerics who had borne arms *and* committed murder, the penalties he imposed were milder than those customarily prescribed (40 days' imprisonment, public humiliation, and fourteen years of fasting commuted to two during Lent).[46] Gregory himself was prepared to lead some kind of 'crusade' in 1074, believed prelates could organize and direct campaigns against the enemies of the Church, and was certainly perceived by hostile churchmen like Wibert of Ravenna and the monk of Hersfeld as commissioning bishops not merely to lead troops, but to shed blood.[47]

---

[45] Jonathan Riley-Smith, in a review of Hehl's *Kirche und Krieg* in the *JEH* 33 (1982):290–1. Although Brundage, 'Holy War,' pp. 116–25, believes that the medieval lawyers considered holy wars as a subset of the just war and that not every just war was a holy war, the evidence he provides of such a clear and sharp distinction is not very convincing.

[46] *The Epistolae Vagantes of Pope Gregory VII*, ed. and tr. H. E. J. Cowdrey (Oxford, 1972), pp. 151–2, no. 68.

[47] Erdmann, *Origin*, pp. 179, 256–61. Brundage, 'Holy War,' pp. 104–5, essentially agrees with historians like Erdmann who see the role of Gregory VII as crucial in the evolution of the idea of holy war, for he went beyond the defensive emphasis of those of his predecessors, who connected fighting for righteousness with the remission of sin, to embrace more aggressive wars on behalf of

Now this changing atmosphere in which religion and war drew ever closer together perhaps need not have necessarily have engaged the clergy, but it did. Parish priests were increasingly ordered to participate in the peace militias enforcing the Peace and Truce of God. Although required only to organize parishioners and carry banners, they were sometimes so easily swept into a more combative role in these righteous wars that the provisions of the Peace and Truce of God came routinely to stipulate that only 'clerics not bearing arms' were entitled to protection.[48] This vigorous clerical engagement reached its denouement around 1044, when a rampaging peace army, originally launched in 1038 by Archbishop Aimo of Bourges, was savagely crushed by Odo of Deol. According to the chronicler, André of Fleury, more than 700 clerical dead lay on the battlefield.[49] It was in part against such conduct that the reformers directed their repeated renewal of the ancient prohibition between 1049 and 1079.

Nevertheless, it was, as we have seen, on the battlefields of the holy wars of the next century, especially those fought in the Holy Land itself, that clerical armsbearing came to be legally sanctioned in two different ways. First, in the presence of King Baldwin II of Jerusalem, Patriarch Warmund of Jerusalem presided at a council at Nablus (the biblical Sichem) in 1120. Following the slaughter of Roger of Antioch's army in June 1119, described above, Patriarch Bernard was able, 'with his armed clergy and knights,' to save the city until the arrival of King Baldwin of Jerusalem.[50] In the patriarch's mind, evidently, necessity knew no law. Aside from the fact that this was the first instance in the history of Christianity permitting clerical resort to arms, the reason granted was rather sweeping, for it did not specify whose defense – of the cleric himself, of others, or of the *patria*? Nor, despite the emphasis on defense, did it restrict the kinds of arms which might be used or the ways in which they could be wielded. Finally, a cleric who took up the arms of a knight might, if penitent, revert to clerical status at the discretion of the patriarch (and the king). Dispensation from excommunication was explicitly conceded. Whether or not these canons became the law of the kingdom of Jerusalem has been a matter of considerable debate.[51] These epoch-making precedents were in any event not to be followed in Europe itself for many decades.

The second development is much better known and was beginning on

Christianity and the papacy. On Gregory's hope to personally lead an army of 50,000 men to aid the Byzantines, see H. E. J. Cowdrey, 'Pope Gregory VII's "Crusading" Plans of 1074,' in Benjamin Kedar et al., eds, *Outremer* (Jerusalem, 1982), pp. 27–40.

[48] A list of no fewer than seven such conciliar decrees is given by Hans-Werner Goetz, 'Protection of the Church, Defense of the Law, and Reform. On the Purposes and Character of the Peace of God,' in Head and Landes, *Peace of God*, p. 266.

[49] Erdmann, *Origin*, pp. 63–4.

[50] Kedar, 'Origins,' pp. 324–5.

[51] Ibid., pp. 310–35, who believes that they did. One reason for doubt is that William of Tyre, the greatest crusade historian who wrote his chronicle between c.1170 and 1184, not only did not list the canons of Nablus, but also expressed directly and indirectly his disapproval of armsbearing clergy (ibid., pp. 328–9).

the crusading frontiers at about the same time as the synod of Nablus: the emergence of the military-religious orders. Complex in origin and constitution, all these orders had as one of their constitutive elements (besides priest-chaplains, working lay brothers, and usually also physicians) professed lay brothers who were warriors who also took vows, lived according to a monastic rule, sang the divine office, and submitted themselves to canonical discipline. However much the popes may have disapproved of such developments and the canonists avoided talking about them,[52] the fact is that the popes did allow them to come into existence and remain in existence, and they marked yet another stage in the disintegration of the old barriers between religion and war.

Insofar as one may assign personal responsibility to particular individuals in bringing about such a sea change, two usually attract attention. The first is, again, Pope Gregory VII, who not only linked force and the pursuit of justice in an original way, but also gave the old concept of the *miles* or *militia Christi* a decidedly new twist. Instead of identifying these terms in the traditional metaphorical ways with spiritual struggle, monasticism, or the clergy, he consistently employed them literally with reference to knights fighting on the battlefields of Christendom. Furthermore, as Ian Robinson has convincingly argued, Gregory viewed this as *the* new way for laymen to gain absolution from sin and hence salvation. This connection lent distinctive definition to the 'lay order' and undercut the customary course of withdrawing from the world into the cloister, the better to insure one's salvation. By implication, the lay Christian warrior, rightly ordered, was elevated partly at the expense of the monk.[53] It took some time for the implications of such ideas to sink in and work themselves out, but they did by the second quarter of the twelfth century. It is significant that Bernard of Clairvaux (1090–1153), the most influential man of the second quarter of the twelfth century, both wrote the Rule of the Templars and defended this new phenomenon against its critics with words powerful, novel, and ominous:

This is, I say, a new knighthood and one unknown to the ages gone by. It ceaselessly wages a twofold war against both flesh and blood and against a spiritual army of evil in the heavens. When someone strongly resists a foe in the flesh, relying solely on the strength of the flesh, I would hardly remark it, since this is common enough. And when war is waged by spiritual strength against vices or demons, this, too, is nothing remarkable, praiseworthy as it is, for the world is full of monks. But when one sees a man powerfully girding himself with both swords and nobly marking his belt [with the cross], who would not consider it worthy of all wonder, the more so since it has been hitherto unknown? He is truly a fearless knight and secure on every side, for his soul is protected by the armor of faith just as his body is protected by armor of steel. He is thus doubly armed and need fear neither demons nor men.

52 See Jonathan Riley-Smith, *What were the Crusades?* (Totowa, N.J., 1977), pp. 70–3; Russell, *Just War*, p. 296; and Helen Nicholson, *Templars, Hospitallers and Teutonic Knights. Images of the Military Orders 1128–1291* (Leicester, 1993).
53 I. S. Robinson, 'Gregory VII and the Soldiers of Christ,' *History* 58 (1973):169–92.

> Not that he fears death – no, he desires it. Why should he fear to live or fear to die when for him is to live in Christ, and to die is to gain?[54]

Aside from Bernard's offhand suggestion that monks are commonplace, his words pulsate with an attraction to the warrior which earlier monks might well have found unseemly and even scandalous. Yet no matter how powerful Bernard's voice and persuasive his words, he needed ripe ground on which to scatter his seed. He found it in a Europe ready to hear such words, and in fact similar sentiments were voiced by some of the other most significant men of his age – Abbot Peter the Venerable of Cluny, Prior Guigo of La Grande Chartreuse, Bishops Otto of Freising and Anselm of Havelberg, and monks like Orderic Vitalis. Crusading was increasingly spoken of as an act of love and even as a form of the imitation of Christ.[55] Behind all of these novel ways of thinking was the consistent support of the popes, whatever misgivings they had from time to time.[56]

Aside from the extraordinary ability of men like Gregory VII and Bernard of Clairvaux both to direct and to give ringing expression to the most deeply felt sentiments of their times, there were two larger factors at work. One of them was the abiding belief, in medieval culture, in the superiority of the religious life, which was not about to be easily displaced in anyone's mind by consecrated knighthood as a superior form of religious life. Jonathan Riley-Smith has discerned the implications of Gregory VII's conception of a new Christian knighthood:

> But so dominant was the appeal of the religious life and so superior was its status that, within twenty years of the capture of Jerusalem [in 1099], professed religious were themselves taking on the role of warriors, usurping the special function of the laity. All contemporaries were struck by the fact that a new kind of religious life had come into being, in which the brothers could hardly have acted in a more secular way.[57]

This could not have happened, however, had there not been yet another factor which permitted and perhaps even encouraged the incorporation of the fully armed, fully consecrated knight within the framework of organized religious life: *the structure of the clergy itself.* As was indicated in the Introduction, the boundaries between the 'clergy' and the laity in the Middle Ages were more permeable than we can imagine today. Clerical status was

---

54   Bernard of Clairvaux, 'In Praise of the New Knighthood,' tr. C. Greenia, in *Treatises III*, Cistercian Fathers Series 19 (Kalmazoo, 1977), ch. 1, pp. 129–30.
55   Jonathan Riley-Smith, 'Crusading as an Act of Love,' *History* 65 (1980):182; William J. Purkis, *Crusading Spirituality in the Holy Land and Iberia c.1095-c.1187* (Woodbridge, 2008), passim. The significance of Purkis' examination of crusading as a form of the *imitatio Christi* is underscored by the fact that this theme is scarcely mentioned in the otherwise very thorough treatment by Giles Constable, 'The Ideal of the Imitation of Christ,' in his *Three Studies in Medieval Religious and Social Thought* (Cambridge, 1995), pp. 143–248.
56   See Hehl, *Kirche und Krieg*, pp. 117–120; Nicholson, *Templars, Hospitallers and Teutonic Knights*, pp. 10–41; Barber, *The New Knighthood*, pp. 38–63.
57   Riley-Smith, 'Crusading as an Act of Love,' 182.

relatively easy to achieve by way of tonsure and ordination in one of the minor orders. It imposed no vows or systematic formation, training, or other requirements, while it conferred many potential benefits (clerical status at law, entitlement to benefices, and hope of preferment) and did not exclude marriage. Many clergy in the sacred or major orders had no specifically 'clerical' training, had few if any obligations, and led largely secular lives. Even within the more disciplined monastic world the boundaries were also problematic, for professed lay brothers (*conversi*) ordinarily took the same vows as fully professed monks, who technically did not have to take any clerical order except monastic tonsure – which even in the clerical order was itself not an order! Despite efforts on the part of the official Church to exclude clergy from secular occupations, the evolution of the 'tertiaries' or 'third orders' in connection with the mendicants in the later thirteenth century reveals only that such fluid boundaries became less porous rather than impermeable. It should thus not be surprising that easy interchanges between the two worlds occurred in the High Middle Ages.

The crusades, the emergence of the military-religious orders, and the articulation of the theory of the just war in the High Middle Ages are all dimensions of a larger acceptance of legitimate violence, which in turn depended on a major shift away from an earlier medieval focus on the objective act of violence itself to more subjective considerations, above all the intention which lay behind the act. Indeed, from the eleventh century onward one witnesses *an unprecedented emphasis on intention in theology and law*. It is well known that Peter Abelard, in his typically provocative manner, held that intention is the sole determinant of the morality of an act, but he differed from his contemporaries only in the extremity of his opinion, not its novelty.[58] Before 1047 Raoul Glaber had defended monks who had taken up arms for the right reason, love of their brothers, not of glory. Behind the success of the crusades in theory lay a partial triumph of Augustine's idea of a just war conducted out of love.[59] Such ideas, increasingly diluted, one can find in ever expanding concentric circles in the course of the twelfth century. Typical is John of Salisbury's passing comment in his *Historia pontificalis* on the discussions at the council of Rheims in 1148 on those who laid violent hands on clerics: 'Indeed everything which is not done maliciously, or with evil intent, ought by no means to incur such a penalty [as requiring papal absolution], and no hand should be called violent which helps to ensure another's well-being or good behavior.'[60]

---

[58] See the remarks of D. E. Luscombe, ed. and tr., *Peter Abelard's Ethics* (Oxford, 1971), pp. xxxii–xxxiii, and Allen J. Frantzen, *The Literature of Penance in Anglo-Saxon England* (New Brunswick, 1983), pp. 202–8. More generally, see *DTC* 7:2267–80; *DDC* 5:1462–64; *Dictionnaire de spiritualité* (Paris, 1937-) 7/2:1838–58; O. Lottin, *Psychologie et morale au XIIe et XIIIe siècles* (Louvain, 1942–60), 4/1:309–486.

[59] See Riley-Smith, 'Crusading as an Act of Love,' especially pp. 188–9 for references to Anselm of Lucca, Ivo of Chartres, and Gratian. Augustine, however, had stressed love of the enemy, whereas thinkers of the twelfth century thought in terms of love of one's fellow Christians.

[60] John of Salisbury, *Historia pontificalis*, ed. and tr. Marjorie Chibnall (corrected ed., Oxford, 1986), p. 10, c. 3.

Even earlier, St Anselm, archbishop of Canterbury (†1109), had in his own way stressed the necessity for the confessor to bear in mind individual psychology and similar considerations, the uniqueness of which R. W. Southern exaggerated.[61] For if one looks to Anselm's predecessor at Canterbury (also an Italian), one finds not only a harmony of approach, but also the applicability of such considerations to the clergy as well as to the laity. A remarkable instance of this new kind of thinking appears in a letter from Archbishop Lanfranc of Canterbury to the archdeacons of Bayeux sometime between 1082 and 1087:

> The bishop of Coutances has told me in his letter that a certain priest on an estate of his that lies within your jurisdiction has personally committed homicide in defending himself and his father against the man who subsequently died ... [A]fter how long a time, if ever, can a homicide be permitted to celebrate Mass[?] It is hazardous, my brothers, for me to give you an answer on this point when I know nothing whatever about the guilty man or his manner of life. If I could gain some knowledge of his life either by personal interview or by a report from trustworthy witnesses, I should be able to give you a ruling with much greater security, my brothers, on so grave a question. So examine his life, for that is one of the duties of your office: in other words, how he has lived in the past, how he is living now, whether he is doing penance with humility, whether he grieves and weeps, and above all whether he is determined to maintain physical chastity from now on and promises that he will maintain it until the end of his life. If you discern in him these and other similar signs that he is penitent, you can give him permission to celebrate Mass when his penance is complete. But if not, it will be hazardous for you and disastrous for him if with unclean hands he dare to sanctify the body and blood of Christ.[62]

This passage contains an enormous amount of material for rumination. What is central here is Lanfranc's genuine pastoral concern about the quality of this priest's whole life and the genuineness of his remorse, the principal considerations informing Lanfranc's penitential advice about what was a homicide, even though the priest had acted both in self-defense and in defense of another. While most people today would probably approve of Lanfranc's approach, we should remember that such a shift of focus away from the objective act itself toward intention, context, and other such subjective factors inevitably opened up large possibilities for misinterpretation, misuse, and perversion, especially in the long run (as the rationalizations, self-deceptions, and excuses offered for the Fourth Crusade would prove[63]).

Two other observations are worth making. First, Lanfranc knew his law, both canon and Roman, which he had learned in the schools of northern

---

[61] R. W. Southern, *Saint Anselm and His Biographer* (Cambridge, 1963), p. 125.

[62] *The Letters of Lanfranc Archbishop of Canterbury*, eds and trs. Helen Clover and Margaret Gibson (Oxford, 1979), no. 51, pp. 162–5.

[63] See Raymond H. Schmandt, 'The Fourth Crusade and the Just-War Theory,' *Catholic Historical Review* 61 (1975):191–221, and Alfred J. Andrea, 'Conrad of Krosigk, Bishop of Halberstadt, Crusader and Monk of Sittichenbach, His Ecclesiastical Career, 1184–1225,' *Analecta Cisterciensia* 43 (1987):26–46, especially 45–6.

Italy (especially Pavia) before his departure for Normandy around 1030.[64] We shall see shortly that it was very possibly Roman law in some form that for him mitigated the harsh provisions of canon law on this matter.[65] Second, Lanfranc specifically tied his willingness to be lenient to the priest's readiness to observe his vow of celibacy. Although Lanfranc had perfectly understandable reasons for making this connection between sex and violence, the fact that he did so and in this way was emblematic of major changes in attitude and policy in the Latin Church on both subjects which would foreshadow long-term themes in western civilization.

Oddly enough, perhaps the greatest combination of impulses promoting the taking up of arms by the clergy was a series of unintended, unforeseen, even ironic *consequences of the ecclesiastical reform movement itself.* Although many aims and themes impelled and undergirded this revolution, one dominant one is that the reformers sought to disentangle the Church from secular involvements and achieve its 'liberty,' its freedom *from* external control.[66] This was not peculiar, for this was also the aim of the aristocracy and of the newly emergent sector of society in the High Middle Ages, the burghers or bourgeoisie, who wished as far as possible not to be dominated or effectively ruled by anyone else. Similarly, the reformers wanted liberty for the Church as well, which resulted in the first set of ironic consequences of the movement. For from this determination to liberate the Church flowed a fundamental premise of the reform effort which then remained a keystone of Roman policy down through Vatican II: official and institutionalized mistrust of the laity. Among the more obvious results by the twelfth century was the exclusion of the laity from ecclesiastical elections and the withholding of the chalice from them in the sacrament of the Eucharist. Another was that since the laity could not necessarily be relied upon any longer to protect the clergy, the clergy might have to defend themselves. The popes found not only that they had lost the German emperors in this capacity, but also that their new 'protectors,' the Normans, were worse, with few redeeming virtues if any; and it is probable that, even if not easily documentable, that long experience shaped papal legislation on armsbearing.

But the consequences of this mistrust of the laity went much farther. As Pope Boniface VIII put it in the opening words of his bull *Clericis laicos* in 1296: 'That laymen have been very hostile to the clergy antiquity relates; and it is clearly proved by the experiences of the present time.' Even when one discounts here for rhetorical exaggeration and deep personal feeling, Boniface placed his finger on a long-term reality consequent upon the reform

---

[64] *Letters*, pp. 84–7, no. 14, and Margaret Gibson, *Lanfranc of Bec* (Oxford, 1978), pp. 36–7, 139–40, 143, 150.

[65] See below, pp. 126–7.

[66] The classic presentation of this aspect of the reform movement is still Gerd Tellenbach, *Church, State and Christian Society at the Time of the Investiture Contest*, tr. R. F. Bennett (Oxford, 1940). Another useful compendium containing many sources in translation is by Brian Tierney, *The Crisis of Church and State 1050–1300* (Englewood Cliffs, N.J., 1964).

movement and the intensely divisive issues it raised: hatred of the clergy. Who could blame the laity for anger at the clergy for wanting to have their cake and eat it too – independence from the laity and substantial control over the property which the laity had donated to the clergy? Violence against the clergy was the result, and about that councils and synods in the High Middle Ages complained at great length. Although it is impossible to prove quantitatively that violence against the clergy was more acute in the early or late Middle Ages than in the High, there is no question about the violent confrontations which occurred again and again in the twelfth and thirteenth centuries over elections and the other explosive issues involved. In the Anglo-American tradition one thinks immediately of Thomas Becket, but one should also ask: Who was there to protect him against assassins unleashed by royal drunkenness? Only clerics, whom Becket in curious fashion dismissed. In any event, Becket was scarcely unique in his exposure to lay violence.[67]

Becket was the odd man out, however, in his defiance of the compromises which inevitably had to be worked out with the secular powers and lay society; and these compromises, too, inadvertently sanctioned, not merely allowed, clerical engagement in military affairs. For in decisions made in the early twelfth century, above all in 1111, it was accepted that the Church would not surrender the lands and rights it had received from the rulers of Europe and that in return the Church was prepared to fulfill the obligations required or implied by such possessions, including military service. However fretfully, virtually all canonists in the twelfth century and thereafter came to accept this compromise and its implications. Needless to say, those men who rose to the episcopate were generally even more so inclined.

The shift in thinking and feeling on the part of bishops and abbots took place slowly and often subtly and can be illustrated in the testaments of two men separated by a half-century. The great Suger, abbot of the royal abbey of St Denis (1122–51), regent of France, and builder of the first great Gothic church, died in 1151. In his tract on his administration of St Denis he alludes to himself as a 'man of blood' and hopes for divine forgiveness.[68] In an 'Ordinance' issued in 1140/41 he is more specific, discussing the domain of Le Vexin 'which we, God helping, have rescued in the early days of our prelacy with great expense, and with a strong and (a fact now aggravating my conscience) armed hand, from the oppression of the bailiffs and other evildoers.'[69] Elsewhere he is more plainly factual in his accounts of involvement in military action and the work of fortification.[70] Nevertheless, nowhere

---

[67] One unexplored dimension of this problem in the twelfth century was whether a Christian killed by another Christian could be a martyr, which I suspect was part of the 'Becket problem,' which has been traditionally misdiagnosed by Anouilh and others as a problem of 'play acting' by Becket.

[68] *Abbot Suger on the Abbey Church of St.-Denis and its Art Treasures*, ed. and tr. Erwin Panofsky (Princeton, 1946), c. 25, pp. 44–5.

[69] Ibid., pp. 122–4.

[70] In c. 21 of his *Deeds of Louis the Fat*, trans. R. Cusimano and J. Moorhead (Washington, 1992), pp. 95–103, and in c. 12 of the 'De administratione' in *Oeuvres complètes de Suger*, ed. A. Lecoy de la Marche (Paris, 1867), p. 172 (a chapter which is not translated in the Panofsky edition).

does he seek to excuse himself or express any pleasure he found in wielding the secular sword. It weighed heavily on his mind and made him fear for his salvation.

Such dilemmas continued to bother more scrupulous consciences, but in a different kind of way by the end of the twelfth century. The change is beautifully illustrated by a fascinating letter written toward the end of the year 1200 by John of Canterbury (or Belmeis), a friend of Becket, canon of Lincoln, treasurer of York, bishop of Poitiers by the grace of Henry II in 1164, archbishop of Lyons by the grace of God from 1184 to 1193, and a monk of Clairvaux in his last years until his death around 1203. In response to an inquiry from William, bishop of Glasgow, he reflected on his own experiences as temporal administrator of the church of Lyons for nine years:

> I had a seneschal to whom I entrusted the responsibility and care for legal business, who according to the nature of the business dealt not merely with pecuniary causes but saw to the punishment of crimes and serious offenses in accordance with the custom of the country . . . But if the nature of the offense implied either the penalty of the gibbet or the cutting off of members, I took care that not a word about this was brought to me. It was he with his assessors who decided about such matters, since it was done without consulting me; of course I knew that it was I who gave him authority both to take up such cases and to decide them. But it gave me some confidence in ignoring the fact, that the holy men who were my predecessors in the see had followed this usage without being blamed for it . . . Next we proceed to your second inquiry. Clerics and such as have been advanced to holy orders, must be strictly prohibited from prosecuting in a secular court robbery or theft committed at their expense; or if they absolutely cannot be kept from so doing, then let them on no account venture to proceed to single combat, or the ordeal of red-hot iron, or of water, or any procedure of that sort . . . On account of the above-mentioned causes, and several others which were very strongly borne in on me, I decided, reverend priest of God, to offer in penitence and tears the little remainder of life which is granted to me by God, my Maker, and, if it may be, to have a foretaste of the joys of the contemplative life. For so long as I exercised the office of Archbishop of Lyons, it was inevitable that I should be involved in responsibility for secular warfare: constrained to pursue with the armed hand robbers and church-breakers and those infringing the peace of the highways, and to besiege, set on fire, and demolish their strongholds and castles; in accomplishment whereof the deaths from time to time occurred, not merely of the malefactors themselves, but of those who were in command. Wherefore now, throwing myself at the feet of your sanctity as a miserable sinner, I humbly beseech you to honor me for the pardon of my transgressions. Farewell.[71]

---

[71] The letter is translated in full in David Patrick, ed. and tr., *Statutes of the Scottish Church 1225–1559, being a Translation of 'Concilia Scotiae,'* Scottish Historical Society 54 (Edinburgh, 1907), App. 2, no. 30, pp. 288–92, where John is referred to by his other common suffix, of Belesmains (sometimes given elsewhere as Belmeis). He was apparently of comparatively humble birth and not related to the Belmeis family of Normandy; but his talents were such that Archbishop Theobald of Canterbury (1138–61), whose eye for ability was considerable, singled him out, along with John of Salisbury and Thomas Becket, for great careers in the Church. See Adrian Morey and C. N. L. Brooke, *Gilbert Foliot and His Letters*, Cambridge Studies in Medieval Life and Thought n.s. 11

Archbishop John reflects a new kind of 'two hats' thinking which resulted from the ecclesiastical revolution and its long-term effects. On the one hand, he was aware that as a cleric he was now held to a stricter standard than had been his holy predecessors with respect to the canonical prohibition on the shedding of blood in any form, and so he was accordingly more scrupulous. Yet at the same time in his 'temporal' capacity as administrator and protector of the lands of the archbishopric he had little compunction about wielding force to enforce the peace. The word 'temporal' is used here with caution, for his language is distinctly reminiscent of the righteous vigor with which the Peace of God had been, and was still being, enforced. (It had in fact been renewed by the first three Lateran Councils of 1123, 1139, and 1179.[72]) This splicing of the sacred and the secular, now dating back two hundred years to the beginnings of the Peace and Truce of God, had blurred the boundaries between the two realms to such an extent that Belmeis clearly, if not consciously, relished the task of destroying the fortresses of violators of the peace. He was of course genuinely distressed by the deaths of those who fell as a result of his commands, but such doubts were insufficient to restrain him from action. A bishop had two distinct jurisdictions, each with its rightful claims: In obedience to his royal master, he could now with good conscience participate fully in peacekeeping or military affairs as a baron of the realm short of actually spilling blood or encouraging others to kill.

The emergence of such ways of thinking and acting is nicely documented at about the same time in a chronicle covering the early years of King Richard's reign by Richard of Devizes, the sardonic monk of Winchester who reviled the archbishop of Rouen, Walter of Coutances, as a coward for reneging on his crusading vow. Once the king had departed, Richard of Devizes records that William, bishop of Ely and chancellor, expelled Hugh of Le Puiset, bishop of Durham, from the Exchequer: 'Scarcely leaving the bishop the bare sword with which the king's hand had girded him a knight, he took away from him the honour of the earldom, which he had held only a short time.'[73] Later, William had Hugh arrested with these words: 'I seize you, not as a bishop seizing another bishop, but as the chancellor seizing another castellan.'[74] Whether or not William actually said this, the words were entirely plausible by the end of the twelfth century.

The great reform effort resulted not only in antagonisms produced by disentanglement and in compartmentalized thinking encouraged by divided jurisdictions, but in the Church's achievement of its own jurisdictional sphere as well. As Maitland put it, the Church became a State.[75] The reasons

---

(Cambridge, 1965), pp. 43–7, 93–4, 203–4, 206–7, 286; and *The Letters of John of Salisbury*, 1, eds W. J. Millor, S.J., and H. E. Butler, rev. by C. N. L. Brooke (Oxford, 1986), pp. xxvii–xxviii.

[72] DEC, pp. 193, c. 15; 199–200, cc. 11–12; 222, c. 21.

[73] *The Chronicle of Richard of Devizes of the Time of King Richard the First*, ed. and tr. John Appleby (London, 1963), p. 10.

[74] Ibid., p. 12.

[75] F. W. Maitland, *Roman Canon Law in the Church of England* (London, 1898), p. 100.

for this development are complex: the jurisdiction which flowed from the possession of land, the jurisdiction which was logically implied over certain kinds of persons (clergy) and cases (marriages, wills, and, theoretically, anything involving sin), the highly indefinite jurisdiction implied by Christ's words to the Apostles ('Whatsoever you shall bind on earth . . .' [Mt. 16.18]), and also the pressure from people below looking to the ecclesiastical judicial system for justice because of the humaneness of its punishments and their hope of finding justice in that distant Eternal City, Rome. For all these reasons, and in intricate ways, the Church emerged from the conflict not only with a great deal of jurisdiction in the first instance, but also at the appellate level. The pope became the highest legislator and judge in Europe, the only monarch whose jurisdictional authority touched everyone in some manner or other; and he in his court became the supreme court of Europe until the Reformation. Analogously, many bishops (and some abbots) emerged from the conflict with heightened authority which resembled, even if it did not rival, that of the bishop of Rome. In all these instances one could and did infer implied powers to tax for the common good and to declare and conduct just war. All of this emphasized not only the what we today would view as the 'temporal' aspects of papal and prelatical power. It also stressed the importance of law in both resolving the prolonged conflicts over jurisdiction and, once the lines of demarcation had been drawn, making the system of ecclesiastical jurisdiction work. In a variety of ways, then, the reform movement inexorably elevated the role of law and of legal thinking in the Church, and for this reason what had earlier been handled as problems of morals or theology could be transformed into primarily problems of law. By 1150 Bernard of Clairvaux saw the danger that the Church was becoming a legal machine, but he protested against it in vain.[76] But he had also not denied the authority of the pope to launch just wars, and he had passionately espoused the new institution of the warrior-monk.

The Changing World of Law

This brings us to the actual realm of law itself, which, whatever its connections with the larger context in which it operated and evolved, also moved according to its own logic and rules. Now concurrent with – and partly stimulated by – the papal reform movement, a revival of legal science or jurisprudence was taking place in Italy in the eleventh century.[77] It came to center on the study of the *Corpus of Civil Law* compiled at the direction of Justinian (527–65), especially the *Digest*. To appreciate the full significance

[76] Bernard of Clairvaux, *Five Books on Consideration. Advice to a Pope*, tr. John D. Anderson and Elizabeth Kennan (Kalamazoo, 1976).

[77] For an excellent, brief introduction by a great master, see Stephan Kuttner, 'The Revival of Jurisprudence,' in Robert Benson and Giles Constable, with Carol Lanham, eds, *Renaissance and Renewal in the Twelfth Century* (Harvard, 1982), pp. 299–323.

of this revival is hard but crucial. For Roman law was not merely another legal system, not just the product of a defunct ancient empire, but the living law of the Roman Empire which had been legally resuscitated in the West on Christmas Day in the year 800. It had also been living administrative law in the Papal States for some time and thus had a particularly close identity with the Roman Church.[78] At the same time, the clarification of jurisdictions taking place from the later eleventh century onward prompted churchmen to develop an equally impressive *Corpus* of ecclesiastical or canon law.

Roman law provided several maxims which bore specifically on clerical armsbearing. Although the legal adage 'Necessity knows no law ' (*Necessitas non habet legem*) had some roots in Roman thinking and law, it was, as we shall see, Christian churchmen and thinkers in the Middle Ages who force-fully articulated this crisp principle of law.[79] The more evidently pertinent Roman one, acknowledging the right of everyone to self-defense, occurs in the *Digest*:

> ... all laws and all legal systems allow one to use force to defend oneself against violence. But if in order to defend myself I throw a stone at my attacker and I hit not him but a passerby, I shall be liable under the *lex Aquilia*; for it is permitted only to use force against an attacker and even then only so far as is necessary for self-defense and not for revenge.[80]

Both the careful restrictions hedging the right of self-defense and the refer-ence to the *lex Aquilia* should be noted, for they will reappear later. But the *Digest* also contained the same principle enunciated without restrictions: 'Cassius writes that it is permissible to repel force by force [*vim vi repellere*], and this right is conferred by nature. From this it appears, he says, that arms may be repelled by arms.'[81] Finally, a related principle of Roman law recorded in the *Code* recognized the right to use force to defend property, but again with restrictions: 'A person lawfully in possession has the right to use a mod-erate degree of force to repel any violence exerted for the purpose of depriv-ing him of possession, if he holds it under a title which is not defective.'[82]

The ease with which these principles entered ecclesiastical thought and discourse in the twelfth century rested in good part on their derivation from other legal traditions as well, not merely the Roman.[83] Most significantly,

---

[78] See Knut Wolfgang Nörr, 'Institutional Foundations of the New Jurisprudence,' in ibid., pp. 324–38 at 329.

[79] Kenneth Pennington has rejected the common misconception ascribing this maxim to the Romans, and pointed instead to its medieval elaborations: 'Innocent III and the Ius commune,' in Richard Helmholz et al., eds., *Grundlagen des Rechts. Festschrift für Peter Landau zum 65. Geburtstag* (Paderborn, 2000), pp. 349–66.

[80] *The Digest of Justinian*, 9.2.45.4, Latin text ed. Theodor Mommsen and Paul Krueger, English tr. ed. Alan Watson (Philadelphia, 1985), 1:291.

[81] *Digest* 43.16.1.27 (4:584).

[82] *Code* 8.4.1, in *The Civil Law*, tr. S. P. Scott (Cincinnati, 1932; repr., New York, 1973), 14:238.

[83] See Gaines Post, *Studies in Medieval Legal Thought. Public Law and the State, 1100–1322* (Princeton, 1964), pp. 8–9, 20–1, 241–309. The neglect of this enormously important subject in medieval legal research has been noted by Adalbert Erler, *Aegidius Albornoz als Gesetzgeber des Kirchenstaates*

the idea that necessity knows no law was discerned in Jesus' sharp and anti-Pharisaical views on the law and necessity (Mt. 12.3–8, 11–12; Mk. 2.23–3.6; and Lk. 6.1–9, 13.14–6, 14.3–6). The articulation of the principle underlying Jesus' words went back at least as far as Bede (†735) in his commentary on Mark, who found additional support in the Old Testament in the exculpation of the Maccabees for fighting on the Sabbath. It was this text from Bede which was formally incorporated in the *Decretales* of Gregory IX in 1234, significantly in the final section entitled 'On the Rules of Law.'[84] Here the pope was merely setting the final seal of approval on a principle which had long since triumphed in ecclesiastical thinking and was taken for granted by such diverse spokesmen as Bernard of Clairvaux, Francis of Assisi, and St Albert (†1214), the founder of the Carmelites.[85] Such thinking could also take a more modulated form, as in 'except for good reason'; in the legislation of the general councils, the breakthrough came in canons of the Fourth Lateran Council of 1215, where such exceptive phrases occur at least seven times.[86]

A more restricted application of this principle, but one with far-reaching effects in the history of the Latin Church, was the dispensatory character of the hardships imposed by travelling. As early as 397 a council held in Carthage in north Africa had accepted this principle thrice within two pages with reference to travel and absolution;[87] and it had also appeared slightly earlier in the so-called Apostolic Canons.[88] This frequency suggests that this was probably

(Berlin, 1970), pp. 74–82, especially 75. In the useful work by Johannes Pichler, *Necessitas. Ein element des mittelalterlichen und neutzeitlichen Rechts* (Berlin, 1983), the emphasis falls on the very late medieval and early modern periods.

[84] *Decretales* 5.41.4 (*CIC* 2:927): 'Quod non est licitum, necessitas facit licitum. Nam et sabbatum custodiri praeceptum est; Maccabei tamen sine culpa sua in sabbato pugnabant; sic et hodie, si quis iejunium fregerit aegrotus, reus voti non habetur.'

[85] Bernard of Clairvaux, 'Book on Precept and Dispensation,' in *Treatises I*, tr. C. Greenia (Spencer, Mass., 1970), p. 108; *S. Francis of Assisi. His Life and Writings as Recorded by His Contemporaries*, tr. Leo Sherley-Price (London, 1959), p. 213 (The First [unapproved] Rule of 1221, c. 9: 'And in times of obvious need all the brethren are to satisfy their wants in whatever way the Lord shall direct them, for necessity knows no law'); *The Rule of Saint Albert*, ed. and tr. Bede Edwards, O.D.C., Vinea Carmeli 1 (Aylesford-Kensington, 1973), c. 13, pp. 86–7 ('unless bodily sickness or feebleness, or some other good reason, demand a dispensation from the fast; for necessity overrides every law'). Even that stern pope, Nicholas I (858–67), accepted the principle in his own way in a text which Gratian adduced in his discussion of the clergy and war (C.23.8.15) [*CIC* 1:956]): 'Si ulla urget necessitas, non solum quadragesimali tempore, sed etiam omni tempore est a preliis abstinendum.'

[86] *DEC*, pp. 237–56, cc. 7, 9 ('urgent necessity'), 16, 21, 33 ('without a clear and necessary reason'), 35 ('without a reasonable cause'), 47 ('without manifest and reasonable cause'). By comparison, such phrases are absent from the decrees of the first three Lateran Councils of the twelfth century. It should also be noted that these provisions did not require obtaining the permission of a superior.

[87] *Acta et symbola conciliorum quae saeculo quarto habita sunt*, ed. E. J. Jonkers, Textus minores 19 (Leiden, 1954), pp. 127–8, cc. 27, 30 (both concerning travel), and 32 ('Ut presbyter inconsulto episcopo non reconciliet poenitentem, nisi absente episcopo et necessitate cogente'). C. 27 was incorporated in Gratian's *Decretum* in D. 44 c. 4 (*CIC* 1:157).

[88] 'The Ecclesiastical Canons of the Same Holy Apostles,' (p. 94 n. 11 above), c. 54, p. 265: 'If any one of the clergy be taken eating in a tavern, let him be suspended, excepting when he is forced to wait at an inn upon the road.' But whether this particular canon was influential on the West is problematical, for it appears that only the first fifty of the 85 'Apostolic Canons' were received there: see *Decretales Pseudo-Isidorianae et capitula Angilramni*, ed. Paul Hinschius (Leipzig, 1863; repr., Aalen, 1963), pp. 27–30.

not a great innovation even then. In any event, as will be seen, the necessities imposed by traveling would, from the thirteenth century onward, come to be applied routinely to clerical armsbearing.

The other, more specific principle of the right of everyone to self-defense was held to be the common heritage of the law of all nations and of natural law. Isidore of Seville had regarded it that way and was cited by Gratian at the very outset of his *Decretum*.[89] The more restricted case of the inculpability of killing a thief at night illustrates the circuitous paths of legal influence. St Augustine had already noted the parallels on this point between Roman law and Mosaic law,[90] and so with this triple authority behind it this principle, too, would pass into the corpus of canon law, although its applicability to the clergy had yet to be demonstrated. That also would occur in a circuitous fashion yet to be explained.

A related, yet even more indirect way in which Roman legal influence shaped the canon law on self-defense in the High Middle Ages was by way of the so-called 'Roman Penitential.' Although modern scholars have shown that this was composed around 830 by Halitgar, bishop of Cambrai, as a supplementary sixth book for his five-book tract on penance, Halitgar claimed that he had taken this extra book 'from a book repository of the Roman Church' (*ex scrinio Romanae ecclesiae*).[91] This, then, was no ordinary penitential, but one associated with the Roman see and easily thought to be its principal or sole penitential. The status of this penitential would presumably rise with the ascent of the papacy from the later eleventh century, and its influence would spread with the centralizing, regularizing tendencies of the papal monarchy. Significantly, on the issue of self-defense the Roman Penitential was milder than most other medieval penitentials, or at least it came to be by later addition.

> If anyone slays a man in a public expedition without cause, he shall do penance for twenty-one weeks; but if he slays anyone accidentally in defense of himself or his parents or his household, he shall not be under accusation. If he wishes to fast, it is for him to decide, since he did the thing under compulsion.[92]

---

[89] D.1.7 (*CIC* 1:2): 'Ius naturale est commune omnium nationum, eo quod ubique instinctu naturae, non constitutione aliqua habetur, ut uiri et feminae coniunctio, liberorum successio et educatio, communis omnium possessio et omnium cum libertas, acquisitio eorum, quae celo, terra marique capiuntur; item depositae rei uel commendatae pecuniae restititio, uiolentiae per uim repulsio. 1. Nam hoc, aut si quid huic simile est, numquam iniustum, sed naturale equumque habetur.'

[90] Post, *Studies*, p. 21.

[91] John T. McNeill and Helena M. Gamer, eds and tr., *Medieval Handbooks of Penance. A Translation of the Principal Libri poenitentiales and Selections from Related Documents* (New York, 1938, repr. 1965), pp. 295–7. The text of the Roman Penitential is on pp. 297–314.

[92] Ibid., p. 310, c. 79. The Latin text is printed in Hermann Schmitz, *Die Bussbücher und die Bussdisciplin der Kirche* (Mainz, 1883; repr., Graz, 1958), 1:485, who lists this passage exculpating self-defense as a later addition. By comparison, the penitential of St Columban (c.600) ordered that a cleric who kills his neighbor was to perform penance for ten years in exile (*Handbooks of Penance*, p. 252), while the later *Confessional of Egbert* (c.950–1000) prescribed degradation for any priest who killed someone, irrespective of circumstance or motive (ibid., p. 245). As late as the early fifteenth century the Penitential of Ciudad (c.1410–14) declared that 'A priest who slays a robber in self-defense shall do penance for two years' (ibid., p. 363, c. 124).

One senses that Lanfranc knew this passage and took it into account in deciding the case described above of the priest who killed in self-defense someone attacking both him and his father.

In applying so many disparate texts to contemporary issues the canonists discovered that everywhere they had to harmonize real or apparent discrepancies again and again. They may have been so inspired by the newly regnant obsession with logic or, more particularly, by Justinian's assertion that his *Code* contained no contradictions.[93] Whatever the reason, the canonists were moved to resolve such problems, and the principal tool they employed in the newly emerging culture of Scholasticism was the distinction – to distinguish again and again, in other words to divide and fragment.[94] It was above all Ivo of Chartres (1040–1115) who laid down this crucial pattern of harmonization by employment of distinctions.

One central distinction on which Ivo relied, which applied to the question of clerical armsbearing, was that between precepts and counsels. How were the words of Christ on turning the other cheek, or those of Paul on not defending oneself, to be construed? Christ Himself had implied such a distinction between precepts and counsels.[95] Instead of relying on the metaphorical mode of interpreting such words favored since at least the time of Augustine, the canonists of the High Middle Ages approached the matter in a more juridical way. Were these words to be understood as minimal mandates or laws binding on all, or instead as counsels or recommendations to those seeking perfection and perhaps capable of approximating it? Were they, in other words, obligations or options? When the issue is stated this way, the only sensible, seemingly humane, and perhaps even scripturally defensible answer to that question was that these were counsels. And that, with a few significant exceptions, was the answer that most theologians and canonists accepted in the twelfth century.

But was this a counsel binding on the 'elect of Christ' (*sors Christi*) dedicated to ministry and to following the evangelical counsels of perfection, that is, the clergy and, in particular, monks? This was a question which the thinkers of the High Middle Ages seem not to have asked, not necessarily out of hypocrisy or avoidance, but probably and simply because since Christian antiquity the evangelical counsels had consisted of poverty, chastity, and obedience. Given this background, it makes sense that it would have occurred to no one in the twelfth century to ask whether turning the other cheek was demonstrably a mandate binding on the clergy.

[93] Noted by Kuttner, 'Revival of Jurisprudence,' p. 310.
[94] See Stephan Kuttner, *Harmony from Dissonance. An Interpretation of Medieval Canon Law*, Wimmer Lecture 10 (Latrobe, Penn., 1960).
[95] See Mt. 19.11–12, and cf. Mt. 19.21 with Mk. 10.21 and Lk. 18.22.

The Response of the Canonists

Let us now turn to the changes which did take place in canon law affect-ing armsbearing.[96] Interestingly, the canonists proved more conservative than one might have expected, given the changes taking place within and without the world of law. Burchard of Worms (†1025) and the anonymous compiler of the *Collection of Canons in Five Books* (third quarter of the elev-enth century) adhered to the old prohibition and cited appropriate texts.[97] However much Ivo of Chartres developed the theory of crusading waged as an act of love, he also reiterated the ancient ban at the turn of the twelfth century.[98] One canonist who did not was Anselm of Lucca, whom Erdmann called the first great Gregorian canonist. Citing Gregory the Great, Anselm argued that churchmen could under certain circumstances declare war, not to mention encouraging troops to fight and ordering pursuit and spoliation of the enemy.[99]

Although Anselm was too partisan to command universal respect, the texts he cited were taken over a few decades later by the preeminent canonist of the century, the elusive Camadolese monk of Bologna, Gratian.[100] Gratian, too, wanted to hold back, but for various reasons he could not. Around 1140 he issued his *Concordance of Discordant Canons* or, as it is usually known, the *Decretum*. It was soon accepted as the definitive *summa* or handbook of canon law, even though it lacked official character, since it had been neither commissioned nor promulgated by the pope. But Gratian was balanced in his treatment, came along at the right time after decades of furor had quieted down, provided for canonists the counterpart to Abelard's *Sic et non* and Peter Lombard's *Books of Sentences* for theologians, and was prodigiously learned. He cited many more sources – scriptural, patristic, conciliar, and papal – and worked more successfully to resolve their discrepancies than had any of his predecessors. The result was a volume which exceeded in length all the official papal collections of the next two centuries put together.[101]

Gratian dealt with most of the issues relating to the clergy and arms in the two major parts of his work, the Distinctions (D.) and the Causes or Cases

---

[96] For a succinct yet thorough survey of medieval canon law, see James A. Brundage, *Medieval Canon Law* (London-New York, 1995). There is also a good, short article in *DMA* 7:408–17.

[97] Burchard of Worms, *Decretorum libri XX*, 2.201–2, in PL 140:661–2; *Collectio canonum in V libris (Lib. I-III)*, ed. M. Fornasari, CCCM 6 (Turnhout, 1970), 3.249, p. 436.

[98] Ivo of Chartres, *Decretum* 5.332, 6.120 and 286, and *Panormia* 3.168, in PL 161:424, 474, 504–5, 1169.

[99] See Erdmann, *Origin*, pp. 241–7, and Kathleen Cushing, *Papacy and Law in the Gregorian Revolution. The Canonistic Work of Anselm of Lucca* (Oxford, 1998), pp. 129–38.

[100] On his much debated identity, see Kuttner, 'Revival of Jurisprudence,' pp. 320–22; René Metz, 'Regard critique sur la personne de Gratien, auteur du Decret (1130–1140), d'après les résultats des dernières recherches,' *Revue des sciences religieuses* 58 (1984):64–76. For a report on Gratian's relationship to his predecessors, see Peter Landau, 'Neue Forschungen zu vorgratianischen Kanonessammlungen und den Quellen des gratianischen Dekrets,' *Ius Commune* 11 (1984):1–30.

[101] See, most recently, *Le Décret de Gratien revisité. Hommage à Rudolf Weigand*, a special issue of *Revue de droit canonique* 48/2 (1998), and Anders Winroth, *The Making of Gratian's Decretum* (Cambridge, 2000).

(*Causae*) (C.). In the very first Distinction Gratian cited Isidore of Seville's definition of natural law which included the principle of legitimate repulse of violence with violence.[102] How this affected Gratian's method of reconciling oppositions became clear in Distinction 50, where he considered impediments to priestly ordination. At one point he confronted contradictory statements on whether a priest who had shed blood remained irregular for life. Pope Nicholas I, ever tough-minded, had decided that a priest who had killed a pagan, even in self-defense, had to be degraded to a lower order and remain in it for life, whereas a synod of Lerida of 524 had permitted a cleric who had been forced to shed blood during a siege (*in obsessionis necessitate*) could resume his office after doing penance for two years. Gratian bridged the discrepancy by viewing the possibility or impossibility of escape as the linchpin. If killing were unavoidable to save one's life, then punishment should not be for life. In his determination to harmonize opposing texts Gratian thus introduced the criterion of unavoidability and thus mitigated the harshness of the old rule.[103] Most later canonists accepted this solution,[104] and 175 years later a pope would draw the logical corollary from this premise and retreat another step from the rigor of the old law.[105]

In the Causes Gratian treated at some length thirty-six particularly thorny problems. In Cause 23 he addressed the matter of war and the Church in its full range in eight questions, in the last of which he took up the specific issue of the clergy and arms. In this question alone he cited thirty-four authorities, to which he added introductory comments or glosses. Scholars who have studied Gratian's positions intensively have not reached complete accord, and no attempt will be made here to supersede or harmonize them.[106] It seems fair to say, however, that in his heart Gratian was decidedly conservative. The prefatory statement (*principium*) begins with the assertion that 'It is easily proved that neither bishops nor any other clerics may take up arms either on their own authority or that of the Roman Pontiff' and ends with the two most favored texts invoked in this connection, Ambrose's 'The arms of a bishop are tears and prayers' and Paul's 'Do not defend yourselves, my brothers' (Rom. 12.9).[107] It is intriguing to note that Gratian the canonist adhered stubbornly to these words, whereas theologians like Abelard were already beginning to skirt them.[108] Finally, neither here nor anywhere else

---

102   D. 1.7 (*CIC* 1:2), citing *Etymologies* 5.4.
103   D. 50.6 and 36 (*CIC* 1:179 and 194). Stephan Kuttner, *Kanonistische Schuldlehre von Gratian bis auf die Dekretalen Gregors IX.*, Studi e testi 64 (Vatican City, 1935, repr. 1961), p. 360, points up and discusses fully the significance of Gratian's treatment here; and in general Kuttner's explanation of the evolution of the canonists' consensus on self-defense is by far still the best available (ibid., pp. 334–379).
104   Ibid., pp. 360–3.
105   See below, pp. 141.
106   Cf. Russell, *Just War*, pp. 72–85; Hehl, *Kirche und Krieg*, pp. 76, 90–105; Brundage, 'Holy War,' pp. 106–9.
107   C.23 q.8 *principium* 1 (*CIC* 1:953): 'De episcopis uero uel quibislibet clericis, quod nec sua auctoritate, nec auctoritate Romani Pontificis arma arripere ualeant, facile probatur.'
108   For Abelard on Rom. 12.19, see *Petri Abaelardi opera theologica*, 1, *Commentaria in epistolam*

in the initial redaction of the *Decretum* did Gratian adduce any references to Roman law; these would be introduced only later.[109]

Nevertheless, despite his conservatism, Gratian opened a Pandora's box on these issues. This followed from his position as a scholar attempting to bring coherence out of the mass of texts he had assembled (as we have seen with Distinction 50); as a canonist or, more precisely, ecclesiastical crown lawyer attempting to conceptualize what the pope and other prelates were doing in a constantly evolving legal sphere; and as a churchman of the 1130s who had no choice but to accept what was and what was going to be. Thus he treated as a given the right of the pope as the supreme *princeps* of Christendom to declare wars and to authorize others to do so and to fight them, although he denied the authority of the pope to order other clerics so to fight. The authority of the emperor was another matter entirely.[110] At the outset of Cause 23 Gratian had announced that in question 8 he would ponder the problem 'Whether it is permitted to bishops or any other clergy to take up arms on their own authority or on command of the pope *or of the emperor?*'[111] Yet the initial sentence of the discussion in question 8 itself – 'It is easily proved that neither bishops nor any other clerics may take up arms either on their own authority or that of the Roman Pontiff'[112] – passes over imperial or royal authority in silence. Nevertheless, however reluctantly, Gratian accepted the duty of bishops to obey their royal masters in return for donations to churches, although he assiduously avoided the word *regalia*, tried to distinguish carefully among the obligations entailed by the possession of different kinds of property and rights, and stipulated that bishops had to secure the permission of the pope before accompanying royal military expeditions. Citing Christ's words to 'Render unto Caesar the things that are Caesar's,' Gratian thus acknowledged the legitimate claims of the temporal realm and rejected the arguments of his contemporary Gerhoh of Reichersberg that royal donations to the Church automatically shed regalian responsibilities. Nevertheless, although Gratian seems to have conceded implicitly that bishops might declare war only in virtue of their temporal jurisdiction, he denied to bishops and priests the right to bear arms with reference to Christ's warning about those who live by the sword, even though they could exhort others to fight in a just war.[113]

Pauli ad Romanos. Apologia contra Bernardum, ed. E. M. Buytaert, O.F.M., CCCM 11 (Turnhout, 1969), pp. 283–5 (= PL 178:944–5).

[109] See Kuttner, 'Revival of Jurisprudence,' (n. 77 above), p. 320 and n. 73, who summarizes the fundamental contribution of Adam Vetulani on this point.

[110] By using only the word 'emperor' Gratian reflects his own position in time and place – in northern Italy, legally part of the revived Roman Empire, in the early twelfth century, when the concept, later a commonplace, of 'the king as emperor in his own kingdom' was only about to be born. It is probably safe to assume that canonists outside the empire read the terms interchangeably.

[111] *CIC* 1:889: '(Qu. VIII.) Octauo, an episcopis uel quibuslibet clericis sua liceat auctoritate, uel Apostolici, uel inperatoris precepto arms mouere?'

[112] Ibid., 1:953: 'De episcopis uero uel quibuslibet clericis, quod nec sua auctoritate, nec auctoritate Romani Pontificis arma arripere ualeant, facile probatur.'

[113] The best discussion of Gratian's positions on these issues is in Hehl, *Kirche und Krieg*, pp. 76, 90–105.

Canonistic Thinking from Gratian through the Decretales

Gratian's *Decretum* set a new stage in the development of canon law. He completed the process, inadvertently triggered by the Peace and Truce of God movements, of neutralizing war as a moral and theological issue and transforming it into a legal one. With respect to the sources of that law, the *Decretum* essentially closed the book save for the decrees of general councils and papal legislation or decisions, which in the manner of the Roman emperors were usually communicated in letters or 'decretals.' Until the last quarter of the twelfth century canonists commented primarily on Gratian's *Decretum* and so are called Decretists. Thereafter their attention shifted more and more to the latest sources of law, papal decretals, whence the commentators from the late twelfth century onward are called Decretalists. With the issuance of the *Decretales* at the command of Pope Gregory IX in 1234 the terminology becomes a bit more confusing, for canonists after that date are variously called both 'decretalists' and 'later decretalists'.

Canonists were stimulated on a large scale – in Bologna, Paris, Oxford, Cologne, and many other places – to study the *Decretum* and these later sources. It is important to have some sense of chronological development here, because once a particular question or topic seemed settled or exhausted, they rarely looked back. Like modern scholars, they were interested in the latest debates and issues rather than old ones like the nature of precepts and counsels. This common tendency was reinforced both by the 'creeping legalism' of the Church in thought and practice and by the flood of papal legislation which required that canonists keep abreast of the newest developments. Little or nothing impelled thinkers, even theologians, to look farther back in time or to ask whether something was morally right. It is important, however, to remember that this transformation of habits of mind and outlook took place subtly and slowly, so slowly that few people if any before the late Middle Ages seemed to be sharply aware of, or disturbed by, what had happened.

The discussions conducted among the decretists and decretalists reveal this gradual yet steady erosion of the old prohibition on clerical armsbearing. For despite their many disagreements with each other, these scholars reached a kind of consensus on several issues which pushed beyond the barriers retained by Gratian. Since their ideas have been treated at considerable length by many fine scholars, it will suffice here to summarize the shifts that took place and to illustrate some of the variety in their thinking. On the matter of the regalian responsibilities of bishops, for example, the canonists dropped Gratian's fine distinctions among kinds of property and instead simply emphasized the distinction between bishops with and without regalia. Although they continued to insist that bishops on royal military expeditions not fight themselves, they dropped Gratian's insistence on their obtaining prior papal permission to join such campaigns.[114] As for the jurisdictional

---

[114]   Russell, *Just War*, pp 105–112, 115–6; Hehl, *Kirche und Krieg*, pp. 188–9, 221–5. John W. Baldwin,

authority to declare a just war, the decretists conceded that this belonged to all *principes* without specifying just who *principes* were.[115] The decretalists of the later thirteenth century were prepared to admit more: not only the right of prince-bishops to declare war, but even, in the opinion of one scholar, the authority of an ecclesiastical judge to declare a just war.[116]

On the more general principle of self-defense, the canonists continued to be aware of the seeming contradiction between Scripture and the principles of Roman and of natural law. With the principal exception of Huguccio, who rejected self-defense for the clergy on the basis of Scripture, the canonists by stages argued away the problem and arrived at the legitimacy of self-defense for all. It is worth stressing that they habitually construed this within the strict limits set out in Roman law: one may defend oneself only against illegal and immediate force, using minimal or proportionate response, only with defensive rather than vengeful intent, and never after the fact in reprisal. Those canonists who conceded the use of weapons by clerics in their own defense (and a few did not) stressed that such weapons had to be defensive in character. If someone happened to kill an assailant, even in case of necessity, the canonists generally concluded that this constituted an impediment to the ordination of a layman and to the promotion of a cleric to a higher order; but they failed to agree on whether a cleric was thus automatically suspended from his order.[117]

There were, furthermore, special circumstances to be considered, such as the killing of a non-Christian or of a thief at night, not to mention the larger issues of defense not of self, but of others (especially those on whom an injustice was being inflicted) and of things (especially ecclesiastical property or rather the property of the saint to whom the property had been given). On this kind of problem the decretist Master Roland had proposed a sharp distinction between clergy in major orders and those in minor orders. The latter, he held, since they could marry and revert to lay status, could carry weapons for the defense of the Church, whereas those in sacred orders could not at all.[118] This view did not win wide acceptance among canonists, although it would sporadically appear in diocesan legislation much later. Rufinus, writing around 1164, for example, dismissed Master Roland's position and maintained that the general prohibition on arms applied to all clerics except

Masters, Princes, and Merchants. The Social Views of Peter the Chanter and His Circle (Baltimore, 1970), 1:206, remarks that 'the primary concern of the Paris theologians was to investigate the military duties of prelates,' but devotes only four pages to this issue in a twenty-two-page chapter on 'Service in the Field' (1:205–27; see 209–10, 216–7). Of these Parisian theologians, only one, Robert of Courson, denied any episcopal obligation of military service derived from regalian lands, and that he did in a single passage which he elsewhere tempered.

115   Hehl, *Kirche und Krieg*, pp. 206–7, 248–51.

116   Brundage, 'Holy War,' pp. 110–1.

117   Kuttner, *Schuldlehre*, pp. 334–79; Hehl, *Kirche und Krieg*, pp. 133, 194–9, 236–8; Brundage, 'Holy War,' pp. 111–2; Russell, *Just War*, p. 107; Wolfgang Müller, *Huguccio. The Life, Works, and Thought of a Twelfth-Century Jurist*, Studies in Medieval and Early Modern Canon Law 3 (Washington, 1994), p. 137.

118   *Summa Magistri Rolandi*, ed. F. Thaner (1874; repr., Aalen, 1962), on C.23.8, p. 98.

for self-defense in extreme necessity and against pagans at the command of a superior (*contra paganos iussu maioris*). Johannes Faventinus and the anonymous author of the tract *Omnis qui iuste iudicat* followed Rufinus' way of thinking.[119] Sicard of Cremona, writing around 1180, allowed an even wider exception for clergy: defense of the faith.[120] But on the defense of property the canonists generally took a rather conservative line, inspired in part by a stringent decision by Pope Alexander III which was later incorporated into the *Decretales*.[121] Nevertheless, Raymond of Pennafort, the Dominican compiler of the *Decretales*, granted that clerics might fight in a just war when absolutely necessary.[122]

What is so striking in all these debates about self-defense, stretching over many decades, is that acceptance of the general principle for the clergy meant that killing in self-defense constituted *only* an irregularity and was not necessarily a sin. By the thirteenth century this kind of thinking was not peculiar to canon lawyers. St Thomas Aquinas is often cited for his denial that clerics, by the nature of their calling, could bear arms or kill malefactors.[123] What is far less frequently noticed is that on homicide in self-defense he took the same position as the lawyers (not that he had any choice about the law of the Church):

> A single act may have two effects, of which one alone is intended, while the other is incidental to that intention. But the way a moral act is to be classified depends on what is intended, not on what goes beyond such an intention, since this is merely incidental thereto, as we have seen already. In the light of this distinction we can see that an act of self-defense may have two effects: the saving of one's life, and the killing of the attacker. ... the controlled use of counter-violence constitutes legitimate self-defense, for according to the law 'it is legitimate to answer force with force provided it goes no further than due defense requires.'
>
> It remains nevertheless that it is not legitimate for a man actually to intend to kill another in self-defense, since the taking of life is reserved to the public authorities acting for the common good, as we have seen ... A person who kills another incurs a technical irregularity even if there is no sin, as in the case of a judge who condemns a man to death justly. That is why even a cleric who kills somebody in self-defense, intending only to protect himself, not to kill, incurs an irregularity.[124]

Thus the thinking of churchmen, whether they were secular or religious, canonists or theologians, had obviously come a long way from the tenth and eleventh centuries, when anyone, cleric or layman, who had killed another, even in battle, could still be subjected to long penances and harsh

---

[119] Brundage, 'Holy War,' pp. 111–2.
[120] Russell, *Just War*, p. 98.
[121] See Kuttner, *Schuldlehre*, pp. 377–9, on *Decretales* 5.12.10, which is discussed below on p. 139.
[122] Russell, *Just War*, pp. 128 n. 5, 187.
[123] *Summa theologica* 2a.2ae.64.4. For an extended discussion of Aquinas' distinctive position, see Russell, *Just War*, pp. 282–91, 300.
[124] *Summa theologica*, 2a.2ae.64.7. For accessibility's sake, I have used the translation of the English Dominican Fathers (here, 38:41–5). The legal text quoted is *Decretales* 5.12.18, which will be discussed shortly.

punishments. Furthermore, the seriousness of irregularity as sufficient punishment could be easily undermined if the dispensing powers of the pope, which were rapidly developing at precisely this same time, were ever to be exercised lightly.

What encouraged all these thinkers to go beyond Gratian, to take such additional liberties with the ancient prohibition? Did they do so on their own authority, or were they inspired by official legislation which guided the evolution of their ideas?

Canonical Legislation, 1123–1317

One almost looks in vain for such inspiration if one turns to the general councils of the High Middle Ages which were so numerous and acted on so many matters. Of the total of twenty-one ecumenical councils of the Christian Church held between 325 and 1965, exactly a third – seven – convened in the two centuries between 1123 and 1311. They have almost nothing to say about clerical armsbearing, in striking contrast to the repeated denunciations of the practice by the reformers between 1049 and 1079 (and again by Urban II at Clermont in 1095). Neither the first three Lateran Councils convened in Rome in 1123, 1139, and 1179, nor the two councils of Lyons of 1245 and 1274 addressed the issue. The greatest of all, the Fourth Lateran in 1215, *seemed* to offer no encouragement, for in canon 18 it not only renewed the old prohibition on clerical shedding of blood in any form, but also stipulated that 'no clerk be put in command of mercenaries or crossbowmen or suchlike men of blood' – a curious choice of words.[125] Canon 16 on the deportment of clerics passes over arms in silence, although it does contain two significant exceptive clauses. First, clergy were to avoid taverns 'unless by chance they are obliged by necessity on a journey.' Second, priests and minor dignitaries were not to wear cloaks with hoods during divine office or anywhere else, 'unless a justifiable fear requires a change of dress.'[126] These two major exceptions, travel and legitimate fear, would within a few decades come to be carried over to armsbearing.

A century later, however, the general council of Vienne in 1311–12 condemned clerics engaged in all manner of secular pursuits, including 'those

---

[125] *DEC*, p. 244, c. 18: 'Nullus quoque clericus rotariis aut balistariis aut huiusmodi viris sanguinum praeponatur.' These restrictions on command are undoubtedly significant. Mercenaries are soldiers whose services have been bought, while the Second Lateran Council had vigorously condemned the crossbow in 1139 (*DEC*, p. 203, c. 29). Clerics who found themselves, say, leading fellow inhabitants of their town in its defense could well have argued that this canon did not apply to them. So, too, might bishops who were commanding their own knights. Had the Fourth Lateran wanted to prohibit all command of troops by clerics, it could have said so.

[126] *DEC*, p. 243, c. 16. The principal glosses on the decrees of Fourth Lateran have been edited by Antonio Garcia y Garcia, *Constitutiones concilii quarti Lateranensis una cum commentariis glossatorum*, Monumenta iuris canonici A/2 (Vatican City, 1981); see especially pp. 64, 66, 206–8, 310–12, 427–8 for the glosses on cc. 16 and 18.

bearing arms.'[127] Oddly, however, a decree promulgated by the same council for the reform of Benedictine monks pronounced automatically excommunicated any monk who bore arms within the precincts of a monastery without the permission of his abbot.[128] What are we to make of these apparently contradictory texts? And how are we to explain the ever-widening loopholes of exceptions to the ancient prohibition by the canonists?

For the solution we must turn to the decisions or decretals of the popes themselves, the ultimate lawgivers and judges in western Christendom. Modern scholars have an occupational inclination to center on the works of other scholars, often to the exclusion or slighting of other sources;[129] and one sometimes gets the impression from studies in the history of canon law that canonists were 'in dialogue' with the pope (to use fashionable contemporary idiom), who seems to be treated as if he were but the first among equals (if that). Fascinating as the ideas and speculations of the canonists may be to later scholars, the canonists themselves knew perfectly well from whom they were taking their cues – the bishop of Rome, whose 'fullness of power' (*plenitudo potestatis*) they themselves articulated and whose crown lawyers they were. They paid very close attention to the words and deeds of the papal monarchs and sought to understand them and their implications. On the other hand, it will not do simply to say that the job of the canonists was to ratify and justify the pronouncements of their masters, for canonists like Bernard of Pavia and Bernard of Parma, at least on the matter of armsbearing, exerted some authority in their selection and interpretation of definitive texts, although their choices could have been overridden by popes had they transgressed acceptable bounds.

The popes were astonishingly active in their issuance of such decretals, usually in response to inquiries or problems remitted to them. The first great lawyer-pope, Alexander III (1159–81), sent out nearly 4,000 of them, while Innocent III (1198–1216) issued over 5,000.[130] Given the difficulties of transcription and communication in that age, it is small wonder that the canonist Stephen of Tournai pronounced Alexander III's epistolary legislation 'an impenetrable forest.'[131] This mass of material had to be reduced to manageable size again and again if the courts of the Church were to function effectively and in an up-to-date fashion, all the more so if the canonists were to isolate the fundamental principles governing papal judicial activity.

---

127 *DEC*, p. 364, c. [8]. This, like all the decrees of this council, was incorporated in the *Clementines* (at 3.1.1 [*CIC* 2:1157]).

128 *DEC*, pp. 370–4, c. [14] at 372 (*Clementines* 3.10.1 [*CIC* 2:1166–8]): 'Praefatae quoque sententiae [i.e., automatic excommunication] monachos infra septa monasterioroum sine licentia abbatum suorum arma tententes decernimus subiacere.'

129 For similar criticisms made in a different context, see my 'Fear and Confession on the Eve of the Reformation,' *Archiv für Reformationsgeschichte* 75 (1984):153–75.

130 *CLCE*, p. 27. Of the 1,963 chapters in the *Decretales* of 1234, 1,148 came from these two popes (ibid., p. 29).

131 Quoted in Robert Benson, *The Bishop-Elect. A Study in Medieval Ecclesiastical Office* (Princeton, 1968), p. 387.

Between c.1191 and 1226 five such collections of the most significant decretals were compiled (the *Quinque compilationes antiquae*).[132] The first was undertaken by the canonist Bernard of Pavia, and it was only the third, ordered by Innocent III, which was technically the first official digest authorized by the papacy (1209). Thereafter additions came with some speed for a while. The first comprehensive and authorized corpus was done by the Spanish Dominican Raymond of Pennafort and issued by Gregory IX in 1234 as the *Decretales*. Boniface VIII promulgated the *Sext* in 1298, and John XXII the *Clementines* in 1317. There were two later medieval collections as well, which were not officially issued and which contain nothing on arms.

Now if we look to these texts for the official law on clerical armsbearing, we may be initially quite misled. For in the section of the *Compilatio prima* treating clerical life and habits, Bernard of Pavia chose around 1191 to repeat the decree of the legatine council of Poitiers of 1078: 'Clerics bearing arms and usurers are excommunicated.'[133] This text was authoritatively repeated in turn in the *Decretales* in 1234 and has always been cited since then as *the* law of the Latin Church on the subject.[134] Yet if we turn to the commentary which came to be accepted as *the* interpretation of the *Decretales* in the second half of the thirteenth century, the *Glossa ordinaria* of Bernard of Parma, we read the following: 'Clergy may not bear arms except for just cause. Understand just cause as meaning that if they are travelling through dangerous places, they may then carry weapons to scare off robbers, but they may still not strike them.'[135] Bernard has here evidently extended to armsbearing the exceptive phrases of canon 16 of the Fourth Lateran concerning travel and fear, but this still does not answer the question why Bernard of Parma dared to make such a leap.

The heart of the answer lies, I believe, in the third quarter of the twelfth century, and the man more responsible than any other was Pope Alexander III (1159–81). The reconstruction offered here is only partial and tentative. We know that Gratian's *Decretum* as it left his atelier around 1140 contained no citations from Roman law and that these were added at some later point.[136] We know that Rolando Bandinelli, Chancellor of the Roman Church and the

---

[132]   *Quinque compilationes antiquae nec non collectio canonum Lipsiensis*, ed. E. Friedberg (Leipzig, 1882; repr., Graz, 1956). These will be cited as 'I Comp.,' 'II Comp.,' etc., followed by the book, title, and chapter numbers and by the page number in this edition.

[133]   I Comp. 3.1.2, p. 25. It would be interesting to know why Bernard chose this one of all the eleventh-century condemnations, which, incidentally, was the only one from the pontificate of Gregory VII.

[134]   *Decretales* 3.1.2 (*CIC* 2:449).

[135]   *Decretales D. Gregorii Papae IX . . . cum glossis restitutae* (Augustae Taurinorum, 1588), col. 1110, on *Decretales* 3.1.2: 'Clerici arma portare non debent. 23. quaest.ult.clerici. & cap.quicunque. sine iusta causa 2. Iustam causam intellige si per loca periculosa transitum faciant, tunc possunt portare arma ad terrorem latronum, licet percutere non debeant. argum.23.quaestio 3.' The legal references given are to C. 23 of the *Decretum*. Bernard of Parma (c.1200-c.1264), canon of Bologna and papal chaplain, prepared at least four recensions of his definitive *glossa ordinaria* on the *Decretales* between 1245 and 1263. On Bernard's gloss, especially its 'posthumous' history, Stephan Kuttner has remarked that 'nearly everything remains to be done' ('Notes on the Glossa ordinaria of Bernard of Parma,' *Bulletin of the Institute of Medieval Canon Law* n.s. 11 [1981]:86–93, at 87).

[136]   See the discussion in Müller, *Huguccio*, pp. 109–35.

future Pope Alexander III, when he was papal legate read at an imperial diet at Besançon in 1157 – over which Frederick Barbarossa presided – a provocative letter from the reigning pope (Adrian IV) concerning the source and nature of imperial authority in its relation to the papacy. We believe that Cardinal Bandinelli was somehow physically threatened by the German princes in their furor.[137] We know that it was in these years that Frederick Barbarossa came to rely on Roman lawyers at Bologna and that for the very first time the term Sacred Empire (*Sacrum imperium*) was officially used, implying sacral parity with the Holy Roman Church (*Sancta Romana ecclesia*). We know that when Rolando Bandinelli was elected Alexander III in 1159, some of the cardinals refused to accept him and elected instead a pro-imperial candidate, Victor IV, whose successor (Pascal III) in 1165 acceded to Barbarossa's wishes and canonized Charlemagne. We know that Alexander's entire pontificate was dominated by his struggle with Barbarossa, especially when the emperor was on Italian soil trying to make real there the claims of empire. Finally, we know that Alexander was an extraordinary lawgiver and that he, more than anyone else, shaped the canon law on canonization, the conferral of benefices, the system of vicars, marriage, papal electoral procedure, judges delegate, and papal appellate jurisdiction for hundreds of years to come.[138]

One salient facet of this struggle between Alexander and Frederick and, more abstractly, the Holy Roman Church and the Sacred (Roman) Empire was which of the two powers would be the more successful in appropriating Roman law and so, in a way, vindicating its claims to true 'Romanness.' As Hans Wolter has observed, 'As Frederick's idea of the function of the imperial office in the Christian world was largely shaped by the revived Roman law as modified by Justinian and Christianity, so did the pontificate of Alexander III seem to be determined by a canon law, developing consistently and establishing itself in practice, which was entirely able to make methodical use of Roman juristic categories.'[139] More specifically, Alexander's personal endangerment at Besançon may have triggered fears, later corroborated by the assassination of Archbishop Becket, that the clergy simply could not look to the laity for their protection and must instead look to themselves.

While some of these observations are speculative and probably would find only slippery grounding in the available sources, one fact is indisputable: from at least the pontificate of Alexander III onward the popes accepted the applicability of the right of self-defense to the clergy.[140] This

---

[137] For a brief account of the 'incident at Besançon,' together with excerpts from the sources, see Tierney, *Crisis*, pp. 100–1, 105–9.

[138] See now Anne J. Duggan, 'The Master of the Decretals. A Reassessment of Alexander III's Contribution to the Development of Canon Law', in Peter D. Clarke and Anne J. Duggan, eds, *Pope Alexander III (1159–81). The Art of Survival* (Farnham-Burlington, Vt, 2012), pp. 365–417.

[139] Hans-Georg Beck et al., *From the High Middle Ages to the Eve of the Reformation*, Handbook of Church History 4, tr. A. Biggs (New York-London, 1970), p. 58.

[140] Kuttner, *Schuldlehre*, pp. 344–6, 349–54, consistently identifies Alexander as the pope initiating these new developments; and in 1988 Kuttner confirmed in conversation with me what he had written in the 1930s about Alexander.

fact lends additional support to the convincing arguments that reject the traditional identification of Master Roland with Rolando Bandinelli or Alexander III,[141] for none of Alexander III's decretals employed Master Roland's crucial distinction between clergy in major orders and those in minor orders so far as armsbearing was concerned. Further research may reveal that an earlier pope made this crucial choice, but I suspect not. Incidentally, the texts discussed below only are those papal letters which passed through the filtration process of popes and canonists and were incorporated into the *Decretales*. They would not, of course, have survived this process of selection had the principles they embodied been in any way unacceptable.[142]

In this mass of texts, the principle at Roman and natural law of repelling violence with commensurate violence was accepted again and again – for the clergy as well as for the laity. An early decretal of Alexander III gave his reply to an inquiry as to whether someone who injures a clerical assailant needed to beseech papal absolution (since canon law ordinarily required papal absolution for someone who physically harms a cleric). No, Alexander replied, since all laws acknowledge the right to repel violence with violence.[143] Any ambiguity about the inclusion of the clergy under this ruling was implicitly resolved in a case, adduced in the same title, which concerned a priest who had led an armed rebellion, was captured and racked by the local count, died and was buried. The pope (it is unclear whether it was Alexander III, Clement III [1187–91], or Celestine III [1191–98]) absolved the count of the obligation of papal absolution, since the priest had transgressed all bounds in 'bearing arms not to repel but to inflict injury.'[144] The unqualified inclusion of the clergy under this principle appeared in a later decretal used in an entirely different context, the title treating the restitution of spoils. In it (*Olim causam quae*) Innocent III applied the Roman principle on violence to a case involving clerics on both sides.[145] It was this text which Pope Innocent IV later employed as a springboard for his consideration of a cleric's right to self-defense.[146] Finally, Innocent III also explicitly cited in another decretal (*Significasti nobis*) the principle in the *Code* of Justinian of responding to violence with proportionate violence.[147]

Interestingly, although this passage in the *Code* dealt primarily with the defense of property, Innocent's decretal was placed in the *Decretales* in Book

---

[141] John T. Noonan, Jr, 'Who was Rolandus?' in Kenneth Pennington and Robert Somerville, eds., *Law, Church and Society. Essays in Honor of Stephan Kuttner* (Philadelphia, 1977), pp. 21–48; Rudolph Weigand, 'Magister Rolandus und Papst Alexander III,' *Archiv für katholisches Kirchenrecht* 149 (1980):3–44. The conflation nevertheless continues, as witness Filippo Liotta, ed., *Miscellanea Rolando Bandinelli, Papa Alessandro III* (Siena, 1986).

[142] See Walther Holtzmann, 'Die Register Papst Alexanders III. in den Händen der Kanonisten,' *Quellen und Forschungen aus italienischen Archiven und Bibliotheken* 30 (1940):13–87.

[143] I Comp. 5.34.4, p. 63 = *Decretales* 5.39.3 (*CIC* 2:890).

[144] II Comp. 3.21.4, p. 87 = *Decretales* 5.39.23 (*CIC* 2:897).

[145] III Comp. 2.6.2, p. 112 = *Decretales* 2.13.12 (*CIC* 2:285–6).

[146] See Russell, *Just War*, pp. 134–5, 187.

[147] IV Comp. 5.6.2, p. 148 = *Decretales* 5.12.18 (*CIC* 2:800–1).

5, title 12, 'On voluntary or accidental homicide,' which was far more serious than self-defense.[148] The title consists of twenty-five chapters, each based on a different text: one each from Exodus, the Roman Penitential, Augustine's commentary on Exodus, Jerome, and a council held at Worms; then six decretals from Alexander III, one from Clement III, nine from Innocent III, three from Honorius III, and one from Gregory IX. This title provided much to choose from. The selection from the Roman Penitential (*Interfecisti*) declared that if someone killed a thief who could have been captured without killing, he should be barred from church for forty days and from all food and drink and contact with his horse and weapons. If he were a priest, he was not to be deposed, but instead should do lifelong penance.[149] There follows a conclusion by Augustine in his commentary on Exodus that he who kills a thief by day was a homicide, but not he who kills one at night.[150] Despite the implications of such texts, early decretalists of rigorous disposition often focused on c. 7, in which Alexander III decided that a priest who strikes a blow from which the victim subsequently dies is to be removed altogether from the service of the altar, or on c. 10, in which Alexander III had ruled that a monk who had killed two robbers lest they kill him was both irregular and guilty of sin.[151] On the other hand, in c. 9 Alexander decided that a cleric whose knife had accidentally killed another while they were playfully tousling was not at fault and therefore could be promoted to sacred orders.[152] Alexander also advised judges to take circumstances into consideration,[153] and he was already far from prescribing the stark punishments common until a century before.

Later popes retreated even further from any residual severity. In one letter Innocent III, who more than any other pope advanced the theory of the fullness of power inherent in the papal office, including the right to dispense from the law, responded to the archbishop of Besançon, in whose diocese a young monk had killed a young boy moving surreptitiously about the church and had hence become irregular. The archbishop wanted to know whether the monk ought to seek a dispensation, and Innocent was amenable to granting it if the monk had believed this action 'necessary and useful' under the circumstances.[154] A comparable reliance on the conscience and judgment of the accused can be discerned in a verdict from Pope Honorius III (1216–27). A priest named Pelagius was staying at a castle attacked by enemies of the faith, and in its defense he had killed someone. Moved by remorse and fear of irregularity, he had written to the pope, who answered that under these circumstances 'you should reverently abstain from the ministry of the altar,

---

[148] *CIC* 2:793–804.
[149] *Decretales* 5.12.2 (*CIC* 2:793–4).
[150] Ibid. 5.12.3 (*CIC* 2:794).
[151] *Decretales* 5.12.7 and 10 (*CIC* 2:796, 797).
[152] Ibid. 5.12.9 (*CIC* 2:797).
[153] Ibid. 5.12.6 (*CIC* 2:794–6).
[154] *Decretales* 5.12.15 (*CIC* 2:799).

since it would be more advisable, when in this kind of doubt, to refrain rather than celebrate boldly [the Mass].'[155] Honorius not only did not inform the priest that this action automatically rendered him irregular at canon law, but essentially left the judgment up to him. Furthermore, in this, as in almost all the other cases, the focus fell on irregularity rather than sinfulness, and in no case was excommunication cited as an automatic punishment.

The next official addition to the corpus of canon law was the *Liber sextus* or *Sext* of Boniface VIII (1298). It bore the strong impress of Pope Innocent IV (1243–54), the most distinguished of the later decretalists. He often commented on his own decisions as pope and issued his own learned commentary on the *Decretales* in 1250. On his own authority, Innocent believed, a prelate could declare and conduct wars, but not fight directly in them. He could exhort soldiers to fight and take prisoners, but not to kill; and if ignorant of any death resulting from his orders, he was not guilty of homicide and left to his conscience. As for self-defense, a cleric could legitimately throw stones to protect himself and others and did not incur irregularity as long as he killed no one.[156] These views both summarized the consensus among canonists and doubtless overcame residual doubts, and it was presumably Innocent's expression of his own views which permitted Bernard of Parma to gloss the *Decretales* as he did sometime before his own death in 1263.[157]

Innocent's own decretals, however, constituted official legislation, and one in particular which Boniface VIII incorporated in the *Sext* had tremendous significance with reference to arms and the clergy. Entitled *Dilecto*, it was, according to many manuscripts, promulgated as a decree of the First Council of Lyons in 1245. Although it was not in fact, it won wide circulation and was dated to the early years of Innocent's pontificate. It was addressed to the dean of Orleans or Arles, who had asked what measures he could employ against a bailiff despoiling ecclesiastical property. Innocent replied that since all laws permit the repulsion of force by force, it was entirely licit to have recourse to violence in this case; but since temporal force does not always suffice, only then it is permissible to deploy spiritual weapons such as excommunication against the bailiff. Innocent's advice to use temporal force first, so as not to vitiate the spiritual, runs contrary to what many people today would probably expect and provides a startling insight into the attitudes of a central pope of the thirteenth century, but his assumption of the legitimacy of using physical force went back at least to the time of Alexander III.[158]

---

[155] *Decretales* 5.12.24 (CIC 2:803–4).

[156] The Latin text, together with summary, is given in large part in Russell, *Just War*, p. 187.

[157] See above, p. 136.

[158] The principal glossator of the *Sext*, Johannes Andrea, on this passage opined that (1) although it was licit to defend not only one's person, but also property, it was not licit to resort to quite the same extreme measures to defend property as to protect life; and (2) everyone is bound to defend his neighbor (which he furthermore asserted twice and grounded in C.23.3). See *Liber sextus decretalium . . . Clementis papae V. constitutiones. Extravagantes. .* (Augustae Taurinorum, 1588), cols. 777–9. The relevant passages are as follows: 'ergo licet defendere non solum personam: sed bona: tamen pro defensione bonorum non licet se seuire, sicut pro defensione personae'; 'Not.

The final official addition to the corpus, the *Clementines*, was initially drawn up by Clement V (1309–14), who seems to have issued them tentatively at the Council of Vienne, but whose death precluded their definitive declaration; and the text as finally promulgated by John XXII (1316–34) in 1317 doubtless includes some additions and emendations.[159] Two relevant sections were decrees of the Council of Vienne briefly discussed above. The first, treating clerical deportment on a broad scale, in one phrase condemned clerical armsbearing without qualification. The second forbade Benedictine monks to bear arms within the confines of their monasteries without the permission of their abbots. The most curious text of all in the *Clementines* is incorrectly listed by many manuscripts as a decree of Vienne, but it was not. Like so many other texts germane to armsbearing, it does not touch the issue directly, although its bearing is obvious. Entitled *Si furiosus*, it read this way:

> If a madman, a child, or someone sleeping should wound or kill a man, he incurs no irregularity. And we think the same about him who, unable to escape death otherwise, kills or wounds an attacker.[160]

The source of this terse passage deserves brief speculation. Was Pope Clement drawing the logical corollary of Gratian's resolution of conflicting texts in D. 50 over a century and a half earlier by using the criterion of unavoidability? The explicit allusion to this criterion makes this connection very likely, but two alternatives seem possible as well. The first is the passage from the Roman Penitential adduced above which entirely exculpates someone who must kill in defense of himself or of someone else. Giovanni da Legnano, writing about half a century after the issuance of the *Clementines* and probably inspired by the reference given in the passage from the *Digest* quoted above, found here an application of the *lex Aquilia* in the *Institutes* of Justinian concerning legal responsibility.[161] It is of course possible that the cumulative weight of thinking represented by these different sources and legal traditions, rather than any one particular text, shaped the formulation of this decree. In any event, the pope had now dropped the automatic irregularity previously

---

quod quilibet tenetur defendere suum proximum ab iniuria eidem proximo illata'; and 'ergo quilibet tenetur vicinum suum, & amicum suum defendere, ut 23.q.3. non inferenda.'

159 See Jacqueline Tarrant, 'The Clementine Decrees on the Beguines: Conciliar and Papal Versions,' *Archivum historiae pontificiae* 12 (1974):301, and 'The Manuscripts of the Constitutiones Clementinae. Part I: Admont to München,' *ZRG KA* 70 (1984):68.

160 *Clementines* 5.4.c.un.: 'Si furiosus, aut infans seu dormiens hominem mutilet vel occidat: nullam ex hoc irregularitatem incurrit. Et idem de illo censemus, qui, mortem aliter vitare non valens, suum occidit vel mutilat invasorem' (*CIC* 2:1184).

161 Legnano, *Tractatus*, p. 264: 'But can a clerk be blamed who does not flee, but waits for one who is attacking and kills him in self-defence? It seems that he must be, by the text of Clement, where he says 'who could not avoid death by other means'; this is proved by ff. Ad leg. Aquil., l. *scientiam, qui cum aliter*, whence the passage in Clement was taken.' The *lex Aquilia* is remembered in the *The Institutes of Justinian*, tr. J. B. Moyle, 5th ed. (Oxford, 1913), 4.3.2, pp. 166: 'To kill unlawfully is to kill without any right; thus a man who who kills a robber is not liable to this action, if he could in no other way escape the danger [*periculum*] by which he was threatened.' *Si furiosus*, however, significantly changes 'escape danger' to 'escape death.'

incurred by *anyone* who had no way to save his own life except to kill or wound an assailant. The word 'anyone' is emphasized to call attention to the fact that this ruling did not apply to the clergy alone, but to anyone seeking ordination who might have been previously rendered irregular in some such manner. It was thus in this oddly oblique way that yet another facet of the ancient prohibition fell away.[162]

From this great distance in time, we can see that by the early fourteenth century, then, canon law had slowly but decisively changed over the course of about two centuries on several central issues related to the use of arms and violence by the clergy. Broadly speaking, the law of the Latin Church now took these as givens: the *authority* of the pope and of other prelates wielding the two swords to declare and direct just wars; the *obligation* of bishops and other clergy to obey legitimate royal demands to serve in the military sphere as a consequence of their possession of lands donated by the laity; and the *right* of every cleric to defend himself against attack and even to kill or wound if necessary to preserve his own life without fear of irregularity, much less of sin.

If we adjust our focus slightly to look at the penumbral worlds between the 'clergy,' the regular clergy, and the laity in the twelfth and thirteenth centuries, we can achieve a different kind of retrospective clarity. However initially reluctant in the twelfth century, the popes came to approve a new form of organized religious life in the so-called military-religious orders. In the thirteenth century, lay confraternities came to be associated with the newly emerging forms of religious life, particularly the friars or mendicants. For the first time, the male branch came to be called the 'first order,' that for females the 'second order,' and that for affiliated laypersons seeking to live a modified form of disciplined religious life the 'third order' (whose members were therefore called tertiaries). The earliest and most conspicuous of these third orders developed in connection with the Franciscans, who happened to also have the most revealing legislation on armsbearing. The initial proposal of 1221 was drawn up by or under the supervision of Ugolino Cardinal di Conti, cousin of Pope Innocent III, dean of the College of Cardinals, protector of the Franciscans, and the future Pope Gregory IX (1227–41), who would issue the *Decretales* in 1234. The germane passage of this document (usually called the *Memoriale Propositi* or, sometimes, the Capistrano Rule) is c. 16 (out of 39): 'They shall not accept lethal weapons against anyone nor carry them on their persons.'[163] Here the concern was to try to exempt members of

---

[162] The gloss of Johannes Andrea is more noncommital on this canon than on Innocent IV's *Dilecto* (see above, p. 140 and n. 158). He simply notes that it is complex, involving three different cases in the first clause and four in the second; that distinctions are to be drawn between those already in orders (*susceptos*) and those to be ordained (*suscipiendos*) and between cases dispensable and indispensable; and that a great variety of opinions already obtained among the canonists. *Liber sextus decretalium . . .* , cols. 307–9.

[163] *History of the Third Order Regular Rule. A Source Book*, eds Margaret Carney et al. (St Bonaventure, NY, 2008), pp. 66–67: 'Arma mortalia contra quempiam non accipiant vel secum deferant.'

this third order from civilian military service, apparently a papal policy from at least 1226 through 1252.[164] On the other hand, in keeping with the spirit of the already well-established military orders, the popes were also harnessing pious bellicose energies to the defense of the Church in one form or another. Thus in 1261 Pope Urban IV approved the Rule of the Militia of the Blessed Virgin, article 23 of which declared it licit for the members 'to bear arms for the defense of the Catholic faith and of ecclesiastical liberty when it is specially demanded of them by the Roman Church.'[165] It was evidently under the influence of this kind of legislation, approved by the popes, that the definitive Rule of the Third Order Regular of the Franciscans was promulgated in 1289 by Nicholas IV, the first Franciscan to ascend the Throne of St Peter (1288–92). His bull, entitled *Supra montem*, contained twenty articles, of which the sixth stipulated: 'Let the brothers not carry offensive weapons with themselves, unless in defense of the Roman Church, the Christian faith, or their country, or with the permission of their ministers.'[166] This remained the Rule of the Franciscan Third Order until 1887.

If this sounds strange, even unbelievable, we have only to turn to turn to Thomas Aquinas, who had already died in 1274 and had asked, in one of the less familiar parts of his *Summa theologica*, 'Whether a religious institute [i.e., order] can be founded for military service?' Citing Augustine, Aquinas answered affirmatively that

> a religious institute can be founded not only for the works of the contemplative life but also for those of the active life, if they have to do with help to one's neighbor and the service of God, and not for obtaining some worldly good. But military service can be directed to the assistance of one's neighbors, not only as private persons, but also for the defense of the entire nation ... Consequently, a religious institute can be fittingly founded for soldiering, not for worldly goods, but for the defense of divine worship and the public good, or of the poor and oppressed, as stated in Psalms: 'Rescue the poor, and deliver the needy out of the hand of the sinner.'[167]

The logic of this position was carried out over two hundred years later in the legislation for the *First* Order of the Franciscans enacted in 1500, usually called the Alexandrine Constitutions after Pope Alexander VI. The very first statute ordered that, 'on pain of imprisonment, no one is to retain any

---

164 *Dossier de l'Ordre de la Pénitence au XIIIe siècle*, ed. G. G. Meersseman, O.P., Spicilegium Friburgense 7 (Fribourg, 1961), pp. 42–45, 61–64, nos. 3–4, 30–35.
165 Ibid., p. 298: 'Licet autem eis arma portare pro defensione catholice fidei et ecclesiastice libertatis, cum eis per Romanam Ecclesiam fuerit specialiter demandatum.' This is c. 23 out of a total of 89 articles (ibid., pp. 295–307).
166 *History of the Third Order Regular Rule*, pp. 76–77: 'Impugnationis arma secum fratres non ferant, nisi pro defensione romane ecclesie, cristiane fidei, vel etiam terre ipsorum, aut de suorum licentia ministrorum.' This repeated exactly the language in c. 28 of the provisional Rule drawn up by the Franciscan Apostolic Visitor Caro in 1284 (*Dossier*, p. 133, where this Rule is printed in its entirety on pp. 128–38).
167 Thomas Aquinas, *Summa theologiae*, 2a.2ae, q. 188, art. 3 ad (tr. by the English Dominican Fathers [New York-London, 1964–], 47:191).

offensive arms whatever or cause them to be made.'[168] Note that the prohibition applied to offensive weapons only. A later statute, 'On going about in the world,' threatened with excommunication and deposition from office those Franciscans 'who have discharged the office of spy, guard, notary, knight, and the like. And all the more so those who have taken up arms and made other signs of unsuitable defense, *except for the safety of the faith, their order, and their country in a way which is fitting for religious when and where it is necessary.*'[169] In short, the members of the First Order of the Franciscans had now largely been granted allowances for armsbearing very similar to those conceded to the Third Order in 1289.

How, then was this mass of complex legislation to be interpreted and taught by bishops, canonists, and theologians, particularly since it appeared that, oddly, the religious orders were evidently given greater scope to bear arms than the ordained clergy were? And has the Roman Catholic Church at any time subsequently rejected or modified these positions and principles, this 'revolution in law' which incrementally took place in the High Middle Ages? These are the subjects of the next chapter.

---

[168] *Chronologia historico-legalis seraphici Ordinis fratrum minorum* (Naples, 1650), 1:178.
[169] Ibid., 1:158: 'nisi pro fidej, religionis, atque patriae salute: eo tamen modo, quo religiosos decet, & quando, & ubi oportet' (emphasis added). For reasons of space, the subject of the legislation of the religious orders on armsbearing must be deferred to another volume.

CHAPTER 5

THE CANON LAW OF THE ROMAN CATHOLIC CHURCH (III): SINCE 1317

NEEDLESS to say, all the provisions and concessions outlined in the previous chapter were carefully restricted in ways which could be spelled out in academic treatises and judicial decisions, but not so easily in the decrees of provincial councils and diocesan synods. How were they to be interpreted as living law for the ordinary clergy? Before proceeding to those texts, we will do well to note that legislation which allowed such considerable room for argument, perplexity, and abuse could be interpreted in ways both unconscious and undocumented. Let two examples suffice. First, although popes and canonists held through the High Middle Ages that regalian bishops might lead their troops and direct them in operations, these bishops were not to exhort the soldiers to kill, nor were they to fight themselves. But how exactly were these pious exhortations to be reconciled with the principle, explicitly conceded again and again from Alexander III onward, of the right of every cleric to defend himself against attackers, a principle extended even further by the *Clementine* text *Si furiosus*? Although I have never encountered in writing an example of a canonist linking the separate canonical possibilities of a cleric's presence at a battle and of his right to self-defense, it is entirely reasonable to suppose that such advice was given at least orally, especially to bishops and others who wanted to hear this kind of advice and were served by canonists who knew what their lords wanted to hear.

Another kind of interpretive problem was this. The canonists admitted the right of every *princeps* to declare a just war. But who were the *principes*? This the canonists did not define as clearly, which by default allowed any cleric exercising any degree of lordly authority to see himself in this position, and not only by reason of the failure of the lawyers to draw a distinct line. For the question of what constituted 'war' in the Middle Ages was an even more open invitation to misinterpretation. Even if the canonists thought they understood it in terms recognizable to the Romans and to us as an affair only of the public realm declared by a legitimately constituted authority, the average medieval person, clerical or lay, was bound to conceive of it in terms of a world in which there existed no sovereign authority, but rather many levels of power and authority arising from the possession of land and the exercise of lordship, and a world in which feuds and the right of legitimate armed resistance were simply taken for granted.[1] Two telling instances from the fourteenth century underscore the tenacity of this outlook. In the Golden Bull of 1356 the Emperor Charles IV forbade only 'every unjust war and feud' and sought to define the limits within which feuds could be lawfully conducted.[2] At about the same time the government in Renaissance Florence in 1378 authorized a family to conduct a just vendetta against another which had wronged it.[3]

The canonists, who were born into and raised in this world, shared such cultural presuppositions. This helps explain some of the curious categories they devised in arriving at a scholastic understanding of war. Thus in the thirteenth century Hostiensis divided wars into seven categories that elude us: Roman, judicial, presumptuous, licit, casual, voluntary, and necessary.[4] A century later Giovanni da Legnano went even further. One of the many questions he set for discussion was this: 'Whether a cleric may declare a war of self-defense?' (Legnano also called this a 'necessary' or 'particular' war.) His unequivocal answer was 'Yes.'[5] Evidently not satisfied with the legitimacy of the right of self-defense, he subsumed self-defense under the theory of the just war and thereby granted to every single person the potential right to declare a just war. Legnano was hardly eccentric in this respect. He probably derived this idea from Innocent IV,[6] and the foremost moral theologian of the late Middle Ages, St Antoninus of Florence (1389–1459), adopted Legnano's concept of 'particular war' and of the right of every cleric to declare it.[7]

How to Interpret this Legislation?
The Response of One Professor of Law

Caught between the few legislators on high and the many clergy down below were the teachers of canon law, who were those clerics who, with more and more legal training, dominated the running of the Church from the twelfth

---

[1] For a simplified presentation of the right of resistance in the Middle Ages, Fritz Kern, *Kingship and Law in the Middle Ages*, tr. S. B. Chrimes (Oxford, 1948), pp. 81–133, 194–7, is still useful; but it must be supplemented by the far richer work by Otto Brunner, *Land and Lordship. Structures of Governance in Medieval Austria*, trans. H. Kaminsky and J. V. H. Melton (Philadelphia, 1992), especially ch. 1, 'Peace and Feud,' pp. 1–94. For numerous examples of clerical property-holders legitimately resorting to 'feud,' see ibid., p. 45, n. 151. The importance of this classic is, however, scarcely confined to Austrian history. For examples from English and French history, see R. W. Kaeuper, *War, Justice, and Public Order. England and France in the Later Middle Ages* (Oxford, 1988), pp. 225–67, who however falls into the same 'statist' trap which Brunner criticized by labeling feuds 'private war.'

[2] *Select Historical Documents of the Middle Ages*, tr. and ed. E. F. Henderson (London, 1910), pp. 246–7, c. 17.

[3] Gene Brucker, ed. and tr., *The Society of Renaissance Florence* (New York, 1971), p. 113; see also pp. 65–6, 105, 116.

[4] See the discussion in Brundage, 'Holy War,' pp. 117–19.

[5] Giovanni da Legnano, *Tractatus de bello, de represaliis et de duello*, tr. F. W. Kelsey, ed. T. E. Holland, Classics of International Law (Oxford, 1917), pp. 280–1.

[6] See the discussion in Brundage, 'Holy Wars,' pp. 110–111 and the material cited in n. 76 on p. 130.

[7] *Sancti Antonini summa theologica* (Verona, 1740; repr., Graz, 1959), 3.4.3, 3:225–6.

century onward. How were teachers to make intelligible for their students what was, on the point of arms as on so many other issues, already by 1300 a highly complex legal tradition?[8] The difficulty is nicely illustrated by the *Tract on War, Reprisals, and Duels* by Giovanni da Legnano, from 1360 until his death in 1383 professor of canon and civil law at Bologna, the leading law school of Europe for half a millennium. Although this particular text has been chosen because of its availability in modern printed form and English translation, it falls solidly within the canonistic tradition and so is worth examining at some length. These and the following excerpts are meant to convey some sense of the character of the debates among academics, the task confronting the lawmaker at the local level, and the levels of acceptable clerical violence in the minds of canonists by the fourteenth century.

To the one question, 'Whether clerics may participate in war?' Legnano devotes four close paragraphs, more than a page of printed text.

There have been various opinions on it. For some say that clerks may use arms of defence, but not of offence, and so may make a defensive war. Others say that they may use all kinds of arms, provided that they attack at once, and only in defence of themselves, and not of others, and when they are placed in a position of imperative necessity . . . Others say that they may only do so with the authority of the Pope.

We may conclude this question by saying that clerks summoned by the Pope may participate; for the prince has authority to make war . . . But in a war they may not kill even a pagan, because of the fear of 'irregularity,' . . . If summoned by others, especially by secular princes, they ought not to go to war. But for their own defence, when they cannot escape save by other means, they may even kill, even without fear of 'irregularity'; Clem., De homicidio, *si furiosus*. And I say defence of their own person advisedly; it is otherwise if they are defending another, even on the instant, such as a father, a brother, and the like . . .

But can a clerk be blamed who does not flee, but waits for one who is attacking and kills him in self-defence? It seems that he must be, by the text of Clement, where he says 'who could not avoid death by other means'; this is proved by ff. Ad leg. Aquil., l. *scientiam, qui cum aliter*, whence the passage in Clement was taken. And this is following the example of our Saviour, who fled into Egypt: [C.] xxxiii, q. iii, []i. And this is noted by Bernard [of Parma] in De homicidio, ch. *suscepimus*.

I believe the contrary to be true on the authority of ff. Ex quibus causis maiores, l. in eadem; for there these two things, not to be able to withdraw, and not to be able to withdraw without dishonour, are treated as the same. I am confirmed by the consideration that danger might occur in flight, for instance, if he were to fall, as often happens in flight, and therefore he ought not to expose himself to such a danger; Vt lite non contestata, accedens. But in this I think we must weigh all the circumstances, the danger of flight, the quality of the person fleeing, and of the person attacking, so that, if by flight a man would probably incur a danger of death, then he is not to be blamed; otherwise he is.[9]

---

8 A comparable mass of canonical legislation of no less complexity is analyzed by Darrel W. Amundsen, 'Medieval Canon Law on Medical and Surgical Practice by the Clergy,' *Bulletin of the History of Medicine* 52 (1978):22–44.
9 Legnano, *Tractatus*, ch. 52, pp. 264–5.

Legnano dwells at substantial length on three cases of clerics defending themselves in unusual circumstances, in all of which he accepts without demur the general right of clerics to self-defense, even to the point of killing their assailants. The first concerns 'Whether, although a clerk may defend himself even by killing another, he may do this in a church?' In good scholastic fashion Legnano adduces the passages and principles supporting the negative position, particularly those concerning brawling in churches and the pollution of churches; but in the end he answers positively,

> since the action arises from natural law, and it is not disapproved by divine law, and the reason of the law sanctioning it is of general application, without distinction of places . . . [Therefore] in the present case, if a man were not allowed to repel force with force in a church, the danger would be immediate, because he would easily be killed at once. As to the other argument, that pollution might follow, the solution is this: The preservation of a man, which cannot be restored, is more to be considered than a church, which may be resanctified.[10]

For Legnano, then, the general precepts of natural law override the particular requirements and corollaries of canon law. His answer to the next question can thus be anticipated: 'Whether a clerk, attacked in the act of celebration [of the Mass], may defend himself, and kill his assailant, and so continue to celebrate the office?' For the negative case he cites canons requiring that a priest celebrate as long as possible and also postpone temporal things for the spiritual; but his much longer argument in support of an affirmative answer draws on many sources, culminating in *Si furiosus*: 'So there seems to be no impediment to prevent him celebrating, as Clement proves in the passage quoted.'[11] Finally, in the absence of a definitive canon, and in a pattern of argumentation similar to that of the first case in which natural law superseded canon law, Legnano offers again a positive answer to the query, 'Whether a monk may defend himself without the licence of his abbot?'[12]

Sometimes Legnano does not come down clearly on one side or the other, as on the questions 'Whether bishops may go to war without the licence of the Pope?' or 'Whether prelates, by reason of temporal jurisdiction, may declare war?'[13] But on one topic his reply is unusually terse and unquivocal: 'Is it lawful to defend the possessions of the Church by corporeal war, and for this purpose to assemble troops? Obviously it is.' As proof he cites various texts from Gratian and Innocent IV's *Dilecto* found in the *Sext* of Boniface VIII.[14] Whatever the later opinions of Erasmus the humanist, for Legnano the legist there existed no doubt whatever on this matter.[15]

---

[10] Ibid., ch. 83, pp. 282–3.
[11] Ibid., ch. 84, pp. 283–4.
[12] Ibid., ch. 87, pp. 286–7.
[13] Ibid., ch. 67 and 72, pp. 273–4.
[14] Ibid., ch. 66, p. 273.
[15] From what has been said thus far and will be revealed below, the following conclusion is demonstrably untenable: 'Following generations of popes, seeing that this aspect of the canon law was unclear, took pains to remedy the defect. A series of conciliar enactments and papal decretals

How to Interpret this Legislation?
The Problem for Bishops

Theologians and canonists like Giovanno da Legnano enjoyed the leisure to dwell at learned length on topics for which ecclesiastical legislators had to produce crisp formulae comprehensible to the average cleric and enforceable by his superiors. Furthermore, these modifications of the old prohibition on arms were being debated and enacted precisely at the same time that two significant changes were occurring at the local level in the governance of the Church. The first has already been alluded to: the rise of the canon lawyer and of the danger that the Church was becoming a legal machine, about which Bernard of Clairvaux warned his protégé, Pope Eugenius III, in 1150. The second development was related to the first: the emergence of provincial councils and diocesan synods as legislative assemblies. The Fourth Lateran Council of 1215 provided the major impulse for this development by requiring all dioceses to hold annual synods for 'the correction of excesses and the reform of morals.'[16] Whereas such convocations until well into the twelfth century had been held irregularly and commonly devoted to only one specific issue (such as the adjudication of a dispute or the foundation of a new monastery), after 1200 they rapidly assumed the character they have retained until this century as forums for the treatment of a broad spectrum of issues and for the issuance of general doctrinal and disciplinary laws. This involved the promulgation of the universally binding legislation of the Church, adaptation of laws and regulations to local needs where modification was prudent and permissible, and formulation of specific local canons to clarify ambiguities or fill in gaps. Although it would in most cases be a long time before councils and synods met annually, they met far more frequently than they ever had before. In France alone, for example, it has been estimated that no fewer than ninety important councils were held during the thirteenth century.[17] Finally, it was in that century that direct lay participation in these assemblies was definitively curtailed.

Here, then, in the diocese and in the ecclesiastical province, was another level of law-making, another source of canon law, which is ordinarily overlooked by historians but just as binding on the clergy unless it clearly contradicted a higher level of law. Since the popes and councils of the High and later Middle Ages did almost nothing to resolve the vagueness and inconsistency of their legislation on arms and the clergy, it was left to the increasingly active bishops to decide the matter for their own clergy.[18] Whether this was by

flatly forbade clerics of whatever rank or grade, to engage in warfare directly or personally, even against the Saracens. Clerics could, however, give aid and counsel in just wars and might thus be indirect participants' (Brundage, 'Holy Wars,' p. 112).

16 *DEC*, c. 6, pp. 236–7.

17 Jean Gaudemet, 'La vie conciliaire en France,' in Ferdinand Lot and Robert Fawtier, *Histoire des institutions françaises du Moyen Age*, 3 (Paris, 1962): 314, n. 1.

18 On the general issue of the 'reception' of Roman canon law at the local level in the Middle Ages, see the excellent explanation of R. H. Helmholz, *Roman Canon Law in Reformation England* (Cambridge, 1990), pp. 4–20.

default or by intention does not matter. The bishops' discretionary authority was of course not absolute, for their decrees had to fall within the range of clearly defined law and canonistic opinion; but, as we shall see, a bishop could be lax, indifferent, or rigorous, and he could also modify, ignore, or overturn the canons issued by his predecessors. Strictly speaking, then, a cleric accused of bearing arms should be judged by what the law of his diocese (or province) was at the time of the delict. Conversely, a cleric in doubt would want to know what the law binding him was, and from a legal point of view he had no reason to give a fig for the opinions of an Aquinas or an Erasmus.

Much of the remainder of this chapter will therefore be devoted largely to a survey of provincial and diocesan legislation on the subject of the clergy in arms from the thirteenth century onward, since the general canon law has directly taken up this subject only once since then and on that occasion refracted what dioceses had been legislating for centuries. A number of the major problems concerning these source materials are mentioned in the Introduction, particularly those relating to transmission, survival, and selectivity. Two additional issues are worth noting. First, from the extant printed sources geographical patterns of legislation may emerge which are more apparent than real. Nevertheless, some tentative observations about geographical differences will be ventured. The second cause for concern is the fact that many dioceses passed over the question of arms in complete silence, and sometimes for very long stretches of time. How is this to be interpreted – that no problem existed, that clerical use of arms was necessary and required no control, that it could not be controlled, that a bishop did not wish to control the problem or preferred to think that none existed, or was there some other reasson? One can only rarely say. But one thing can be safely deduced from this frequent preterition and from the customary terseness with which the subject was treated: clerical use of weapons was only rarely regarded as an issue of the first rank, and it was often treated under the rubric of clothing. In any given age, something else always seems to have been more pressing, be it clerical concubinage, illiteracy, feuds between the diocesan and regular clergy, clandestine marriage, tithes and other payments, or lay recalcitrance. Rarely did any cleric become as exercised on the subject as did Erasmus.

Later Medieval Affirmations of the Ancient Ban

Given the variety of laws and interpretations emanating from the popes, the ecumenical councils, and the canonists on this intricate topic, it is not surprising to find that the dioceses of Europe differed significantly in their approaches in the High and late Middle Ages. A relatively small number evidently took their cue from the categorical prohibition in the *Decretales* and repeated it. The provinces of Trier and Valladolid in fact anticipated the issuance of Gregory IX's collection by several years in 1227 and 1228.[19] The council of Braga simply forbade all armsbearing in 1281, as did that in Leon in 1262/67 and again in 1303.[20] For reasons which will be discussed in Chapter 6, the dioceses of Britain seem to have been most vigorous in restating the old ideal as normative law: Lincoln around 1239/40, St Andrews in 1242, Winchester around 1247, Ely sometime between 1239 and 1256, Wells around 1258, and possibly the important legatine council which met in London in 1268.[21]

In the fourteenth century the unequivocal interdiction appears in a London council in 1342 (or so it seems), the province of Ravenna in 1314 and 1317, the diocese of Olmütz in 1342, the regulations of the bishop of Bath and Wells for thirteen chantry priests in 1347, and the province of Palermo in 1388.[22] On the other hand, few such references occur in the fifteenth century and the first half of the sixteenth before the Council of Trent: in the diocese of Breslau in 1446, the province of Besançon in 1480, and the archdiocese of Tournai in 1481, where Cardinal Ferry de Clugny (bishop 1473–83) took the most unusual, perhaps even unique, step of authorizing lay justiciars to arrest guilty clerics and deliver them up to him.[23] And in 1497 the synod of Salamanca unambiguously forbade clergy to bear arms in or outside their rooms.[24]

Problematical Language

One set of laws sometimes cited as flatly forbidding arms to the clergy are the famous reform constitutions issued for the Papal States by Cardinal Gil Albornoz in 1353. What the statute actually said was this: 'Similarly, we forbid all clerics and religious to carry arms in cities, fortresses, and villages; and if anyone should do the contrary, he is to be punished with a fine of thirty gold florins for each offense and loose the arms.'[25] As will become clear later, the punishment was severe by contemporary standards, but the statute also passes over in complete silence what by then was the most frequently conceded exception, armsbearing while traveling. This preterition was not without precedent. The council of Braga in Portugal in 1281 had been no

---

[19] CG 3:532, c. 9 ('Mansi 23:33); J. Tejada y Ramiro, *Colleccion de canones y de todos los concilios de la Iglesia de Espana y de America* (Madrid, 1859–63), 3:326.

[20] SH 2:22 (c.39); 3:234 (c. 4) and 262 (c.1).

[21] See below, pp. 183–6.

[22] Mansi 25:1170, c. 2; 25:543, 603–4; CG 4:338; Wilkins 2:737; Mansi 26:747.

[23] CG 5:289, 508, 533. On Ferry de Clugny, a member of an ancient Burgundian aristocratic family and of the great council of the dukes of Burgundy, a diplomat, and cardinal as of 1480, see *Nouvelle biographie generale* 10 (1854):919 and *Dictionnaire de biographie française* (Paris, 1933-), 9:52.

[24] SH 4:365, c. 10.

[25] Mansi 26:302: 'Item interdicimus omnibus clericis, & religiosis personis in civitatibus, castris, vel villis arma portare; & si quis contra fecerit, tribus florenis aureis pro vice qualibet puniatur, & arma amittat.'

less puzzling, allowing clerics by its choice of words to infer that travel was not covered by the prohibition. Legislation by later councils of Braga clearly excepted travel, but this was not necessarily the intent in 1281.[26]

Less equivocal, but no less puzzling, are what seem to be prohibitions which qualify the word *arma* in some way, most commonly with the words *illicita, prohibita,* or *offensiva.* Were such modifiers meant to leave open the use of defensive weapons or weapons not explicitly forbidden by spiritual or temporal authority? That was probably the case in most instances, but it is ordinarily impossible to say with any certitude, especially since lists of such weapons are seldom provided before the sixteenth century. And what was considered acceptable in one place was not necessarily so in another. According to the Annals of Waverly, two papal nuncios met with English prelates in 1273 to discuss both a subsidy from the English clergy for King Edward I's crusade and the state of the clergy in England. Near the top of the nuncios' long list of questions was one 'Concerning clerics bearing arms illicitly' (followed immediately by 'Concerning murderous clerics holding churches' and 'Concerning clerical arsonists'). The legates clearly had in mind circumstances in which clerics could bear arms, but whether English bishops did will be explored in Chapter 6.[27]

On the Continent such language was scarcely unusual and often hard to interpret. The diocese of Utrecht condemned *arma illicita* in 1293 and *arma prohibita* in 1294.[28] In 1310 it followed the example of many other dioceses and allowed clerics to carry weapons while traveling, but this does not mean that this exception was implied or understood in the legislation of 1293-4.[29] When an archidiaconal synod of Prague interdicted *arma prohibita* in 1365,[30] we stand on firmer ground in interpreting these words, since the province of Prague had in 1346 and 1355 allowed the clergy weapons when traveling and in case of necessity.[31] Finally, the diocese of Breslau, which had condemned all arms in 1446 (including overly large knives), evidently retreated from that position in 1456 by denouncing only *arma offendendi*; but what exactly these were cannot be said.[32]

Then there are laws which it is difficult to say have been badly or cleverly written or curiously transmitted. The highly influential constitutions of Bishop Eudes de Sully of Paris (1196–1208) include the following: 'It is strictly forbidden for priests or their clerics to carry knives with sharp points.'[33] Did

---

[26] *SH* 2:22, c. 39. For later statutes, see below, p. 156.
[27] *C&S* 2:805, and see below, p. 190.
[28] *CG* 4:17, c. 4, and 4:22, c. 5.
[29] Ibid., 4:169, c. 6.
[30] Ibid., 10:744.
[31] Mansi 26:83 and 390, c. 26.
[32] *CG* 5:289 and 445.
[33] Odette Pontal, ed., *Les statuts synodaux français du XIIIe siècle* (Paris, 1971-), 1:86, c. [91]: 'Item prohibetur districte ne sacerdotes cultellum portent cum cuspide nec clerici eorum' (=Mansi 22:683, c. 40). On the significance of Eudes de Sully, C. R. Cheney has remarked that his *prohibitiones et precepta* 'came to be a model for many statutes of the didactic sort throughout northern Europe' (*Medieval Texts and Studies* [Oxford, 1973], p. 143).

Bishop Eudes have in mind Master Roland's distinction between clergy in major and minor orders? If so, why mention only priests and the clerics in their service, who could have been in minor orders or even only tonsured? Or could he have meant 'priests' as a synonym for all in major orders or even all clerics? If the latter, why add 'and their clerics'? And did he really mean to outlaw even simple eating knives which were a personal necessity well into the early modern period?[34]

Somewhat clearer was a statute from Bordeaux in 1234. It forbade priests, other clerics in sacred orders, and beneficed clergy to carry sharp knives and wear various kinds of unseemly raiment. While unambiguous about which ranks of the clergy were affected by this legislation, did it mean to pass over the unbeneficed clergy in minor orders in silence? And, as with Eudes de Sully's enactment, was the intent to interdict *only* sharp knives or anything more dangerous *as well*?[35]

Or consider the synod of Clermont in 1268, which ordered the beneficed parish clergy not to carry weapons in suspect places at night on pain of deprivation of benefice for a year.[36] It was a commonplace of ecclesiastical legislation to discourage clergy from unnecessary travel, particularly at night and in dangerous places; but, as will be seen shortly, it was rapidly becoming equally commonplace to allow clergy to carry weapons when traveling or in dangerous places. What was the exact intent of this canon? And was it really intended to bind only clergy holding benefices with the cure of souls, but not incumbents of benefices without pastoral responsibility? A third problematical case: The synod of Sodor on the Isle of Man in 1292 banned clerics from bearing arms in church.[37] Only in church? Could they take up their weapons again outside the door? Evidently so. A fourth instance, related to the one above from Clermont: The diocese of Mainz in 1299 forbade clerics to bear arms at night in lay habit.[38] Although one end may have been served by this phrasing – to dissuade clerics from wearing disguises for whatever purposes – it only muddied the waters otherwise. A different kind of problem was raised by the provincial council of Milan in 1311, which specified that only on occasions permitted by law could a cleric appear armed in public.[39] Whose law? That of the city, the surrounding territory, the archdiocese, or the province? And was a cleric otherwise entitled to bear arms as long as he did so discreetly? Many pages later the same council largely resolved these quandaries by stating that clerics could bear arms only with episcopal permission except

34 On the problems of his legislation, see L. Guizard, 'Les statuts d'Eudes de Sully,' *Revue historique de droit français et étranger*, ser. 4, 33 (1955):623–33; Joseph Avril, 'Naissance et evolution des legislations synodales dans les diocèses du nord et de l'ouest de la France (1200–1250),' *ZRG KA* 72 (1986):155–67.
35 Pontal, *Les statuts synodaux, 2, Les statuts de 1230 à 1260* (1983), p. 76, c. 34: 'Item statuimus ne sacerdotes vel clerici beneficiati vel in sacris ordinibus constituti cultellos accutos defferant.'
36 Mansi 23:1203.
37 Wilkins 2:179.
38 Mansi 24:1210.
39 Ibid., 25:481.

when traveling, a clarification which should have appeared much earlier in the decrees.[40] Even within the strict canon law, what has been said so far should suggest that the bishop of Brixen was possibly slightly evasive in 1419 when his synod decreed that clergy 'are not to bear arms in accordance with the sanctions of the canons.'[41]

There are in fact comparatively few examples of such vague language. Considering the many gray areas created by the complexity of the general canon law on clerical arms, the canons promulgated in synods and councils were normally clear even if they did not anticipate all situations or questions, such as the kinds of weapons that might be carried, the ways one ought to employ them, or the penalties to be inflicted on violators. In addition, we do well to remember that what seems like fuzzy language to us was possibly either understood fairly well in a particular area at a particular time on the basis of custom or unrecorded 'common understanding,' or else was deliberate imprecision arising from several possible motives – unwillingness or inability to resolve what the popes and canonists had not clarified, a desire or willingness to leave certain matters to the judgment of individuals, or an intent to leave some areas of law penumbral so as to enjoy greater flexibility in the disposition of individual cases. Many motives are possible, but very few are documented.

Finally, to reiterate a point which can never be forgotten, the documents themselves can be highly problematical as a result of their transmission over many centuries. With respect to the clergy and arms, two important decrees from thirteenth-century England – the diocese of Norwich in 1240/3, and the legatine council of 1268 – will be treated at some length in the English context in Chapter 6.[42] On the Continent, the statutes of the diocese of Cambrai before 1260 are particularly difficult. In the textual tradition of the first half of the thirteenth century a statute is recorded which forbade 'clergy, on pain of excommunication, to bear arms or sharp knives'; but one manuscript states that 'clergy are not to bear arms of aggression (*arma impugnationis*) or sharp knives on pain of excommunication.'[43] The editor rejects this variant for reasons unknown. If he thought such an alteration uncanonical, he was wrong, for a synod could well have amended earlier legislation in this way. It is, of course, possible that a scribe unilaterally did so at some later point. It is impossible to verify any of these possibilities by checking later statutes. The ten sets of synodal changes made between 1260 and 1288 contain nothing on armsbearing,[44] while in 1312 the bishop decreed that no cleric was to bear

---

[40] Ibid., 25:492.
[41] G. Bickell, ed., *Synodi Brixinenses saeculi XV* (Innsbruck, 1880), p. 2. I thank the Austrian Embassy in Washington for obtaining a xeroxed copy of this work for me.
[42] See below, pp. 186–9.
[43] P. C. Boeren, 'Les plus anciens statuts du diocèse de Cambrai,' *Revue de droit canonique* 3 (1953):152 and n. 159: 'Prohibemus sub pena excommunicationis ne clerici arma ferant vel cultros acutos,' which the discordant manuscript modifies as reading 'ne clerici ferant arma impugnationis nec cultros acutos.' On the textual tradition, see ibid., 3:1–32.
[44] Ibid., 3:377–415, 4 (1954):131–47.

arms without the permission of the bishop or his official.[45] None of this sheds any light on the early legislation of the church of Cambrai or its evolution.

Episcopal Discretionary Control over Armsbearing

The extent of the discretionary authority vested in, or assumed by, bishops and ecclesiastical superiors is revealed in the single most common form of later medieval legislation when arms were not totally forbidden to the clergy: clergy were not to bear arms without the permission of their superiors. Bishop Bonfiglio of Siena (1216–52) in 1232 went so far as to permit the carrying of only defensive weapons with episcopal permission, but this was an unusual proviso at such an early date.[46] A council in Arles convened in 1260 lamented that in many places disputes over benefices had moved secular clerics and even monks to take up arms, drag their friends and families into disputes, and spill much blood. Instead of outlawing any resort to weapons by clerics, the council forbade any arms to any secular or regular cleric without a license from his bishop or a competent judge.[47] Similar legislation was passed in Vienne 1289, Anse in 1300, Avignon in 1326, and Saint-Ruf in 1339.[48] In 1267 another council in Arles declared incorrigible any cleric who without the permission of his superior carried a sharp pointed knife or offensive weapons.[49]

Caution and some confusion characterize the relevant decrees of a national council of the church of Hungary meeting at Buda in 1279. Canon 7 forbade clerics to engage in war or fighting of any sort 'except perhaps for the defense of their churches and the country, not for offense or repulsion, but solely for defense, if necessity shall require it; and then they shall not fight in their own persons.' Canon 11 went on more directly to forbid clergy to carry sword or knife 'unless a case of clear peril should befall them; nor may they then without the permission of superiors.' In short, the clergy of Hungary were not to bear arms except in dangerous circumstances, and then only with permission.[50]

Elsewhere, however, bishops were generally less inclined so to restrict their own discretionary authority or that of other prelates. Without episcopal leave

---

[45] CG 6:711.
[46] Mansi 23:244: 'Item praecipimus, quod nullus clericus portet arma mortifera, nec etiam arma defensionis sine licentia sui episcopi.'
[47] Ibid., 23:1011–12, c. 17.
[48] Louis Boisset, 'Un concile provincial au treizième siècle, Vienne 1289. Eglise locale et société,' *Theologie historique* 21 (Paris, 1973), pp. 286–8, c. 44.
[49] Ibid., 23:1180, c. 4: 'Ut nullus clericus cultellum cum cuspide seu arma impugnationis ferat, sine praelati sui licentia.'
[50] Mansi 24:275–6, c. 7 ('nisi forte pro ecclesiarum suarum & patriae defensione, non ad impugnandum vel propulsandum, sed ad defensionem tantum, si necessitas eos compellat: & tunc in propriis personis non pugnent') and c. 11 ('[ne] gladium vel cultellum, quod vulgariter dicitur bord, portent, nisi eis manifesit temporis causa ingruerit: nec tunc absque licentia praelatorum portent').

no cleric was to presume to bear weapons according to canons of the synods of Cambrai in 1312, Perugia in 1320, Ferrara in 1332, and Padua in 1339,[51] and of the great council which assembled at Avignon to legislate for three ecclesiastical provinces in 1326.[52] Several synods allowed the one exception that clerics when traveling could arm themselves without first securing permission: the dioceses of Valentine in 1262, Lucca in 1308 and 1351, Utrecht in 1310 (possibly), and Florence in 1346,[53] and the provinces of Milan in 1311, Etruria in 1327, and Florence in 1517.[54] The council of Milan in 1311, however, noted that abuses easily arose from this privilege, and in 1339 the bishop of Padua, openly voicing his scepticism about the alleged need to have weapons for travel, insisted on the requirement of episcopal license in such cases.[55]

Italian bishops predominate among these examples of insistence on episcopal prerogative. Perhaps this impression is accidental, flowing from those sources which happen to have survived and been printed. Only in Iberia did bishops similarly insist so much on their authority with respect to armsbearing, and there they did so only in the later fifteenth and sixteenth centuries. Episcopal permission was required for armsbearing while traveling in the legislation of the sees of Orense in 1471/91, Porto in 1496, Braga in 1505, and Mondonedo in 1534.[56] Necessity could also justify armsbearing, but again only with permission, in Orense (1508/11 and 1538-9), Astorga (1553), and Oviedo (1553).[57] But other Iberian dioceses allowed arms for travel without permission: Salamanca in 1451, Braga in 1477, Tuy in 1482 and 1528, and Orense in 1539/42.[58]

Why this pattern in Italy so early and so consistently? Here one can only speculate on some of the possible reasons. Bishops elsewhere had on average much larger dioceses to administer, while Italy had as many bishops as most of the rest of Latin Christendom combined. Italian administrative practices were also the most advanced in Europe. Perhaps in the rest of Europe quotidian violence was either more common or at least more 'acceptable.' Bishops elsewhere may also have anticipated that their clergy were likely either to resist openly or to ignore such assertions of episcopal prerogative. Finally, Italian bishops were perhaps more inclined than non-Italians to imitate the papal prerogative to dispense from all laws and rules except those of strictly divine origin. Whatever the reasons, non-Italian bishops seem to have been less interested in pressing this issue, at least on the issue of arms control.

---

[51] CG 6:711; Mansi 25:641, 919–20, 1141.
[52] Ibid., 25:765. This decree was renewed at a similar council at Avignon in 1337: ibid., 25:1098.
[53] Mansi 23:1056-7 and 25:184 (c. 40) and 190 (c. 60); CG 4:169; Mansi 26:36.
[54] Mansi 25:481 and 820; 35:225 (c. 17).
[55] Ibid., 25:1141, c. 23.
[56] SH 1:56; 1:118; 2:145–6; 2:360–1.
[57] Ibid., 1:183–4, 192; 3:85, 506–7.
[58] Ibid., 1:186–7, 356, 448; 2:122–3; 3:506–7; 4:308.

Other Exceptions in the Later Middle Ages

Various exceptions to the general prohibition were enacted in many dioceses from the thirteenth century onward without any reference to bishops or other superiors. In such cases, the implication was that the use of arms was left to the decision of the individual cleric.

A few dioceses in the thirteenth century took the extreme course of authorizing armsbearing in any necessity as decided by the cleric. Bishop Walter de Cantilupe of Worcester in 1240 forbade the bearing of any arms 'except perhaps defensive weapons when necessity evidently requires this.'[59] The synod of Le Mans in 1247 allowed all clergy and religious to carry a knife (*cultellum*) only when 'just cause for fear' existed.[60] The diocese of Nimes in 1252 denied to all clergy, particularly those in sacred orders, the use of daggers, sharp knives, lances, and sickles 'except perhaps for probable cause of fear or war.'[61] A synod in Münster in 1279 forbade the use of arms 'except for necessity,' but in an earlier canon it had stipulated that armsbearing by clergy required both 'legitimate cause and the explicit permission of prelates.'[62] The province of Soissons in 1403 allowed the use of arms in case of 'pressing necessity and for useful and honest cause.'[63] A council in Salamanca in 1410 authorized clergy to carry weapons in cases of fear or travel.[64] Fear was also sufficient reason for the synod of Amiens in 1454.[65]

Travel was by far the most common exception which bishops left to the discretion of their clergy, a concession sometimes qualified or extended by permission to bear arms in dangerous or suspect places. The synod of Valentine in 1262 reported many complaints, from laymen and clerics alike, about clerics, 'forgetful of their honor and ecclesiastical simplicity,' bearing arms, including swords larger than those worn by the laity. The bishop's response was to forbid clerics to wear arms day or night except when traveling. Then they might wear a winged or Segovian sword which, however, they must remove as soon as they arrive at a place of hospitality.[66] Synods in some dioceses granted simple dispensations for travel or danger: the provinces of Benevento in 1331 and 1378 and of Prague in 1346 and 1355;[67] the dioceses

---

59   *C&S* 2:307, c. [43]: 'Nec arma portent clerici, cum hoc clericalem non deceat honestatem, nisi forsan arma defensionis cum hoc necessitas exegerit evidenter.' For further discussion of this statute, see below, p. 182.

60   Avril, 'Naissance et évolution,' p. 240.

61   Pontal, *Les statuts synodaux*, 2:352, c. 103: 'clerici universi, presertim in sacris ordinibus constituti, ... enses non deferant, nec cultellos acutos, nec lanceas, nec fausones, nisi forte ex causa probabili timoris seu guerre.' The statutes of this synod were copied in the neighboring dioceses of Arles, Béziers, Lodève, and Uzès (ibid., p. 239).

62   Mansi 24:312, c. 2 ('Clerici, volentes privilegio clericali ... arma non ferant, nec gladios, nisi hoc faciant ex causa legitima et expressa licentia praelatorum') and c. 20 ('Item ne arma portent praeter necessitatem').

63   Gousset 2:635, c. 84.

64   *SH* 4:365, c. 2.

65   Gousset 2:690 c.1.8.

66   Mansi 23:1056–7.

67   Mansi 25:960 (c. 46) and 26:643 (c.38); 26:83 and 390 (c.26).

of St Andrews in the early fourteenth century,[68] Olmütz in 1342, Eichstätt in 1354, and Halberstadt in 1408;[69] the representatives of the Danish church gathered in Copenhagen in 1425;[70] and the council convened by Cardinal Lorenzo Campeggio in Regensburg in 1524 for the reform of the German clergy.[71] In 1410 the bishop of Speyer went so far as to forbid the wearing of knives, especially in public, except when travel required it, a statute which was essentially repeated in 1412, 1465, and 1544.[72]

As early as the thirteenth century several dioceses had been willing to allow armsbearing for a considerably vaguer reason: just cause for fear. The province of Rouen enacted this single exception to the prohibition in 1231, as did the dioceses of Le Mans in 1247 and Gerona in 1274.[73] A possible fourth instance comes from Norwich between 1240 and 1243 and illustrates beautifully the hazards of textual transmission.[74] Interestingly, after these thirteenth-century occurrences this broad exception, which accorded the ordinary cleric so much latitude, was rarely enacted on the Continent in the late Middle Ages. A synod of Eichstätt did so in 1354, but by then this was most unusual.[75]

It is curious in all this local legislation that very few overt acknowledgments appear of the right of self-defense granted by virtually all the Decretists and Decretalists. The diocese of Gerona did so in 1274.[76] The constitutions issued by William Durandus, bishop of Mende (1285–96), declared excommunicated a cleric guilty of a whole range of offenses, including severe assault and battery, 'unless he did it in defending himself and repelling force' and it is judicially determined that it was necessary to repulse violence in this way.[77] Durandus knew his law well. Most famous for his *Rationale divinorum officiorum* on liturgy, he was also a distinguished canonist who had probably

---

[68] David Patrick tr., *Statutes of the Scottish Church 1225–1559*, Scottish Historical Society 54 (Edinburgh, 1907), pp. 70–1: 'Item we enact that no priest shall wear the long knife which is called a *hangar*, save when he is equipped for a journey, under the fine of half a merk.' The original Latin texts which Patrick translated were edited by Joseph Robertson, *Concilia Scotiae. Ecclesiae Scoticanae statuta tam provincialia quam synodalia quae supersunt MCCXXV–MDLIX*, 2 vols. (Edinburgh, 1866), and this statute appears on 2:67.

[69] *CG* 4:337, 371; 5:14.

[70] Mansi 28:1087.

[71] Ibid., 32:1084.

[72] *Collectio processuum synodalium et constitutionum ecclesiasticarum dioecesis Spirensis ab anno 1397 usque ad annum 1720* (Bruchsal, 1786), pp. 53, 63, 73, 277.

[73] Mansi 23:216 (c. 20), 755, 936. A more modern edition of the 1247 synodal of Le Mans was published by Joseph Avril, 'Naissance et evolution des legislations synodales' (c. 140 on p. 240: 'Districte precipitur ne presbiteri vel clerici atque religiosi cultellum . . . nisi justa causa timoris').

[74] See below, Chapter 6, pp. 186–7.

[75] *CG* 4:371.

[76] Mansi 23:936.

[77] Joseph Berthelé, 'Les instructions et constitutions de Guillaume Durand, le Spéculateur,' *Académie des sciences et lettres de Montpellier. Mémoires de la section des lettres*, 2nd ser. 3 (1900–07):101: 'vel aliquem atrociter, nisi se defendendo et vim repellendo fecerit, vulnerasse vel mutilasse . . . et captus ad officialem nostrum per clericos adducatur, adjunctis sibi aliquibus laicis, si opus fuerit ad repellendam violentiam, si forte inferri per aliquos timeatur.'

helped draft the decrees of the ecumenical council of Lyons in 1274.[78] The council of Tarragona in 1317 evidently chose to follow Master Roland's interpretation by allowing only the clergy in minor orders the right to use weapons to defend themselves or their churches.[79] The province of Mainz in 1423 was more latitudinarian in conceding to all the clergy the right to protect themselves, their property, and their churches – but only with the permission of their superiors.[80]

No council or synod explicitly empowered clerics on their own initiative to take up arms on behalf of the defenseless or what were often called *miserabiles personae* (widows, orphans, the aged, the infirm, and the like). In a pinch, of course, concerned clerics probably could have devised some justification for acting on their behalf, employing, for example, the commonly enacted canon that clerics ought not to dispute in public or appear before secular courts except to protect such *miserabiles*. If a cleric could speak up for them, was it not just as reasonable to be able to fight for them? Still, it is an interesting omission. Perhaps bishops wished to reserve this category for their own discretionary power or feared giving their priests too many pretexts for resorting to violence. Or perhaps they unreflectively accepted the minimalist nature of law, which focuses on what people are required or forbidden to do rather than on what they ought to do.

Again, despite texts incorporated into the *Sext* and elsewhere, there apparently existed at the local level a marked reluctance to admit the right of clerics to come armed to the aid of other clerics or of their churches. As has already been seen, the general council of the church in Hungary in 1279 allowed clergy to rise to the defense of their churches or their fatherland, but not to fight in their own persons;[81] and the province of Tarragona in 1317 allowed only the clergy in minor orders to fight for their churches. Only three late medieval ecclesiastical assemblies permitted the clergy in general this right to protect with arms the persons and property of their churches. All three were German, and all required the prior permission of superiors: the province of Mainz in 1423, the diocese of Constance in 1463 and 1483, and the diocese of Hildesheim in 1539.[82]

Nor did ideas about the just war appear in local and provincial statutes. On this matter bishops would have been understandably loath to water down any of their authority either to declare a just war or to judge one waged by others, or, to put the matter differently, to cater to the readiness of most of their contemporaries, including the clergy, to regard their causes as unquestionably just and hence worthy of recourse to violence. When the bishops and barons of England met in London in October 1264 to discuss the public disorder which had obtained during the recent civil war, the behavior of

[78] *ODCC*, s.v..
[79] Mansi 25:630, c. 7.
[80] *CG* 5:210, c. 5.
[81] Mansi 24:275, c. 7.
[82] *CG* 5:210, 458, 553, and 6:321.

clerical murderers, arsonists, and pillagers was the object of special concern. The ecclesiastical respondent distinguished sharply between clergy who 'were promoting justice and repelling violence' with their weapons and those who gave themselves over to rapine. The latter, he said, would of course be subjected to deprivation of benefice and harsher penalties; but even the first were automatically suspended from their offices, to which they could be eventually restored so long as they had struck or wounded no one during the conflict.[83] While the respondent phrased all this carefully to placate the barons, his position was consonant with that of the English church and of canon law, especially the two principles, reconcilable only with some difficulty before *Si furiosus*, of repelling violence with violence and of the automatic irregularity of a clerical *percussor* who harmed the person of another.

A few synods allowed clerics to carry weapons during wartime, and all had comprehensible reasons for doing so. In 1233 the papal legate in southern France convened a council for the province of Béziers. The region had recently witnessed twenty years of intermittent but bloody crusades against the Cathars and was now the proving-ground for the newly-created Inquisition. Canon 13 threatened with the loss of benefit of clergy any cleric who carried sharp knives, swords, lances, or other offensive weapons 'except perchance in time of war.'[84] In the diocese of Durham, the bishop of which was effectively a viceroy in the dangerous march along the Scottish border, a synod convened sometime in the 1240s forbade the clergy to bear arms except defensive weapons in time of war and for reasonable cause.[85]

A number of canonists allowed that clerics could take arms for the defense of their *patria*, and on the matter of bishops and their military obligations to the crown a clear consensus among the canonists developed: regalian bishops had to discharge their duty, and non-regalian bishops could serve if they wished. They could exhort others to fight but not to kill, and they should not fight themselves. These were sensitive issues usually not raised at the local level, and when they were one often notices the presence of the king at such deliberations. The conflict was sometimes openly registered in the record. Thus the council of Palencia in 1129 was presided over by King Alfonso I (1104–34), the 'Warrior.' Canon 14 enjoined on all obedience to the king on pain of excommunication; canon 15 forbade anyone to require the clergy to go on campaign, carry weapons, or do anything contrary to canon law.[86] Such resistance to royal or princely pressure weakened in the later Middle Ages. The case of the general council of the Hungarian church in 1274 has already been discussed: although the clergy were not to participate personally in warfare, they could otherwise aid in the defense of the *patria*. In 1473 the council of Toledo, the primatial see of Spain, condemned at some length the

---

[83] *C&S* 2:696–7.
[84] Mansi 23:273.
[85] *C&S* 2:431: 'ne clerici arma portent, presertim aggressionis, nisi forsan arma defensionis tempore belli ingruente et causa rationabili compellante.'
[86] Mansi 21:387.

absurd and dishonorable practice of the clergy's serving in the military entourage of any secular lord – except that of the king and of other royal persons.[87] Isabella and Ferdinand, married four years earlier and fighting with the aristocracy a civil war that would last another six, were determined to subjugate the Spanish church to their rule alone and, like Pepin and Charlemagne long before, to harness ecclesiastical military power to royal purposes.

The Council of Trent

Thus far this survey has not gone beyond the early sixteenth century, when the Reformation movement permanently shattered western Christianity and forced the Roman Catholic Church to confront problems and abuses which had long needed reform. After several decades of delay, an ecumenical council convened at Trent in 1545 and, in four major sessions spread over the next eighteen years, debated and enacted a whole series of decrees and reforms touching all aspects of church life. In countless ways this council constituted a decisive turning-point in the history of the Church, even if some of its objectives took centuries to achieve. It addressed the issues it believed needed attention, even if it often had to accept compromises. Interestingly, on the issue of the clergy and arms it said nothing. None of the canons and decrees drawn up in Session 23, which treated holy orders, or in Session 25, which handled general reform, mentions the issue. A tangential issue was raised in Session 14 in 1551, which was concerned with the sacraments of penance and extreme unction. Chapter 7 of the decree on reform excluded permanently from ordination to any ecclesiastical order anyone who had committed voluntary homicide. 'If, however,' it went on,

> it is reported he has killed someone not intentionally but by accident, or in repelling force by force as when one protects oneself from death, and for that reason a dispensation is needed by law in some way for holy orders and the ministry of the altar, and for any kind of benefices and dignities; then let the matter be committed to the local ordinary or, as the case may be, to the metropolitan or the neighboring bishop, who shall be able to dispense only after studying the case and testing the petitions and reports, and not otherwise.[88]

Aside from the fact that the fathers of Trent had to deal with far more serious and pressing problems, the allusion to the principle of the right of everyone to repel force with force and, more specifically, to *Si furiosus* suggests that in the minds of the bishops and theologians at Trent there existed no substantial need for reform in law or behavior.[89]

[87] Mansi 32:394.
[88] *DEC*, Sess. 14, de ref. c. 7, p. 717.
[89] Nor does the subject appear in the series of supplementary materials published by the Görresgesellschaft, *Concilium Tridentinum. Diariorum, actorum, epistularum, tractatuum nova collectio*, 5 vols. (Freiburg, 1963–).

This inference is confirmed by the synodal activity of two distinguished reforming prelates shortly after the conclusion of the council in 1563. A year or two later Stanislaus Cardinal Hosius (1504–79), the leading Polish reformer and one of the presiding officers at the last session of the Council of Trent, presided over a synod of the diocese of Ermland which decreed what had become the single most important legal tradition in the later medieval Church on the subject of arms: clergy are not to bear arms except when traveling.[90] The second prelate was the most impeccable model reformer of the second half of the sixteenth century, a source of inspiration to uncounted numbers of other bishops for several hundred years: Carlo Borromeo (1538–84), archbishop of Milan from 1560 to 1584 (although he did not take up his duties there until September 1565). He conducted his work of reform on many levels, one of which was the holding of six provincial councils and eleven diocesan synods. The very first council in late 1565 treated arms and the clergy at some length. It is worth quoting in full:

> The arms of the clergy are tears and prayers.
> Therefore we decree that clerics are not to bear weapons of any sort for offense or even defense, excepting little knives designed for domestic use; unless by chance they must undertake a journey outside a city in suspect places.
> If a bishop has decided to grant permission to them for probable and just cause, then this permission, having been requested in writing, may be granted to them to use it; but not publicly unless necessity requires it.
> We forbid entirely crossbows, spears, arquebuses, daggers, and other weapons of this sort.[91]

However lacking in elegance, this decree is one of the most precise and thorough decrees on the whole issue ever promulgated in the history of Christianity. In allowing little knives for domestic use only, requiring submission of a written request to a bishop, reminding the bishop to accede only for 'probable and just cause,' avoiding publicity, and banning all offensive weapons, it falls entirely within the late medieval tradition of exempting travel from the prohibition and within the Italian tradition of requiring prior episcopal consent. Of all the later councils and synods Borromeo convoked, only the diocesan synod of 1578 alluded to the subject again in any way, and then by tersely referring the clergy to the relevant provincial decree.[92]

---

[90] CG 7:598: 'Tabernas nunquam ingredietur, nec arma gestabit, nisi viator fuerit.' On Cardinal Hosius, see George H. Williams, 'Stanislas Hosius,' in Jill Raitt, ed., Shapers of Religious Traditions in Germany, Switzerland, and Poland 1560–1600 (New Haven, 1981), pp. 157–74.

[91] Acta ecclesiae Mediolanensis, ed. A. Ratti, 3 vols. (Milan, 1890–92), 2:72: 'Clericorum arma sunt orationes et lachrymae. Idcirco edicimus, ne clerici cuiusvis generis ad offensionem, vel etiam ad defensionem ferant, exceptis cultellis ad domesticum vitae usum accomodatis; nisi forte extra civitatem suspectis locis iter eis faciendum sit. Quod si episcopus probabili iustaque de causa id eis permittendum iudicaverit; tunc, scripto impetrata venia, ipsis uti liceat; non tamen publice, nisi rei, aut facti necessitas postulet. Omnino balista, hastis et sclopeto, telis aliisque huius generis instrumentis ipsis interdicimus.' The older text, which differs in no essential respect, is printed in Mansi 34:37.

[92] Acta ecclesiae Mediolanensis, 2:1–1094, with the exception of p. 942 (1578): 'Cleri familiae delectus

In other words, Borromeo apparently never saw fit to change his legislation on this topic once he had issued it. Although strict, it was also essentially conventional.

The Early Modern Period

Since Trent did nothing to change canon law on armsbearing, it comes as no surprise that the pattern that had emerged in the later thirteenth, four- teenth, and fifteenth centuries continued substantially unchanged in the early modern period: occasional assertion of the ideal, but habitual modification on the local or regional level, particularly for traveling. Impressions of some later change do emerge, however. Never a matter of central concern, cleri- cal armsbearing gradually receded further into the background, especially in the eighteenth century. Thus the tenth volume of the *Concilia Germaniae*, the great collection of German synodal texts, covers the years 1662–1768. Arms are treated with some frequency until 1713, but not at all thereafter. What becomes relatively more important is hunting – not a new issue by any means, but one which figures more conspicuously in ecclesiastical legislation in Germany and elsewhere than it had before.[93]

Without attempting to explain this phenomenon in detail, one can hazard some guesses as to why it occurred. The climate of opinion was changing, but as usual it is hard to pinpoint who was changing it. Perhaps the satire directed at figures like Julius II and Christoph von Galen was beginning to make itself felt. Certainly clerical expectations of the clergy were rising, for diocesan legislation conveys the sense of a concern with clerical decorum palpably stronger than ever before. Bishops were not alone in this respect. At this moment historians may be more preoccupied with order in early modern Europe than people really were then, but in Catholic and Protestant lands the domestication of the clergy was an important theme. The instrument for that domestication was the seminary, an institution unknown for the secular clergy in the Middle Ages, where the clergy were to live an ordered, peaceful life and learn systematically theology, canon law, homiletics, and the clerical ideal.[94] Meanwhile, in the world outside, the need for carrying weapons slowly declined as the conditions of life became gradually more settled. Finally, as armies became more professional and more distinctive in their uniforms, the need for clerical participation may have declined while its conspicuousness in dress would surely have risen.

---

decretis provincialibus praescriptis, et vestitus item ratio servetur, de armis item non ferendis.' These diocesan statutes are not printed in Mansi 34.

[93] Timothy Tackett, *Priest and Parish in Eighteenth-Century France* (Princeton, 1977), pp. 166–7, finds that among the clergy of eighteenth-century France hunting and the wearing of wigs elicited more episcopal notice than did gambling, violence, or excessive bibulousness. The same is gener- ally true of Germany.

[94] On this large topic, see Michael Arneth, *Das Ringen um Geist und Form der Priesterbildung im Säkularklerus des siebzehnten Jahrhunderts* (Würzburg, 1970).

The Augsburg Interim of 1548 forbade the clergy to go about girded with swords.[95] Whether or not this influenced ecclesiastical legislation very much seems doubtful. A few dioceses in the early modern period followed the example of some late medieval ones and now forbade clerical bearing of arms without qualification. The synod of Tournai did this in 1574, but it had already done so in 1481.[96] Such prohibitions were new in the New World province of Lima in 1582[97] and the Italian province of Fermo in 1590 (excepting knives for food) and 1726.[98] The synod of Osnabrück in 1628 forbade to the clergy 'swords, pikes, arquebuses, and the like.'[99] One synod of Münster enacted such a blanket ban in 1668,[100] but this may have been directed at Bishop von Galen, who in his many pastoral addresses to his synods never once mentioned the subject.[101] The archdiocese of Besançon renewed in 1560 and 1648 the complete prohibition enacted in 1480, but the statutes passed in 1707 applied only to clerics in holy orders and had mostly to do with hunting.[102] Hunting seems also to have been the background of the condemnations issued at Metz in 1604 and 1699 and at Eichstätt in 1713.[103] French bishops directed their attention to firearms, which were outlawed in Beauvais (1646 and 1669), Rheims (1647), Chalons (1657), Noyon (1673 and 1690), and Amiens (1696).[104]

Other qualifications appeared as well, sometimes different from those of the late Middle Ages. The diocese of Haarlem outlawed *arma illicita* in 1564,[105] while the neighboring diocese of Utrecht in 1565 ordered the beneficed clergy and those in major orders not to go about at night with swords.[106] In 1580 the synod of Breslau reversed the normal concern of authorities and forbade the clergy to retain arms at home.[107] The diocese of Namur in 1698 banned the bearing of arms by the clergy in processions.[108] In 1699 the province of Naples denied the clergy the right to bear arms prohibited to the laity.[109] Did this apply only to weapons banned by the kingdom of Naples? The same council also excepted the needs of travel and then threatened all clerics with severe and arbitrary punishment if they kept weapons at home. In 1726 the exception for traveling here was abolished, at least in the diocese of Naples. Violators were threatened with five years' imprisonment if they were nobles, galley-service if

[95]   CG 7:759, tit. 17 ('De disciplina cleri & populi'): 'nec incedant Clerici cum multi famulitii strepitu, aut gladiis accincti terribiles, sed venerabiles, qualiter se contemptibiles reddunt.'
[96]   CG 5:533, c. 8, and 7:780, c.12.4.
[97]   Mansi 36Bis:216, c. 16.
[98]   Ibid., 36Bis:899, 10.2; 37:663, 9.3.
[99]   Acta synodalia Osnabrugensis . . . MDCXXVIII (Cologne, 1653), 2.1.9., p. 38.
[100] CG 10:29.
[101] See ibid., 9:786-92, 836-40, 874-6, 893-8, and 10:16-18, 21-3, 31-2.
[102] CG 5:508, 8:12, 10:289-90 (where it is noted that the statute of 1571 was renewed in 1648).
[103] Ibid., 10:770 (c. 61), 244 (c.10.8), and 382 (c. 21), respectively.
[104] Gousset 4:134, 142, 170, 276-7, 344, 503, 545.
[105] CG 7:24.
[106] Ibid., 7:137.
[107] Ibid., 7:897.
[108] Ibid., 10:228, c. 105.
[109] Mansi 36Ter:780-1.

they were not.[110] In 1699 the council of Tarragona declared that clerics bearing arms forbidden by law would be subject to loss of clerical privileges, fines, and additional arbitrary punishments; but in 1717 the province interdicted weapons entirely for all clergy except the military-religious orders.[111]

Many Italian provinces continued the tradition of reserving the whole matter to the discretion of superiors: Sorrento in 1584, Trani in 1589, Siena in 1599, and Benevento in 1599 and 1693.[112] The latter council marked a change by limiting bishops' licensing authority to those instances permitted by law. And very few Italian dioceses allowed the exemption for travelers without the obligation to secure prior permission from an ecclesiastical authority. The bishop of Imola in 1693 spelled out in detail that under no circumstances were clergy to use any kind of weapons without securing episcopal permission in cases of anticipated fear or need.[113] In 1624 and again in 1793 the diocese of Padua required written permission, to be issued only for 'just and probable cause,' and completely prohibited the use of crossbows, pikes, and arquebuses.[114] One of the few sees north of the Alps to take a comparable stance was Prague in 1605, which required episcopal permission for all uses of arms except domestic small knives.[115] The bishop of Laon in 1696 also made mandatory his license, which could be granted only in the cases permitted in law.[116]

Only three Italian provinces evidently did not require episcopal license for armed travel: Florence in 1517, Genoa c. 1574, and Naples in 1699.[117] As in the late Middle Ages, this automatic exception was far more readily granted in Northern Europe. Interestingly, whereas few sees in German Europe had mentioned this exception in the late Middle Ages, its concession by Cardinal Campeggio's reform council at Regensburg in 1524, combined with the turbulence of the Reformation, appears to have unleashed a great flood of such enactments in the Empire during the next century: Hildesheim in 1539, Mainz in 1549, Ermland in 1564 or 1565 and 1610, Constance in 1567 and 1609, Salzburg in 1569, Olmütz in 1591, Brixen in 1603, Chur in 1605, Augsburg in 1610, Cologne in 1662, Trier in 1678, Paderborn in 1688, and Eichstätt in 1700.[118] Elsewhere this concession appears in Arras in 1570, Namur in 1604 (but with required episcopal license), and Liège in 1618.[119] The national synod of Albania in 1703 allowed clergy to carry weapons in areas where danger to life existed, especially the mountains.[120]

---

[110] *Synodus dioecesana ab. . . . cardinali Pignatello celebrata . . . M.DCC.XXVI.* (Rome, 1726), 4.1.8, p. 153.

[111] Mansi 36Ter:849 and 966.

[112] In the order given, Mansi 36Bis:277 (5.29), 877, 544 (17.8), 428 (8), and 564 (17.12).

[113] *Synodus dioecesana Imolensis anno 1693* (Imola, n.d.), 3.1.9., pp. 32–33.

[114] *Constitutiones et decreta . . . Patavini. .anno MDCXXIV. Nunc demum confirmata . . .* (Padua, 1793), 2.1., p. 57,

[115] CG 8:735.

[116] Gousset 4:70 c. 30.

[117] Mansi 35:225 (c.17), 36Bis:586 (23.2), 36Ter:780–1 (9.5.9).

[118] CG 6:321, 584; 7:299, 539, 598; 8:354–5, 575, 637–8, 891; 9:56, 132, 1007; 10:59, 170, 273.

[119] Ibid., 8:271, 622, and 9:294.

[120] Mansi 35:1418–19, 4.1.

In 1569 the province of Salzburg, after denouncing clerical bearing of arms at great and unusual length, parenthetically admitted that the clergy could carry weapons in the event of travel and the danger of hostilities.[121] Only rarely do the exceptions for 'necessity' or just cause for fear, occasionally granted in the late Middle Ages, explicitly appear in the last centuries of the Ancien Regime. The synods of Beauvais in 1554 and Chalons in 1557/72 allowed arms in the event of necessity as well as in other cases permitted by law, while in 1673 Soissons forbade all weapons, including firearms, except for 'pressing necessity.'[122] One striking exception to this generalization and to a larger pattern of slowly restricting clerical armsbearing occurs in the diocese of Speyer in 1593. Whereas the bishops had four times between 1410 and 1544 forbidden even knives except for travel, in 1593 Bishop Eberhard condemned the wearing in public of all manner of secular garb, including 'swords and arms (unless reasonable cause exists).'[123] This was the last statute on clerical armsbearing enacted in the diocese of Speyer.[124]

Early Modern Papal Legislation

Although the early modern popes did not legislate for the whole Church on clerical armsbearing, they did for Rome and for the Papal States. In December 1706, Clement XI, through his Vicar-General for Rome, Cardinal Gasparo, published an edict on the deportment of the clergy, who were expected to serve as a model for clergy throughout the Christian world. They were not to go armed within or without the city, not even on the pretext of hunting, without the written permission of the pope or of the Vicar-General – in short, the standard Italian stipulation. Offenders faced imprisonment, fines, and forfeiture of weapons.[125] This decree was renewed in 1724.[126] Although the council of Rome in 1725 issued no specific legislation on arms, it referred constantly to the edict of 1724 and evidently accepted all its provisions on clerical discipline.[127]

In the larger area of the Papal States, the popes had long pursued a different policy. As far back as the Aegidian Constitutions of Cardinal Albornoz in 1357, armsbearing by the clergy had been forbidden in cities, fortresses, and

---

[121] *CG* 7:299.

[122] Gousset 3:137 c. 12., 356 c. 5; 4:315, c.13.18.

[123] *Collectio processuum*, p. 401.

[124] The *Collectio processuum*, which ends in 1720, was supplemented by the *Sammlung der Bischöflich. Speirischen Hirtenbriefe und Diocesan-Verordnungen von den Jahren 1720 bis 1786* . . . (Bruchsal, 1786), which contains nothing about arms, but does in 1720 record a vigorous denunciation of tobacco snuffing (p. 5). It also ardently condemns clerical wearing of wigs in 1724, 1745, and 1784 (ibid., pp. 19, 180–1, and 427–8).

[125] *Magnum Bullarium Romanum, seu ejusdem continuatio* (Luxembourg, 1727–58), 8:252–3.

[126] The latter decree is printed in *Acta et decreta sacrorum conciliorum recentiorum. Collectio Lacensis*, 7 vols. (Freiburg, 1870–90), 1:438–41, as Appendix XVIII; the paragraph on arms is no. 12 on col. 440.

[127] Ibid., 1:371–3; Mansi 34:1879–81. Mansi did not reprint the edict of 1724 here.

villages. While the Constitutions lacked any provision for episcopal licensing, they also had none governing armsbearing outside these inhabited places. Rather than openly allowing arms for travel or danger, or at least creating a legal possibility subject to episcopal regulation, the Constitutions effectively turned a blind eye on the matter. Alexander VIII reissued this law in 1690, and Benedict XIV in 1753 extended it explicitly to the military-religious orders.[128] But, as this learned, humane, and highly respected pope noted in his famous treatise *On the Diocesan Synod* (1748), this legislation applied only to the Papal States and was not meant for the rest of the Church.[129] In 1755 Benedict renewed papal legislation, going as far back as Pope Pius V (1566–72), which authorized the personnel of the Inquisition (but only if they belonged to the secular and not the regular clergy) and their servants to carry weapons, offensive as well as defensive, to defend themselves and the work of the Holy Office – but not in the Papal States.[130]

What was papal policy in the eighteenth century on clerical armsbearing for the rest of the Church? That depends on where one looks; and the more one looks, the more bewildered one is likely to become. In 1723 Innocent XIII issued a constitution entitled *Apostolici ministerii* in which all manner of clerical misbehavior was condemned in one long paragraph, including 'bearing arms.'[131] Yet when in 1759 Clement XIII sent *Cum primum* to all prelates, reminding them to enforce observance of the canons prohibiting clerical participation in business and secular affairs, he made no mention of armsbearing.[132] Small wonder, then, that Benedict XIV received an inquiry from a professor of philosophy concerning the irregularity incurred by a cleric for specific kinds of military service and armsbearing. Small wonder, too, in view of the increasing complexities of canon law on these issues since the High Middle Ages, that the pope's answer ran to eight double-columned pages replete with the learning and sense for which he was so famous.[133]

Benedict's reply alluded again and again to one institution in Rome which did after a fashion legislate for the entire Church on this and many other matters – the Sacred Congregation of Cardinal Interpreters of the Sacred Council of Trent. Although Trent had not declared anything on arms, the cardinals nevertheless received petitions and problems on the question of arms, and their responses reflected the complexity of ecclesiastical thinking and policy on the subject. Thus on 3 February 1635, to discourage the clergy from daring to take up arms, the Congregation conceded that in exceptional

128 *Magnum Bullarium Romanum*, 19:21–2.
129 Benedict XIV, *Opera omnia in unum corpus collecta . . . Editio novissima* (Venice, 1787–88), 12:4 (10.2.3).
130 *Magnum Bullarium Romanum*, 19:146.
131 Ibid., 13:61 (8): 'Ubi vero reperiantur clerici . . . concubinarii, aut foenatores, vel ebrietati, ludisve alearum dediti, vel satores rixarum, vel negotiatores, vel arma gestantes, vel incertis sedibus vagantes.'
132 *Bullarii Romani continuatio . . .* , ed. Andreas Barberi, 19 vols. (Rome, 1835), 1:227–31, no. 87.
133 *Institutiones ecclesiasticae*, no. 101, in *Opera omnia, editio novissima*, 17 vols. in 18 (Prato, 1839–46), 10:432–9.

circumstances secular authorities could be temporarily authorized to seize the offending clerics to be delivered up to an ecclesiastical judge. The cardinals revealed their severe mood by demanding on the same day the strict enforcement of all the canons and Apostolic Constitutions concerning the bearing of arms by the regular clergy, especially in public, for decency's sake; offenders should be incarcerated. But two years later, in 1637, the cardinals exempted from the prohibition on *arma prohibita* the sub-collectors of tenths on *spolia* and other commissioners of the Nunciature of Trani in the exercise of their office. And in decisions handed down in 1609, 1627, and 1634 the cardinals declared that bishops not only could have armed households or entourages (*familiae*), but ought to; that these could be increased in size, but only moderately so; and that the size of these *familiae* should be determined not only by that of the corresponding secular prince, but by the discretion of the bishop as well.[134] To be sure, this group of decisions did not necessarily have anything to do with the clergy; but they do mirror facets of the thinking of Roman prelates and the conventions of the age. Few if any thought it inappropriate for a bishop to process in armed company.

As for the participation of clerics in warfare, Benedict XIV in his reply to the professor adduced a decision of the Sacred Congregation of 1701–02 in the case of Henricus Boffaert, a deacon and canon of Ypres, who under an assumed name had served in the army of the emperor in warfare, but without killing or wounding anyone, and who now sought ordination to priesthood. The Congregation decided that he had become irregular and so required dispensation and that, in view of his sworn oath that he had not exercised any sacred functions since his military service, he ought to be granted the dispensation.[135] The Congregation ruled in 1778 no less strictly that any cleric who volunteered for secular military service forfeited clerical status and therefore all offices and benefices. Yet in 1781, while reiterating that clerics were not to participate in war and that even in a just war they were to discharge only spiritual tasks like preaching and ministering the sacraments, the cardinals also bowed to the opinion of 'some learned men' by granting that clerics did not incur irregularity by bearing arms in a just and defensive war *if* the number of laymen was insufficient to conduct that defense and *as long as* the clerics so engaged neither killed nor wounded nor exhorted anyone else to do so.[136]

In short, even though 'Rome' seems in certain respects to have been

---

[134] All these decisions are abstracted in Salvator Pallottini, *Collectio omnium conclusionum et resolutionum quae in causis propositis apud S. Cong. Cardinalium S. Concilii Tridentini interpretum prodierunt ab anno 1564 ad annum 1860*, 17 vols. (Rome, 1868–93), 2:512–13, s.v. 'Arma.' While I have not been able to work directly with the 167 volumes of the *Thesaurus resolutionum Sacrae Congregationis Concilii* (Rome, 1718–1908), undoubtedly most bishops and their legal advisers, and possibly even a few scholars, would have relied heavily on such distillations as these by Pallottini and Zamboni.

[135] Cited in 'Institutio 101' in *Opera omnia*, 10:437.

[136] J. F. de Comitibus Zamboni, ed., *Collectio declarationum Sacrae Congregationis Cardinalium Sacri Concilii Tridentini interpretum*, 4 vols. (Arras, 1860–68), 4:146–7.

taking a somewhat stronger stance on clerical arms, there was a fundamental continuity here between the late medieval and early modern periods.

Punishments for Armsbearing

The continuity between the late medieval and early modern periods on clerical armsbearing is underscored in yet another way: the punishments incurred by, or imposed on, offenders. The well-known text in the *Decretales* decreed excommunication, although it did not specify whether the excommunication was automatic (*latae sententiae*) or had to be declared by proper ecclesiastical authority (*ferendae senteniae*).[137] The *Clementines* ordered bishops to proceed canonically against those who infringed ecclesiastical discipline (triple admonition to desist, and so on), but whether this canon clearly resolved the problem posed by the earlier one is doubtful, especially if one supposes that rigorist bishops would have preferred that clerics toting arms in violation of the canons be automatically excommunicated.[138]

Local canons sometimes threatened some kind of loss of clerical status, temporary or permanent, but usually without being as precise as they might have been. Between 1176 and 1298 the popes came to distinguish four penalties: suspension (from office), privation (of income), deposition, and degradation. Deposition intensified the effects of suspension and privation because it could be removed only by formal restitution and often involved incarceration. Only degradation entailed loss of the privileges of the clerical estate. It was administered only for spiritual crimes, including relapse of an already deposed cleric (defined as 'incorrigibility'), and required a formal procedure. In practice, most degraded clerics were heretics who were then, as laymen, handed over to secular authorities for condign punishment, usually death. As for armsbearing, deposition was thus ordinarily the harshest of these punishments which could be imposed.[139]

On the level of the province and diocese, penalties are often not spelled out and commonly less severe when they are. Sometimes statutes threaten the 'canonical punishments,' either assuming that the clergy knew what these were or else deliberately remaining vague. Excommunication was not often mentioned as such. One of the strongest and clearest statements came from the legatine council of London in 1268, which possibly implied that all clerical armsbearing incurred automatic excommunication. Furthermore, if the guilty cleric did not satisfy the requirements of his superior within the time specified, he would be deprived of his benefice or, if he had none, be barred from receiving one for five years.[140] Another synod of London several decades

---

137   *Decretales* 3.1.2.
138   A good introduction to the complexities of excommunication is by Elizabeth Vodola, *Excommunication in the Middle Ages* (Berkeley-Los Angeles, 1986).
139   For an excellent brief summary, see the article by Bernhard Schimmelpfennig in *DMA* 4:133–4.
140   *C&S* 2:751–2, c. 4. For a more detailed discussion, see below, pp. 187–91.

later (1280/90) imposed the same penalties, but only for bearing arms of aggression.[141] The province of Milan in 1311 believed that excommunication *ferendae sententiae* was the proper procedure, to be followed by deprivation in the case of the unrepentant.[142] The synod of Arras in 1570 imposed excommunication and a fine of twenty pounds on clerics carrying weapons other than knives, daggers, or misericords while traveling or otherwise without special permission.[143]

In some places the bishop reserved the right to punish as he saw fit, although sometimes additional penalties were explicitly listed: Wells in 1258, Sodor (Isle of Man) in 1291, the province of Lima (Peru) in 1582 (plus loss of arms), Siena in 1599, Liège in 1618, the provinces of Naples (and confiscation of weapons) and Tarragona (plus fines) in 1699, and Eichstätt in 1700 (and forfeiture of arms).[144] Although the right of bishops to determine and license permissible cases of armsbearing was a particularly Italian phenomenon, this was not so much the case when it came to episcopal discretion in meting out punishment.

Loss of benefice (or blacklisting in the case of non-incumbents) was, as has been seen already, specified as an additional punishment in London in 1268 and Milan in 1311. It is found also in the statutes of Clermont in 1268 (one year), Gerona in 1274, Palermo in 1388, and Constance in 1463 and 1483 (one month).[145]

But by far the most common penalty held out before the clergy was fines, again a strongly Italian tendency in the late Middle Ages. Occasionally further punishments were listed, but usually not. Fines varied considerably. The following is a list, admittedly incomplete, in chronological order of dioceses or provinces which levied fines: Cambrai in 1312 (50 gulden plus confiscation), Ravenna in 1317 (40 solidi), the three provinces meeting at Avignon in 1326 (100 solidi for a daytime offense, ten pounds for a night-time one), Ferrara in 1332 (ten pounds), Padua in 1339 (whatever the Commune of Padua assessed against lay offenders), Florence in 1346 (ten pounds by day, ten gold florins by night, plus loss and sale of weapons), Lucca in 1351 (ten pounds), the Papal States in 1357 (three florins and forfeiture), Benevento in 1378 (15 gold carolini), Arras in 1570 (unspecified, as well as excommunication), Namur in 1604, Metz in 1604 (twenty francs), Besançon in 1694 and 1707 (thirty pounds), Tarragona in 1699 (ten pounds plus episcopal discretion), and Rome in 1706 and 1725.[146]

Incidentally, bishops in the later Middle Ages have often been roundly criticized for relying on fines as a way of increasing revenue as well as

---

[141] Ibid., 2:657, c. 110.
[142] Mansi 25:492.
[143] CG 8:271.
[144] C&S 2:602; Wilkins 2:179; Mansi 36Bis:214 and 544; CG 9:294; Mansi 36Ter:780–1 and 849; CG 10:273.
[145] Mansi 23:936, 1203, and 26:747; CG 5:458, 553.
[146] CG 6:711; 8:271, 622; 10:290, 770; Mansi 25:603–4, 765, 919–20, 1141; 26:36, 267, 302, 643; 36Ter:849.

punishing criminous clerks. The charge is not entirely fair, for fines were habitually assessed throughout the Middle Ages and early modern period, were decidedly more humane than many of the cruelties inflicted by secular justice (which were ordinarily not options open to the ecclesiastical judicial system), affected offenders more concretely than abstract punishments, and were sometimes to be distributed to the poor. At the same time, it must also be admitted that it may well be that the imposition of fines rather than of stiffer penalties mirrored the attitudes of the legislators, in other words, that even illegal armsbearing by clergy was often accepted as a fact of life more than one might suppose.

Finally, although clerics were doubtless sometimes imprisoned for illegal use of arms, it was a form of punishment rarely mentioned in statutes: imprisonment was used in the diocese of Liège in 1618, the province of Cambrai in 1631, the city of Rome in 1706 and 1724, and Naples in 1726.[147] Since the early Middle Ages prelates had sometimes sought to punish, isolate, and rehabilitate recalcitrant clerics by packing them off to monasteries and monastic penitentiaries. The province of Milan prescribed incarceration for *clerici militares* who neglected their benefices to pursue worldly ways, engage in tournaments and other military activities, and then impudently expected to be able to return to their posts. This statute was repeated, more or less verbatim, in Mainz in 1310, Magdeburg in 1370, 1403, and 1485, and Würzburg in 1485. In 1631 the council of Cambrai ordered imprisonment and other condign punishments for clerics engaging in brawling and assault. These cases, however, transcended armsbearing and do not permit us to infer anything about the frequency of incarceration to control it among the secular clergy.[148]

The Nineteenth Century

The nineteenth century brought enormous changes to European society, including the Church, but little to the law of arms for the clergy. Because only a minute fraction of the statutes of the thousands of synods held are easily accessible, even though so many were printed, it would require enormous (and probably largely fruitless) additional research to determine in any quantitative way how important the issue seemed to be and how synods ruled on it. No clear pattern emerges. Total prohibitions were enacted in the provinces of Pisa in 1850, Urbino in 1859, and Kolozsvàr in Hungary in 1863,[149] while the diocese of Rome in 1804 forbade all weapons except for small knives required

---

147 CG 9:294; Mansi 36Ter:186; *Acta et decreta . . . Collectio Lacensis*, 1:439; *Synodus dioecesana . . . Neapolitanae celebrata M.DCC.XXVI* (n.p., n.d.), p. 153.

148 Robert Rodes, Jr., *Ecclesiastical Administration in Medieval England* (Notre Dame, 1977), pp. 65–99, especially 89–98, has argued that 'canon law' was not a legal system in the usual sense in that penance rather than punishment was its object. This helps explain the apparent leniency of the prescribed punishments.

149 Mansi 47:854, 893, and 48:555.

for daily use.[150] On the other hand, the provinces of Esztergom and Vienna in 1858 allowed armsbearing in case of necessity.[151]

The case of the Roman Catholic Church in the United States illuminates the complexities of the issue in the nineteenth century. Plenary councils began to convene in 1791 in Baltimore to treat issues of nationwide concern. None of these councils before 1866 acted on armsbearing.[152] Until just before the Civil War the Catholic Church in the United States was very much a minority church which carefully kept aloof from the political realm. If Catholic priests during the Civil War bore arms, little evidence of it has turned up.[153] The distance of the Catholic clergy from the passions of the war encouraged some self-righteous commentary from one bishop, Martin John Spalding of Louisville (1848–64).[154] An exchange which was more revealing both of the absence of the Catholic clergy among the combatants and of the opacity of canon law on the subject took place in 1863 between two Southern Catholic bishops, Patrick Lynch of Charleston (1858–82) and John McGill of Richmond (1850–72). They discussed the theoretical possibility of conscription of the clergy and wondered about the germane canon law. Lynch believed that the clergy were simply forbidden to bear arms, but McGill did not. In a long letter, dated 17 December 1863, he wrote:

> Suppose a law is passed requiring priests as well as preachers to enter the army, and a law against procuring substitutes, what are we to do? I hope it 'will exempt ministers of religion,' but suppose it does not, what are the priests to do? There is no law direct and positive forbidding priests to bear arms under all possible circumstances, as far as I can discover. And writers on Canon Law say that a priest who carries arms and fights a *just defensive* war *pro ecclesia vel pro patria* does not therefore become irregular. We ought to have some understanding on this subject and I would wish very much to have your views and the views of other B[isho]ps of the South. It is true priests might possibly be appointed Chaplains if called into service, and thus be non combattant [*sic*]. But, also some if made to enter the ranks, might rather choose to bear arms than apply for a Chaplaincy.[155]

[150] *Synodus dioecesana . . .* (Rome, 1804), 1.16, p.155.
[151] Ibid., 47:687, 823–4.
[152] The decrees of these councils are printed in Mansi 39:293–394, 966–70.
[153] The only instance I have uncovered is Father John Bannon (1829–1913), an Irish diocesan priest who served as chaplain to the First Missouri Confederate Brigade. So brave under fire that his commanding general called him 'the greatest soldier I ever saw,' he at least twice helped work artillery pieces in March 1862 and June 1863. In the following year he returned to Ireland and entered the Jesuits (Phillip Tucker, *The Confederacy's Fighting Chaplain. Father John B. Bannon* [Tuscaloosa, 1992], pp. ix, 1, 52, 128). Two Southern Jesuits were noted in a letter of 22 November 1861 as liking to dress up as Confederate officers, but the author, a fellow Jesuit, added that 'to my knowledge, they are the first and only Catholic chaplains to wear a military uniform' (*A Frenchman, a Chaplain, a Rebel. The War Letters of Pere Louis-Hippolyte Gache, S.J.*, trans. Cornelius Buckley, S.J. [Chicago, 1981], pp. 60–62). That was still early in the war, and further research may well reveal much more activity on the part of the Catholic clergy.
[154] David Spalding, C.F.X., 'Martin John Spalding's "Dissertation on the American Civil War",' *Catholic Historical Review* 52 (1966): 66–85. Spalding sent this document (pp. 70–85) in 1863 as a letter to the Congregation on the Propagation of the Faith, of which he was an alumnus.
[155] Willard E. Wight, 'War Letters of the Bishop of Richmond,' *Virginia Magazine of History and Biography* 67 (1959):268–70. The emphases are in the original.

Nothing in this letter suggests that this was anything more than a theoretical discussion.

The only peculiar note appears in the decrees of the Second Plenary Council of Baltimore held in October 1866, which condemned clerical arms-bearing in general, threatened excommunication for offenders, and declared that clerics who voluntarily rendered military service were irregular, in contempt of the canons, and therefore deposed. In support of these positions the council referred to classic texts in Gratian, the *Clementines*, and treatises by Pope Bendict XIV. The final quotation was drawn from the first provincial council of Milan held by Carlo Borromeo in 1565, which vigorously forbade the bearing of any kind of defensive or offensive arms 'unless perhaps they [clerics] must undertake a journey outside cities in suspect places.'[156] It is intriguing not only that the exemption for travel, a commonplace in diocesan legislation by the fourteenth century, was still being repeated in the last third of the nineteenth century, but also that it was here enacted for the first time in the history of the U. S. Catholic Church, which evidently still found the legislation of Carlo Borromeo relevant and prudent. Perhaps the formulation of this decree was precipitated by the kinds of exchanges of views desired by Bishop McGill, although I know of no treatment of this topic.[157]

The only ecumenical council of the nineteenth century was Vatican I (1870), which the Franco-Prussian War caused to be prorogued indefinitely after it had issued decrees only on the faith and on papal infallibility. A proposed schema on clerical life, however, elicited speeches from thirty-eight prelates which are printed in Mansi.[158] Neither the schema nor the orators addressed the matter of arms directly, and only one bishop did so obliquely. In a discussion of hunting (which continued to arouse interest here and elsewhere), Bishop Joseph Urguinano of the Canary Islands, pressing for a total ban on hunting, remarked in passing that it was unbecoming for priests to use arms.[159]

The New Code of 1917–18

When Pope Pius X in 1904 declared that the reordering of canon law was going to be 'a difficult task indeed' (*arduum sane munus*), he might well have had this topic alone in mind. How were the commissioners he appointed to reduce all this to a few simple, comprehensible rules? Their work went on for over a decade and was delayed by the First World War. Nevertheless, in an

---

[156] Mansi 48:937–8, 3.6.153.
[157] Nor did the late Monsignor John Tracy Ellis, who kindly responded to my inquiries at some length. It should be noted that a sermon on priesthood and the life of the clergy preached before the council by the archbishop of San Francisco, Joseph Alemany (1853–85), twice alluded to the principle that the clergy ought have nothing to do with arms (Mansi 48:869–73, at 869 and 872).
[158] Mansi 50:517–700, especially 522–70.
[159] Ibid., 50:555.

effort which may be compared with the accomplishment of Tribonian and his small team of jurists during the reign of Justinian in the 530s, by 1917 the accumulated legislation of more than eight hundred years had been stream-lined and reduced to a manageable Code of Canon Law.[160] It was promul-gated in that year and took effect on Pentecost 1918, completely superseding the old *Corpus*.

Out of a total of 2,414 canons, parts of two treated armsbearing by the clergy. Canon 141 handled the question of military service and involvement in civil disturbances:

> 1. [Clerics in major orders] are not voluntarily to take up military service unless they do it with the permission of their ordinary [i.e., bishop] for the purpose of freeing themselves earlier from military obligations; nor are they to participate in any way in civil wars or disturbances of public order.
> 2. A cleric in minor orders who in violation of the above regulation voluntarily enlists in the military ipso facto loses his clerical status.[161]

The verb rendered here as 'take up' is *capessere*, which in classical Latin has the force of 'eagerly take up' or 'embrace' and was presumably meant to dis-courage among clergy the kind of eagerness to enlist so common during the First World War. Whatever their zeal, clerics could in any case canonically volunteer only in anticipation of being called up for service and only with the permission of their bishop, who on a strict reading could grant permission for this reason alone. As for participation in any sort of civil disturbances, an unqualified prohibition applied to all in major orders, although *ex silentio* not necessarily to those in minor orders. Nevertheless, even though punish-ments are not spelled out, the tone throughout is stern and unyielding and suggests a lesson well learnt from the engagement of clergy in the civil wars and uprisings of the previous century.

By comparison, canon 138, which treats all activities incompatible with clerical status in six lines, subsumes all other armsbearing possibilities under these terse words: 'nor are [clerics] to bear arms, except when a just cause for fear exists.'[162] Far from constituting any kind of general prohibition, these few

---

[160] The work of the papal commission was recorded by its head, Pietro Cardinal Gasparri, and is now available in English translation in *The 1917 or Pio-Benedictine Code of Canon Law*, ed. and tr. E. N. Peters (San Francisco, 2001), pp. 1–19.

[161] *Codex* c. 141: '1. Saecularem militiam ne capessant voluntarii, nisi cum sui Ordinarii licentia, ut citius liberi evadant, id fecerint; neve intestinis bellis et ordinis publici perturbationibus opem quoque modo ferant. 2. Clericus minor qui contra praescriptum 1. sponte sua militiae nomen dederit, ipso iure e statu clericali decidit.' My rendering differs slightly from the first translation into English ever officially allowed: '1. [Clerics] should not volunteer in secular armies, except with the permission of the local Ordinary, which they might do in order to be free of an earlier draft; nor should they become involved in civil wars or disturbances of the public order in any way. 2. A minor cleric who freely gives his name to the army in violation of the prescription of 1. falls by law from the clerical state' (*Pio-Benedictine Code*, p. 71.)

[162] Ibid., c. 138: 'Clerici ab iis omnibus quae statum suum dedecent, prorsus abstineant: indecoras artes ne exerceant; aleatoriis ludis, pecunia exposita, ne vacent; arma ne gestent, nisi quando iusta timendi causa subsit; venationi ne indulgeant, clamorosam autem nunquam exerceant; tabernas aliaque similia loca sine necessitate aut alia iusta causa ab Ordinario loci probata ne

words open up at the level of universal canon law many more possibilities than had ever existed before. Several points are worth noting about the exceptive clause: first, it is vague and could be invoked to justify armsbearing in many circumstances, certainly for all instances of self-defense and for many more than mere travel; second, it says nothing about securing the permission of superiors and leaves the matter tacitly to the judgment of the individual cleric; third, it thus ignores and in fact reverses historic tendencies toward gradually greater restriction and greater control from above; and fourth, it raises to the level of universal law for the Catholic clergy of the whole world a broad concession – 'just cause for fear' – which only a few dioceses had been willing to grant in the thirteenth and fourteenth centuries and which almost none had since then.

Several commentaries on the *Code* of 1918 published in the United States confirm that this is no forced interpretation of this passage. One adheres closely to the words in the original: 'Clerics must absolutely refrain from all things that are unbecoming to their state: . . . nor carry weapons (unless there is just cause for fear).'[163] A collaborative commentary by Jesuits changed slightly from one edition to another. In the first one of 1946, 'carrying weapons, unless reasonably necessary,' was interdicted, while in the fourth edition of 1966 clerics were not to 'carry weapons unless upon occasion there is reasonable cause for such precaution.'[164] A third commentary appeared in 1952 with a Preface by the Apostolic Delegate to the United States, Amleto Cicognani, a distinguished canon lawyer in his own right. It provided an explanation which goes straight back to the twelfth century: 'They [clerics] shall not carry arms, unless there is just reason to fear attack, when they may do so because of their natural right of self-defense.'[165]

Why was this clause so formulated? The *acta* of the commission which produced the new *Code* and might produce an answer to that question have yet to be investigated. Nor have most canonists speculated on the possible reasons. One who did (and was a Benedictine monk) ventured this opinion a few years after the conclusion of World War I:

The carrying of arms, fire-arms as well as others, is forbidden also in the Decretals. But we remember that, about ten years ago, when there was a morbid agitation against the clergy in Italy, and especially in Rome, many priests received license

---

ingrediantur.' This is translated as follows by Peters, *Pio-Benedictine Code*, p. 70: 'Clerics shall entirely abstain from all those things that are indecent to their state: they shall not engage in indecorous arts; they shall abstain from gambling games with risks of money; they shall not to carry arms, except when there is just cause for fearing; hunting not be indulged, and [then] never with clamor; taverns and similar places should not be entered without necessity or another just cause approved by the local Ordinary.'

163 Stanislaus Woywod, O.F.M., *A Practical Commentary on the Code of Canon Law*, rev. ed. by Callistus Smith, O.F.M., 2 vols. (New York, 1948), 1:68. On this and the following commentaries, see Peters, 'Researching the 1917 Code in English,' in *Pio-Benedictine Code*, pp. xxxi–xxxiv.

164 Timothy L. Bouscaren, S.J., and Adam C. Ellis, S.J., *Canon Law. A Text and Commentary* (Milwaukee, 1946), p. 115; Bouscaren, Ellis, and Francis N. Korth, S.J., *Canon Law. A Text and Commentary*, 4th ed. (Milwaukee, 1966), p. 118.

165 John A. Abbo and Jerome D. Hannan, *The Sacred Canons. A Concise Presentation of the Current Disciplinary Norms of the Church*, 2 vols. (St. Louis-London, 1952), 1:197.

from the Pretor to carry a revolver. This was purely a means of self-defence; hence the very reasonable clause in the new Code.[166]

Passing over in silence the interesting attitude of the author toward this matter, one may wonder whether one such specific occasion (albeit Roman, and therefore presumably very much on the minds of the commissioners of reform) sufficiently explains the extension of the exceptive clause for the whole life of the Code to all the clergy of the world under all fearful circumstances. Equally plausible as a hypothesis is the First World War, although again one may ask whether such particular circumstances, no matter how grisly, warranted the creation of such a universally binding (or, rather, unbinding) regulation of such flexibility. 'Creation' is the right word here, for even though the significant modifications in the ancient prohibition went back over six hundred years to the twelfth and thirteenth centuries, never had the legislation on arms emanating from the papacy itself conceded so much to so many.

The Code of 1983

The Code of 1917–18 did not survive that long. As Pope John Paul II noted in 1983, Pope John XXIII announced in 1959 his intention to convene an ecumenical council and to overhaul the existing Code.[167] In fact, the new one finally issued in 1983 after twenty years of work completely abrogated that of 1917.[168] An omission in the more recent Code is therefore not automatically covered by the earlier one. Furthermore, whereas the proceedings of the earlier commission are not available in published form, those of the more recent commission are, thus granting us some insight into the thinking of its members. A comparison of the provisions of the 1917 Code, the proposals of the later commissioners, and the results of their labors in 1983 is illuminating.

For on every aspect of clerical armsbearing covered in 1917, the new Code retreats still further from the ban of the first millennium. On military service, for example, an early draft, officially published in 1977, read as follows:

1. Since the military service is hardly becoming to the clerical state, let not clerics go into soldiery as volunteers, unless with the permission of the Ordinary. Clerics and also candidates for sacred ordination are to use the exemptions from military service which civil laws of one's own Nation and agreements, entered between them and competent Church authority, grant in their favor unless the Ordinaries in particular cases have decreed otherwise.

---

[166] Charles Augustine Bachofen, O.S.B., A Commentary on the New Code of Canon Law, 8 vols. (St. Louis-London, 1918–31), 2:87.
[167] Code of Canon Law, p. xi, in the Apostolic constitution Sacrae disciplinae leges.
[168] Ibid., p. 3, c. 6.1. The Commission for the Revision of the Code of Canon Law was established on 28 March 1963 (ibid., p. xix).

2. Clerics, who enjoy political and civil rights as do other citizens, are also to use the exemptions which the same laws or agreements or customs have granted in their favor from exercising duties and public civil offices alien to the clerical state unless the proper Ordinary decrees otherwise.[169]

On 16 January 1980, the commission proceeded to amend the first paragraph. Three members, including the Secretary, argued that the second sentence ('Clerics ... are to use the exemptions from military service ... otherwise') was redundant because its sense was contained in the prohibition on voluntary military service. Even though earlier sessions of the commission had insisted on defining the obligation of clergy to take advantage of possible exemptions,[170] the members of the commission (with one dissenter) now accepted the motions to strike the second sentence entirely and to add to the first sentence after the word 'clerics' the words 'and also candidates for sacred ordination.'[171]

Thus the new law of 1983 reads this way:

1. Since military service is hardly consistent with the clerical state, clerics and candidates for sacred orders are not to volunteer for military service without the permission of their own ordinary.
2. Clerics are to make use of those exemptions from exercising duties and public civil offices alien to the clerical state which laws, agreements or customs grant in their favor, unless in particular cases their own proper ordinary has decided otherwise.[172]

Gone is the earlier restriction which allowed clergy to volunteer only in anticipation of conscription, a condition which bound both bishop and cleric and maintained the integrity of the clerical state. Struck, too, was the proposed injunction that clerics avail themselves of exemptions from conscription permitted in secular law. Now, if a cleric feels that he ought to serve, he can presumably negotiate with his bishop, who has much less sure ground on which to stand if he wishes to decline the request. Section 2 of this canon possibly provides a bishop some support, but it is not nearly as forceful or definite as similar earlier provisions were.

---

[169] Pontificia Commissio codici iuris canonici recognoscendo, *Communicationes* 3 (1971):192, and Pontifical Commission for the Revision of the Code of Canon Law, *Draft of the Canons of Book Two. The People of God* (Vatican City, 1977), p. 66, c. 149. Although the helpful *Incrementa in progressu 1983 Codicis iuris canonici*, comp. E. N. Peters (Montreal, 2005), contains appropriate page references to the material recorded in these *Communicationes*, it regrettably gives no indication of their contents.

[170] *Communicationes* 3 (1971):192 and 9 (1977):244.

[171] *Communicationes* 14 (1982):84: 'Mons. Segretario, il secondo e il sesto Consultore concordano di sopprimere la seconda parte "iidem ... censuerint" perché è sufficiente quanto si dice nella prima parte, dove si proibisce il servizio militare voluntario. La maggioranza dei Consultori, eccetto il Relatore, approva il testo con i seguenti emendamenti.'

[172] *Code*, p. 103, c. 289.

Even more striking is the complete disappearance by 1983 of any prohibition on clerical engagement in civil upheavals, on which the *Code* of 1917 had been quite clear: 'nor are they to participate in any way in civil wars or disturbances of public order.' This suppression happened in an odd way. The reform commission originally not only wanted to retain the prohibition, but also to balance it with a positive stress on the role of the clergy as peacemakers. The official draft of 1977 thus read:

1. By all means let clerics always foster the preservation of peace and concord among mankind. Clerics may in no way have part in internal warfare and disturbances of the public order.[173]

But at the session of the commission on 16 January 1980 the Secretary moved to strike the second sentence because (according to the official minutes) 'there are moments in the history of a country to which clerics cannot remain indifferent.' Two other members also proposed adding the phrase 'based on justice' after 'concord' in the first sentence. Both motions passed unanimously.[174] The final version promulgated in 1983, then, was this:

Most especially, clerics are always to foster that peace and harmony based on justice which is to be observed among all persons.[175]

What is most striking of all about the *Code of 1983*, however, is the complete absence of any kind of ban on armsbearing by clerics. The crucial decision was made by 1971, when the commission concluded that the definition of occupations and activities unbecoming a cleric should be relegated to local ecclesiastical authorities.[176] Thus the first three sections of canon 285, the counterpart to the old canon 138 of 1917, read this way:

1. In accord with the prescriptions of particular law, clerics are to refrain completely from all those things which are unbecoming to their state.
2. Clerics are to avoid those things which, although not unbecoming, are nevertheless alien to the clerical state.
3. Clerics are forbidden to assume public offices which entail a participation in the exercise of civil power.[177]

The explicit enumeration of those activities unbecoming and alien to the clerical state that had characterized the entire tradition of canon law from at

---

[173] *Communicationes* 3 (1971):194; *Draft of the Canons*, p. 65, c. 148.
[174] *Communicationes* 14 (1982):83: 'Mons. Segretario propone di sopprimere la seconda parte: "in intestinis … habeant" perché ci sono momenti nella storia di un paese per cui i chierici non possono restare indifferenti.
  'Vari Consultori (il quinto e il sesto Consultore) propongono anche di aggiungere il concetto di giustizia (opus iustitiae pax) e il Relatore propone di dire, dopo "concordiam", "iustitia innixam"'.
[175] *Code*, p. 101, c. 289.1.
[176] *Communicationes* 3 (1971):194, and *Drafts of the Canons*, p. 65, cc. 145 and 146.1.
[177] Ibid., p. 101, c. 285.1–3.

least the early Middle Ages down to 1917 has disappeared – with the reveal-ing exception of the continuing prohibition on the holding of civil political office. *That* is evidently important enough to require firm legislation and firm action, as witness the forced resignation of Father Robert Drinan, S.J., from his seat in the U.S. Congress in 1980 and the attempt of the Vatican some years later to secure the departure from office of the priests holding ministe-rial office in the government of Nicaragua.[178]

Armsbearing is not canonically forbidden, however, and there thus exists at the moment no general prohibition on clerical armsbearing in Roman Catholic canon law save for the mild provisions concerning volunteering for military service. An appeal might be made to canon 287.1: 'Most especially, clerics are always to foster that peace and harmony based on justice which is to be observed among all persons.' From a legal point of view, especially with respect to the possibility of indicting or suspending a cleric for armsbear-ing, this is nothing more than pious moral exhortation further debilitated, perhaps even emasculated, by the qualifying phrase 'peace and harmony *based on justice.*' Since justice is rarely if ever found on this earth, on the basis of this kind of thinking one can develop a line of reasoning which sub-ordinates the pursuit of peace to the pursuit of justice. It is a line of thinking most conspicuous in Pope Gregory VII, but scarcely peculiar to him. Indeed, as was indicated at the end of the last chapter and will be again in Chapter 7, there have been enough clerical spokesmen for this position in the past century to give reason for pause and reflection.

Why this fateful near-abandonment of any real prohibition on arms-bearing, especially in view of the clear-cut retention of the ban on secular officeholding? This is the commentary offered by The Canon Law Society of America:

> The 1983 Code is content with stating the general rule that clerics should wholly avoid all those things that are unbecoming their state according to the prescripts of particular law. Obviously many of the activities once considered inappropriate for clerics ceased to be so – long before the [Second Vatican] Council. People have grown more tolerant, and clerics are no longer looked upon as semi-cloistered indi-viduals on a pedestal. The Church always expects, however, that they will conduct themselves in such a way as to maintain the respect of the community at large. In their lives they should witness to the higher values and tastes of society. If necessary, particular law [i.e., of dioceses] can specify what activity in a given locality would threaten clerical esteem.[179]

---

178 Canon 282.2, however, stipulates that 'Clerics are not to have an active role in political parties and in the direction of labor unions unless the need to protect the rights of the Church or to promote the common good requires it in the judgment of the competent ecclesiastical authority' (*Code*, p. 103).

179 James A. Coriden, Thomas Green, and Daniel Heintchel, eds., *The Code of Canon Law: a Text and Commentary* (New York-Mahwah, 1985), p. 222. These comments are repeated in John P. Beal, James Coriden, and Thomas Green, eds., *New Commentary on the Code of Canon Law* (New York-Mahwah, 2000), p. 374. In general, from a historical point of view this more recent work is of much less value than the earlier, which focused on the differences between the *Codes*

Now in a way all this accords with some of the leading principles accepted in 1967 to guide the work of revision, in particular the vesting of greater trust and authority in bishops and, instead of reliance on 'unduly rigid norms,' a preference for 'exhortations and persuasions where there is no need of a strict observance of the law on account of the public good and general ecclesiastical discipline.'[180]

Nevertheless, one wonders whether this is not only somewhat naive, but something worse. For the continued inclusion of the interdiction on office-holding (and some other clear prohibitions as well) compared with the disappearance of that on armsbearing suggests that in the eyes of the Vatican officeholding by clergy is more dangerous and offensive than armsbearing and also that bishops cannot be trusted to regulate the former matter in a wise manner. The implications of such law-making have yet to be seen and understood fully, but one thing is clear. Even if the changes in canon law on arms and the clergy in the twentieth century turn out to be unexpectedly flaccid, they are ultimately not inconsistent with the patterns of the last nine hundred years. Once the ancient prohibition was perforated with loopholes, in its official legislation and in the thinking of its canonists the Roman Catholic Church on this matter has in a sense never looked back to the tradition of the first thousand years. Erasmus and Luther protested in vain.

of 1917 and 1983 and on the shaping of the new *Code* after Vatican II. By comparison, the *New Commentary* 'focuses on the lived experience of the canons in use since 1983. It emphasises the contemporary understanding and applications of the canons based on that experience' (p. xx).

[180] Principles 3 and 4 of the ten enunciated in the official Preface to the Latin edition of the Code, p. xxi.

CHAPTER 6

ARMSBEARING IN THE ENGLISH LEGAL TRADITION

ENGLAND and Italy are habitually different – each from the other, each from the rest of Europe.[1] This is conspicuously the case with respect to ecclesiastical legislation on clerical armsbearing. Beginning in the thirteenth century, Italian bishops carved out for themselves a distinctive sphere of reserved jurisdiction normally requiring, frequently in writing, their consent to exceptions from the customary prohibition on clerical armsbearing, even for travel. It was a model imitated nowhere else in Europe save in a few Iberian dioceses in the very late Middle Ages.

The course taken by the English was entirely different. Here the church *seemed* to cleave more faithfully to the ancient ban than did any other in Europe. It was not without significance that the last recorded instance in European history in which all the participants in a battle were obliged to do penance occurred in connection with Battle of Hastings.[2] At this time ecclesiastical legislators everywhere were coming to focus on armsbearing by the clergy in particular, a narrowing which reflected both the reformers' intent to separate and reform the clergy and also the incipient reordering of jurisdiction that dominated so much of the formal political life of the High Middle Ages. In England the early collection of canons of Wulfstan, archbishop of York from 1002 to 1023, survives in two different forms. In both clerical armsbearing is forcefully condemned. Recension A specifies that 'A cleric ought not to wield arms or go out to war, because the canons teach that whatever cleric has died in warfare, there should not be any plea made for him, either at the offering or in prayer; he should not be denied a grave, however.'[3] On the subject of military service the other variation opens by declaring, 'Brothers, know that secular power and spiritual power are separate,' enumerates a great many instances to prove the point, and concludes that 'By these and many other examples it is made clear that bishops, priests, deacons or monks are not to bear any arms in battle, except only those concerning which it is read: In all

---

[1] See Robert Brentano, *Two Churches. England and Italy in the Thirteenth Century* (Princeton, 1968).
[2] See above, p. 98. The text of the penitential articles is in *C&S* 1:581–4.
[3] *Wulfstan's Canon Law Collection*, eds J. E. Cross and A. Hamer, Anglo-Saxon Texts 1 (Cambridge, 1999), p. 98, c. 75.

things taking up the shield of faith, on which you can extinguish all the fiery missiles of the evil one; and take up the helmet of salvation and the sword of the spirit, which is the word of God. Consequently, it is entirely against ecclesiastical rules to go back after ordination to secular military service.'[4]

After the Conquest a council held at Windsor in or before 1071 ordered that 'no cleric shall bear secular arms.'[5] In 1138 the papal legate convened a council at Westminster which quoted at length the letter of Pope Nicholas I of c. 861: 'it is not fitting that a soldier of the church should fight in the world, which must necessarily issue in the shedding of blood ... it is absurd and unseemly that a cleric take up arms and go forth to war, for as the Apostle Paul says, "No one fighting for God involves himself in secular affairs".'[6] And in 1175 a council of the province of Canterbury, also meeting at Westminster in the presence of King Henry II, flatly forbade armsbearing by the clergy on pain of degradation.[7]

To Allow Armsbearing or Not?
The Crisis of c. 1238–68

It was in the course of the thirteenth century that significant modifications of the ancient ban began to crop up at many levels of ecclesiastical thinking and law-making almost everywhere in Europe. Usually, whatever debate may have occurred has left few if any traces. England, as ever, was different. Partly because of the extraordinary wealth of documentation available, partly because of the extraordinary force of character of one churchman, the records suggest that a debate of sorts was conducted in various forums between approximately 1240 and 1268.

The first break with the prohibition, and the first indication of the controversy, comes from the diocese of Worcester, where on 26 July 1240 Bishop Walter de Cantilupe (1236–66) promulgated new statutes. Canon 43 reads as follows: 'Nor are clergy to carry weapons, since this does not redound to clerical honor, unless perchance necessity clearly requires defensive arms.'[8] The second break appears in the statutes issued by Bishop Nicholas de Farnham of Durham (1241–48). Canon 36 forbade the clergy the use of arms, 'especially of aggression, except perhaps for defensive weapons in time of war and for compelling reasonable cause.'[9]

Why this unusual chronological coincidence of such unprecedented character? The dissimilarities in language, content, and geographical origin

---

[4] Ibid., pp. 169–71, c. 165.
[5] C&S, 1:581, c. [12].
[6] Ibid., 1:777, c. 13.
[7] Ibid., 1:988, c. [1].
[8] Ibid., 2:307, c. [43]: 'nisi forsan arma defensionis cum hoc necessitas exegerit evidenter.'
[9] Ibid., 2:431, c. 36: 'ne clerici arma portent, presertim aggressionis, nisi forsan arma defensionis tempore belli ingurente et causa rationabili compellante.'

of the two statutes do not seem to support hypotheses about mutual influence or common source. On the other hand, geography may be a factor, for Worcester and Durham lie on borders, which might help explain the sweeping nature of their exceptive clauses. The background of the two bishops is certainly germane. Both were university graduates as well as administrators and men of wide acquaintance and experience. They had also spent time on the Continent. Cantilupe had been in Rome in 1229 and was consecrated bishop in Viterbo in 1237, while Nicholas de Farnham had studied and taught medicine at Paris and Bologna before returning to Oxford in 1229. Both had served the king, Cantilupe as itinerant justice in 1231, Farnham as Henry III's physician.[10] Both moved in a large world where they could easily have learned of new developments in canon law, even if neither of them was a canonist himself. In any event, their independent introduction into the canon law of the British Isles of the exception for defensive weapons in cases of necessity within the space of a few years represented an important victory of canonistic thinking, particularly since it seemed to fly in the face of the most quoted passage in the recently issued *Decretales* of Gregory IX – 'Clergy bearing arms and usurers are excommunicated' – and also anticipated Innocent IV's later justification of the minimalist, defensive use of weapons by clergy.

These bishops may have been emboldened to act by the council presided over by the papal legate Otto in London in November 1237. One of the issues taken up there was widespread clerical greed over benefices, which had so escalated that benefices were being seized and defended by force of arms. While condemning such practices, the council imposed a surprisingly mild punishment – automatic suspension from office and income of anyone who seized benefices held by another and anyone who, 'after judgment has been made that it belongs to another, relies on arms to defend himself in possession thereof.'[11] What lies behind this confusing misapplication of the concept of self-defense and the implied retreat from the automatic excommunication prescribed by the *Decretales* only three years earlier? How much discussion lay behind this canon? We do not know.

Whether or not this council precipitated debate over clerical armsbearing in England, one can reasonably infer that such a controversy arose within a few years from the statutes given to the diocese of Lincoln by Bishop Robert Grosseteste (1235–53).

> And because in the clergy nothing should shine except the humility of Jesus Christ and evangelical perfection, which counsels 'If anyone should strike you on the right cheek, offer him the other,' we warn in advance that the clergy are not to bear arms, but are to wear tonsure and suitable garb.[12]

---

[10] *DNB* 8:452; Marion Gibbs and Jane Lang, *Bishops and Reform 1215–1272* (1934; repr., London, 1962), pp. 4, 13, 48, 194–5; F. M. Powicke, *King Henry III and the Lord Edward* (Oxford, 1947), p. 293.

[11] *C&S* 2:250, c. [11].

[12] Ibid., 2:272, c. 24.

The dating of this synod is crucial but vexing. The scholar most qualified to decide, Christopher Cheney, once believed it took place sometime between 1240 and 1243, but later pushed the date back to 1239.[13] Cheney also presupposes a general dependence of Grosseteste's legislation on the statutes issued by Cantilupe.[14] On the matter of arms, however, Grosseteste relied on his own 'Constitutions' of c. 1238 for the parochial clergy of the diocese, for he had already published here the forceful text given above.[15] It is striking in its appeal not only to Christ rather than Paul or Ambrose, but also to these specific words of Christ less frequently cited than 'Put away your sword.' While unusual in the history of ecclesiastical legislation on arms and the clergy, this kind of position was characteristic of Robert Grosseteste. R. W. Southern's description of Grosseteste's overall pattern of legislation certainly applies in this instance: 'Here, as so often, Grosseteste was going a little further than any existing ecclesiastical laws on the subject.'[16]

Now whether Grosseteste was also throwing down the gauntlet to Cantilupe and Farnham, or Cantilupe was throwing it down to him, depends in part on the dating of Grosseteste's synod, but only in part. For although Grosseteste often clashed with the papal legate Otto, he got along well with both Farnham and Cantilupe. Grosseteste's intervention had secured the see of Durham for Farnham,[17] while his relationship with Cantilupe was one of mutual deep devotion and admiration. In 1238 Grosseteste and his cathedral chapter both proposed Cantilupe to the papal court as the principal arbiter in their disputes, while Cantilupe turned to Grosseteste three years later for advice as to whether to join the king in his overseas journey. They cooperated in many matters, and Cantilupe followed Grosseteste's methods in dealing with the monasteries in his diocese.[18]

Yet these two bishops also contended over serious issues. Grosseteste opposed any practice, no matter how hallowed by custom, which worked to the detriment of pastoral care. He loathed pluralism, a common practice against which he not only legislated in his synod, but also carefully obtained a papal rescript. Cantilupe, on the other hand, had publicly defended the practice before the papal legate at the council of 1237.[19] These were strong men who knew each other's views on many issues. They were also good friends who know how to disagree.

And so it was also over clerical armsbearing, I think, for the timing of all these decrees and the vigor of Grosseteste's language cannot be dismissed

---

[13] C. R. Cheney, *English Synodalia of the Thirteenth Century* (Oxford, 1941), pp. 110–24; *C&S* 2:266.

[14] Cheney, *Synodalia*, p. 121.

[15] *Roberti Grosseteste episcopi quondam Lincolniensis epistolae*, ed. H. Luard, RS 25 (London, 1861), pp. 154–66, at 159.

[16] R. W. Southern, *Robert Grosseteste. The Growth of an English Mind in Medieval Europe* (2nd ed., Oxford, 1992), p. 262.

[17] Gibbs and Lang, *Bishops and Reform*, p. 85.

[18] *Epistolae*, pp. 259, 302–4, nos. 80 and 99; Francis Stevenson, *Robert Grosseteste, Bishop of Lincoln* (London, 1899), pp. 153 n. 1, 261, 262, 280, 304.

[19] *C&S* 2:266 and 272, c. 25; *DNB* 8:452.

as mere coincidence. Grosseteste the theologian was in confrontational fashion repudiating the 'new thinking' by citing the words of Christ which were the hardest to explain away. This was typical of Grosseteste. Even in his purely legal and jurisdictional disputes with the canons of Lincoln cathedral, Grosseteste argued from the Bible and from Nature rather than from canon law.[20] And as for his courage and his readiness to face any adversary, Grosseteste dispelled any possible remaining doubts a few years later when before the pope himself he blasted the Roman Curia as the font of all corruption in the church.[21] In every way Grosseteste was a worthy successor to an earlier bishop of Lincoln, St Hugh (†1200), before whose holy fierceness kings had trembled.

How exactly this argument progressed among prelates, lawyers, administrators, and diplomats deserves further study, for the larger political world provides some tantalizing corroboration of this hypothesis. Between 1236 and 1245 Grosseteste inveighed against beneficed clergy involved in secular government and warfare. During those years such men became especially prominent in the king's entourage, and a decisive realignment of royal councilors occurred in 1239–40.[22] Henry's tutor, Peter des Roches, had risen in knightly service under King Richard, received the see of Winchester (1205–38), served at the battle of Lincoln, and later led papal troops in Italy.[23] He was no friend of Grosseteste.[24] When des Roches died in 1238, the king wanted the monks of Winchester to elect William of Savoy, bishop-elect of Valence since 1226 and a capable warrior who participated at the siege of Brescia in August 1238. The monks resisted successfully, mainly because William was yet another foreigner. Grosseteste joined their fight by writing two careful letters to the legate, Cardinal Otto, defending the electoral rights of the monks and the necessity of choosing a suitable person. Grosseteste did not explicitly condemn William of Valence as a warrior, but that would have been imprudent in view of the services he was rendering to the papacy.[25] In 1241 Grosseteste rejected a papal provision to a benefice in his diocese for John Mansel, the latest rising star at court who had fought in northern Italy in 1238 and would again in Gascony in 1242.[26] In 1244 Grosseteste was joined by other bishops in scotching Henry's attempt to promote to the see of Chichester Robert Passelew, a protégé of des Roches and a forest judge,

---

20 Southern, *Grosseteste*, pp. 264–65.
21 Ibid., pp. 276–81.
22 See Robert Stacey, *Politics, Policy and Finance under Henry III 1216–1245* (Oxford, 1987), pp. 139–43.
23 *DNB* 15:938–42; Powicke, *Henry III*, pp. 12, 75–6, 736, 738; Nicholas Vincent, *Peter des Roches. An Alien in English Politics, 1205–1238*, Cambridge Studies in Medieval Life and Thought, 4th ser. (Cambridge, 1996), pp. 61–64, 135–40, 232.
24 See Stevenson, *Grosseteste*, pp. 66, 93, 97, 110, 168, for the evidence, which he tends to push too far.
25 *Epistolae*, pp. 182–8, nos. 60–1; Southern, *Grosseteste*, p. 214; Powicke, *Henry III*, pp. 152–3, 270–1, 290; Eugene Cox, *The Eagles of Savoy* (Princeton, 1974), pp. 67–8. The monks won largely because they held out until William died in 1239.
26 *DNB* 12:969–71; Stevenson, *Grosseteste*, pp. 207–9; Powicke, *Henry III*, pp. 153, 294 and n. 2.

and in 1245 Grosseteste refused to install Passelew in a benefice in the royal gift.[27]

Grosseteste was thus campaigning against clerics engaged in secular activities, including warfare, an inference strongly suggested by the subsequent pattern of legislation as well as by these coincidences. Cheney originally thought that Cantilupe's statutes for Worcester in 1240 informed Grosseteste's statutes for Lincoln over the next few years. Although in his reconsiderations on the earlier dating of Grosseteste's synod Cheney abandoned this view, he still maintained that Cantilupe's legislation exerted great influence in later thirteenth-century England.[28] Southern, too, downplays Grosseteste's influence: 'He belonged to and created no school.'[29] However true this may have been on the whole, it was not so with respect to legislation on armsbearing. If anyone 'won' this dispute on arms and the clergy, it was Grosseteste, not Cantilupe, to judge by action taken in other dioceses. Thus, for example, the whole table of contents of Grosseteste's 'Constitutions' of 1238, including the categorical interdiction of arms for the clergy, was incorporated with slight changes in the statutes of the diocese of St Andrews, very possibly by Bishop David de Bernham (1239–53) in a synod held in 1242.[30] Furthermore, the particular canon on armsbearing of the synod of Lincoln of 1240 was quoted verbatim at Winchester (c. 1247), Ely (sometime between 1240 and 1256), and Norwich (between 1240 and 1243).[31] Even if Southern's observation is right that Grosseteste acquired no following as a theologian, he certainly did as a legislator.

The case of Norwich is, fortunately, not so simple, for it tells much not only about the complexities of manuscript transmission, but also of this controversy. Three different manuscript readings of the relevant canon (24) obfuscate the legislative intent of the synod but illuminate the debate posited here. The first manuscript simply repeats the Lincoln decree. The second, after repeating the decree, immediately adds after the word 'arma' the clause 'unless it be necessary to traverse places witnessing hostilities.'[32] Although this reading makes sense and suggests an attempt to bridge the old and the new thinking, the third variation does not, for here the appended clause, 'unless by reason of fear or out of necessity it is required that they

---

[27] *Epistolae*, pp. 348–51, no. 124; *DNB* 15:444–6; Southern, *Grosseteste*, pp. 176, 217; Powicke, *Henry III*, 104–5, 288 n. 2, 363.

[28] Cheney, *Synodalia*, pp. 90–109, 121–4; *C&S* 2:266.

[29] Southern, *Grosseteste*, pp. 230–1. Gibbs and Lang, *Bishops and Reform*, pp. 38–9, on the other hand, consider Grosseteste's authority in the schools and in ecclesiastical affairs to have been immense.

[30] Joseph Robertson, ed., *Concilia Scotiae* (Edinburgh, 1866), 2:52. A translation of these documents was made by David Patrick, *Statutes of the Scottish Church 1225–1559* (Edinburgh, 1907); the text of this passage appears on p. 55. On Bishop Bernham, see Marinell Ash, 'David Bernham, Bishop of St Andrews, 1239–53', *Innes Review* 25 (1974):3–14, who argues that 'There can be little doubt that Bernham consciously modeled his activities on those of Robert Grosseteste' (pp. 5–6), especially in these 'Lothian constitutions' which she dates to 1242.

[31] *C&S* 2:349 (c. 24), 407 (c. 29), 519 (c. 19).

[32] Ibid., 2:349: 'nec arma portent, nisi per loca hostilitatis oporteat eos transire.'

[i.e., clergy] pass through places suspected of hostilities' violates both logic and grammar because the addition is too widely separated from the main passage and because of the excessive heaping up of all possible justificatory words and phrases.[33] It makes sense to suppose that the second and third manuscripts incorporate interpolations designed to accommodate sharply differing viewpoints.

Which viewpoint triumphed in the long run? Grosseteste's, it would seem at first glance, to judge from what came to be the *locus classicus* on this issue in the subsequent history of English canon law. In 1268 the papal legate Ottobono (later the short-lived Pope Adrian V of 1276) convened in London the second great legatine council of the thirteenth century to reform the church and to heal the wounds suffered during the protracted Barons' Revolt. Out of the three days of meeting came fifty-seven canons. The fourth, 'On Clerics Bearing Arms,' must be quoted in full, since it will turn out to be the last and most significant prohibition on clerical armsbearing in the history of the English church. The translation is that of the Rev. John Johnson (1662–1725).

> Since the safety of Christian innocence consists in the arms of virtue, the Apostle teacheth us to put on the armour of God, and the sword of the Holy Spirit; for we wrestle not with flesh and blood, but with the princes of darkness, who are overcome not with arms of steel, but with prayers, and tears, and virtuous actions. Since therefore *the use of offensive and vindictive arms is forbidden to clergymen* who are assumed into the inheritance of Christ by the law of God and man, and that even in a just cause . . . We therefore pursue these clerks that rave with wickedness, yet with a care for their salvation, ordaining that *whoever being an ordained clerk bears arms or offends in the premisses* [sic] *ipso facto incurs excommunication*; and unless he do within a certain term fixed by the bishop make satisfaction at the bishop's discretion, let him from that time be *ipso facto* deprived of every ecclesiastical benefice in the kingdom, and yet be liable to the loss of his order. And if he have no benefice let him be uncapable of obtaining any for five years[34]

This decree attracts attention for several reasons. First, it is unusually lengthy and passionate as canons on this subject go. Second, it declares that armsbearing is entirely (*omnino*) forbidden to the clergy 'by the authority of divine and human law.' Grosseteste, by then dead for fifteen years, might have been pleased, but no specific divine law is cited. Third, Grosseteste's satisfaction would have depended on a crucial word in the text on which

---

33 Ibid.: 'etiam sub pena excommunicationis precipientes ne clerici torniamenta excerceant nec arma portent, sed coronam et tonsuram habeant ordini congruentem et habitum convenientem tam sibi quam suis equitaturis secundum quod determinant sancta consilia nisi timore mortis vel de necessitate per loca hostilitati [sic] suspecta oporteat eos transire.'

34 John Johnson, tr., *A Collection of the Laws and Canons of the Church of England . . .* (Oxford, 1850–1), 2:216–7 (emphases added). The Latin text is in *C&S* 2:751–2, of which the crucial words are: 'usus armorum divini et humani iuris auctoritate sit omnino prohibitus, ita etiam ut pro iustitia eis ad defensionem [offensionem?] aut vindicatam nullatenus sit permissus . . . statuentes ut quicunque in clericali ordine constitutus arma detulerit, vel alias deliquerit in premissis, ipso facto vinculum excommunicationis incurrat.'

basic disagreement has existed to this day: 'offensive' or 'defensive' in the clause interdicting recourse to arms 'even in a just cause.' Grosseteste, like St Boniface, presumably would have rejected self-defense and therefore used the word 'defensionem' to eliminate that potential loophole. The modern editors Cheney and Powicke follow that interpretation and adopt 'defensionem.' Yet Johnson in the early eighteenth century construed the condemnation as applying only to the use of arms for offense or vengeance, even in a just cause, which tacitly permits the defensive usage of weapons. Which is the right reading?

The manuscript tradition provides no definitive way out, for five of the nine manuscripts come down on the side of 'defensionem,' the other four for 'offensionem.'[35] The words of condemnation in the decree are also confusing, since the clause 'or otherwise offends in the premisses' potentially undercuts the outright ban implied in the immediately preceding words. The modern editors Cheney and Powicke plump in favor of 'defense,'[36] but I believe they were wrong to do so for several reasons.

First, the council convened under the presidency of Ottobono Cardinal Fieschi, nephew of Pope Innocent IV, a fellow Genoan, who had promoted him at the Curia and conferred the red hat in 1251. As we have seen, Innocent IV accepted and even widened the scope of clerical recourse to arms in his own legislation and in his commentary on the canon law. Ottobono presumably also had to have acquired some knowledge of canon law in order to function as archdeacon and chancellor of Rheims, archdeacon of Parma, and papal diplomat. Is it likely that the nephew whom Innocent IV had nurtured would have presided over a legatine council in England which would have flatly condemned even the defensive use of weapons by the clergy, thereby contradicting a hundred years of legislative development in the church? No, but this rhetorical argument cannot be definitively proved by recourse to the thirty-six extant letters from his mission to England in 1265–68 or to the work of his brief, five-week pontificate as Hadrian V in the summer of 1276.[37]

Far more compelling is the evidence provided by the English canonistic tradition from the fourteenth through the eighteenth century, represented by John Athon, William Lyndwood, Edmund Gibson, and John Johnson, who all took the disputed word to be 'offense.'[38]

These differences in reading and in interpretation over the course of seven hundred years nicely encapsulate the English ecclesiastical tradition on the

---

[35] C&S 2:752 note a.

[36] Ibid. 2:752 n. 2: 'Athon glosses 'offensionem'; his references are unconvincing.'

[37] Ghislain Brunel, 'Hadrian V,' in *The Papacy. An Encyclopedia*, gen. ed. Philippe Levillain (New York-London, 2002), 2:685–6; Rose Graham, ed., 'The Letters of Cardinal Ottoboni,' *EHR* 15 (1900):87–120.

[38] The definitive compilation is William Lyndwood's *Provinciale (seu Constitutiones)* (Oxford, 1679); the text of this constitution is given in the separately paginated latter part of the volume containing the legatine decrees. The canonists John Athon (Ayton) and William Lyndwood died in 1350 and 1446, respectively.

issue which concerns us. My tentative reconstruction is that at the time of the legatine council there existed genuine disagreement which left a legacy of confusion traceable in the manuscripts; that by the early fourteenth century subsequent papal legislation and canonistic interpretation unquestionably supported the reading of 'offensionem' together with its tacit acceptance of the right of self-defense; that the later medieval English church accepted these interpretative possibilities, even though in its enactments it never openly admitted them for whatever reason; that out of this curious silence there grew up a myth that the church in England faithfully preserved the age-old prohibition on armsbearing, a myth of which Cheney and Powicke were the heirs and which ineluctably guided them toward their emendation of the crucial text, an emendation which conveniently preserves and validates the myth. This catena of facts, inferences, and conjectures will require some explanation.

It may well be that confusion arose at the very outset in the deliberations of the council of 1268, about which we know nothing.[39] The invocation of divine law without citation of any text savors of a sop thrown to the rigorists in the spirit of compromise – thus would run one possible reconstruction. It is also conceivable that the two manuscript readings represent very divergent schools of thought which either did not achieve a compromise or, if they did, a settlement which was not distinctly remembered or which the losing party did not wish to remember.

English politics as well as canon law shaped the background of this council. Ottobono's task was not only to reform the church, but also to bring peace and unity to England after the civil wars in the last part of the reign of Henry III. One relevant incident from that long story had occurred four years before in 1264. A *parlementum* of bishops and barons had assembled in London to consider measures to be taken against leaders and participants in the rebellion, both lay and clerical, who had carried weapons, stolen, plundered, and seized clerics. The bishops responded through one person, whom Powicke tentatively but significantly identified as the bishop of Worcester – Walter de Cantilupe.[40] The portion of the response specifically treating clerics who had borne arms reminds one of the later legatine statute with its reference to those who fight for justice and to repel violence, its insistent condemnation of clerical pillagers, and its punishments for both kinds of offenders.

> To the second point I answer that clerics bearing arms in that conflict are suspended from office for a time and may be restored to office after the elapse of the time of dispensation, if they did so on the side of those who were seeking justice and repelling violence and if they struck or wounded no one in that conflict. From these [words] it should be apparent what I shall say about the others. Those clerics, however, who went about with robbers and pillagers and were party to their plundering, especially of churches and things ecclesiastical, shall be subject to the

---

[39] Powicke, *Henry III*, p. 564.
[40] Ibid., pp. 465–86, especially 484–5.

perils of their order and can be deprived of their benefices to the full extent of the law.[41]

While this particular passage does not indisputably sustain either reading of 'offensionem' or 'defensionem,' later developments all point to 'offense' as the more appropriate word for the legatine legislation, which was thus classifying only the offensive use of weapons by clergy as illegal. For example, the two papal nuncios who met with English prelates in 1273 to discuss a subsidy for Edward I's crusade also inquired about a broad range of issues touching the church. The source (the Annals of Waverly) regrettably lists only the topics covered by their questions. Among those concerning the clergy were clerical homicide, fornication, arson, and marriage; but the list begins with 'On clergy bearing arms illicitly' (*illicite*).[42] While the adverb implies that clergy could use arms under certain conditions, the qualification may reflect only the thinking of the legates, not necessarily that of their English hosts.

More convincing evidence for 'offense' as the correct reading of the 1268 decree dates from sometime in the 1280s, when supplementary statutes for the diocese of London were joined to those promulgated earlier between 1245 and 1259. In terms recalling Ottobono's council, canon 110 declared 'That clergy are not to bear arms of aggression [*arma agressionis*] or, associating with thieves, pillagers, and other evildoers, participate in plunder, rapine, and theft.'[43] The statute pronounced such malefactors *ipso facto* excommunicate and subject to deprivation of benefice for five years, unless they gave satisfaction to their superiors within a specified grace period. It is fairly safe to conclude that this synod would not have limited its condemnation to arms of aggression if the Ottobonian constitution had been intended to apply to all use of arms, even in self-defense.

This inference is strengthened by the mandate issued in 1368 to the bishop of London by Archbishop William Wittlesey of Canterbury out of fear of an imminent French invasion. Although the archbishop spoke of 'manifest necessity,' he did not have to appeal to the principle that 'necessity knows no law' to justify his command, for with one exception ('arms defensive and offensive') what he ordered fell within the limits of the established canon law of the universal church:

> everyone, even those in the clergy, whatever his status or condition, should prepare himself for the defense of his country and his own people with arms defensive and offensive to repel our enemies leaping at the very gates[44]

Similarly, Archbishop Courtenay's fulsome praise in 1383 of Bishop Henry Despenser's zeal in crushing the Peasants Revolt has offended some people, then and more recently, but it did not exceed the bounds of the canon law

[41] *C&S* 2:697.
[42] Ibid., 2:805.
[43] Ibid., 2:657.
[44] Wilkins 3:79.

on 'defense' as many canonists would have interpreted it, particularly as it applied to bishops as magnates of the realm responsible for its internal peace and external defense. Nor is it likely that Courtenay, by reputation by no means a 'corrupt' prelate, would have waxed so enthusiastic if the legal tradition of the church in England had unequivocally outlawed all resort to arms by the clergy. Courtenay, not to mention Despenser, undoubtedly would have construed the canon of 1268 as forbidding only arms of aggression.

Someone who was better placed than either bishop to offer an informed opinion on that canon was John Ayton (Acton, Athon) (†1349), a canonist in the service of Archbishop John Stratford (1333–48). Not only did he gloss the legatine constitution as condemning offensive arms alone; he immediately provided a catena of canonistic sources to demonstrate the permissibility of defense of one's possessions as well as of one's own person.[45] Cheney and Powicke found these references 'unconvincing.' Ayton did not in fact adduce the most compelling citations, but he was certainly right in viewing the weight of law and legal opinion by his time as allowing the defensive employment of weapons by clerics under a variety of circumstances. Offensive weapons were not permitted, but Ayton classifies small knives, clubs, and stones as licit. Whatever unclarity had existed in 1268 had probably in good part disappeared by the second quarter of the fourteenth century. At the very least, then, in his age Ayton was right to read the Ottobonian decree as condemning only arms of 'offense.'

If, then, the council of 1268 interdicted clerical resort to weaponry even 'for attack or revenge on behalf of justice' (which makes more sense than 'defense' in this context), it did not rule out defensive uses of weapons on behalf of persons or property. And even if the council in 1268 meant only to hint at such a prohibition, it was in any case later superseded by the papal enactments of Innocent IV and Clement V incorporated in the *Sext* and the *Clementines*.

Later Medieval Legislation on Arms

The enactments of the church in England in the fourteenth and fifteenth centuries on clerical armsbearing are very patchy indeed. The surviving published evidence from this period is inconclusive, even contradictory in some ways, but in its lumbering, oblique fashion it favors the conclusion that the thirteenth-century English church did not enact a total prohibition on all arms. Indeed, only one, very limited shred of later evidence hints of a total ban. In 1347 the bishop of Bath and Wells issued constitutions for thirteen chantry priests of Wells cathedral in which he forbade them commerce, other

---

[45] In the appendix to Lyndwood's *Provinciale*, p. 86, gloss 'd'. On Ayton, see J. H. Baker, 'Famous English Canonists III: John Ayton (or Acton) U.J.D. (†1349),' *ELJ* 2 (1991): 159–63.

secular activities incompatible with clerical status, and the bearing of arms.[46] How he construed the word *arma* is crucial but indeterminable.

Other evidence is ambiguous. For example, Archbishop John Pecham of Canterbury (1279–92) in 1279 sent to the University of Oxford a letter of protection, according to which any cleric proved guilty of disturbing the peace of the university by arms or any other means was to be stripped of all benefices for three years or barred from all benefice-holding for five years.[47] Pecham, like the bishops of the 1260s and the bishop of London in the 1280s, and like most bishops elsewhere, took a very hard line on clerics who disturbed the public order for their private purposes; but this did not exclude many other, essentially defensive uses of arms. No less subject to misinterpretation are the complaints of some councils that the clergy often dress in 'military' fashion, which may or may not embrace arms. Pecham excoriated such nonsense in 1281, but the details of his decree concern only disguising the tonsure and wearing hats, coifs, and hairpieces;[48] and in the fifteenth century the canonist William Lyndwood glossed the word *militari* in this decree as referring to fabrics and colors rather than to arms.[49]

But six widely spaced decrees over a period of two centuries suggest not only widespread clerical use of knives, daggers, and swords in late medieval England, but also acceptance of such practices by British bishops in at least four of the instances. Even the sole exception here is by no means unequivocal. The University of Oxford in 1414 drew up proposals for the reform of the universal church, two of which are germane only at first glance. The first denounced insolent young clerics acting like *armigeri* 'who do not say the prescribed offices, and are indistinguishable from the laity in clothing and tonsure, yet hold chapels and prebends in the church.'[50] *Armigeri* usually means 'squires' or 'armor-bearers,' but the serious charge in any event is that these youths neither deport themselves as clerics nor discharge their duties, not that they actually bear arms. A later article blasts those who are 'clerics in name only, soldiers in dress,' by which is meant, as in Pecham's decree, ornateness of clothing rather than use of arms.[51]

Even more curious is a canon from the diocese of Sodor on the Isle of Man from 1292. It forbade both clerics and laymen to bear arms in church or to cause disturbances there, particularly during the celebration of the Mass. Those who remained incorrigible after three warnings were to be punished

---

[46] Wilkins 2:737.
[47] C&S 2:852.
[48] Ibid., 2:914, c. 21; translation in Johnson, *Collection*, 2:296–7.
[49] Lyndwood, *Provinciale*, p. 120. Lyndwood (c. 1375–1446) graduated from Cambridge and was appointed Official Principal by Archbishop Chichele in 1414, Keeper of the Privy Seal in 1432, and bishop of St David's in 1442. See *ODCC*, p. 1018; J. H. Baker, 'Famous English Canon Lawyer IV: William Lyndwood,' *ELJ* 2 (1992): 268–72; and Brian Ferme, 'William Lyndwood and the Provinciale,' ibid. 4 (1997): 615–28.
[50] Wilkins 3:362, no. 15.
[51] Ibid., 3:365, no. 45.

with appropriate ecclesiastical censure.[52] Apart from the mildness of the punishments threatened, the decree forbids only armsbearing in church, tacitly leaves open its possible use for self-defense or traveling, and suggests that weapons were routinely carried by many men, clerical as well as lay.

Another incontrovertible fragment also originates outside England proper. Among the fourteenth-century statutes of the diocese of St Andrews in Scotland we find this unique appearance in the British Isles of the exception for travel granted so frequently on the Continent: 'Likewise, we enact that no priest shall wear the long knife which is called a *hangar*, save when he is equipped for a journey, on fine of half a merk.'[53]

Ayton's patron, Archbishop Stratford of Canterbury (1333–48), provides an intriguing case. In the provincial constitutions of 1343 he inveighed against clergy who 'apparel themselves like soldiers rather than clerks.' He spelled out what he meant: long sleeves, powdered hair, lengthy tippets, rings, costly belts, flamboyant shoes and saddles, fur-edged cloaks, and decorated purses 'with knives hanging in the manner of swords' (*cum cultellis, ad modum gladiorum pendentibus*). When he turned to proscription and threatened suspension from benefice for the recalcitrant, he mentioned in particular only long hair and beards, inappropriately long or short upper garments, and rings in public 'excepting those of honor and dignity.' To be sure, the following catchall clause, 'or exceed in any particular before expressed,' could encompass weapons; yet Stratford clearly reserved his special wrath for rings, hair, and sleeves, not arms.[54]

In 1463 Archbishop Thomas Bourchier of Canterbury (1454–86) promulgated a condemnation of excesses in clerical dress similar to Stratford's, including 'a short hood after the manner of prelates and graduates (excepting only the priests and clerks in the service of our lord the king), or gold, or anything gilt on their girdle, sword, dagger, or purse.'[55] Bourchier's manifest objection was to the wearing only of *gilded* cinctures, swords, daggers, and purses, not of those objects themselves.

The final and least equivocal scrap of late medieval evidence derived from episcopal *acta* dates from a century later, the articles of visitation for the diocese of London given by Bishop Edmund Bonner (b. c. 1500, †1569) in 1554. Consecrated bishop of London in 1539, he had already remarked in his injunctions of 1542 that 'I am credibly informed, that certain priests of my diocese and jurisdiction doth use to go in an unseemly and unpriestly habit and apparel, with unlawful tonsures, wearing and having upon them

---

[52] Ibid., 2:179, c. 29.
[53] Robertson, *Concilia Scotiae*, 2:67, c. 152; translation in Patrick, *Statutes of the Scottish Church*, pp. 70–1.
[54] Wilkins 2:703, c. 2; Johnson, *Collection*, 2:381–2. Lyndwood, *Provinciale*, pp. 122–3, unfortunately reproduces only the later, statutory part of the decree, not the introductory arenga, and thus does not gloss the reference to knives hanging in the manner of swords.
[55] *Registrum Thome Bourgchier Cantuariensis archiepiscopi A.D. 1454–1486*, ed. F. R. H. Du Boulay, Canterbury and York Society 54 (Oxford, 1957), p. 110 ('aut in zona, ense vel sica vel marsupio, exterius aureum deauratumve'); Johnson, *Collection*, p. 516.

also armour and weapons, contrary to all wholesome and godly laws and ordinances, more like persons of the laity than of the clergy.'[56] Given this widespread behavior, it is therefore perplexing to read the limited question his inspectors in 1554 were instructed to put to all parsons, vicars, curates, and priests: 'Whether they, or any of them do wear swords, daggers, or other weapons *in times or places not convenient or seemly?*'[57] Can such evidence dating from the Reformation period be admissible in a consideration of the late medieval church in England? Perhaps not at first glance. Bishop Bonner, however, was vigorously advancing Queen Mary's determination to restore the Roman faith and thus acting, as it were, as a late medieval bishop. He also knew the law extremely well. Holder of two degrees in canon and civil law from Cambridge, he had served as Cardinal Wolsey's chaplain, as a member of Doctors' Commons (to be explained below), as a diplomat in the 1530s, and as bishop of Hereford and then London (1539–59). Deprived of his see by both Edward VI and Elizabeth, he used his consummate expertise to escape death only to die in Marshalsea prison in 1569 after ten years' imprisonment.[58]

Given his legal background and his dedication to the restoration of the old church, then, it is highly unlikely that in 1554 Bonner was introducing a novelty on the subject of weapons or making prudent concessions to a clergy lately turned rowdy. He takes it for granted that in dangerous places and other appropriate circumstances the clergy will carry weapons, and not merely small or defensive ones, and his censure falls not so much on the kinds of weapons, however deadly, as on the circumstances under which they are carried. Yet the words 'not convenient or seemly' smack of a latitudinarianism that might have disturbed many a bishop on the Continent, especially in Italy. In this respect, as we shall see, Bonner's indefiniteness foreshadows the later character of English ecclesiastical law-making at least as much as it typifies the late medieval English tradition.[59]

Finally, if we look beyond the realm of episcopal legislation, the evidence is uneven and not always easy to interpret. The *Instructions for Parish Priests* of John Mirk (Myrc) (c. 1400) says little about arms and in words not as strong as one might expect: 'In honest clothes must thou go,/ Baselard nor baldric wear thou none.'[60] A baselard is a kind of sword or dagger, while a baldric is a diagonal strap for hanging a sword and is usually richly ornamented. From this choice of words, admittedly influenced by the poetic form, one cannot

[56] *Visitation Articles and Injunctions of the Period of the Reformation*, ed. W. H. Frere, Alcuin Club Collections 14–16 (London, 1910), 2:86, no. 12.

[57] Ibid., 2:338, art. 32 (emphasis added); Wilkins 4:107.

[58] Besides the entries in the *DNB* and *ODCC*, see also George Townsend, *The Life and Defence of the Conduct and Principles of the Venerable and Calumniated Edmund Bonner . . .* (London, 1842), and Merrill Sherr, 'Bishop Edmund Bonner: A Quasi Erasmian,' *HMPEC* 43 (1974):359–66.

[59] Townsend, *Life of Bonner*, p. 226, notes the report that in his visitation of Hadlam in September 1554 Bonner struck out at the head of the local parson a blow which fell instead on the head of Sir Thomas Joscelyn. It is thus possible that Bonner was more violent than most bishops and hence possibly more tolerant of clerical violence than they were.

[60] John Mirk, *Instructions for Parish Priests*, ed. G. Kristensson, Lund Studies in English 49 (Lund, 1974), ll.47–8, p. 69.

be sure whether Mirk objected to all arms in general or primarily to highly decorated ones.

The English Austin Canons and Arms

Thus far we have examined materials relating to the English secular church, particularly episcopal enactments. What of the regular clergy whose lives were to be governed by a *regula* and might therefore be expected to incline less to armsbearing? The Augustinian canons of later medieval England did not conform to such preconceived notions. In obedience to the decree of the Fourth Lateran Council of 1215, they began to convene regular chapters, first in two separate provinces, later as one united one, and we shall now examine *acta* of these chapters.

Some of the early chapters made striking use of the exceptive possibilities of appeals to 'necessity,' 'common utility,' and 'reasonable cause.' The records of the chapter meeting at St Frideswide's, Oxford, in 1234 employ such phrases seven times in two pages, and the protocol of its northern counterpart is almost as noteworthy. The level of 'exceptive thinking' in these early documents matches anything comparable on the Continent from the same period.[61]

These early sources lack references to arms in any form. The chapter at Newburgh in 1247 berated superiors and canons guilty of 'novelties' such as fancy shoes, ornamented baldrics, 'gilded or silvered sharp bread knives,' and the like.[62] Again, the objection was to the sumptuous decoration of the knives rather than the knives themselves, which had been taken for granted by monastic reformers since St Benedict. Whatever doubts remained on that score were overtaken by the constitutions of Pope Benedict XII for the canons regular in 1339. As *Ne in agro* had done for the black monks, Benedict forbade canons to bear arms within the precincts of their houses except with the permission of their superiors. For canons, as for monks and mendicants, this ambivalent ruling created problems for both the earnest and the mischievous.[63]

What the later chapters general of the English Austins did with this papal legislation is most intriguing. One meeting at Northampton in 1359 forbade canons to bear 'knives of aggression' (*cultellos invasivos*) in future on pain of bread and water.[64] A summary of the duties of the presidents of the chapters, the visitors of the houses, and the definitors drawn up after 1362 inferred from the papal constitution a general right of superiors to dispense and to

---

[61] *Chapters of the Augustinian Canons*, ed. H. E. Salter, Canterbury and York Society 29 (Oxford, 1922), pp. 4–7, 21–4, nos. 4 and 13.
[62] Ibid., p. 31, no. 20.
[63] Ibid., p. 264, c. 34.
[64] Ibid., p. 64.

punish with respect to hunting and the 'retention of arms.'[65] And instructions for visitations from around 1400 listed two pertinent questions together with their legal sources:

> Whether any [canons] carry aggressive knives, who are to fast on bread and water. 11th provincial chap. 'Extra,' on the life and rectitude of the clergy, c. 2. Whether any have weapons in the dormitory without permission? Benedict[ine constitutions], c. 34.[66]

What is ironic here is the misleading citation of the *Decretales* of Gregory IX, which had simply forbidden clerical armsbearing on pain of excommunication, and which therefore had nothing to do with this canon, which in fact was enacted first in 1359 at Northampton and interdicted only offensive small weapons with a lighter threat of punishment than excommunication.

It was, then, fourteenth-century papal legislation for the regular clergy of Europe which enabled the Austin canons of England to define the limits of licit arms usage more accurately than the English bishops had done for the secular clergy, but also to extend both those limits and the authority of abbots and priors. Whether Benedict XII could have foreseen this is doubtful. One can still safely say that what popes explicitly allowed to regulars was bound to influence the thinking and the behavior of the secular clergy, who because of their lack of formal spiritual formation, their dispersion in parishes, and their proximity to the laity simply were not held to as high a standard. It is inconceivable that what was not forbidden to the regular clergy could have been successfully interdicted to the seculars, and it may be this kind of influence which helps account for the apparent latitude of bishops Stratford, Bourchier, and Bonner on the matter of arms and their clergy.

Law and Clerical Society in Pre-Reformation England

What, then, was the position of the English church on clerical armsbearing on the eve of the Reformation? By comparison with what prevailed on the Continent it was vague, even muddled, in a way for which it is hard to account. Whether it was the ghost of Robert Grosseteste, the collective memory of heated disputes or of clerical rebels, or the reluctance of English bishops to concede to their clergy any pretext for armsbearing, the silence of the canons is conspicuous. An oblique approach to the tatters of evidence nevertheless yields a coherent hypothesis. However Ottobono's statute was construed in 1268, within a half-century it was evidently coming to be interpreted as applying only to weapons used for revenge or for offense, even in a just cause. If one can make fair leaps of deduction from the words of Stratford, Bourchier,

---

[65] Ibid., p. 196: 'Item super inhabilitate & suspencione prelatorum & subditorum pro venacione & retencione armorum dispensare & penitencias iniungere salutores Benedict' cap.o Porro.'
[66] Ibid., pp. 201, 203.

and Bonner, English bishops took an increasingly lax stand on the carrying of weapons under a variety of circumstances; and at least in the fourteenth century the bishops themselves habitually showed great zeal every bit as fiery as that of Spanish or German prelates in wielding their own weapons and in summoning up the lower clergy for the defense of the realm.

While it is impossible to estimate comparatively whether English clerics were more peaceful than their Spanish or German counterparts in the four- teenth and fifteenth centuries, it cannot be argued that they were so tran- quil that no legislation was really needed. Aside from bishops like Bek and Despenser (who were barons and great men and entitled to act accordingly), there is too much evidence to the contrary. Let four different sources speak to illustrate the problem, although more could be adduced.

It will come as no surprise to learn that the registers of the Chancellors of Oxford University are filled with entries recording the many scholars, most of them clerics, convicted of armsbearing and violation of the peace of the University and ordinarily subject only to confiscation and fines in accord with royal and Parliamentary enactments rather than any ecclesiasti- cal laws.[67] From the general chapters of the English Benedictines come much more disturbing stories: of the armed rebel monks of Binham Priory in 1320 whose wild living moved the chapter to beg the king to order their arrest; of Thomas Haukesgarth and other armed monks at Whitby who terrorized the abbot in 1366; of the eight monks of Malmesbury who besieged their abbot in 1527 'with bows, arrows, swords, and clubs'; and of the report of the proctor of the order at the papal court around 1378 that English Benedictines are said habitually to shoot with crossbows and longbows, to hunt, and to throw dice, rumors which the proctor did not deny.[68]

The papal registers provide a more concrete glimpse into clerical life in England and Ireland, if probably also a skewed one. Within a period of sixteen months (March 1398–June 1399) no fewer than four cases involv- ing English priests and violence came before the pope for adjudication and dispensation: Richard Tyttesbury of the diocese of Exeter, who had attacked many ecclesiastics; William Beverly of the diocese of Winchester, who got into an argument with and killed another priest who, like himself, was armed; Thomas Baudewy of the diocese of Lincoln, who had killed a layman with a dagger (*baslardum*); and Roger de Stoles, clerk of the diocese of Lichfield, who became involved in a brawl while wearing arms.[69] It would be rash to base generalizations on these scraps, for the fifteenth-century papal regis- ters oddly record only instances of Irish clerics so engaged.[70] Yet there is no

---

[67] *Registrum Cancellarii Oxoniensis 1434-1469*, ed. H. E. Salter, Oxford Historical Society 93–94, 2 vols. (Oxford, 1932), 1:xix–xx et passim.

[68] W. A. Pantin, ed., *Documents Illustrating the Activities of the General and Provincial Chapters of the English Black Monks 1215-1540*, 3 vols., Camden Society, 3rd ser., 45, 47, 54 (London, 1931–37), 1:203–04 and 3:79–80, 126, 279–96.

[69] *Calendar of Entries in the Papal Registers, Relating to Great Britain and Ireland. Papal Letters*, 5, eds. W. Bliss and J. Twemlow (London, 1904), pp. 88–9, 174, 192–3, 204–5, 240, 266, 345.

[70] Ibid., 5:435–6, 9:169, 10:341–2 and 678–9, and 12:89, 137–8, 141–2, 185, 407–8.

denying that these four cases did occur within a remarkably short period, even if they were wholly abnormal in their frequency.

Finally, chronicles and narrative sources corroborate, supplement, and correct this picture. Thus the acts of the chapter of the collegiate church of Ripon between 1452 and 1506 record the testaments of three chaplains who deeded weapons to others. In 1459 Father Forster left to his servant William Webster 'my bow, sword, helmet, and arrows, together with my grammar books.'[71] In 1468 these words of the late priest Thomas Hawk were probated: 'I leave to Robert Markynfeld my jerkin and my helmet, battleaxe, and sword.'[72] And in 1488 John Gregson willed no less than one dagger, and possibly two other ornamented ones as well as some armor.[73] Small wonder, then, that in this kind of atmosphere two priests in 1498 should fall to fighting with their long daggers ('*hyngers vel baselerdys*'). At their arraignment they produced papal letters of absolution. 'But,' the court ruled, 'because the sin was public, a public penance was imposed upon them,' namely that on three successive Sundays they should precede the procession to church barefooted and holding their swords and wax candles. Neither priest appeared at the appointed time, and in the end only one of the two was with some difficulty brought to submit.[74] Several decades later, in 1537, the treasurer of Ripon, Sir Christopher Dragley, was charged with all manner of offenses by the archbishop of York. Among the many punishments imposed on him was that he 'shall wear no dagger at any time.'[75]

From other records one finds more evidence of clergy routinely bearing arms and sometimes doing worse. In the diocese of Hereford in 1312 a priest, William de Winewod, was brought before the papal legate for having served as a soldier, committing homicide, and laying violent hands on other priests and shedding their blood. The legate absolved him of the automatic excommunication he had incurred, allowed him to reenter his church, handed him over to his bishop for penance, but also excluded him forever from the discharge of his priestly functions.[76] During the pontificate of Archbishop Stratford of Canterbury (1333–48), the vicar of Rainham, William Sare, came to the attention of the audience court of the archdiocese. He was a great frequenter of taverns, and on at least one festive occasion he carried about in public a shield and buckler. He even appeared armed in his own church, sometimes carrying arms up to the high altar. The disposition of the case is not recorded.[77] In Bowers Gifford, Essex, on Ascension Day 1512, the rector,

---

[71] *Acts of the Chapter of the Collegiate Church of SS. Peter and Wilfrid, Ripon, A.D. 1452 to A.D. 1506*, ed. J. T. Fowler, Surtees Society 64 (Durham, 1875), p. 86.

[72] Ibid., p. 137. Hawk's profession is not mentioned here, but he is elsewhere referred to as *capellanus* as early as 1452 (see pp. 22, 36).

[73] Ibid., pp. 285–6.

[74] Ibid., pp. 288–9, 303.

[75] *Visitation Articles and Injunctions*, 2:26.

[76] *Registrum Ade de Orleton, episcopi Herefordensis*, ed. A. Bannister, Canterbury and York Society 5 (Oxford, 1908), pp. 166–7.

[77] Roy Haines, *Archbishop John Stratford* (Toronto, 1986), p. 94.

John Baker, fell into an altercation with his neighbors which led to his being clapped in the stocks. The record reveals a man who was rough and tactless; he routinely carried about, and was ready to use, not only a sword but also a staff or rod.[78]

All these scattered shreds of information add up to a picture which corroborates, and is in turn corroborated by, a celebrated piece of Middle English literature which, as a mirror of social reality, must ordinarily be treated with great caution. This is (*The Vision of*) *Piers the Plowman*, usually attributed to William Langland, who was probably an itinerant cleric who died around 1400. In at least two places the text alludes to the wearing of swords or daggers by clerics as a commonplace. In the first, Anima quotes in Latin a passage from John Chrysostom indicting corrupt priests as the font of the church's ills and then says:

> It would no more surprise me to find laymen translating this Latin and naming the author, than it would to see priests going about with Rosaries in their hands and books under their arms, instead of wearing short-swords and trinkets! For it is quite the thing nowadays for Father John, and Monsignor Geoffrey, to wear silver girdles and carry daggers and sheath-knives studded with gilt.[79]

And in the last book the Castle of Unity was being assaulted by Sloth, 'backed by an army of proud priests, at least a thousand strong. They were wearing short jackets and pointed shoes, and carrying long daggers like a band of cut-throats.'[80]

Thus there existed enough of this sort of thing to warrant clarifying legislative action by the bishops of England, yet they seem to have done little or nothing. They neither spelled out nor circumscribed the legitimate uses of arms, nor did they ever at any level renew the old prohibitions on arms of 1070, 1175, and 1268 (insofar as the latter really was a blanket prohibition, which is doubtful). Nor, with two possible exceptions, does any cleric appear to have been prosecuted for armsbearing in later medieval England.[81] In the case of William de Winewod in 1312 the offenses were egregious and surpassed mere armsbearing, so much so that the papal legate dealt with the matter. The other case also went beyond armsbearing to encompass murder. Sometime between 1385 and 1400 the very good and distinguished prior of St Andrews in Scotland, Robert de Monte, was mortally stabbed by a canon, Thomas Platar, who had refused to reform his ways. The bishop condemned Platar to life imprisonment on bread and water, and he died shortly thereafter.[82] Furthermore, not one clergyman has been found to have been prosecuted

---

[78] Peter Heath, *The English Parish Clergy on the Eve of the Reformation* (London, 1969), pp. 10–12.

[79] William Langland, *Piers the Plowman*, tr. J. F. Goodridge, rev. ed. (Harmondsworth, 1966), p. 182.

[80] Ibid., p. 251.

[81] Richard Helmholz informs me that in all his researches in diocesan proceedings he has not found a single instance of such prosecution, although the clergy were often indicted for many other offenses: see his 'Discipline of the Clergy: Medieval and Modern,' *ELJ* 6 (2002):189–98.

[82] *Joannis de Fordun Scotichronicon*, ed. W. Goodall (Edinburgh, 1759), 1:371–2.

in the late medieval English church for extravagance of dress, against which there existed legislation aplenty.[83]

This is odd and cannot be written off as mere oversight. Throughout the history of the Christian church prelates have legislated again and again, often tiresomely so, against clerical abuses and practices which have genuinely disturbed them. The evidence for the later Middle Ages arrayed above ineluctably points toward the conclusion that the bishops of England tolerated a high degree of clerical arms display as a fact of social life, *de facto* regarded certain uses of arms as legitimate (above all the defense of the realm), and did relatively little to check abuses. And insofar as English canon law was affected by the common law emphasis on custom and precedent, the law of the church was diluted still further. In any case, the laws of the universal church modified and tempered whatever rigor ostensibly remained on the books in England. The acceptance of that law and its sources was implied every time a bishop, an abbot, a priest, or a cleric in Britain or Ireland petitioned the court of Rome for a dispensation.[84]

The Reformation and English Canon Law

The ecclesiastical tradition of a thousand years in England was shattered within ten years in two steps which accompanied the introduction of the Reformation in England. In 1535 Cromwell's injunctions for the universities substituted lectures in Roman law for those in canon law, which was no longer to be taught in the realm. The second change followed from the first. In 1545 an act of Parliament (37 Henry VIII, c. 17) allowed laymen who held doctorates only in Roman law to fill judgeships in the ecclesiastical courts. Maitland called this statute Henry VIII's *Unam sanctam*.[85]

The break was in fact less abrupt than it first appeared. The expulsion of canon law from the universities had not resulted in its death, but rather its transferral to, and resuscitation in, Doctors' Commons, which had already emerged as an association of the lay and clerical advocates practicing in the courts ecclesiastical and provided many judges for that system. After 1535 aspirants to that system first acquired at Oxbridge a knowledge of Roman law, which had always been a prerequisite for the study of canon law, and then they moved on to Doctors' Commons to gain a practical working knowledge of canon law. The abiding significance of this system, and therefore of canon law, is underscored when one notes that all marriage and testamentary cases

---

[83] Heath, *English Parish Clergy*, p. 109.

[84] The relationship between the Roman canon law and that of the church in England has now been definitively treated by R. H. Helmholz, *Roman Canon Law in Reformation England* (Cambridge, 1990), which supersedes the old 'Maitland-Stubbs controversy.'

[85] F. W. Maitland, *Roman Canon Law in the Church of England* (London, 1898), p. 94. The two best introductions to the history of English canon law bridging the medieval, Reformation, and post-Reformation periods are the Introduction to *CLCE* and R. C. Mortimer, *Western Canon Law* (London, 1953).

in England fell under the jurisdiction of the courts ecclesiastical until 1857. Doctors' Commons furthermore staffed the Admiralty Court which administered prize law and which therefore required familiarity with maritime and administrative law.[86]

Still, Henry VIII's Reformation had no intention of sweeping away canon law. On the contrary, the authority of the Church to enact canon law was reduced but in no way denied, and it was really only from the later eighteenth century that Parliamentary regulation of the church began to accelerate markedly at the expense of canon law and of ecclesiastical autonomy. More important, the Reformation did not diminish, much less abolish, the binding character of canon law on all subjects of the Crown (except where a canon expressly pertained to the clergy). Convocation of the Clergy still effectively functioned as a third house of Parliament, particularly for the granting of taxation of the Church for the Crown, a right which was surrendered only in 1664.[87] As for the binding nature of the other enactments of Convocation, it is telling that Convocation sat coterminously with Parliament from the Reformation until the twentieth century and that it was only in the eighteenth century that an unequivocal judicial ruling was handed down on the non-obligatory character of ecclesiastical laws unless Parliament also specifically assented to them.

The King did, however, envisage the reformation of the existing canon law. In 1534 the Act for Submission of the Clergy and Restraint of Appeals (25 Henry VIII, c. 19) ordered the revision of canon law, which was to remain in force until the completion of that task except where it ran counter to the laws of the realm or damaged the royal prerogative. The enabling legislation authorized the King to appoint a commission of thirty-two members to compile a corpus for use by the courts ecclesiastical. Delay followed upon delay, and it was only in 1551 that a committee of eight, not of thirty-two, formally began to work. They finished their task by early 1553 and presented it to Parliament in March. Edward VI died that summer, however, and between the religious controversies of the next two decades and the strongly Calvinist flavor of the text, the book did not fare well. Finally, in 1571 Archbishop Matthew Parker gave John Foxe (the famous martyrologist) leave to print it as the *Reformatio legum ecclesiasticarum* or *Reformation of the Ecclesiastical Laws.*[88]

This work recast the 'mountain' (*mons*) which canon law had become into 323 printed pages of text. The guiding spirit behind it was Archbishop Thomas Cranmer, who also put his decisive impress on the Articles of Religion and on

---

[86] *CLCE*, pp. 52–5.
[87] *ODCC*, pp. 416–17.
[88] The Latin text was published under an English title by Edward Cardwell, *The Reformation of the Ecclesiastical Laws* . . . (Oxford, 1850) (hereafter *REL*). A translation of the 1552 version, together with emendations made then and later by Foxe, has been rendered by James C. Spaulding, *The Reformation of the Ecclesiastical Laws of England, 1552*, Sixteenth Century Essays and Studies 19 (Kirksville, Missouri, 1992). See the article in *ODCC* s.v. 'Reformatio legum ecclesiasticarum.'

the Book of Common Prayer. More than any other single person (save Henry VIII and possibly Elizabeth, whose place is still being debated), Cranmer shaped the Anglican form of Christianity. In his search for a *via media* he consciously sought to cull the best from the past while purging those accretions to the tradition which had gone astray. The Preface to the First Book of Common Prayer of 1549 is a remarkable statement of his vision and his goals. Compared with the anti-Roman venom so prominent among most of the earlier Continental Reformers, it is unusually balanced, generous, and far-sighted. The Preface also contains the key to his and subsequent Anglican thinking about law: 'Yet because there is no remedy, but that of necessitie there must be some rules: therfore certein are here set furth, whiche as they be fewe in nombre; so they be plain and easy to be understanded.'[89]

The result, however well-intentioned and successful in other respects, was not necessarily a happy one so far as the discipline of the clergy was concerned. The sections dealing with various punishments – suspension, sequestration, deprivation, and excommunication – are vague and unhelpful in enumerating the offenses for which these penalties could be imposed.[90] And while custom was explicitly rejected where it ran counter to reason and law (positive, natural, or divine), it is also striking that the very first of the 'Rules of Law' which the *Reformatio* carried over from the old law was the principle that 'Necessity makes permissible that which was not permitted in law.'[91] To be sure, this was counterbalanced immediately by another maxim taken from Pope Boniface VIII's 'Rules': 'Those matters which were introduced because of necessity ought not be drawn into argument.'[92] Nonetheless, the principle that 'necessity knows no law' was given a distinctive primacy of place in a proposed code which laid down few precise guidelines on clerical conduct.

The *Reformatio* does describe the duties of each of the three grades of the clergy (bishop, priest, and deacon) and of the other officers of the church, together with the things they are to avoid. The relevant section on priests is specific up to a point: 'Neither should they be drinking companions, nor dicers, nor fowlers, nor hunters, nor sycophants, nor idlers, nor lazabouts . . . [A priest's] dress is to be decorous and grave, as befits his ministry, not that of a soldier, according to the judgment of his bishop.'[93]

Armsbearing as such is thus not prohibited except possibly by inference from the ban on hunting. 'Military' dress, as we have already seen, does not necessarily even include armsbearing. Some latitude is granted to bishops, but for centuries they had shown no sign of caring about arms. And in the end, 'necessity' could be appealed to, especially in that obedience to the

---

[89] *The First and Second Prayer Books of Edward VI* (London, 1910), p. 4.
[90] *REL*, pp. 156–88.
[91] Ibid., p. 319 (Spaulding trans., p. 277). The original text appears in Bede's commentary on Mark and was incorporated in the *Decretales* 5.41.4.
[92] *REL*, p. 319 (Eng. trans., p. 277) (=*Sext* 5.12.post cap. 5).
[93] *REL*, pp. 99–100. The text of the 1552 edition (Spaulding, p. 140) is substantially the same as that of the 1571 ed.

magistrate which the clergy were to inculcate in Her Majesty's subjects and were themselves to practice as examples to their flock.

Even had the *Reformatio* forbidden arms to the clergy, it would never have taken effect because although it was accepted by the Upper Houses of both Convocations, it was not by the Lower House, by Parliament, or by the Queen, and so never became law. And with two exceptions no other attempt was made in the sixteenth century to change or define the law on armsbearing – not in Edward VI's injunctions of 1547, nor in Cardinal Pole's constitutions, nor in the articles of visitation of almost all the bishops.[94] As we have seen, Bishop Bonner's instructions of 1554 constitute one exception, and he forbade arms to his clergy 'in times and places not convenient or seemly.' The other exception was the royal injunctions for St George's Chapel, Windsor (the seat of the Order of the Garter) for 1550, which commanded that 'no prebendary or other inferior minister shall wear any weapon *within the chapel.*'[95]

Viewed in terms of ecclesiastical law and tradition, then, Archbishop Whitgift's summons to the clergy of the province of Canterbury in 1588 canonically hardly differed from Archbishop Wittlesey's to his clergy in 1368. Defense of the *patria* in its hour of need was widely accepted among late medieval canonists as a sound reason for the clergy's taking to weapons, especially in obedience to lawfully established authority. That tradition did not die in England. Although it does not appear to have been much discussed in English circles, or at least scarcely surfaced in the serendipity of the recorded past, the actions of the English clergy, particularly of the hierarchy, at such times indicate that England did not differ that much from the Continent.

If anything, in fact, the English Reformation reinforced such features. By withdrawing obedience to Rome and declaring the monarch head of the church, and by curtailing the scope and autonomy of canon law, Parliament effectively converted the church into a state ministry of prayer and the clergy into ministers of the Crown. Only time would tell whether the episcopate and 'papistical' conceptions of priesthood would survive in England, but there was no question that ministers of the Gospel were to be firmly under the control of the government. 'Puritans' of whatever stripe protested against the princely pretensions of the clergy, and in their way they leveled the clergy by rejecting its sacral character and putting it on an equal footing with the laity. One way or another, the barriers between the clergy and the laity were to be knocked down.

The relevance of the status of the clergy with respect to both the laity and the government becomes apparent in a consideration of the Articles of Religion, which all Anglican clergy since the Reformation have been obliged to swear to uphold. In the draft of 1552, article 36 is germane. The Latin and English texts which follow were published separately in 1553.

---

[94] Wilkins 4:3–8, 23–4, 60, 123, 145–6, 157–8, 169, 183, 263–9, 792–806.
[95] *Visitation Articles and Injunctions*, 2:220, art. 14 (emphasis added).

Christianis licet ex mandato Magistratus arma portare & iusta bella administrare.
It is lawefull for Christians at the commaundement of the Magistrate, to weare weapons, and to serue in lawefull wars.[96]

While 'lawefull' is not the most precise translation of 'just,' what is most intriguing is that in the final and official rendering of the Articles in 1571 (now article 37) the word 'lawefull' disappeared from the English translation, although not from the Latin text.[97] Why Convocation permitted this omission, or whether it was compelled to do so, or whether the church was as much animated as the government by fear of Calvinism and Catholicism – the answers to these questions have yet to be extricated from the complexities of politics and discussion over the course of a significant decade, if they ever can be.[98]

Aside from quietly rendering obsolete the old question whether the wars on which the government was engaged were just or not, all these variants sidestep a question central to our concerns: do the clergy enjoy exemption from the commands of the magistrate to wear weapons and serve in the wars, just or no? Unfortunately, commentaries on the Articles of Religion from all later centuries do not take up these problems.

In fact, although as men of God the clergy enjoyed a certain status at law with particular rights and exemptions, there is little evidence of such an exemption in practice in medieval or early modern English history. In the Middle Ages, when the clergy were the 'elect of Christ' (sors Christi) and officers of two realms, bishops as magnates of the realm routinely served their king, and at least in time of need the secular clergy were ordered to go forth in battle. With the Reformation the clergy lost some of their 'consecration' in the original sense of the word, their 'set-apartness.' No longer under papal jurisdiction, unambiguously officers of the Crown, and less 'priestly,' they became much more like the laity.

And so they were treated, at least in times of emergency. The 'Armada scare' of 1590 produced a command that the clergy again provide 'armor and warlike furniture' as they had two years before. In this instance we have the fascinating returns of the diocese of Lincoln. The 902 incumbent clergy were officially listed as having for the defense of the realm 48 light horses, 9 lances, 46 petronels (large pistols favored by horsemen), 96 muskets, 40 corslets (breastplates), 283 calivers (light muskets or harquebuses), 192 bows, 80 bills, and 5 halberds. Of the 902 clergy, exactly 100 are listed as sharing weapons with others, while thirteen churches are described as without incumbent but

---

[96] The various redactions of the Articles are printed in Appendix III of Charles Hardwick, *A History of the Articles of Religion* (Philadelphia, 1852; 3rd ed., London, 1876), p. 300 in the first edition and p. 344 in the third.
[97] Ibid., pp. 301 and 345.
[98] Although noting the many differences among the texts, Hardwick says nothing about the disappearance of the qualifier (pp. 148–51 in the first edition, 155 n. 5 in the third). Interestingly, the Church of Ireland in its Articles of Religion in 1615 correctly translated the Latin text (ibid., p. 381 in the third ed.).

provided with a weapon.[99] (Presumably many of them would have been used for hunting to supply meat for the table.) Although the Militia Act of 1662 exempted the clergy, the complaint of the Reverend John Johnson in the eighteenth century suggests that the Crown would in a pinch not hesitate as late as 1708 to press the clergy to serve personally or vicariously.[100] It was evidently only by shifting the military obligation from the individual to the parish that the Act of 1757 ended this continuing threat to what some clergymen considered their rightful immunity from military service and armsbearing.

Whether such sentiments were shared by the majority of clergymen is more problematical. Passionate loyalty to the Crown and military zeal moved some clergymen, while simple fear of angering the monarch impelled others. The bishop of Lincoln in 1602 was probably a good barometer of clerical feeling when he sought to expedite the clergy's provision of men, horses, weapons, and money for the expedition to Ireland so that 'wee may bee freed from God and her Ma[jes]tes displesure then the w[hich] twoe there can noe greater plagues fall vppon vs.'[101] This conflation of the divine and royal minds was by now an established pattern in England, especially after the brusque elimination in the 1530s of the Vicar of Christ in Rome as a rival spokesman for the divine will.

Whether out of fear, discretion, indifference, or loyalty as the Established Church, the Anglican Church has never made any attempt to impose even a half-hearted prohibition on armsbearing by the clergy which it could then have fallen back on against the claims of the civil power. This is of great significance. A sufficient number of clergymen, or even a small number of highly-placed or forceful clergymen, believing that it is simply not right for clergy to use weapons, could have proposed such legislation at some time or other, even though it would have required the assent of Parliament, both Convocations, and the Crown for its successful passage. No evidence exists that such an attempt was ever made.

The Constitutions and Canons Ecclesiastical of 1603

All the fruitless efforts to revise canon law in the sixteenth century were finally vindicated in 1603, when the Constitutions and Canons Ecclesiastical received the assent of both Houses of both Convocations and of the Crown, but not of Parliament. The relevant canons are given below:

> 75. Sober Conversation required in Ministers.
>   No Ecclesiastical Person shall at any time, other than for their honest necessities,

99 *The State of the Church in the Reigns of Elizabeth and James I as Illustrated by Documents Relating to the Diocese of Lincoln*, 1, ed. C. Foster, Publications of the Lincoln Record Society 23 (Horncastle, 1926), pp. 145–68.
100 John Johnson, *The Clergy-Man's Vade-Mecum* . . . 4th ed. (London, 1715), 1:147.
101 *State of the Church*, p. 219.

resort to any taverns or alehouses, neither shall they board or lodge in any such places. Furthermore, they shall not give themselves to any base or servile labour, or to drinking or riot, spending their time idly by day or by night, playing at dice, cards, or tables, or any other unlawful games; but at all times convenient they shall hear or read somewhat of the holy Scriptures, or shall occupy themselves with some other honest study or exercise, always doing the things which shall appertain to honesty, and endeavouring to profit the Church of God; having always in mind, that they ought to excel all others in purity of life, and should be examples to the people to live well and christianly, under pain of Ecclesiastical censures, to be inflicted with severity, according to the qualities of their offences.

76. Ministers at no time to forsake their Calling.

No man being admitted a Deacon or Minister shall from thenceforth voluntarily relinquish the same, nor afterward use himself in the course of his life as a layman, upon pain of excommunication[102]

There is nothing here about armsbearing in any form, nor would there be in any of the amendments to these canons enacted in 1640, 1865, 1887, 1936, 1946, or 1948. In 1603, these two canons became the relevant law of the Church of England for the next three-and-a half centuries, until the issuance of a completely new set of canons in 1969.

Although canon 75 does not touch arms (but does cover many other topics treated in medieval disciplinary canons), it might be argued that canon 76 does on the basis of the Pauline or Ambrosian texts on the inherently lay character of warfare. Unfortunately for this line of reasoning, not a single Anglican clergyman has been indicted for 'bearing arms' in any form under either of these canons or any other law since the Reformation. Nothing happened to all those clergymen of the seventeenth century mentioned in the first chapter because they bore arms – Williams, Mews, Compton, and all the others. Under canon 75, they could have been indicted, tried, and punished accordingly if found guilty; none was. Under canon 76, they would have been automatically excommunicated; none was, or rather, no one acted as if any of them had been.

The importance of being clear and explicit in legislation is underscored by considering the related canon (74) on 'Decency in Apparel enjoined to Ministers.' Its length notwithstanding, clergymen are here not enjoined from wearing military dress or even arms. The result was that those who preferred to understand the law *a la moda italiana* ('if it is not forbidden, then it is permitted') rather than *a la moda tedesca* [German] ('if it is not permitted, then it is forbidden') were basically otherwise free to follow fashion. And they did, just as they had in the late Middle Ages. If one Presbyterian, Adam Martindale (1623–86), serves as a reliable guide, the majority of the clergy tended toward a loose rather than a strict construction of the law. In 1642 he chose to surrender his private secretaryship to Col. Moore, commander of

---

[102] *The Constitutions and Canons Ecclesiastical (Made in the Year 1603, and Amended in the Years 1865, 1887, 1936, 1946, and 1948)* (London, 1961), p. 33.

the Parliamentary garrison at Liverpool, because Moore's family 'was such an hell upon earth, as was utterly intollerable,' and a pack of thieves and blasphemers to boot.

> I was therefore well content to come downe a peg lower, accepting of the chief clarke's place in the foot regiment, which place (though belowe the other for profit and credit) gave me better content ... My worke also was easie enough, and such as gave me time for my studies, being onely to keep a list of the officers' and souldiers' names, and to call them upon occasion. Nor was I to carrie either musquet, pike, halbert, or any other weapon, onelie for fashion sake I wore a sword, as even ministers in those dayes ordinarily did.[103]

Martindale was, on his own account, a man of peace and genuine religion, not a devotee of vice and violence; yet he followed contemporary fashion, like most other ministers, in wearing a sword. His words 'in those days' suggest that by the time he wrote several decades later this usage had disappeared. In the mid- and later seventeenth century the 1710s, clergymen could imitate such lay fashions if they so chose because canon law did not forbid them to.

This is scarcely to suggest that canon law and its enforcement had fallen into desuetude in the seventeenth century. One case alone will prove not only the contrary, but also the high degree of continuity of medieval canon law in the Anglican Church. In late July 1621, George Abbot, archbishop of Canterbury, while hunting on his estate in Bramzil Park, accidentally killed a huntsman with an arrow he had fired from his crossbow. The archbishop was charged with irregularity and suspended from office until the resolution of the case. King James I appointed a commission of six clergy and four laymen, who submitted a perfectly split decision on the question. Making up his own mind, therefore, as Head of the Church, the King created a new commission with instructions to prepare the necessary dispensation for Archbishop Abbot. On Christmas Eve, 1621, James signed the dispensation which allowed the Primate to resume his duties.[104]

Archbishop Abbot, then, was prosecuted in the seventeenth-century Anglican Church in a way which reveals not only the legal precision of which that tradition was capable, but also its essential continuity with medieval ecclesiastical law, and its willingness to prosecute offending clerics, even highly situated ones. When this case is set over against what did not happen to any of the seventeenth-century Anglican clerical warriors, one can conclude only that no flat prohibition on arms existed in canon law either before or after the Reformation, not that the Anglican Church had become so flaccid that its own laws were not enforced.

---

[103] *The Life of Adam Martindale, Written by Himself,* ed. Richard Parkinson, Chetham Society Publications 4 (n.p., 1845), p. 37. See also his comments on pp. 194–5. On Martindale, see *DNB* 12:1189–92.

[104] Wilkins 4:462–3; Paul Welsby, *George Abbot. The Unwanted Archbishop 1562–1633* (London, 1962), pp. 91–104; S. M. Holland, 'George Abbot: "The Wanted Archbishop",' *Church History* 56 (1987):172–87.

The Genesis of Anglican Memory on Armsbearing

The modern Anglican tradition 'remembers' that the church in England has 'always' forbidden armsbearing. The curious origins of that myth seem to lie in the later seventeenth and eighteenth centuries. While most commentators on English canon law in the seventeenth, eighteenth, and nineteenth centuries say little or nothing about clerical armsbearing, the most forceful statement happens to have come from the most celebrated work on Anglican canon law by a clergyman, the *Codex juris canonici Anglicani* (1713) of Edmund Gibson, bishop of Lincoln (1716–23) and then London (1723–48). The Archbishops' *Report on Canon Law of 1947* describes Gibson's work as 'still absolutely indispensable to any serious study of the law and constitution of the Church of England.'[105] In title 7 (The Conversation and Apparel of Priests and Deacons), c. 2 (The Conversation of Ministers, with regard to Life and Manners), Gibson reproduces two texts. The second is canon 75 of the Constitutions of 1603, which does not refer to arms. The first text adduced does, but what Gibson does with it is intriguing. The constitution is c. 4 of Ottobono's legatine council of 1268, which Gibson misdates to 1237, obviously conflating Otto and Ottobono and their two councils. Gibson quotes the Latin text of 'De Clericis Arma portantibus' accompanied by the following marginal gloss:

> The Sword of the Spirit, (and not of secular weapons) is the Armour that belongs to Clergymen,
> - notwithstanding which divers do wear Arms,
> - which for the future, none shall do upon pain of Excommunication,
> - and, being Contumacious, of Deprivation,
> - or Incapacity of Promotion for five years.[106]

The Latin text which Gibson quotes reads 'offensionem' in the crucial place discussed earlier, but Gibson ignores or does not see the purely defensive possibilities latent in the canon and interprets it as a blanket prohibition on all armsbearing. Whether his oversimplification derived from innocence, ignorance, haste, or design cannot be said. In view of his authority in the modern Anglican tradition, however, it is fair to observe that if Gibson did not create the myth that the Church in England and the Church of England have always forbidden clerical armsbearing, he at least inadvertently greatly strengthened it and ensured for it long life.

What undoubtedly contributed to the making of that myth was, ironically, the way Lyndwood's *Provinciale* handled some key texts. The long table of contents, which serves also as an index, provides summaries of, or extracts from, the constitutions and canons glossed by Lyndwood and Athon,

---

[105] *CLCE*, p. 55. See also Norman Sykes, *Edmund Gibson. Bishop of London 1660–1748* (Oxford, 1926), pp. 65–71.
[106] Edmund Gibson, *Codex juris ecclesiastici Anglicani*, 2nd ed. (Oxford, 1761), 1:161–2.

including those of 1268. The fourth title, 'De clericis arma portantibus,' significantly omits the introductory passage, including the vexing words about the offensive and defensive usage of arms, and prints only the apparently categorically prohibitory words in the second half of the decree.[107] Anyone reading only this summary, then, without turning to the full text of the constitution, would reasonably infer a complete prohibition on arms from these words; and the probability of this deduction was increased by the English translation of the *Provinciale*, first published in 1534, which does *not* contain the legatine constitutions of 1237 and 1238 and Athon's glosses on them (since these were all additions to the work). A reader using this translation alone would thus be unable to check the fully translated text of the constitution and Athon's comments.[108] Finally, anyone reading Gibson's gloss without checking the complete Latin text, which he did reproduce, would fall into the same trap.

Whether Gibson actually represented the consensus then is hard to estimate, for nearly all other commentators of the seventeenth through nineteenth centuries bypass the issue or fasten only on select facets of the question.[109] Only one followed Gibson directly, and he sounds very much as though he was a victim of Gibson's myth. In 1874 Mackenzie Walcott, precentor of Chichester Cathedral, published his commentary on the constitutions and canons in which he quoted without translation only one sentence from Ottobuono's constitution: 'The use of arms is completely forbidden by the authority of divine and human law to the clergy, who are called to the distinguished inheritance of Christ.' Walcott's citation in Latin of this sentence from the introductory portion of the constitution reveals that he had seen the full original text and did not fall into the trap outlined above by relying on shortcuts. Yet he, too, like Gibson, did not 'see' the qualification governing weapons employed 'for offense and revenge, even in a just cause.' Walcott then cites in abbreviated form the Apostolic Canons, the council of Meaux of 845, and the council of Westminster of 1175, but nothing of later origin.[110] He thus confirms both the binding character of medieval legislation and the absence of any pertinent canons after 1268. His distortion of Ottobono's constitution was doubtless unwitting and expressed the Victorian clerical understanding of the matter. Thus only a year later another Anglican clergyman wrote in an entirely different context: 'Yet in the legatine constitutions clerics were very strictly forbidden to bear arms.'[111] Whether armsbearing was a

---

[107] *Provinciale*, sig. n [3], 'Constitutionum Othoboni Summaria,' tit. 4: 'Quicunque in Clericali Ordine constitutus Arma detulerit, aut deferenti illicite sese immiscuerit, ipso facto excommunicetur.'

[108] *Lyndwood's Provinciale. The Text of the Canons Therein Contained, Reprinted from the Translation Made in 1534*, eds J. V. Bullard and H. C. Bell (London, 1929).

[109] Specifically, Edward Stillingfleet, John Godolphin, William Watson, Richard Zouch, John Ayliffe, Richard Burn, and Thomas Sharp.

[110] Mackenzie E. C. Walcott, *The Constitutions and Canons Ecclesiastical of the Church of England, referred to their original sources, and illustrated with explanatory notes* (Oxford-London, 1874), p. 108.

[111] J. T. Fowler, ed., *Acts of Chapter of the Collegiate Church of Ripon*, p. 286, n. 4.

justiciable offense in the eyes of the ecclesiastical courts at that time is highly doubtful, however, for it is nowhere listed as such in two standard texts of the period.[112]

Further Complication of Ecclesiastical Law

Two developments in the eighteenth and nineteenth centuries sapped the autonomy of canon law in the Church of England. First, the quantity of Parliamentary legislation for the church increased appreciably. The following list shows, according to the calculations of one scholar, the maximum average number of ecclesiastical statutes enacted by Parliament per annum:

1216–1530:	1.5
1530–1760:	2.5
1760–1820:	10
1820–1870:	25

The marked acceleration from the mid-eighteenth century owed less to the intrusiveness of the State than to internecine warfare within the church, above all the Bangorian controversy, which crippled for some time its ability to function effectively.[113] In fact, the backing of Parliament strengthened the position of the laws of the church as long as Parliament and the church agreed and, more specifically, the ecclesiastical courts accepted the validity of Parliamentary statutes (which they did until the decisive parting of the ways over divorce in 1937). On armsbearing, however, none of the pertinent statutes – the Church Discipline Acts of 1840 (3 & 4 Victoria, c. 86) and 1892 (55 & 56 Victoria, c. 32), and the Incumbents Measures of 1945 and 1947 – has a word to say.[114]

The second change in the nineteenth century did adversely affect the workings of the church and its law. In 1833 an Act of Parliament transferred jurisdiction from the Court of Delegates, which since the Reformation had served as the supreme ecclesiastical court of appeals, to the Judicial Committee of the Privy Council. This committee is obliged neither to have any clergymen as members nor to decide cases according to canon law. The Act, furthermore, never received the assent of the Church. For these reasons many churchmen have since 1833 refused to recognize this jurisdiction of the Judicial Committee, and in consequence since then there has existed no generally accepted supreme court of appeal in the Church of England. The

---

[112]   Robert Phillimore, *The Ecclesiastical Law of the Church of England*, 2nd ed. by W. G. F. Phillimore and C. F. Jemmett (London, 1895), pp. 473–81, 836–911, 1064–1107; Henry Cripps, *A Practical Treatise on the Law Relating to the Church and Clergy*, 8th ed. by K. M. Macmorran (London, 1937), pp. 59–63, 67–70.

[113]   *CLCE*, p. 50.

[114]   The texts are all contained in *Halsbury's Complete Statutes* (London, 1929–31), vol. 6 ('Ecclesiastical Law').

result, according to one authority, is 'disciplinary chaos tempered by episcopal good advice and a practical disuse of ecclesiastical courts.'[115] It was only
after World War II that the church undertook fundamental reform of its
court system.[116]

The Church of England and World War I

The responses of the Church of England during the First World War revealed
how thoroughly muddled the law concerning the clergy and arms had
become. The Church of England was in 1914 more than ever the church of
the Establishment, and the links with the army were particularly close. On the
outbreak of war, thirty percent of all officers in the royal army were the sons of
clergymen, and the ranks of the theological colleges of the realm were swiftly
thinned by a good third by the prompt enlistment of over 400 seminarians.[117]
Nevertheless, even though the church gave every sign of its loyalty, it was put
under considerable pressure to do more, especially to allow clergy to be conscripted, even perhaps for combat service. With one exception, no churchman ever publicly responded to such demands by adducing the irrefutable
trump card, the canon law of the church which supposedly forbade the clergy
to take up arms. Even the exception put the case anonymously and weakly. In
February 1916 *The Times* published a letter, signed 'A Bishop,' on the subject
of 'Theological Students as Combatants': 'There has been much discussion on
the subject of priests enlisting as combatant soldiers. Personally, I feel sure
that it is ecclesiastically wrong, but it has been done.'[118] Far from quoting a
canon or law of which he is certain, the bishop instead relies on his personal
feelings about the matter. It is useless to speculate whether the clergy acted
so timidly out of patriotism, fear, or confusion, for all three motives, far from
being incompatible, mutually reinforce each other.

Ironically, one layman did forthrightly cite the ancient prohibition. Sir
Lewis Dibdin (1852–1938) was no ordinary layman, however. Son of a clergyman, chancellor of numerous dioceses from 1886 onward, he was an out-
standing ecclesiastical judge, lawyer, and administrator, and thus in a good
position to know.[119] In February 1916 he had the following exposition published in the *Guardian*:

> The general Canon Law again and again forbade Clerks to bear arms. In England
> the prohibition is to be found so early as Archbishop Theodore's Penitential (668–

---

[115]   E. J. Bicknell, *A Theological Introduction to the Thirty-Nine Articles of the Church of England*, 3rd
         ed. rev. by H. J. Carpenter (London, 1955), pp. 433–5.
[116]   *The Ecclesiastical Courts. Principles of Reconstruction* . . . (London, 1954).
[117]   Albert Marrin, *The Last Crusade. The Church of England in the First World War* (Durham, N.C.,
         1974), pp. 187–8.
[118]   *The Times*, 23 Feb. 1916, p. 9.
[119]   *DNB* (1931–40), pp. 224–5; E. S. S. Sutherland, *Dibdin and the English Establishment* (Durham,
         N.C., 1995).

90) and is formally laid down in Provincial and Legatine Canons by Archbishop Lanfranc (1070), by the Legate Alberic at Westminster (1138), by Archbishop Richard (1175), and by the Legate Othobon (1268).

That the rule was frequently broken is as true of this as of other laws, but its existence was never open to doubt. That it was not abrogated at the Reformation as 'contrarient or repugnant to the laws, statures, and customs of this realm' we have the authority of Coke himself, who, writing in the seventeenth century, lays it down as clear law that clergymen 'ought not in person to serve in war.' Thus whether you inquire as to English ecclesiastical law (for instance, the constitutional conditions under which the Established Church enjoys its status and property), or as to English Canon Law pure and simple, or as to the general Canon Law of the West, the answer is the same.[120]

There is no need to dwell here on the flaws in this reading of the past, for our concern is with Dibdin's understanding of the matter and with the fact that he, a layman, was the only prominent person to state the canonical case publicly.

Sir Lewis was also uniquely placed, for he advised the archbishop of Canterbury almost daily on most issues except patronage, at least when the archbishop resided at Lambeth. The archbishop before, during, and after the war was Randall Davidson (b. 1848, archbishop 1903–28, †1930), who as the man at the top was pivotal on the question of the clergy and armsbearing. The entry in the *Oxford Dictionary of the Christian Church* accurately characterizes Davidson this way: 'He possessed the courage necessary in a leader, even if he more often preferred to exercise the caution of a chairman.'[121] Yet although he acted as a leader during the General Strike of May 1926, he chose the role of 'denominational executive' on the matter of arms and the clergy during the war. What would have happened had he publicly and consistently stated the case advanced by his principal legal adviser cannot, of course, be said. Leaders cannot lead where they will not be followed, but in this instance Davidson cannot be said to have tried.

Within a few days of the outbreak of war, both clergy and laity began pressing the archbishop on the status of the clergy respecting military service, both as non-combatants and combatants. The latter, more controversial question arose partly because of deep feelings held by some laymen and clergy, partly because of the more practical problem that by 1 September 1914 so many clergy had volunteered for chaplaincies that places could not be found for 900 of them. What were these enthusiastic priests to do? Archbishop Davidson wrote on the following day to the bishops of his province:

> I recognize the *prima facie* arguments which can be used by the younger clergy, or by others on their behalf, in support of such action at a moment like the

---

[120] Quoted in G. K. A. Bell, *Randall Davidson, Archbishop of Canterbury*, 3rd ed. (Oxford, 1952), p. 775, n. 1. The reference to Sir Edward Coke is to *The Second Part of the Institutes of the Laws of England* (London, 1641), p. 4.

[121] ODCC, p. 457.

present ... By every line of thought which I have pursued, I am led to the conclusion that I have been right in maintaining from the first that the position of an
actual combatant in our Army is incompatible with the position of one who has
sought and received Holy Orders. The whole idea which underlies and surrounds
Ordination implies this ... Under this obligation those who have been ordained
to the Ministry of Word and Sacrament ought, even in time of actual warfare, to
regard that Ministry, whether at home or in the field, as their special contribution
to the country's service.[122]

Criticisms and inquiries did not abate, so less than a year later Davidson
joined the archbishop of York in issuing a joint declaration:

We still hold that it is unsuitable for the Clergy to serve as combatants, and we
believe that, at the present juncture, the work of the Clergy in their parishes is
certainly as necessary as other kinds of 'necessary work' which exempt from Army
service those who are so employed. The task of the Clergy is a task which no other
man can discharge.[123]

Within a few months strong pressure came from a different direction as
Lord Derby undertook a new Recruiting Scheme to raise a sufficient number
of troops without conscription. All men of military age, including clergy, were
asked whether they would enlist. Derby discretely wrote the archbishop, in a
letter intended for publication, that the clergy, 'however much they may wish
to enlist, equally do their duty when obeying the directions of those who are set
in authority over them.'[124] Davidson's noncommittal reply left the situation so
open that while some bishops openly favored combatant service, others were
perceived as so hindering recruitment that one M.P. on 30 November 1915
requested that the appropriate provisions of the Defence of the Realm Act be
set in train against them. Just a week before, Derby had privately told Davidson
that 'I find there is a very strong feeling growing up on this subject, not only
amongst those who are opposed to our Church, but also amongst those who
are its chief supporters. They feel the Church is being very much weakened
by this exceptional treatment that is being meted out to the Clergy.'[125] After
further discussion the two men publicly exchanged letters dated 3 December
1915. The pertinent portion of the archbishop's inquiry follows:

... I and other Bishops have instructed clergy who have sought our advice that
they are following a perfectly legitimate course if, in reply to recruiting officers,
they say that acting under the instruction of their Bishops, they are unable to offer
themselves for combatant service. I now learn that clergy who have so acted are
in some cases informed that their names, not having been starred by the local
tribunals, will be placed on the list of those who while at liberty to offer themselves
for service have declined to do so – in other words among those who are popularly

---

[122] Quoted in Bell, *Davidson*, p. 739.
[123] Quoted in ibid., p. 762.
[124] Quoted in ibid., p. 765.
[125] Quoted in ibid., p. 765.

described as 'shirkers.' This seems to be an intolerable position in which to place men who are eager and willing in whatever way is fitting to serve their country at this time. It is obvious that Parliament alone can ultimately decide on the terms of any Compulsion Act, should such an Act become necessary . . . We have repeatedly drawn the distinction between such combatant service and the non-combatant branches of Army work. In such work clergy who can rightly be spared from their parishes may, in our judgment, most properly take their part.[126]

Interestingly, in the same month 1,000 junior clergy of the diocese of London petitioned their bishop to arrange things so that they could do work related to the war and to consider waiving the rule barring them from combatant service. He declined to do the latter on the grounds that the diocese could not afford their loss and the army did not require their service – yet.[127]

When conscription was enacted in February 1916, it exempted the clergy and all regular ministers of religious denominations. Archbishop Davidson chose this occasion to address the House of Lords. While alluding to the argument from canon law which his counsel Dibdin had set out, Davidson expressly refused to rely on it: 'it is not upon that that I, and those who think with me, rest in our concurrence in the provision which this Bill makes.' Instead, he pressed home the special duties of the clergy and the acute need for them at home.[128]

What effect this exhortation worked on the clergy may be seen in an incident at the Convocation of York meeting at the same time. In the Upper House the bishop of Liverpool on 16 February raised the problem of the shortage of clergy. Although considerable discussion ensued, no action was taken. Not so in the House of Laymen, where on the same day the Viscount Halifax, acting president, delivered a speech ending with this motion:

> That in the opinion of this House the primary duty of the Clergy at the present time is not to act as combatants in the war, but to fulfill the spiritual duties of their vocation whether among the King's forces or in their own parishes.
> That in the faithful discharge of these duties they will also be best serving their country; and by preaching repentance for all that may have been amiss in the past and exhorting to amendment of life, which may plead with God for relief in present distress, they will be taking their part in helping the nation to be worthy of such a peace as will vindicate the cause of right against might, and promote the spread of the Kingdom of God upon earth.

The motion was seconded and unanimously passed. Two points are worth recording: the indication that noticeable numbers of clergy were volunteering as combatants to the apparent detriment of parochial life, and significant lay opposition to such priestly zeal in the face of inaction on the part of Lambeth Palace and the episcopal bench. Unlike Dibdin, who grounded his opposition

---

[126]   Quoted in ibid., pp. 765–6.
[127]   Marrin, *Last Crusade*, p. 193.
[128]   Bell, *Davidson*, p. 775.

solidly on what he believed was the canon law, Halifax argued on more practical grounds for the usefulness of the clergy as recruiters on the home front.
Yet both were laymen, and Halifax's motion won the unanimous support of
the House of Laymen.[129]

Nevertheless, exactly a year later the clergy in the Convocation of
Canterbury also showed priestly zeal on behalf of the war, even at the expense
of parochial work. On 8 February 1917, in the Upper House (of bishops) the
bishop of Winchester moved

> That in view of the existing stress, and of the desire of the Bishops and Clergy to do
> their utmost for National Service, and of the Laity to support them in so doing, this
> House would welcome some arrangement whereby the Bishops with the necessary
> legal sanction should be enabled during the continuance of the war to suspend
> or modify where necessary existing obligations as to the performance of Divine
> Service in the Parish Church or elsewhere . . . with the view simply of enabling the
> Clergy under the guidance and approval of the Bishops to offer their services more
> freely and in a greater variety of ways.[130]

This resolution passed the Lower House (of clerical deputies) the next day.
The House of Laymen, recorded as having met only on 8 February, took no
action.[131]

What in February seemed like a motion designed to remove obstacles to
enlistment by eager clergy was soon apparently transformed into an enlistment campaign actively conducted by the bishops. On 1 May the bishop of
Truro moved this resolution in the Upper House:

> That this House expresses its satisfaction at the prompt response made by the Clergy
> to the Bishops' appeal to them to volunteer for National Service, especially for
> Chaplaincies at the Front, and while regretting that in several directions unexpected
> difficulties have arisen . . . in no way abates its desire that the Clergy should be used
> for such service, provided it does not hinder the spiritual work of the Church.[132]

The unspeakable slaughter which occurred on the battlefields of France
over the next two years, culminating in the nearly successful German counter-
offensive in the spring of 1918, frightened the British government into forcing
through Parliament on 9 April 1918 a new conscription bill which raised
the age for compulsory service and abolished the clerical exemption from
non-combatant service.[133] Archbishop Davidson supported the repeal of the

---

[129]   *The Official Year-Book of the Church of England. 1917* (London, 1917) (hereafter *OYB* followed by
the year), pp. 290, 292, 294 (the quotation appears on p. 294); *Manchester Guardian*, 17 February
1916, p. 2. The latter article also recounts misgivings expressed in the York House of Laymen
about a national mission of 'repentance and hope,' which one delegate, evidently representing
the feelings of many others, charged had been decided upon by a 'secret meeting of Bishops.' The
vote on Halifax's motion may thus to some extent have served to express lay resentment against
the hierarchy.

[130]   *OYB 1918*, p. 288.

[131]   Ibid., pp. 289, 295–6.

[132]   Ibid., p. 289.

[133]   There is much confusion about this act. Denys Hayes, *Conscription Conflict* (New York, 1973),

exemption. Six days later the repeal was repealed, as Davidson explained to some of his bishops in a confidential letter:

> I do not think the House of Lords will take this peaceably, and I myself should feel bound, I think, to make it very clear that it was not being done by our wish, and possibly should feel bound to say that we ought to bid the clergy, who are willing to do so, volunteer for service, *preferably non-combatant, but not exclusively so.*[134]

Two days later he addressed the Lords upon the Second Reading of the Military Service Bill. After emphasizing yet again that the clergy had not sought the exemption in 1916, he passed on to the extraordinary developments of the previous week and his letter to the Prime Minister, in the course of which he had written:

> We clergy, in face of an emergency so great, are ready, I firmly believe, to answer with whole-hearted loyalty to any new call that the nation through its responsible spokesmen makes upon us. The hour is too grave for any reply but one, and the very sacredness of our distinctive trust deepens our sense of responsibility for seeing that no detriment or lack accrue by any default on our part, or on the part of those whom we can influence[135]

Davidson concluded by promising 'to see what we can do voluntarily under conditions so different – and this is the real point – from those of 1915–16 as to justify a different attitude on our part from that which we took up at that time.'[136] He kept his promise. Five days later he called a special meeting of the seventeen bishops of the province at which they agreed to create in their dioceses arrangements for the clergy to join the services. Significantly, combatant as well as non-combatant service was allowed. The Primate of England, who until then had spoken of armsbearing by the clergy as 'incompatible,' 'incongruous,' and 'unsuitable,' finally chose to cave in to a host of pressures at the very height of the war.[137]

Davidson's want of decisive leadership had permitted the bishops and the clergy to think and act as they wished, and few if any of them had asserted that canon law forbade armsbearing to them. Bishop Charles Gore of Oxford (1911–19) attempted to dissuade clergy and ordinands from enlisting as combatants. The Warden of Chaplains School in France from 1917 to 1919, B. K. Cunningham, put the case against clerical military service slightly more

---

p. 306, points out that the bill stipulated that clergy were to be assigned non-combatant duties unless they volunteered for combat service. Cf. Bell, *Davidson*, p. 887; Marrin, *Last Crusade*, p. 193; and Alan Wilkinson, *The Church of England and the First World War* (London, 1978), p. 40.

[134] Quoted in Bell, *Davidson*, p. 888 (emphasis added).

[135] Quoted in ibid., p. 889.

[136] Ibid., p. 889.

[137] Ibid., pp. 889–90. In fairness, one must remember that the situation was so tense that a few weeks later (2 May) the Lower House of the Convocation of York passed this motion concerning conscientious objectors: 'That this House does not feel able to justify the actions of those citizens who, while enjoying the full rights and benefits of citizenship, yet decline to render the State the services which the State demands of them in time of war' (*OYB 1919*, p. 297).

forcefully than Davidson had by calling it 'particularly incongruous.' Bishop Handley Moule of Durham (1901–20) held that the clergy should fight only in cases of 'extreme necessity,' but, like Davidson and the bishops of the southern province, he felt that that hour had indeed arrived in April 1918 and wrote to his clergy accordingly.[138] William Temple, later archbishop of York (1929–42) and then of Canterbury during the Second World War (1942–44), argued in a lecture series delivered in New York that the separateness of the church required the separateness of its official representatives, whose functions were therefore 'incompatible with others' and thereby 'deprived [the clergy] of the right to take part in many worldly activities, though these in themselves are right enough.' As for 'the question whether a priest should serve as a combatant in his country's army,' Temple felt that this would violate the international witness of the church, which 'exists to bind the nations of the earth in one.' Responsibility for 'national witness' lay rather with the church's 'lay, or unofficial, members,' who were subject to 'the freedom of the State to act in its own sphere.'[139]

Other clergy saw things very differently. Soon after the declaration of war four bishops agreed that after Trinity Sunday 1915 they would not normally accept for ordination any men fit for military service.[140] More lay behind this announcement than a simple concern with interdicting the clerical profession as a haven for draft-evaders. The Dean of Emmanuel College, Cambridge, Charles Raven, attempted to enlist as a combatant on four occasions, but was rejected for medical reasons each time.[141] By 1918 the bishops were even more fired up. *The Times* published on 19 April 1918 letters from three bishops lamenting the government's withdrawal of the clause imposing compulsory military service on the clergy.[142] Within a few days they were allowing and even enabling clergy to volunteer as combatants. The bishop of London granted 'special dispensations' to clergy willing to fight, 'now that the lives and honour of women and children depend upon the courage and skill of their menfolk.'[143]

Although we know much less about them, the rank-and-file clergy responded with similar diversity. Father John Groser, a chaplain, finally and very reluctantly yielded to a great deal of pressure from his commanding officer that he lead combat troops with the proviso that he himself should not have to bear arms. On the other hand, a member of a religious order, the Community of the Resurrection, Father Hubert Northcott, secured the permission of the bishop of Wakefield in early 1918 to enlist as a private in the artillery. Yet another member of the same order who served only as a

138 Wilkinson, *Church of England*, p. 41.
139 William Temple, *Church and Nation. The Bishop Paddock Lectures for 1914–15* (London, 1915), pp. 95–7.
140 Marrin, *Last Crusade*, p. 189; Wilkinson, *Church of England*, p. 37.
141 Ibid., p. 140.
142 *The Times*, 19 April 1918, p. 8, col. 1. The bishops were those of Bristol, Chichester, and Salisbury.
143 Quoted in Bell, *Davidson*, p. 890.

chaplain was perplexed by a priest he had met who celebrated the Eucharist for his men and then led them into battle. The chaplain wrote to his home community in 1916: 'I wish I knew if he is right to go on like this, as it seems to me so incongruous.' No such doubts clouded the judgment of Father Robert Callaway, who was killed in the Somme offensive in September 1916. A few days before he died, he described in a letter to his wife his revulsion at a lecture he had just heard on how to kill with a bayonet: 'but I shudder merely with the natural instinct of repulsion, which is common to at least all educated people. I don't shudder because I think it any more wrong of me as a priest. I have never for a single moment regretted becoming a combatant.'[144]

Given such a range of opinion among the clergy and also the absence of any clear assertion of a simple canonical prohibition on armsbearing, it is not surprising that no Anglican clergyman who did take up arms in World War I seems to have been prosecuted.[145] The only instance in which some kind of disciplinary action may have been taken is that of Eric Milner-White. As a chaplain in 1917 he was said to have agreed to assume command of his unit after all the other officers had been killed or wounded and to have been sent back to base as a result. The precise facts in his case are, however, quite unclear;[146] and even if true, such treatment was highly unusual if not unique.

Although it may be impossible to determine how many Anglican clergy served in a combatant capacity during the Great War, the figures on the chaplains in National Service compiled within a few months of the Armistice may be helpful. The total number of clergy who had offered their services was 7,169, of whom 3,030 had served or were still serving. In all, 888 had been killed or had died in service, and 176 were wounded. Among them, they had won 245 crosses, medals, and distinctions.[147] It is interesting to compare these statistics with those of Roman Catholic priests in the French army during the war. There the clergy were not only conscripted, but generally compelled to serve as combatants. Of the 32,699 mobilized, 4,618 were killed.[148] Although the number of French clergy killed was thus over five times as high as the number of Anglican clergy, the ratios between the enlisted and the killed were completely different: almost 30% of the Anglicans (most of whom were not combatants), as opposed to about 14% of the French priests (most of whom were). This is a matter worth further study.

---

[144] All the material in this paragraph appears in Wilkinson, *Church of England*, pp. 42–3, 142. The Callaway quotation is on p. 43.

[145] This impression is confirmed by *CLCE*, pp. 67–8, and the entry on 'War, Participation of the Clergy in,' in *ODCC*, s.v.

[146] Wilkinson, *Church of England*, p. 143.

[147] *OYB 1920*, p. 190.

[148] Wilkinson, *Church of England*, p. 42.

The Archbishops' Commission to Reform Canon Law

Some Anglican clergymen took arms in World War II as well – an undeter-mined number, but probably not a large one. What is especially arresting is the source of this information: the Archbishops' Commission for the reform of canon law which formed in 1939 and delivered its Report in 1947. In con-sidering the status and enforceability of laws which had fallen into desuetude, the Commission chose significantly to focus on the canonical prohibition on clerical armsbearing. The passage deserves extensive quotation:

> Long-continued non-user and custom to the contrary have the power of abolish-ing a canon, if the non-observance has received the tacit or expressed approval of authority. In such a case the law ceases to be obligatory, in the sense that those who do not observe it cannot be punished. For example, by the Canon Law it is not lawful for the clergy to wear weapons and to serve in the wars. The State has observed this by exempting the clergy from the provisions of the Conscription Acts. Yet in both the last two wars some clergy have served as combatants and have not been subjected to canonical penalties. It is probable, therefore, that this particular law is in desuetude. Probable, but not certain, because the time is doubtfully suf-ficient to establish desuetude, and because it is not certain that the law has never during this period been enforced, and that therefore the non-user is unbroken.[149]

What is even more extraordinary is that, despite this awareness of the recent conduct of some clergy and a conviction of the unenforceability of the old law against it, the Commission did nearly nothing to restore the ancient ban. In its proposed Constitutions and Canons Ecclesiastical, the Commission offered this as canon 83, 'Of the Manner of Life of Ministers':

1. No Bishop, Priest, or Deacon shall give himself to such occupations, habits, or recreations as do not befit his sacred calling, or tend to be a just cause of offence to others ... But at all times he shall be diligent to frame and fashion his life according to the doctrine of Christ, and to make himself, as much as in him lies, a wholesome example and pattern to the flock of Christ.
2. No Bishop, Priest, or Deacon shall accept or undertake any office, work, or duty which is incompatible with his sacred calling or detrimental to the performance of the duties of the ecclesiastical office to which he has been appointed.[150]

This laid the basis for discussions within and between the two Convocations. Although no agreement on this canon had been reached by 1954,[151] these revisions were accepted by 1959:

---

[149] *CLCE*, pp. 67–8.
[150] Ibid., p. 174.
[151] See the comment in *The Revised Canons of the Church of England Further Considered* (London, 1954), p. 111: 'Both Canterbury and York have deferred consideration of this Canon.'

C 27.2. A Minister shall not give himself to such occupations, habits, or recreations as do not befit his sacred calling, or may be detrimental to the performance of the duties of his office, or tend to be a just cause of offence to others ...

C. 28. The apparel of a Bishop, Priest, or Deacon shall be suitable to his office; and, save for purposes of recreation and other justifiable reasons, shall be such as to be a sign and mark of his holy calling and ministry as well to others as to those committed to his spiritual charge.[152]

Still under consideration was a new provision which would have allowed bishops to grant dispensatory licenses to clergy to do work affecting the discharge of their responsibilities:

C. 29.1. No Minister holding ecclesiastical office shall engage in trade or any other occupation in such manner as to effect [sic] the performance of the duties of his office except so far as he be authorized so to do under the statutory provisions in this behalf for the time being in force or he have a licence to do so granted by the Bishop of the Diocese.[153]

This last item was incorporated in the final form of the revised canons, promulgated in 1969, which supersedes all earlier canon law in the Church of England. Under the new numbers c. 26.2, 27, and 28.1, the last three canons quoted above are the relevant canons germane to clerical armsbearing.[154]

It seems fair to say in conclusion that these canons do not in any explicit way prohibit any manner of armsbearing, that one would be hard put to defend such an interpretation as implied by the language of the canons, and that, in any case, in a pinch or a doubt a dispensation could be enacted by statute or granted by episcopal dispensation. Such is the law of the Church of England in force at the moment.

[152] Canon Law Revision 1959 (London, 1960), pp. 178, 180.
[153] Ibid., p. 182.
[154] The Canons of the Church of England. Canons Ecclesiastical Promulged by the Convocations of Canterbury and York in 1964 and 1969 (London, 1969), pp. 51–2.

CHAPTER 7

CONCLUSION

FOR over a thousand years the Christian churches, Latin and Greek, maintained an ancient prohibition on armsbearing by the clergy, no matter how much individual clerics failed to observe it. The Eastern Church appears never to have relaxed that standard. In the West, on the other hand, in the kingdom of the Franks during the Carolingian period there developed a tacit narrowing in the interpretation of the word 'clericus' to exclude bishops and abbots from the ban so as to allow them to discharge their military obligations to the king with something like a clear conscience. Such artful legislation was in any event not promulgated by an independent church, was not imitated elsewhere in Europe, and perhaps inspired a sharp reaction in the ninth and tenth centuries.

Hostility to clerical armsbearing also in part animated the great reform movement which climaxed under papal leadership from the mid-eleventh century onward. One of the objectives of the reform movement was the restoration of the ancient canons. On the issue of clerical armsbearing the reformers renewed and reiterated the prohibition in the most vigorous, unambiguous terms in the whole history of Christianity. No fewer than twelve times in thirty years (1049–79), councils and synods declared flatly that clergy were not to bear arms. Furthermore, popes or their legates presided over eight of those twelve councils. Their intention was clear.

Yet within three hundred years a whole series of complex modifications of that ban had been woven into the new corpus of canon law of the Latin Church. The most striking admission was that clerics, like anyone else, had the right, according to natural law, to defend themselves against violence. This principle was, to be sure, circumscribed in theory by significant restrictions largely taken over from Roman law: a cleric could not resist lawfully exercised force by a lawfully constituted authority; he could resist only on the spot and not seek revenge after the fact; he could employ only minimal or proportional response with respect to both weapon and intended effect (for example, to ward off rather than wound an attacker); and if he shed blood, even unintentionally, he automatically incurred irregularity, which suspended him from the exercise of his sacred functions and barred his promotion to higher orders until he had been absolved by dispensation. Yet in practice these restrictions were not, and could not be, repeated each time the simple principle of the right of self-defense was invoked, which effectively allowed more latitude of action to a cleric on the spot than was presumably ever intended. Furthermore, by the early fourteenth century the popes conceded that killing in self-defense did not result in irregularity if no other way existed of saving one's own life.

As for the defense by violence or by arms of other persons or causes, here too complex possibilities developed. While much thinking had been devoted since Christian antiquity to whether Christ's injunction to turn the other cheek was a literal command binding on all, not nearly as much attention was given to Christ's words that 'Greater love hath no man than that he lay down his life for his neighbor' (John 13.15), which John significantly interpreted as meaning that 'We ought to lay down our lives for the brethren' (1 John 3.16). Although St Ambrose not only rejected the right of a Christian to self-defense, but also asserted the obligation of a Christian to defend others, most prelates and thinkers did not take Christ's words as a command. Furthermore, the task of protecting the defenseless, especially widows and children, properly fell to rulers (including bishops with princely responsibilities), to knights, and, from the twelfth century onward, to some extent to the fighters in the military religious orders, so that ordinary clerics need not have concerned themselves with this issue. But what of extraordinary circumstances when no one else except a cleric could aid the helpless except by recourse to arms? Legislation rarely provided for this possibility, although by comparison it often did allow clerics to stand up for the defenseless in secular courts of law, which they otherwise were to avoid.

The defense of ecclesiastical property, of the faith, and of *patria* were other matters entirely. Protection or recovery of ecclesiastical property by clerical arms was becoming a well-established principle of canon law by the mid-thirteenth century, though theoretically subject to the defensive and minimalist restrictions governing individual self-defense. Defense of the faith was more problematical and tended to fall to members of the large, gray world between 'clergy' and 'laity,' including the knights in military-religious orders and tertiaries of the Franciscan and Dominican orders. As for *patria*, although canonists were more prepared to allow a cleric's rush to arms on behalf of the community than of isolated individuals in it, in the High Middle Ages ecclesiastical legislators were understandably loath to admit openly these claims of Caesar or of secular loyalty as far as the lower clergy were concerned.

On the other hand, the two hats worn by many bishops and abbots as prelates and princes became less of a problem because of the division of jurisdiction which resulted from the revival of Roman law and of jurisprudence and from the effort of the ecclesiastical reformers of the eleventh and twelfth centuries to liberate the church from entanglements in secular society. Caesar's claims, no less than the Church's, achieved greater clarity and autonomy as a result, and prelates could with good conscience separate their two offices more easily than their early medieval predecessors had. Although they were still not to bear arms or fight or shed blood, they could certainly lead troops to the battlefield in obedience to their royal masters and direct military operations. Once there at the scene of fighting, they could have invoked the canonical principle of the validity of self-defense and, after 1317, even have killed an assailant without irregularity if survival had been otherwise out of the question. (Although I have discovered nowhere in canonistic writings this splicing of principles, there surely must have existed canon lawyers who so counseled their bishops verbally, if not in writing.)

Although according to the sharp division between the 'public' and 'private' realms embodied in Roman and modern law bishops and abbots did not ordinarily have the right to 'declare war,' from the perspective of medieval customary law they had the right to declare a 'feud' when their rights had been violated. Thus the concession by canon law of the right, grounded in Roman law, to defend ecclesiastical property, or to recover it if lost, was inadvertently widened when interpreted by medieval bishops, abbots, or, for that matter, any other cleric or layman according to their habitual ways of thinking. On this particular point canon law inadvertently opened a large hole in the dike.

Why or how did all these departures from the ancient ban come about over the course of about two hundred years? These changes in ecclesiastical law in the High Middle Ages took place within a much larger context of thought and action which helped to shape the direction taken by the rapidly evolving canon law. With the possible exception of the Napoleonic Code, there has never been a period in western history of such rapid change in law and legal thinking as in the High Middle Ages. Men then sought to bridge the distance between idea and action – to clarify, redefine, and reorder law in the light of emerging ideals, expectations, and perceptions. One relevant dimension of moral theology involved a shift away from an objectivisitic approach focusing on the act itself towards a greater stress on subjective considerations such as the circumstances surrounding a delict, the intention of the sinner, or even the moral quality of his whole life. This emphasis on intention could take many forms, some more curious than others, as in the popularity in the twelfth century of the view of crusading as 'an act of love.' With respect to arms and the clergy, it opened up possibilities for much wider considerations than the act itself of bearing arms. Such considerations found their way into canon law in both general rules and the adjudication of individual cases.

A second aspect of the interrelationship between law and society in both thought and action concerned the legitimate uses of violence. By imposing limits on warfare the Peace and Truce of God movements of the late tenth and eleventh centuries inadvertently prepared the way for the crusades by effectively declaring warfare legitimate as long as it was conducted within those limits. The crusading movement went well beyond this implicit legitimation of warfare to sanctify both warfare rightly directed and the warrior acting rightly to aid fellow Christians and to recover lost Christian territory. The sanctification of such warfare was particularly significant if, as has been suggested, the distinction customarily drawn between 'holy wars' and 'just wars' did not really exist before the sixteenth century. And even if theologians and canonists had insisted on the distinction, had the question been put to them, the climate of opinion was such in the High Middle Ages that it would have probably have been difficult for someone waging a 'just' war not to feel it somehow or other to be 'righteous' or 'sacred.' Two previously antagonistic realms, war and the holy, now thoroughly interpenetrated each other. In human terms this gave birth to a new consecrated knighthood, another *militia Christi* taking both individual and corporate forms as crusading pilgrims and as military-religious orders dedicated to defending Christian possessions, recuperating lost ones, protecting Christians, and aiding Christian missionary activity. This was, in Bernard of Clairvaux's view, not merely a new *militia Christi*, but a higher one.

This incarnation of the warrior element within the ranks of the visible Church need not necessarily have affected the 'clergy' proper. On the face of it, to use the medieval organic image, this growth could have turned out to be encapsulated within, but safely isolated from, the rest of the body. But it did not turn out that way, in good part because the boundaries between the 'clergy' and the 'laity' were too porous. Although the distinction between the ordained and the unordained seems pellucid, it was not that simple. Even within the strictly defined ordained clergy, there existed the division between those in major or sacred orders, bound to celibacy and a lifelong commitment, and those in minor orders, who were not so obliged and could revert to lay status. In the wider meaning of the word 'clergy' which embraces the religious orders, beside the professed monks or friars, who theoretically need not have been ordained but in practice ordinarily were, there stood the lay *conversi* whose daily round of prayer, discipline, and work differed but little from that of the professed religious. In the military-religious orders the 'clerical' status of the 'brethren in arms' is a vexing problem to which their varied rules and constitutions provided no uniform answers. Finally, besides *conversi* who lived with and worked for the religious, there were lay tertiaries or members of third orders who lived in the world but solemnly promised to live an ordered life largely modeled on that of the First Order (for men) or Second Order (for women). Significantly, the Rules for the Dominican and Franciscan tertiaries promulgated in the 1280s allowed them to bear arms, if only for the defense of the faith, their *patria*, and their religion. Within a few decades both the regular Dominicans and Franciscans, admittedly in response to more recent papal legislation as well as to these stipulations of the 1280s, were allowing armsbearing to their members under certain conditions; and in 1500 the Franciscan chapter general extended to all friars the right, previously reserved to the tertiaries, to use weapons for the defense of the faith, their religion, and their *patria*.[1]

Another germane sector of life in the High Middle Ages concerned the

---

[1] See my forthcoming *Legislation of the Medieval and Early Modern Religious Orders on Armsbearing*.

largely unforeseen and unintended consequences of the ecclesiastical reform movement, often misleadingly called the Gregorian Reform or the Investiture Controversy. The first result, flowing from that official mistrust of the laity which was an operating premise of the movement, was hostility to laymen as reliable protectors of ecclesiastical property and persons. Clerics were thus encouraged to fall back on their own resources. Ironically, the effort to liberate the Church from entanglement in secular society promoted a certain secularization of the clergy, who had earlier relied on laymen for their defense. The second consequence, which caused far more open conflict, was the problem of jurisdiction over ecclesiastical persons and cases, and of supreme jurisdiction in one Christian society. However much the reformers sought to extricate the Church from worldly entanglements, the fact was that by 1150 the bishop of Rome was emerging as the supreme monarch of Europe, its supreme judge and lawgiver, while ecclesiastical officials and courts dispensed justice on matters which touched everyone. Since justice was the most important prerogative of medieval rulers (inherent in their central task of creating and maintaining order), the resulting conflicts were bound to be bitter until workable compromises could be worked out, which often took a century or much more. This accentuated the enmity between clerics and laymen and, even more importantly, it magnified the centrality of law and of legal thinking. For even if the reform movement had not resulted in a struggle over jurisdiction as such, the resolution of the many particular controversies which did arise could only have been achieved and sustained by detailed legal compromises in which all sides got something in both substance and shadow. Law, lawyers, and legalistic thinking triumphed of necessity in such an atmosphere.

This brings us to the developments in canon law itself, which between roughly 1100 and 1300 came to sanction clerical resort to arms in specified circumstances. Although influenced in profound and often indiscernible ways by the society in which it lives and grows, law, like art, has a rhythm and a logic of its own, especially at a time when its practitioners seek to establish new order and clarity. This was particularly true in the later eleventh and twelfth centuries, when the compilers of, and commentators on, Roman law, canon law, and customary and feudal laws sought to bring 'harmony out of dissonance,' a task which of its nature requires simplification. In the first instance, this meant determining what were valid laws and what relationships existed among the different sources of law. The revival of Roman law not only gave great impetus to this codifying impulse; it was the law of the Roman Empire, which legally still lived, and it was the law with which the Holy Roman Church identified, particularly in the protracted struggles of the bishops of Rome with the (Holy) Roman emperors. In a way, the crucial legal question involved in this conflict was whether the Holy Roman Church or the Sacred Roman Empire would succeed in appropriating Roman law as its own, thereby anointing its own claims.

On the matter of clerical armsbearing, the principle that everyone had the right to defend himself against force was to be found not only in Roman law, but in the law of all peoples and in natural law, which itself was created by God and thus an aspect of divine law. Over and against this weight of laws were the words of Christ, echoed by St Paul, about turning the other cheek and not seeking revenge. Were these injunctions laws or commands binding on all, or counsels only for those striving for perfection? This was the great question posed not only by canonists, but by theologians as well. Although he seemed to come down on the side of the former view, Abelard the theologian rehearsed the arguments pro and con, some of them raised already in late Christian antiquity, and by implication said that here was a genuine problem with considerable room for debate. Interestingly, Gratian the lawyer stoutly denied a cleric's right to self-defense, even though in many other ways he opened up many related issues. It was Pope Alexander III (1159–81) who in his disposition of several cases clearly accepted the applicability to the clergy of the right of self-defense and so, by implication, settled the debate about the universally binding character of the words of Christ as law – they were not. Alexander's decision made sense from the narrow viewpoint of law, which is after all concerned with what is minimally required. Later canonists had no choice but to proceed from this given. Nor, really, did theologians, since the pope had decided the question. In sticking to his guns on the issue of clerical armsbearing, Aquinas was in effect criticizing a legal principle which had passed into the system nearly a century before he was writing. He was entitled to his opinion, but his opinion was not the law. For the canon lawyers, however, once the papal decision had been taken, no choice existed between a principle of Roman, 'international,' and natural law on the one hand and, on the other, an exhortation of Christ which the great majority could not be expected to obey and which Christ did not declare a prerequisite for salvation. To the legal mind pondering the minimal rules applicable to all, a moral injunction, even when expressed by the Savior of humankind, naturally carried little weight against a universally accepted maxim of law, especially of the divinely created natural law.

But were not the clergy as the 'elect of Christ' (*sors Christi*) precisely that class of people pledged to follow the counsels of Christ? Although to my knowledge no one directly addressed this question, I suspect that the tradition of the ancient canonical 'evangelical counsels' which the clergy were committed to obey – obedience, chastity, and (in the case of religious) poverty – won out and possibly even precluded the raising of the question. This is only speculation, however, on an important topic which requires more investigation.

In any case, once the essential breakthrough had been made that a cleric could wield arms under certain conditions, the focus of discussion among canonists shifted understandably, decisively, and almost exclusively to what those circumstances were, and all earlier doubts and reservations began to recede quickly into the background. It was here that the 'tunnel vision' of legal thinking took over, moving according to its own internal logic. To illustrate the point, two factors may be singled out here, one in a sense pro-cedural, the other substantive. The overwhelming desire in twelfth-century theology and law to bring harmony out of dissonance, to reconcile apparently contradictory texts, could sometimes result in a modification or watering down of what had earlier been clear-cut norms. Thus, in his prodigious and unprecedented assemblage of texts on the clergy and war, Gratian uncov-ered evident discrepancies among sources which he sought to reconcile. In general he thereby opened up the whole question for fresh reconsideration, and in particular he laid the compromise foundation for the Clementine text *Si furiosus*, which admitted that a cleric who had no other way of saving his life except to kill an assailant did not incur irregularity. It took over a century and a half for this logical corollary to be inferred from Gratian's solution, but it was drawn in good time.

What undoubtedly also widened the scope of debate was the substantive principle that 'necessity knows no law,' which was to be found in different forms not only in Roman law and thinking, not only in the Old Testament, but in the New Testament in Jesus' own teaching. It is remarkable how often this precept was quoted or alluded to by ecclesiastics in the High Middle Ages, even by St Francis himself in his original Rule for his followers. Although the maxim was not often invoked in its bald form in connection with armsbear-ing, it did clear the way for other general exceptive clauses (especially 'for just cause for fear') and above all for the most common exemption from the ban, the dangers associated with travel. Since late antiquity, travel, with its associated inconveniences and perils, had again and again provided the major exception to ecclesiastical legislation on fasting, parochial obligation, and other matters. In this context, its extension to clerical armsbearing made good sense, especially in a legal atmosphere suffused with the notion that necessity truly knows no law.

How all these complexities regarding but one small aspect of ecclesiasti-cal legislation were to be interpreted by and for the ordinary cleric was no easy matter. But it was a crucial one nevertheless, because here lay the heart of what the clergy would learn to be the law of the Church on armsbear-ing. The intricacies of legislation and thought at the top were such that they left considerable scope at the diocesan level for bishops to devise their own rules governing the use of arms by their subject clergy. Flat prohibitions still occurred with some frequency in the thirteenth century, but became less and less frequent thereafter. Conversely, the explicit concession for travel appeared with increasing frequency from the later thirteenth century onward. Otherwise, both prohibitions and exceptions tended to be somewhat more general in nature, whether in the form of interdictions on *arma offensiva* or dispensations for dangerous places or other reasonable cause for fear. By implication, much was left to the conscience and judgment of the individual cleric, who was rarely obliged to obtain the prior permission of his superior except in Italy. On the whole, there was a gradual widening of the possibilities until approximately the sixteenth century. Although from about then onward there are scattered indications of a new restrictiveness on the part of some bishops, the far more common phenomenon in early modern ecclesiastical legislation on clerical armsbearing was the progressive recession of the topic from the public arena, notwithstanding considerable continued participation of the clergy in civil conflicts in both the seventeenth and nineteenth centuries.

But neither the topic nor the activity has disappeared, nor have the traditions of the High Middle Ages which peppered the ancient prohibition with numerous loopholes. When the throughly revised *Code of Canon Law* was promulgated in 1917, the two pertinent canons (138 and 141) neatly tied up the past and the present. Clergy were not to participate in civil wars and disturbances at all, they were not to volunteer for military service unless threatened by conscription and permitted by their religious superiors, and otherwise they were not to bear arms 'unless reasonable cause for fear exists.' The sweeping nature of this concession should be clearly understood. A wide exception that was rather seldom conceded by a few bishops between the thirteenth and the seventeenth centuries was in 1917 granted to the clergy of the Roman Catholic Church throughout the world, who were, furthermore, in no way required to consult a superior, much less secure his permission. A more generous loophole for a cleric determined to bear arms could scarcely have been provided – until, that is, the new *Code* issued in 1983. This continues to require episcopal permission for clerics volunteering for military service, but the earlier reference to the imminence of conscription as a condition has been dropped (c. 289.1). Gone, too, is the explicit prohibition on engagement in civil disturbances – and by conscious choice, as the minutes of the reform commission reveal. Canon 287 addresses this matter only indirectly and in a manner which plays straight into the hands of Liberation Theologians and their most ardent adherents: 'Most especially, clerics are always to foster that peace and harmony *based on justice* which is to be observed among all persons.' Pope Gregory VII in the eleventh century and Bishop William Thomas Manning of New York in the twentieth might well have felt a profound sense of vindication in these words suggesting the establishment of justice as a prerequisite of peace. Finally, the *Code* of 1983 contains nothing at all on armsbearing, either explicitly or in any form reasonably enforceable in an ecclesiastical court. Armsbearing priests in Latin America, the Phillipines, or elsewhere in the world today may be prosecuted by the state, but they may not be by the Roman Catholic Church, which conveys the appearance of being indifferent on the matter.

The church in England has followed a similar if eccentric course to that taken by the church of Rome. After having been routinely forbidden for hundreds of years, arms and the clergy suddenly became a subject of intense interest in certain episcopal circles around 1240. In the light of developments on the Continent, two bishops enacted substantial modifications of the ancient ban, while Bishop Robert Grosseteste of Lincoln enacted the most stirring condemnation of clerical use of arms in the history of the English Church.

It was also the last unequivocal one. The famous legatine decree of 1268, the one always cited for the last seven hundred years, is so confusing that it smacks of the urgent need for compromise and the heavy hand of a committee. Thereafter the dioceses of England, unlike those on the Continent, enacted almost nothing on the issue – such, at least, is the historical record at the present. Nevertheless, the few scraps of pertinent evidence suggest that only offensive weapons were condemned and that armsbearing was widely tolerated and almost never prosecuted, if ever. In his visitation injunctions of 1554 Bishop Edmund Bonner of London perhaps expressed the reigning spirit of the late medieval English church when he set this question for the parochial clergy: 'Whether they, or any of them do wear swords, daggers, or other weapons in times or places not convenient or seemly?'

With the Reformation, the Church in England, nominally subject to the pope as well as the king, became the Church of England subject to the king alone. To it abiding change came slowly and fitfully in canon law as well as in theology and liturgy. By Parliamentary statute the old canon law remained in force until superseded by a new corpus. Although that finally came forth in 1603–04, neither it nor any preceding or subsequent proposal or enactment has ever touched the issue of arms and the clergy. The old canon law thus remained living law. But what exactly was that law? And how binding was the old 'Roman' canon law of the pre-Reformation era? On these issues some revealing historical memories and myths developed. A century ago Maitland exploded the conventional wisdom that Roman canon law had received its validity in England only when 'received' or otherwise acted on by English authorities. Although the archbishops' commission for the reform of canon law of 1939–47 accepted Maitland's position, it nevertheless perpetuated another, more stubborn myth, viz. that the English church has always forbidden armsbearing by the clergy. Curiously, although the commission admitted at the same time that that prohibition had lapsed into desuetude and that Anglican priests had borne weapons in the two World Wars of the twentieth century, the commission proposed no restoration of the prohibition, and none has been enacted to this day by the Church of England. Given this conscious acknowledgment on the part of the Anglican hierarchy, one can only conclude here a considered refusal to tell the clergy that they may not use weapons.

The Episcopal Church in the United States of America is in a similar position, but by way of a very different route. Here a conspicuous number of its clergy, including one bishop, participated actively as soldiers in the great Civil War a hundred-fifty years ago. The General Convention of 1865, held in Philadelphia six months after the conclusion of the war, entertained a motion to enact a canon forbidding the clergy to bear arms in the military, a motion which by implication meant that no prohibition existed. One senses from the record of the convention that the motion embarrassed the delegates, who in the end watered it down well beyond the point of innocuousness. The nearest which any subsequent legislation has come to any kind of prohibition was the canon, drawn up by the General Convention of 1892, listing 'conduct unbe-coming a clergyman' as a judicable offense.[2] Whether an armsbearing cleric would be arraigned, much less convicted, under this canon is highly doubtful, given what happened during and after the U. S. Civil War. It is not unfair to conclude that a guntoting Episcopal clergyman is no more likely to be tried than is his counterpart in England. As for his Roman Catholic counterpart, he could simply not be tried under the new *Code*, which essentially ignores the issue.

The resulting possibilities can be glimpsed, at least in part, in a story. An Irish Columban priest, Niall O'Brien, worked in the Philippines for about twenty-five years. In 1987 he published a book tracing the progress of his mind and heart toward non-violence as the best way of dealing with the intolerable circumstances there. He had to discover this principle for himself, however, because it was not part of his tradition, not even as a priest. He reveals all this in one place in particular:

> When we Columbans met every couple of weeks at our central house in Batang, everyone had gruesome stories from their parishes of the latest atrocities against the people. I said little about non-violence because I feared that it would sound unrealistic – another foreign theory being applied to the Philippine culture, even a ploy to distract us from the task at hand.[3]

It is telling that Father O'Brien believes that his fellow priests would react to the idea of non-violence as 'another foreign theory, . . . even a ploy.' Perhaps these priests would not themselves employ violence, although nothing in canon law would stop them from doing so. One wonders what Pope Alexander III would have thought. One wonders what Christ might have thought. Finally, one wonders what, if anything, the bishops of Rome and Canterbury will do to correct such ultimately singular consequences of the changes their predecessors gradually enacted eight hundred years ago.

[2] See my forthcoming article on this subject in *Anglican and Espiscopal History*.
[3] Niall O'Brien, *Revolution from the Heart* (New York-Oxford, 1987), p. 109. My thanks to Rowan Greer of Yale Divinity School for bringing this book to my attention.

BIBLIOGRAPHY

Primary Sources

(a) Legal

Abbo, John A. and Jerome D. Hannan. *The Sacred Canons. A Concise Presentation of the Current Disciplinary Norms of the Church*. 2 vols. St Louis-London, 1952.

Acta Apostolicae Sedis. Rome, 1909–.

Acta ecclesiae Mediolanensis. A. Ratti, ed. 3 vols Milan, 1890–92.

Acta et symbola conciliorum quae saeculo quarto habita sunt. E. J. Jonkers, ed. Textus minores, 19. Leiden, 1954.

Acta et decreta sacrorum conciliorum recentiorum. Collectio Lacensis. 7 vols. Freiburg, 1870–90.

Acta synodalia Osnabrugensis . . . MDCXXVIII. Cologne, 1653.

Acts of the Chapter of the Collegiate Church of SS. Peter and Wilfrid, Ripon, A.D. 1452 to A.D. 1506. J. T. Fowler, ed. Surtees Society, 64. Durham, 1875.

The Anglican Canons, 1529–1947. Gerald Bray, ed. Church of England Record Society, 6. Woodbridge-Rochester, 1998.

Bachofen, Charles Augustine, O.S.B. *A Commentary on the New Code of Canon Law*. 8 vols. St Louis-London, 1918–31.

Beal, John P., James A. Coriden, and Thomas J. Green. *New Commentary on the Code of Canon Law*. New York-Mahwah, 2000.

Berthelé, Joseph, ed. 'Les instructions et constitutions de Guillaume Durand, le Spéculateur'. *Académie des sciences et lettres de Montpellier. Mémoires de la section des lettres* 2nd ser. 3 (1900–07).

Blumenthal, Uta-Renate. 'Ein neuer Text für das Reimser Konzil Leos IX. (1049)?' *DA* 32 (1976): 23–48.

Boeren, P. C., ed. 'Les plus anciens statuts du diocèse de Cambrai'. *Revue de droit canonique* 3 (1953): 1–32.

Bouscaren, Timothy L., S.J., and Adam C. Ellis, S.J. *Canon Law. A Text and Commentary*. Milwaukee, 1946.

_____, and Francis N. Korth, S.J. *Canon Law. A Text and Commentary*. 4th ed. Milwaukee, 1966.

Bullarii Romani continuatio . . . Andreas Barberi, ed. 19 vols. Rome, 1835–57.

Burchard of Worms. *Collectio canonum in V libris (Lib. I-III)*. M. Fornasari, ed. CCCM, 6. Turnhout, 1970.

_____. *Decretorum libri XX*. PL 140: 537–1058.

The Canon Law Digest. Officially Published Documents Affecting the Canon Law. Milwaukee, 1934–.

Canon Law Revision 1959. London, 1960.

The Canons of the Church of England. Canons Ecclesiastical Promulged by the Convocations of Canterbury and York in 1964 and 1969. London, 1969.

Cartulaire general de l'ordre des Hospitaliers de St-Jean de Jerusalem (1100-1300). J. Delaville Le Roulx, ed. 4 vols. Paris, 1894-1906.

Chapters of the Augustinian Canons. H. E. Salter, ed. Canterbury and York Society, 29. Oxford, 1922.

Chronologia historico-legalis Seraphici Ordinis Fratrum Minorum. Michele Angelo da Napoli et al., eds. 4 vols. in 5. Naples, 1650–1797.

The Civil Law. S. P. Scott, tr. 17 vols. Cincinnati, 1932; repr., New York, 1973.

Code of Canon Law. Latin-English Edition. Canon Law Society of America, ed. Washington, 1983.

Codex iuris canonici Pii X Pontificis Maximi iussu digestus . . . [1917]. Vatican City, 1974.

Coke, Edward. *The Second Part of the Institutes of the Laws of England*. London, 1641.

Colleccion de canones y de todos los concilios de la Iglesia de Espana y de America. J. Tejada y Ramiro, ed. 6 vols. Madrid, 1859–63.

Collectio declarationum Sacrae Congregationis Cardinalium Sacri Concilii Tridentini interpretum. J. F. de Comitibus Zamboni, ed. 4 vols. Arras, 1860–68.

Collectio omnium conclusionum et resolutionum quae in causis propositis apud S. Cong. Cardinalium S. Conciliii Tridentini interpretum prodierunt ab anno 1564 ad annum 1860. S. Pallottini, ed. 17 vols. Rome, 1868–93.

Collectio processuum synodalium et constitutionum ecclesiasticarum dioecesis Spirensis ab anno 1397 usque ad annum 1720. Bruchsal, 1720.

A Collection of the Laws and Canons of the Church of England. John Johnson, trans. 2 vols. Oxford, 1850–51.

Les conciles de la province de Tours. Concilia provinciae Turonensis (Saec. XIII-XV). Joseph Avril, ed. Paris, 1987.

Concilia Germaniae. J. F. Schannat and J. Harzheim, eds. 11 vols. Cologne, 1759–63. Repr., Aalen, 1970–96.

Concilia Scotiae. Ecclesiae Scoticanae statuta tam provincialia quam synodalia quae supersunt MCCXXV-MDLIX. J. Robertson, ed. 2 vols. Edinburgh, 1866.

Concilium Tridentinum. Diariorum, actorum, epistularum, tractatuum nova collectio. Görresgesellschaft, ed. 13 vols in 20. Freiburg, 1961–2001.

Constitutiones concilii quarti Lateranensis una cum commentariis glossatorum. Antonio Garcia y Garcia, ed. Monumenta iuris canonici, A/2. Vatican City, 1981.

Constitutiones et decreta . . . Patavini . . . anno MDCXXIV. Nunc demum confirmata . . . Padua, 1793.

The Constitutions and Canons Ecclesiastical of the Church of England, referred to their original sources, and illustrated with explanatory notes. Mackenzie E. C. Walcott, ed. Oxford-London, 1874.

The Constitutions and Canons Ecclesiastical (Made in the Year 1603, and Amended in the Years 1865, 1887, 1936, 1946, and 1948). London, 1961.

Consuetudines canonicorum regularium Springersbacenses-Rodenses. S. Weinfurter, ed. CCCM, 48. Turnhout, 1978.

Coriden, James A., Thomas Green, and Daniel Heintchel, eds. *The Code of Canon Law. A Text and Commentary.* New York-Mahwah, 1985.

Corpus iuris canonici. E. Friedberg and E. L. Richter, eds. Leipzig, 1979. Repr., Graz, 1959.

Councils and Synods, with Other documents Relating to the English Church. Vol. 1, *A.D. 871–1204.* D. Whitelock, M. Brett, and C. N. L. Brooke, eds. Oxford, 1981. Vol. 2, *1205–1313.* F. M. Powicke and C. R. Cheney, eds. Oxford, 1964.

Cripps, Henry. *A Practical Treatise on the Law Relating to the Church and Clergy.* 8th ed. by K. M. Macmorran. London, 1937.

Decrees of the Ecumenical Councils. Giuseppe Alberigo et al., eds. Norman Tanner, S.J., et al., trans. 2 vols. London and Washington, 1990.

Decretales D. Gregorii Papae IX . . . cum glossis restitutae. Augustae Taurinorum, 1588.

Decretales Pseudo-Isidorianae et capitula Angilramni. Paul Hinschius, ed. Leipzig, 1863; repr. Aalen, 1963.

The Digest of Justinian. Theodor Mommsen and Paul Krueger, eds. Alan Watson, tr. 4 vols. Philadelphia, 1985.

Documents Illustrating the Activities of the General and Provincial Chapters of the English Black Monks, 1215–1540. W. A. Pantin, ed. 3 vols. Camden Society, 3rd ser., 45, 47, 54. London, 1931–37.

Dossier de l'Ordre de la Pénitence au XIIIe siècle. G. Meersseman, O.P., ed. Spicilegium Friburgense 7. Fribourg, 1961.

'The Ecclesiastical Canons of the Same Holy Apostles'. In *Ante-Nicene Christian Library. Translations of the Writings of the Fathers down to A.D. 325,* 17:257–69. Alexander Roberts and James Donaldson, eds. Edinburgh, 1867–72.

Extrauagantes Iohannis XXII. Jacqueline Tarrant, ed. Monumenta iuris canonici, B/6. Vatican City, 1983.

Ferraris, Lucio, O.F.M. *Bibliotheca canonica iuridica moralis theologica nec non ascetica polemica rubricistica historica.* New ed. 9 vols. Rome, 1884–99.

The First Book of Discipline. With Introduction and Commentary by James K. Cameron. Edinburgh, 1972.

Gibson, Edmund. *Codex juris ecclesiastici Anglicani.* 2nd ed. Oxford, 1761.

Gousset, Thomas, ed. *Les actes de la province ecclésiastique de Reims.* 4 vols. Reims, 1842–44.

Halsbury's Complete Statutes of England. 22 vols. London, 1929-31.

Incrementa in progressu 1983 Codicis iuris canonici. E. N. Peters, comp. Montreal, 2005.

The Institutes of Justinian. J. B. Moyle, tr. 5th ed. Oxford-New York, 1913.

Ivo of Chartres. *Decretum* and *Panormia.* PL 161–162.

Liber sextus decretalium . . . Clementis papae V. constitutiones. Extravagantes. . . . Augustae Taurinorum, 1588.

Lyndwood, William. *Provinciale (seu Constitutiones).* Oxford, 1679.

Lyndwood's Provinciale. The Text of the Canons Therein Contained, Reprinted from the Translation Made in 1534. J. V. Bullard and H. C. Bell, eds. London, 1929.

Magnum Bullarium Romanum, seu ejusdem continuatio. 19 vols. Luxembourg, 1727–58.

Mansi, G. D., ed. *Sacrorum conciliorum nova et amplissima collectio.* Continued by L. Petit and J. B. Martin. 60 vols. Paris, 1899–1927.

McNeill, John T. and Helena M. Gamer, eds and tr. *Medieval Handbooks of Penance. A Translation of the Principal Libri poenitentiales and Selections from Related Documents.* New York, 1938, repr., 1965.

Monumenta Germaniae historica. *Concilia aevi merovingici.*

_____. *Concilia aevi karolini.*

The 1917 or Pio-Benedictine Code of Canon Law. E. N. Peters, ed. and tr. San Francisco, 2001.

The Official Year-Book of the Church of England. 1917–20.

Pontifical Commission for the Revision of the Code of Canon Law. *Draft of the Canons of Book Two. The People of God.* Vatican City, 1977.

Pontificia Commissio codici iuris canonici recognoscendo. *Communicationes.* 1969–.

Quinque compilationes antiquae nec non collectio canonum Lipsiensis. E. Friedberg, ed. Leipzig, 1882; repr., Graz, 1956.

The Reformation of the Ecclesiastical Laws... E. Cardwell, ed. Oxford, 1850.

The Reformation of the Ecclesiastical Laws of England, 1552. James C. Spaulding, tr. Sixteenth Century Essays and Studies 19. Kirksville, Mo., 1992.

Registrum Ade de Orleton, episcopi Herefordensis A.D. MCCCXVII-MCCCXXVII. A. Bannister, ed. Canterbury and York Society, 5. Oxford, 1908.

Registrum Cancellarii Oxoniensis 1434-1469. H. E. Salter, ed. Oxford Historical Society 93-94. 2 vols. Oxford, 1932.

Registrum Thome Bourgchier Cantuariensis archiepiscopi A.D. 1454-1486. F. R. H. Du Boulay, ed. Canterbury and York Society, 54. Oxford, 1957.

The Revised Canons of the Church of England Further Considered. London, 1954.

The Rule of Saint Albert. Bede Edwards, O.D.C., ed.and tr. Vinea Carmeli, 1. Aylesford-Kensington, 1973.

The Rule of Saint Benedict. Justin McCann, ed. and tr. London, 1952.

Sammlung der Bischöflich. Speierischen Hirtenbriefe und Diocesan-Verordnungen von den Jahren 1720 bis 1786 . . . Bruchsal, 1786.

Statutes of the Scottish Church 1225–1559. David Patrick, trans. Edinburgh, 1907.

Les statuts synodaux français du XIIIe siècle. Odette Pontal, ed. Paris, 1971–.

Summa Magistri Rolandi. F. Thaner, ed. 1874; repr., Aalen, 1962.

Synodi Brixinenses saeculi XV. G. Bickell, ed. Innsbruck, 1880.

The Synodicum Nicosiense and Other Documents of the Latin Church of Cyprus, 1196–1373. C. Schabel, ed. and trans. Texts and Studies in the History of Cyprus, 39. Nicosia, 2001.

Synodus dioecesana ab . . . cardinali Pignatello celebrata . . . M.DCC.XXVI. Rome, 1726.

Synodus dioecesana Imolensis anno 1693. Imola, n.d.

Synodus dioecesana . . . Neopolitanae celebrata M.DCC.XXVI. N.p., n.d.

Synodus dioecesana . . . Rome, 1804.

Tudor Church Reform. The Henrician Canons of 1535 and the Reformatio Legum Ecclesiasticarum. Gerald Bray, ed. and tr. Church of England Record Society, 8. Woodbridge, 2000.

The Visigothic Code. S. P. Scott, tr. Boston, 1910.

Visitation Articles and Injunctions of the Period of the Reformation. W. H. Frere, ed. Alcuin Club Collections 14-16. London, 1910.

Wilkins, David, ed. *Concilia Magnae Britanniae et Hiberniae A.D. 446-1717.* 4 vols. London, 1737. Repr., Brussels, 1964.

Woywod, Stanislaus, O.F.M. *A Practical Commentary on the Code of Canon Law.* Rev. ed. by Callistus Smith, O.F.M. 2 vols. New York, 1948.

Wulfstan's Canon Law Collection. J. E. Cross and A. Hamer, eds. Anglo-Saxon Texts, 1. Cambridge, 1999.

(b) Non-legal

The Anglo-Saxon Missionaries in Germany. C. H. Talbot, ed. and tr. New York, 1954.

Anna Komnene. *The Alexiad.* E. R. A. Sewter, tr., rev. Peter Frankopan. Harmondsworth, 2009.

The Anonimalle Chronicle, 1333 to 1381. V. H. Galbraith, ed. Yorkshire Archaeological Society, 147. Manchester, 1970.

The Apostolic Tradition of Hippolytus. B. Easton, ed. and tr. 1934; repr., New York, 1962.

Benedict XIV, Pope. *Opera omnia in unum corpus collecta . . . Editio novissima.* Venice, 1787-88.

_____. *Opera omnia, editio novissima.* 17 vols. in 18. Prato, 1839-47.

Bernard of Clairvaux. 'Book on Precept and Dispensation'. In *Treatises I*, C. Greenia, tr. Spencer, Mass., 1970.

_____. *Five Books on Consideration. Advice to a Pope.* John D. Anderson and Elizabeth T. Kennan, tr. Kalamazoo, 1976.

_____. 'In Praise of the New Knighthood'. C. Greenia, tr. In *Treatises III*, Cistercian Fathers Series, 19. Kalamazoo, 1977.

_____. *The Letters of Bernard of Clairvaux.* Bruno James, tr. Chicago, 1953; repr., New York, 1980.

Between Honesty and Hope. Documents from and about the Church in Latin America. Issued at Lima by the Peruvian Bishops' Commission for Social Action. John Drury, tr. Maryknoll, 1970.

Boniface. *The Letters of Saint Boniface.* Ephraim Emerton, tr. New York, 1940, repr., 1976.

Brucker, Gene, ed. and trans. *The Society of Renaissance Florence.* New York, 1971.

Burnet, Gilbert. *Bishop Burnet's History of His Own Time: with the Suppressed Passages of the First Volume . . . [and] the cursory Remarks of Swift, and Other Observations.* 6 vols. Oxford, 1823.

Caesarius of Heisterbach. *The Dialogue on Miracles.* H. von E. Scott and C. C. Swinton Bland, tr. 2 vols. London, 1929.

Calendar of Entries in the Papal Registers, Relating to Great Britain and Ireland. Papal Letters. W. Bliss and J. Twemlow, eds. 19 vols. London, 1904; repr., Nendeln, 1971-.

Camoens, Luis Vaz de. *The Lusiads*. W. Atkinson, tr. Harmondsworth, 1952.

Caskey, Thomas W. *Caskey's Last Book. Containing an Autobiographical Sketch of His Ministerial Life, with Essays and Sermons*. B. J. Manire, ed. Nashville, 1896.

Chronica monasterii de Melsa. E. A. Bond, ed. RS, 43. London, 1866-68.

The Chronicle of Bury St Edmunds 1212–1301. Antonia Grandsden, ed. and tr. London-Edinburgh, 1964.

The Chronicle of Jocelin of Brakelond. H. E. Butler, tr. Nelson's Medieval Texts. Edinburgh, 1949.

The Chronicle of Richard of Devizes of the Time of King Richard the First. J. T. Appleby, ed. and tr. London, 1963.

Chronicles of Matthew Paris. Monastic Life in the Thirteenth Century. R. Vaughan, ed. and tr. New York, 1984.

Chronicles of the Reigns of Stephen, Henry II., and Richard I. R. Howlett, ed. RS, 82. 4 vols. London, 1884–89.

The Correspondence of Pope Gregory VII. Selected Letters from the Registrum. E. Emerton, tr. New York, 1932.

The Diary of Dudley Rider 1715–1716. W. Mathews, ed. London, 1939.

The Diary of Henry Teonge, Chaplain on Board H.M.'s Ships Assistance, Bristol, and Royal Oak 1675–1679. G. Manwaring, ed. London, 1927.

Dino Compagni's Chronicle of Florence. D. Bornstein, tr., Philadelphia, 1986.

Dobson, R. B., ed. and tr. *The Peasants' Revolt of 1381*. London, 1970.

Documentary Annals of the Reformed Church of England. Edward Cardwell, ed. 2 vols. Oxford, 1844.

The Ecclesiastical History of Orderic Vitalis. M. Chibnall, ed. and tr. 6 vols. Oxford, 1969–78.

English Historical Documents. D. C. Douglas, gen. ed. London, 1953–.

The Epistolae Vagantes of Pope Gregory VII. H. E. J. Cowdrey, ed. and tr. Oxford, 1972.

Erasmus, Desiderius. 'Julius Excluded from Heaven: A Dialogue'. In *Collected Works of Erasmus*, 27, ed. A. H. T. Levi, tr. M. J. Heath, pp. 155–97. Toronto, 1986.

The First and Second Prayer Books of Edward VI. London, 1910.

Florence of Worcester. *Chronicon*. B. Thorpe, ed. London, 1848; repr., Vaduz, 1964.

S. Francis of Assisi. His Life and Writings as Recorded by His Contemporaries. Leo Sherley-Price, tr. London, 1959.

A Frenchman, a Chaplain, a Rebel. The War Letters of Pere Louis-Hippolyte Gache, S.J. Cornelius Buckley, S.J. tr. Chicago, 1981.

Froissart, Jean. *Chronicles*. G. Brereton, tr. Harmondsworth, 1968.

Fulcher of Chartres. *A History of the Expedition to Jerusalem, 1095–1127*. F. R. Ryan, trans. Knoxville, 1969.

Galterius Cancellarius. *Bella Antiochena*. Heinrich Hagenmeyer, ed. Innsbruck, 1896.

Gerald of Wales. *Autobiography*. H. E. Butler, ed. and tr. London, 1937.

Gilbert Foliot and His Letters. A. Morey and C. N. L. Brooke, eds. Cambridge Studies in Medieval Life and Thought, n.s. 11. Cambridge, 1965.

Gooch, Thomas. *A Sermon Preached ... July 26, 1713. On Occasion of the much-lamented Death of the ... Late Lord Bishop of London*. London, 1713.

Gregory of Tours. *The History of the Franks*. Lewis Thorpe, tr. Harmondsworth, 1974.

Roberti Grosseteste episcopi quondam Lincolniensis epistolae. H. Luard, ed. RS 25. London, 1961.

Guibert of Nogent. *The Deeds of God Through the Franks.* R. Levine, tr. Woodbridge, 1997.

Helmold of Bosau. *The Chronicle of the Slavs by Helmold, Priest of Bosau.* F. J. Tschan, tr. Columbia University Records of Civilization, 21. New York, 1935.

Henry of Livonia. *The Chronicle of Henry of Livonia.* J. A. Brundage, tr. Madison, 1961.

Joannis de Fordun Scotichronicon. W. Goodall, ed. Edinburgh, 1759.

John of Salisbury. *Historia pontificalis.* M. Chibnall, ed. and tr. Corrected ed., Oxford, 1986.

_____. *The Letters of John of Salisbury,* vol. 1. W. J. Millor, S.J., and H. E. Butler, eds., rev. ed. by C. N. L. Brooke. Oxford, 1986.

Johnson, John. *The Clergy-Man's Vade Mecum . . .* 4th ed. London, 1715.

Joinville, Jean de and Geoffrey de Villehardouin. *Chronicles of the Crusades.* Caroline Smith, tr. Harmondsworth, 2008.

Langland, William. *Piers the Plowman.* J. F. Goodridge, trans. Rev. ed. Harmondsworth, 1966.

Legnano, Giovanni da. *Tractatus de bello, de represaliis et de duello.* T. E. Holland, ed. F. W. Kelsey, tr. Classics of International Law. Oxford, 1917.

The Letters of Gerbert with His Papal Privileges as Sylvester II. H. P. Lattin, tr. Records of Civilization Sources and Studies, 60. New York, 1961.

The Letters of Lanfranc Archbishop of Canterbury. H. Clover and M. Gibson, eds and tr. Oxford, 1979.

The Letters of Robert Grosseteste, Bishop of Lincoln. F. A. C. Mantello and Joseph Goering, tr. Toronto, 2010.

Lettres et memoires d'Adam Schall, S.J. Henri Bernard, S.J., ed. Tientsin, 1942.

Lowrey, M. P., General. 'An Autobiography [September 1867]'. *Southern Historical Society Papers* 16 (1888): 365–76.

Luther, Martin. *Works.* 6 vols. Philadelpha, 1915–43.

The Life of Adam Martindale, Written by Himself. R. Parkinson, ed. Chetham Society Publications, 4. N.p., 1845.

McKim, Randolph. *A Soldier's Recollections.* New York, 1910.

The Memorials of St Edmund's Abbey. 3 vols. RS, 96. London, 1890–96.

Michelangelo. *Complete Poems and Select Letters.* Creighton Gilbert, tr. New York, 1963.

Mirk, John. *Instructions for Parish Priests.* G. Kristensson, ed. Lund Studies in English, 49. Lund, 1974.

Monumenta Franciscana. J. S. Brewer, ed. RS, 4. London, 1858.

Monumenta Germaniae historica. *Epistolae Karolini aevi.*

_____. *Scriptores.*

_____. *Scriptores rerum Germanicarum.*

_____. *Scriptores rerum Merovingicarum.*

Orderic Vitalis. *The Ecclesiastical History of Orderic Vitalis.* M. Chibnall, ed. and tr. 6 vols. Oxford, 1969–78.

A Parisian Journal, 1405-1449. J. Shirley, tr. Oxford, 1968.

Peter Abelard's Ethics. D. E. Luscombe, ed. and tr. Oxford, 1971.

Petri Abaelardi opera theologica, 1, *Commentaria in epistolam Pauli ad Romanos. Apologia contra Bernardum.* E. M. Buytaert, O.F.M., ed. CCCM, 11. Turnhout, 1969.

Peters, Edward, ed. *The First Crusade. The Chronicle of Fulcher of Chartres and Other Source Materials.* 2nd ed. Philadelphia, 1998.

Reminiscences of an American Loyalist 1738–1789, Being the Autobiography of the Rev.d Jonathan Boucher, Rector of Annapolis in Maryland and Afterwards Vicar of Epsom, Surrey, England. Jonathan Boucher, ed. Boston, 1925.

Rodolfus Glaber. *The Five Books of the Histories.* John France, ed. and tr. Oxford, 1989.

St Odo of Cluny. Gerard Sitwell, O.S.B., ed. and tr. London-New York, 1958.

Sancti Antonini summa theologica. 4 vols. Verona, 1740; repr., Graz, 1959.

Scottish Annals from English Chroniclers, A.D. 500 to 1286. A. O. Anderson, tr. London, 1908.

Scriptores rerum gestarum Willelmi conquestoris. J. A. Giles, ed. Caxton Society, 3. London, 1845; repr., New York, 1967.

Select Historical Documents of the Middle Ages. E. F. Henderson, ed. and trans. London, 1910.

Las Siete Partidas. S. P. Scott, tr. Chicago, 1931.

Somerville, Robert, ed. *The Councils of Urban II.* 1, *Decreta Claromontensia.* Annuarium historiae conciliorum, Supplementum 1. Amsterdam, 1972.

The Song of Roland. D. Sayers, tr. Harmondsworth, 1957.

The State of the Church in the Reigns of Elizabeth and James I as Illustrated by Documents Relating to the Diocese of Lincoln. Vol.1. C. Foster, ed. Publications of the Lincoln Record Society, 23. Horncastle, 1926.

Suger. *Abbot Suger on the Abbey Church of St.-Denis and Its Art Treasures.* E. Panofsky, ed. and tr. Princeton, 1946.

_____. *The Deeds of Louis the Fat.* R. Cusimano and J. Moorhead, tr. Washington, 1992.

_____. *Oeuvres complètes de Suger.* A. Lecoy de la Marche, ed. Paris, 1867.

Swift, Jonathan. *Prose Works.* 14 vols. H. Davis, ed. Oxford, 1939–68.

Swift, Louis J., ed. *The Early Fathers on War and Military Service.* Wilmington, Del., 1983.

Synesius of Cyrene. *The Letters of Synesius of Cyrene.* A. Fitzgerald, tr. Oxford, 1926.

Temple, William. *Church and Nation. The Bishop Paddock Lectures for 1914–15.* London, 1915.

Theodoret. *Ecclesiastical History.* B. Jackson, tr. 1892; repr., Grand Rapids, 1979.

Thomas à Kempis. *The Chronicle of the Canons Regular of Mount St Agnes.* J. P. Arthur, tr. London, 1906.

Thomas Aquinas. *Summa theologica.* English Dominican Fathers, tr. 60 vols. to date. Cambridge-New York, 1964–.

Tierney, Brian, ed. *The Crisis of Church and State, 1050–1300.* Englewood Cliffs, N.J., 1964.

The Western Fathers. Being the Lives of Martin of Tours, Ambrose, Augustine of Hippo, Honoratus of Arles, and Germanus of Auxerre. F. R. Hoare, tr. New York, 1954.

William of Malmesbury. *Vita Wulfstani*. R. R. Darlington, ed. Camden Society, 3rd ser., 40. London, 1928.

William of Tyre. *Chronicon*. R. B. C. Huygens, ed. CCCM 63–63A. Turnhout, 1986.

_____. *A History of Deeds Done Beyond the Sea*. E. A. Babcock and A. C. Krey, tr. 2 vols. New York, 1941; repr., 1976.

Wyclif, John. *Iohannis Wyclif sermones*. J. Loserth, ed. London, 1887–90.

_____. *Tractatus de officio regis*. A. Pollard and C. Sayle, eds. Wyclif's Latin Works, 8. London, 1887.

Secondary Works

Alföldi, Lászlo. 'The Battle of Mohács, 1526'. In János Bak and Béla Király, eds., *From Hunyadi to Rákóczi. War and Society in Late Medieval and Early Modern Hungary*, pp. 189–201. New York, 1982.

Althoff, G. 'Nunc fiant Christi milites, qui dudum extiterunt raptores. Zur Entstehung vom Rittertum und Ritterethos'. *Saeculum* 32 (1981): 317–33.

Alvarez, David J. *The Pope's Soldiers. A Military History of the Modern Vatican*. Lawrence, Kan., 2011.

Amundsen, Darrel W. 'Medieval Canon Law on Medical and Surgical Practice by the Clergy'. *Bulletin of the History of Medicine* 52 (1978): 22–44.

Anders, Leslie. 'His "Radical Reverence" John H. Cox'. *Missouri Historical Review* 65 (1971): 139–58.

Anderson, Charles. 'Presbyterian Personalities'. *Journal of the Presbyterian Historical Society* 23 (1945): 48–54.

Andrea, Alfred J. 'Conrad of Krosigk, Bishop of Halberstadt, Crusader and Monk of Sittichenbach, His Ecclesiastical Career, 1184–1225'. *Analecta Cisterciensia* 43 (1987): 26–46.

Appleton's Cyclopaedia of American Biography. J. Wilson and J. Fiske, eds. 6 vols. New York, 1886–89.

Arneth, Michael. *Das Ringen um Geist und Form der Priesterbildung im Säkularklerus des siebzehnten Jahrhunderts*. Würzburg, 1970.

Arnold, Benjamin. 'German Bishops and Their Military Retinues in the Medieval Empire'. *German History* 7 (1989): 161–83.

Artonne, André, Louis Guizard and Odette Pontal. *Répertoire des statuts synodaux des diocèses de l'ancienne France du XIIIe à la fin du XVIIIe siècle*. 2nd rev. ed. Paris, 1969.

Asbridge, Thomas. 'The Significance and Causes of the Battle of the Field of Blood'. *JMH* 23 (1997): 301–16.

Ash, Marinell. 'David Bernham, Bishop of St Andrews, 1239–53'. *Innes Review* 25 (1974): 3–14.

Aston, Margaret. 'The Impeachment of Bishop Despenser'. *Bulletin of the Institute for Historical Research* 38 (1965): 127–48.

Atwood, Craig. *Handbook of Denominations in the United States*. 13th ed. Nashville, 2010.

Avril, Joseph. 'Naissance et évolution des legislations synodales dans les diocèses du nord et de l'ouest de la France (1200-1250)'. *ZRG KA* 72 (1986): 155-67.

Bainton, Roland. *Christian Attitudes Toward War and Peace*. Nashville, 1960.

Baker, J. H. 'Famous English Canon Lawyer IV: William Lyndwood'. *ELJ* 2 (1992): 268-72.

Baldwin, Alice. *The Clergy of Connecticut in Revolutionary Days*. New Haven, 1936.

Baldwin, John W. *Masters, Princes, and Merchants. The Social Views of Peter the Chanter and His Circle*. 2 vols. Baltimore, 1970.

Bates, David. 'The Character and Career of Odo, Bishop of Bayeux (1049/50–1097)'. *Speculum* 50 (1975): 1–20.

Barber, Malcolm. *The New Knighthood. A History of the Order of the Temple*. Cambridge, 1994.

Barlow, Frank. *The English Church, 1000–1066*. London, 1979.

Bartlett, Robert. *Gerald of Wales*. Oxford, 1982.

Baum, Wilhelm. *Nikolaus Cusanus in Tirol*. Bozen, 1983.

Beck, Hans-Georg. *Nomos, Kanon und Staatsraison in Byzanz*. Vienna, 1981.

_____, et al. *From the High Middle Ages to the Eve of the Reformation*. Handbook of Church History, 4. A. Biggs, tr. New York-London, 1970.

Becker-Huberti, Manfred. *Die tridentinische Reform im Bistum Münster unter Fürstbischof Christoph Bernhard von Galen, 1650 bis 1678*. Westfalia Sacra, 6. Münster, 1978.

Bell, G. K. A. *Randall Davidson. Archbishop of Canterbury*. 3rd ed. Oxford, 1952.

Benson, Robert. *The Bishop Elect. A Study in Medieval Ecclesiastical Office*. Princeton, 1968.

_____, Giles Constable, and Carol Lanham, eds. *Renaissance and Renewal in the Twelfth Century*. Cambridge, Mass., 1982.

Bernstein, David. *The Mystery of the Bayeux Tapestry*. London, 1986.

Bicknell, E. J. *A Theological Introduction to the Thirty-Nine Articles of the Church of England*. 3rd ed. rev. by H. J. Carpenter. London, 1955.

Bloch, Herbert. *Monte Cassino in the Middle Ages*. 3 vols. Cambridge, Mass., 1986.

Boisset, Louis. 'Un concile provincial au treizième siècle, Vienne 1289. Eglise locale et société.' *Théologie historique*, 21. Paris, 1973.

Borosy, András. 'The *Militia Portalis* in Hungary before 1526'. In Bak and Király, ed., *From Hunyadi to Rákóczi*.

Boynton, Lindsay. *The Elizabethan Militia 1558–1638*. London, 1967.

Brentano, Robert. *Two Churches. England and Italy in the Thirteenth Century*. Princeton, 1968.

Briden, T., and B. Hanson, eds. *Moore's Introduction to English Canon Law*. 3rd ed. London, 1992.

Briggs, Robin. *Early Modern France 1560–1715*. Oxford, 1977.

Brooks, Nicholas. 'The Development of Military Obligations in 8th and 9th Century England'. In P. Clemoes and K. Hughes, eds., *England Before the Conquest. Studies in Primary Sources Presented to Dorothy Whitelock*, pp. 69–84. Cambridge, 1971.

Broué, Pierre and Emile Témine. *The Revolution and the Civil War in Spain*. T. White, tr. Cambridge, Mass., 1970.

Brown, Lawrence. 'Henry Compton, 1632–1713, Bishop of London 1675–1713. Pioneer Leader in the Expansion of the Anglican Communion'. *HMPEC* 25 (1956): 7–71.

Brundage, James A. 'Holy War'.' In Thomas P. Murphy, ed., *The Holy War*, pp. 99–140. Columbus, 1976.

_____. *Medieval Canon Law*. London-New York, 1995.

_____. *Medieval Canon Law and the Crusader*. Madison-London, 1969.

Brunner, Otto. *Land and Lordship. Structures of Governance in Medieval Austria*. H. Kaminsky and J.V.H. Melton, trans. Philadelphia, 1992.

Brydon, G. Maclaren. 'The Clergy of the Established Church in Virginia and the American Revolution'. *Virginia Magazine of History and Biography* 41 (1933): 11–23, 123–43, 231–43, 297–309.

_____. 'The Diocese of Virginia in the Southern Confederacy'. *HMPEC* 17 (1948): 384–410.

Bueno de Mesquita, D. M. *Giangaleazzo Visconti, Duke of Milan (1351–1402)*. Cambridge, 1941.

Burckhardt, Jacob. *The Civilization of the Renaissance in Italy*. S. G. C. Middlemore, tr. 2 vols. New York, 1958.

Burger, Nash. 'The Diocese of Mississippi and the Confederacy'. *HMPEC* 9 (1940): 52–77.

Callahan, William J. *Church, Politics and Society in Spain, 1750–1874*. Cambridge, Mass., 1984.

Carpenter, Edward. *The Protestant Bishop. Being the Life of Henry Compton, 1632–1713, Bishop of London*. London, 1956.

Castillo Lara, Rosalio. *Coaccion eclesiastica y Sacro Romano Imperio. Estudio juridico-historico sobre la podestad coactiva material suprema de la Iglesia en los documentos conciliares y pontificios del periodo de formacion del derecho canonico clásico como un presupuesto de las relaciones entre Sacerdotium e Imperium*. Turin, 1956.

Chambers, D. S. *Popes, Cardinals and War. The Military Church in Renaissance and Early Modern Europe*. London-New York, 2006.

Cheney, C. R. *English Synodalia of the Thirteenth Century*. Oxford, 1941.

_____. *Hubert Walter*. London, 1967.

_____. *Medieval Texts and Studies*. Oxford, 1973.

Cheshire, Joseph Blount. *The Church in the Confederate States*. New York, 1912.

Chibnall, Marjorie. *The World of Orderic Vitalis*. Oxford, 1984.

Clarendon, Edward, Earl of. *The History of the Rebellion and Civil Wars in England Begun in the Year 1641*. W. Macray, ed. 6 vols. Oxford, 1888, repr., 1958, 1969.

Clifton, Robin. *The Last Popular Rebellion. The Western Uprising of 1685*. London, 1984.

Constable, Giles. 'The Historiography of the Crusades'. In *Crusaders and Crusading in the Twelfth Century*, pp. 3–44. Farnham-Burlington, Vt, 2008.

_____. 'The Ideal of the Imitation of Christ'. In *Three Studies in Medieval Religious and Social Thought*, pp. 143–248. Cambridge, 1995.

_____. 'Medieval Charters as a Source for the History of the Crusades'. In *Crusaders and Crusading*, pp. 93–116.

_____. 'An Unpublished Letter by Abbot Hugh II of Reading Concerning

Archbishop Hubert Walter.' In *Cluniac Studies*. Collected Studies, 109. London, 1980.

Contamine, Philippe. *Guerre, état et société à la fin du moyen age*. Paris, 1972
_____. *War in the Middle Ages*. M. Jones, tr. Oxford, 1984.

Coolidge, Robert. 'Adalbero, Bishop of Laon'. *Studies in Medieval and Renaissance History* 2 (1965): 1–114.

Corbet, Patrick. *Les saints ottoniens*. Beihefte der Francia, 15. Sigmaringen, 1986.

Coriden, James A. *An Introduction to Canon Law*. London, 1990, and New York-Mahwah, 1991.

Corvisier, André. *Armies and Societies in Europe, 1494–17890*. A. Siddell, tr. Bloomington, 1979.

Cowdrey, H. E. J. 'Bishop Erminfrid of Sion and the Penitential Ordinance following the Battle of Hastings'. *JEH* 20 (1969): 225–42.
_____. 'Cluny and the First Crusade'. *Revue bénédictine* 83 (1973): 285–311.
_____. 'Martyrdom and the First Crusade'. In P. W. Edbury, ed., *Crusade and Settlement*, pp. 46–56. Cardiff, 1985.
_____. *Pope Gregory VII, 1073–1085*. Oxford, 1998.
_____. 'Pope Gregory VII's "Crusading" Plans of 1074'. In B. Z. Kedar et al., *Outremer*, pp. 27–40. Jerusalem, 1982.
_____. *Popes, Monks and Crusaders*. London, 1984.

Cox, Eugene. *The Eagles of Savoy*. Princeton, 1974.

Cruickshank, C. G. *Elizabeth's Army*. 2nd ed. Oxford, 1966.

Curtis, Catherine Mary. 'Richard Pace on Pedagogy, Counsel and Satire'. Cambridge University Ph.D. dissertation, 1996.

Cushing, Kathleen. *Papacy and Law in the Gregorian Revolution. The Canonistic Work of Anselm of Lucca*. Oxford, 1998.

Daniel, W. Harrison. 'Chaplains in the Army of Northern Virginia. A List Compiled in 1864 and 1865 by Robert L. Dabney'. *Virginia Magazine of History and Biography* 71 (1963): 327–40.

Le Décret de Gratien revisité. Hommage à Rudolf Weigand. Revue de droit canonique 48/2 (1998).

Dictionary of the Middle Ages. Joseph Strayer, gen. ed. 12 vols. New York, 1982–89.

Dictionnaire de biographie française. Paris, 1933–.

Dictionnaire de droit canonique. R. Naz, ed. 7 vols. Paris, 1935–65.

Dictionnaire de théologie catholique. A. Vacant et al., eds. 18 vols. 1903–72.

Dictionary of American Biography. New York, 1927–.

Dictionary of Canadian Biography. Toronto-Quebec, 1966–.

Dictionary of National Biography. London, 1885–.

Dimier, Anselme. 'Violences, rixes et homicides chez les Cisterciens'. *Revue des sciences religieuses* 46 (1972): 38–57.

Dizionario degli istituti di perfezione. 10 vols. Rome, 1974–2003.

Doe, Norman. *Canon Law in the Anglican Communion. A Worldwide Perspective*. Oxford, 1998.
_____. *The Legal Framework of the Church of England*. Oxford, 1996.

Donaldson, G. and R. S. Morpeth, comps. *Who's Who in Scottish History*. New York, 1973.

Donovan, John Thomas. *The Clerical Obligations of Canons 138 and 140*. Catholic University of America Canon Law Studies, 272. Washington, 1948.

Duggan, Anne J. 'The Master of the Decretals. A Reassessment of Alexander III's Contribution to the Development of Canon law', pp. 365–417 in Peter D. Clarke and Anne J. Duggan, eds, *Pope Alexander III (1159–81). The Art of Survival*. Farnham-Burlington, Vt, 2012.

Duggan, Lawrence G. 'Fear and Confession on the Eve of the Reformation'. *Archiv für Reformationsgeschichte* (1984): 153–75.

_____. '"For Force Is Not of God"? Compulsion and Conversion from Yahweh to Charlemagne'. In James Muldoon, ed., *The Varieties of Religious Conversion in the Middle Ages*, pp. 49–62. Gainesville, 1997.

_____. 'Was Art Really the "Book of the Illiterate"?' *Word & Image* 5 (1989): 227–51, repr. in *Reading Texts and Images. Medieval Images and Texts as Forms of Communication*, eds. Marielle Hageman and Marco Mostert, pp. 64–103. Utrecht Studies in Medieval Literacy, 8. Turnhout, 2005.

Dussel, Enrique, ed. *The Church in Latin America, 1492–1992*. Tunbridge Wells-Maryknoll, 1992.

_____, gen. ed. *Historia general de la iglesia en America Latina*. 9 vols. Salamanca, 1981–95.

_____. *A History of the Church in Latin America. Colonialism to Liberation (1492–1979)*. A. Neely, tr. Grand Rapids, Mich., 1981.

The Ecclesiastical Courts. Principles of Reconstruction . . . London, 1954.

Edbury, Peter, ed. *Crusade and Settlement. Papers Read at the First Conference of the Society for the Study of the Crusades and the Latin East and Presented to R. C. Smail*. Cardiff, 1985.

Encyclopaedia of Religion and Ethics. James Hastings, ed. 13 vols. 1908–26; repr., New York, 1961.

Engels, Odilo. 'Der Reichsbischof in ottonischer und frühsalischer Zeit'. In Irene Crusius, ed. *Beiträge zu Struktur und Struktur der mittelalterlichen Germania Sacra*. Göttingen, 1989.

Erdmann, Carl. *The Origin of the Idea of Crusade*. Marshall Baldwin and Walter Goffart, tr. Princeton, 1977.

Erichson, L. A. *Zur 400 jährigen Geburtsfeier Zwingli's*. Strasbourg, 1884.

_____. *Zwingli's Tod und dessen Beurtheilung durch Zeitgenossen*. Strasbourg, 1883.

Erler, Adalbert. *Aegidius Albornoz als Gesetzgeber des Kirchenstaates*. Berlin, 1970.

Essen, Alfred van der. *Le Cardinal-Infant et la politique européene de l'Espagne 1609–1641*, 1. Brussels, 1944.

Esteban, Carro Celada. *Curas guerrilleros en España*. Madrid, 1971.

Fairbank, John K., Edwin O. Reischauer and Albert M. Craig. *East Asia. The Modern Transformation*. Boston-Tokyo, 1964.

Farriss, Nancy. *Crown and Clergy in Colonial Mexico, 1759–1821. The Crisis of Ecclesiastical Privilege*. London, 1968.

Ferme, Brian. 'William Lyndwood and the Provinciale'. *ELJ* 4 (1997): 615–28.

Firth, C. H. *Cromwell's Army*. 4th ed. London, 1962.

Fisher, Josephine. 'Bennet Allen, Fighting Parson'. *Maryland Historical Magazine* 38 (1943): 299–322 and 39 (1944): 49–72.

Ford, Henry. 'A Revolutionary Hero: James Caldwell'. *Journal of the Presbyterian Historical Society* 6 (1911): 260–66.

France, John. 'War and Christendom in the Thought of Rodulfus Glaber'. *Studia monastica* 30 (1988): 105–119.

Frantzen, Allen J. *The Literature of Penance in Anglo-Saxon England.* New Brunswick, 1983.

Fraser, C. M. *A History of Antony Bek, Bishop of Durham, 1283–1311.* Oxford, 1957.

Freeman, Edward A. *The History of the Norman Conquest of England.* 6 vols. Oxford, 1870–79.

Gaudemet, Jean. 'La vie conciliaire en France'. In Ferdinand Lot and Robert Fawtier, *Histoire des institutions françaises du Môyen Age,* 3. Paris, 1962.

Geary, Patrick. *Before France and Germany.* New York, 1987.

Gibbs, Marion and Jane Lang. *Bishops and Reform 1215–1272.* 1934, repr. London, 1962.

Gibson, Margaret. *Lanfranc of Bec.* Oxford, 1978.

Gilchrist, John. 'The Erdmann Thesis and the Canon Law, 1083–1141'. In P. Edbury, *Crusade and Settlement,* pp. 37–45.

_____. 'The Reception of Pope Gregory VII into the Canon Law'. *ZRG KA* 69 (1973):35–82 and 76 (1980):192–239.

_____. 'The Papacy and War Against the "Saracens", 795–1216'. *International History Review* 10 (1988): 174–97.

Goetz, Hans-Werner. 'Protection of the Church, Defense of the Law, and Reform. On the Purposes and Character of the Peace of God'. In Head and Landes, *Peace of God,* pp. 259-79.

Greenaway, G. W. *Arnold of Brescia.* Cambridge, 1931.

Gribbin, William. *Churches Militant. The War of 1812 and American Religion.* Yale, 1973.

Guizard, L. 'Les statuts d'Eudes de Sully'. *Revue historique de droit français et étranger* ser. 4, 33 (1955):623–33.

Gwatkin, H. M. *Church and State in England to the Death of Queen Anne.* London, 1917.

Haines, Roy. *Archbishop John Stratford.* Toronto, 1986.

Hale, John. *Renaissance War Studies.* London, 1983.

_____. *War and Society in Renaissance Europe 1450–1620.* Leicester, 1985.

Haller, Johannes. *Das Papsttum. Idee und Wirklichkeit.* Rev. ed. 6 vols. Munich, 1965.

Hamilton, Bernard. *The Latin Church in the Crusader State. The Secular Church.* London, 1980.

Hardwick, Charles. *A History of the Articles of Religion.* Philadelphia, 1852. 3rd ed. London, 1876.

Harnack, Adolf. *Militia Christi. The Christian Religion and the Military in the First Three Centuries.* D. Gracie, tr. Philadelphia, 1981.

Hauck, Albert. *Kirchengeschichte Deutschlands.* 8th ed. 1922; repr., Berlin, 1954.

Hay, Denys. *The Italian Renaissance in its Historical Background.* Cambridge, 1961.

Hayes, Denys. *Conscription Conflict.* New York, 1973.

Head, Thomas and Richard Landes, eds. *The Peace of God. Social Violence and Religious Response in France Around the Year 1000*. Ithaca, 1992.

Headley, Joel T. *The Chaplains and Clergy of the Revolution*. New York, 1864.

Heath, Peter. *The English Parish Clergy on the Eve of the Reformation*. London, 1969.

Heathcote, Charles W. *The Lutheran Church and the Civil War*. New York, 1919.

Heers, Jacques. *Genes au XVe siècle*. Paris, 1961.

Hefele, Karl von. *The Life of Cardinal Ximenez*. Rev. Canon Dalton, tr. London, 1860.

Hehl, Ernst-Dieter. *Kirche und Krieg im 12. Jahrhundert. Studien zu kanonischem Recht und politischer Wirklichkeit*. MGM, 19. Stuttgart, 1980.

Heinzelmann, Martin. 'Bischof und Herrschaft vom spätantiken Gallien bis zu den karolingischen Hausmeiern'. In Prinz, *Herrschaft und Kirche*, pp. 23–82.

Helmholz, Richard, ed. *Canon Law in Protestant Lands. Comparative Studies in Continental and Anglo-American Legal History*. Berlin, 1992.

_____. 'Discipline of the Clergy: Medieval and Modern'. *ELJ* 6 (2002): 189-98.

_____. *Roman Canon Law in Reformation England*. Cambridge, 1990.

_____. *The Spirit of Classical Canon Law*. Athens, Ga., 1996.

Hiestand, Rudolf. 'Kardinalbischof Matthäus von Albano, das Konzil von Troyes und die Entstehung des Templerordens'. *Zeitschrift für Kirchengeschichte* 99 (1988): 295–325.

Highfield, J. R. L. 'The English Hierarchy in the Reign of Edward III'. *TRHS* 5th ser. 6 (1956): 115–38.

Hill, Christopher. *The World Turned Upside down*. New York, 1972.

Hill, Mark. *Ecclesiastical Law*. London, 1995.

_____, *Faithful Discipleship. Clergy Discipline in Anglican and Roman Canon Law*. Cardiff-Rome, 2001.

Hillgarth, J. N. *The Spanish Kingdoms, 1250–1516*. 2 vols. Oxford, 1976–78.

Hinschius, Paul. *Das Kirchenrecht der Katholiken und Protestanten in Deutschland*. Berlin, 1869–97; repr., Graz, 1959.

Hoffmann, Hartmut. 'Petrus Diaconus, die Herren von Tusculum und der Sturz Oderisius' II von Monte Cassino'. *DA* 27 (1971): 1-109.

Holdsworth, Christopher. 'Orderic, Traditional Monk and the New Monasticism'. In D. Greenway, C. Holdsworth and J. Sayers, eds., *Tradition and Change. Essays in Honour of Marjorie Chibnall*. Cambridge, 1985.

Holland, S. M. 'George Abbot: "The Wanted Archbishop"'. *Church History* 56 (1987):172–87.

Holmes, David. 'The Episcopal Church and the American Revolution'. *HMPEC* 47 (1978): 261–92.

Holt, J. C. *Robin Hood*. London, 1982.

Holtzmann, Walther. 'Die Register Papst Alexanders III. in den Händen der Kanonisten'. *Quellen und Forschungen aus italiensichen Archiven und Bibliotheken* 30 (1940): 13–87.

Howard, Michael. *War and the Liberal Conscience*. London, 1978.

Hsü, Immanuel C. Y. *The Rise of Modern China*. 3rd ed. Oxford, 1983.

Hughes, Robert. *The Fatal Shore*. New York, 1987.

Humphrey, Edward F. *Nationalism and Religion in America, 1774–1789*. Boston, 1924.

Huscroft, Richard. *The Norman Conquest. A New Introduction*. Harlow, 2009.

Hussey, J. M. *The Orthodox Church in the Byzantine Empire.* Oxford, 1986.

Jacob, E. F. 'Wilkins's *Concilia* and the Fifteenth Century'. *TRHS* 4th ser., 15 (1932):91–131.

Jenal, Georg. 'Gregor der Grosse und die Stadt Rom (590–604)'. In Prinz, *Herrschaft und Kirche*, pp. 108–45.

Jones, J. William. *Christ in the Camp; or, Religion in Lee's Army.* Richmond, 1887.

Jones, Rhidian. *The Canon Law of the Roman Catholic Church and the Church of England. A Handbook.* Edinburgh, 2000.

Joyce, Lester. *Church and Clergy in the American Revolution.* New York, 1966.

Kaeuper, R. W. *War, Justice, and Public Order. England and France in the Later Middle Ages.* Oxford, 1988.

Kaiser, Reinhold. 'Königtum und Bischofsherrschaft im frühmittelalterlichen Neustrien'. In Prinz, *Herrschaft und Kirche*, pp. 83–108.

Kamen, Henry. 'Clerical Violence in a Catholic Society: The Hispanic World, 1450–1720'. In W. J. Shiels, ed., *The Church and War*, pp. 200–16. Studies in Church History, 20. Oxford, 1983.

_____. *The War of Succession in Spain 1700–15.* Bloomington, 1969.

Kapitanovic, Vicko, O.F.M. 'Die Stellung der Franziskaner zur Gewaltanwendung im Freiheitskampf in Bosnien und Hercegowina, 1875'. *Archivum Franciscanum historicum* 76 (1983): 355–62.

Katzir, Yael. 'The Patriarch of Jerusalem, Primate of the Latin Kingdom'. In Edbury, ed., *Crusade and Settlement*, pp. 169-75.

Kedar, Benjamin. 'On the Origins of the Earliest Laws of Frankish Jerusalem: the Canons of the Council of Nablus, 1120'. *Speculum* 74 (1999): 310–36.

_____, Hans Eberhard Mayer, and R. C. Smail, eds. *Outremer. Studies in the History of the Crusading Kingdom of Jerusalem.* Jerusalem, 1982.

Kempshall, Everard. *Caldwell and the Revolution.* Elizabeth, 1880.

Kern, Fritz. *Kingship and Law in the Middle Ages.* S. B. Chrimes, tr. Oxford, 1948.

Kirsten, Klaus-Peter. *Die lateinischen Patriarchen von Jerusalem. Von der Eroberung der Heiligen Stadt durch die Kreuzfahrer 1099 bis zum Ende der Kreuzfahrerstaaten 1291.* Berliner Historische Studien, 35. Berlin, 2002.

Kramer, Leonard. 'Muskets in the Pulpit: 1776–1783'. *Journal of the Presbyterian Historical Society* 31 (1953): 229–44 and 32 (1954): 37–52.

Kuttner, Stephan. *Harmony from Dissonance. An Interpretation of Medieval Canon Law.* Wimmer Lecture, 10. Latrobe, Pa., 1960.

_____. *Kanonistische Schuldlehre von Gratian bis auf die Dekretalen Gregors IX.* Studi e testi, 64. Vatican city, 1935; repr., 1961.

_____. 'Notes on the Glossa ordinaria of Bernard of Parma'. *Bulletin of the Institute of Medieval Canon Law* n.s. 11 (1981): 86–93.

_____. 'The Revival of Jurisprudence'. In Benson et al., *Renaissance and Renewal in the Twelfth Century*, pp. 299–323.

Landau, Peter. 'Neue Forschungen zu vorgratianischen Kanonessammlungen und den Quellen des gratianischen Dekrets'. *Ius Commune* 11 (1984): 1–30.

Lang, Peter. 'Würfel, Wein und Wettersegen. Klerus und Gläubige im Bistum Eichstätt am Vorabend der Reformation'. In Volker Press and Dieter Stievermann, eds., *Martin Luther. Probleme seiner Zeit*, pp. 219–43. Stuttgart, 1986.

Lapsley, Gaillard T. *The County Palatine of Durham*. Harvard, 1924.

Le Patourel, John. 'Geoffrey of Montbray, Bishop of Coutances'. *EHR* 59 (1944): 129–61.

Levillain, Philippe, gen. ed. *The Papacy. An Encyclopedia*. 3 vols. New York-London, 2022.

Leyser, Karl. 'Early Medieval Canon Law and the Beginnings of Knighthood'. In Lutz Fenske, Werner Rösener, and Thomas Zotz, eds. *Institutionen, Kultur und Gesellschaft im Mittelalter. Festschrift für Josef Fleckenstein zu seinem 65. Geburtstag*, pp. 549–66. Sigmaringen, 1984.

Liebeschuetz, J. H. W. G. *Barbarians and Bishops. Army, Church and State in the Age of Arcadius and Chrysostom*. Oxford, 1990.

Liotta, Filippo, ed. *Miscellanea Rolando Bandinelli, Papa Alessandro III*. Siena, 1986.

Lottin, Odon. *Psychologie et morale au xiie et xiiie siècles*. 6 vols in 8. Louvain, 1942–60.

Loud, G. A. *Church and Society in the Norman Principality of Capua*. Oxford, 1985.

————. 'The Church, Warfare and Military Obligation in Norman Italy'. In W. J. Shiels, ed., *The Church and War*. Studies in Church History, 20. Oxford, 1983.

Macaulay, Thomas Babington. *The History of England from the Accession of James the Second*. C. H. Firth, ed. 6 vols. London, 1914.

Maitland, F. W. *Roman Canon Law in the Church of England*. London, 1898.

Mampoteng, Charles. 'The New England Anglican Clergy in the American Revolution'. *HMPEC* 9 (1940): 267–304.

Manning, Eug. 'La signification de "militare-militia-miles" dans la regle de Saint Benoit'. *Revue Bénédictine* 72 (1962): 135–8.

Marrin, Albert. *The Last Crusade. The Church of England in the First World War*. Durham, N.C., 1974.

Maurer, Helmut. 'Zu den Inskriptionen der Mainzer Provinzialstatuten von 1310'. *ZRG KA* 53 (1967): 338–46.

Maurer, Wilhelm. 'Reste des kanonischen Rechtes im Frühprotestantismus'. *ZRG KA* 51 (1965): 190–253.

Mayer, Hans Eberhard. 'The Concordat of Nablus'. *JEH* 33 (1982): 531-43.

McKeel, Arthur. *The Relation of the Quakers to the American Revolution*. Washington, 1979.

McManners, John. *Church and State in France, 1870–1914*. London, 1972.

McNab, Bruce. 'Obligations of the Church in English Society: Military Arrays of the Clergy, 1369–1418'. In William C. Jordan, Bruce McNab, and Teofilo F. Ruiz, eds, *Order and Innovation in the Middle Ages. Essays in Honor of Joseph R. Strayer*, pp. 293–314. Princeton, 1976.

Metz, René. 'Regard critique sur la personne de Gratien, auteur du Decret (1130–1140), d'après les résultats des dernières recherches'. *Revue des sciences religieuses* 58 (1984): 64–76.

Minninger, Monika. *Von Clermont zum Wormser Konkordat. Die Auseinandersetzungen um den Lehnsnexus zu König und Episkopat*. Cologne-Vienna, 1978.

Morris, John E. *The Welsh Wars of Edward I*. Oxford, 1941, repr., 1968.

Mortimer, R. C. *Western Canon Law*. London, 1953.

Müller, Wolfgang. *Huguccio. The Life, Works, and Thought of a Twelfth-Century Jurist.* Studies in Medieval and Early Modern Canon Law, 3. Washington, 1994.

Murdock, Eugene. *One Million Men. The Civil War Draft in the North.* Madison, 1971.

Murphy, DuBose. 'The Protestant Episcopal Church in Texas during the Civil War'. *HMPEC* 1 (1932): 90–101.

Murphy, Thomas P., ed. *The Holy War.* Columbus, 1976.

Nadro, Silvino da, O.F.M.Cap. *Sinodi diocesani italiani. Catalogo bibliografico degli atti a stampa 1534–1878.* Studi e testi, 207. Vatican City, 1960.

Nelson, Lynn H. and Arnold H. Weiss. 'An Early Life of Francisco Jimenez de Cisneros'. *Franciscan Studies* 42 (1982): 156–65.

New Catholic Encyclopedia. 16 vols. Washington, 1967.

The New Century Italian Renaissance Encyclopedia. C. Avery, gen. ed. New York, 1972.

The New Schaff-Herzog Encyclopedia of Religious Knowledge. 13 vols. New York, 1908–14.

Newlin, W. H. et al. *A History of the Seventy-Third Regiment of Illinois Infantry Volunteers.* N.p., 1890.

Nicholl, Donald. *Thurstan, Archbishop of York (1114–40).* York, 1964.

Nicholson, Helen. *Templars, Hospitallers and Teutonic Knights. Images of the Military Orders, 1128–1291.* Leicester, 1993.

Nörr, Knut Wolfgang. 'Institutional Foundations of the New Jurisprudence'. In Benson et al., *Renaissance and Renewal*, pp. 324–38.

Noonan. John T., Jr. 'Who was Rolandus?' In Kenneth Pennington and Robert Somerville, eds. *Law, Church and Society. Essays in Honor of Stephan Kuttner*, pp. 21–48. Philadelphia, 1977.

Nouvelle biographie générale. 46 vols. Paris, 1853–66.

O'Brien, Niall. *Revolution from the Heart.* New York-Oxford, 1987.

O'Callaghan, Joseph. *A History of Medieval Spain.* Ithaca, 1975.

O'Connell, D. P. *Richelieu.* Cleveland-New York, 1968.

Oerter, Herbert. 'Campaldino, 1289'. *Speculum* 43 (1968): 429–50.

O'Malley, John W., S.J. *Giles of Viterbo on Church and Reform.* Leiden, 1968.

_____. *Praise and Blame in Renaissance Rome. Rhetoric, Doctrine, and Reform in the Sacred Orators of the Papal Court, c. 1450–1521.* Durham, N.C., 1979.

Oman, Charles. *A History of the Art of War in the Middle Ages.* 2 vols. London, 1924.

_____. *A History of the Art of War in the Sixteenth Century.* 1937; repr, New York, 1979.

The Oxford Dictionary of the Christian Church. F. L. Cross and E. A. Livingstone, eds. 3rd ed. rev. Oxford, 2005.

Pagès, Georges. *The Thirty Years War.* D. Maland and J. Hooper, tr. New York 1970.

Partner, Peter. *Renaissance Rome, 1500–1559.* Berkeley-Los Angeles, 1976.

Pastells, Pablo, S.J. and F. Mateos, S.J. *Historia de la Compañia de Jésus en la provincia de Paraguay . . .* 8 vols. in 9. Madrid, 1912–49.

Peck, Epaphroditus. *The Loyalists of Connecticut.* New York, 1934.

Pennington, Kenneth. 'Innocent III and the Ius commune'. In Richard Helmholz et al., eds, *Grundlagen des Rechts. Festschrift für Peter Landau zum 65. Geburtstag*, pp. 349–66. Paderborn, 2000.

Perroy, Edoard. *The Hundred Years War*. W. B. Wells, tr. New York, 1965.

Perry, William Stevens. *The Bishops of the American Church Past and Present*. New York, 1897.

Phillimore, Robert. *The Ecclesiastical Law of the Church of England*. 2nd ed. by W. G. F. Phillimore and C. F. Jemmett. London, 1895.

Phillips, Jonathan. *Defenders of the Holy Land. Relations Between the Latin East and the West, 1119–1187*. Oxford, 1996.

Pichler, Johannes. *Necessitas. Ein Element des mittelalterlichen und neuzeitlichen Rechts*. Berlin, 1983.

Plöchl, Willibald. *Geschichte des Kirchenrechts*. 5 vols. Vienna-Munich, 1952–68.

Poggiaspalla, Ferminio. 'La Chiesa et la partecipazione dei chierici alla guerra nella legislazione conciliare fino alla Decretali di Gregorio IX'. *Ephemerides iuris canonici* 15 (1959): 140- 53.

Post, Gaines. *Studies in Medieval Legal Thought. Public Law and the State, 1100–1322*. Princeton, 1964.

Potter, G. R. *Zwingli*. Cambridge, 1976.

Powicke, F. M. *King Henry III and the Lord Edward*. Oxford, 1947.

Powicke, Michael. *Military Obligation in Medieval England*. Oxford, 1962.

Prescott, William H. *History of the Reign of Ferdinand and Isabella the Catholic*. J. F. Kirk, ed. 3 vols. Philadelphia, 1872.

Prinz, Friedrich. 'Die bischöfliche Stadtherrschaft im Frankenreich vom 5. bis zum 7. Jahrhundert'. *Historische Zeitschrift* 217 (1973): 1–35.

_____. 'King, Clergy and War at the Time of the Carolingians.' In Margot King and Wesley Stevens, eds., *Saints, Scholars and Heroes. Studies in Medieval Culture in Honour of Charles W. Jones*, 2:301–329. Collegeville, Minn., 1979.

_____, ed. *Herrschaft und Kirche. Beiträge zur Entstehung und Wirkungsweise episkopaler und monastischer Organisationsformen*. MGM, 33. Stuttgart, 1988.

_____. *Klerus und Krieg im frühen Mittelalter*. Stuttgart, 1971.

Purkis, William J. *Crusading Spirituality in the Holy Land and Iberia, c. 1095-c. 1187*. Woodbridge-Rochester, NY, 2008.

Ranke, Leopold von. *A History of England Principally in the Seventeenth Century*. Oxford, 1875.

Reid, Charles J., Jr. 'The Papacy, Theology, and Revolution. A Response to Joseph L. Soria's Critique of Harold J. Berman's *Law and Revolution*'. SC 29 (1995): 433-80

Reynolds, Roger. *Clerical Orders in the Early Middle Ages. Duties and Ordination*. Aldershot, 1999.

Richard, Jean. 'Hospitals and Hospital Congregations in the Latin Kingdom in the Early Days of Frankish Conquest', in *Croisés, missionaires et voyageurs. Les perspectives orientales du monde latin medieval*, II, 89-100. Variorum Reprints CS 192. London, 1982.

Richardson, R. K. 'The Bishopric of Durham under Anthony Bek, 1283-1311'. *Archaeologia Aeliana* 3rd ser. 9 (1913): 89–229.

Richter, Aemelius Ludwig. *Lehrbuch des katholischen und evangelischen Kirchenrechts. Mit besonderer Rücksicht auf deutsche Zustände*. 8th ed. Leipzig, 1886.

Rightmyer, Nelson Waite. *Maryland's Established Church*. Baltimore, 1956.

Rightmyer, Thomas. 'The Holy Orders of Peter Muhlenburg'. *HMPEC* 30 (1961): 183–97.

Riley-Smith, Jonathan. *The Crusades. A History*. 2nd ed. New Haven, 2005.

_____. 'Crusading as an Act of Love'. *History* 65 (1980): 177-192.

_____. *The First Crusade and the Idea of Crusading*. Philadelphia, 1985.

_____. *The First Crusaders, 1095-1131*. Cambridge, 1997.

_____. *The Knights of St John in Jerusalem and Cyprus, c. 1050-1310*. London, 1967.

_____, ed. *The Oxford Illustrated History of the Crusades*. Oxford, 1997.

_____. *What Were the Crusades?* Totowa, N.J., 1977.

Roberts, B. Dew. *Mitre and Musket. John Williams. Lord Keeper, Archbishop of York, 1582-1652*. Oxford, 1938.

Robinson, I. S. 'Gregory VII and the Soldiers of Christ'. *History* 58 (1973): 169–92.

_____. 'Pope Gregory VII (1073–1085)'. *JEH* 36 (1985): 439–83.

Rodes, Robert, Jr. *Ecclesiastical Administration in Medieval England*. Notre Dame, 1977.

Romero, Sidney. 'The Confederate Chaplain'. *Civil War History* 1 (1955): 127–40.

_____. 'Louisiana Clergy and the Confederate Army'. *Louisiana History* 2 (1961): 277–300.

Runciman, Steven. *The Eastern Schism*. Oxford, 1955.

Rupp, E. Gordon. *Patterns of Reformation*. Philadelphia, 1969.

Russell, F. H. *The Just War in the Middle Ages*. Cambridge Studies in Medieval Life and Thought, 3rd ser. 8. Cambridge, 1975.

Säbisch, Alfred. 'Drei angebliche Breslauer Diözesansynoden des 15. Jahrhunderts'. *ZRG KA* 50 (1964): 272–8.

Saenger, Paul. 'Silent Reading: Its Impact on Late Medieval Script and Society'. *Viator* 13 (1982): 367–414.

Sanchez, Jose. *The Spanish Civil War as a Religious Tragedy*. Notre Dame, 1987.

Sanders, Vivienne. 'John Whitgift: Primate, Privy Councillor and Propagandist'. *Anglican and Episcopal History* 56 (1987): 385–403.

Sawicki, J. T. *Bibliographia synodorum particularium*. Monumenta iuris canonici, C/2. Vatican City, 1967.

Schenck, Robert L., ed. *Constitutions of American Denominations*. 3 vols. Buffalo, 1984.

Schmandt, Raymond H. 'The Fourth Crusade and the Just-War Theory'. *Catholic Historical Review* 61 (1975): 191–221.

Schmitt, Karl M. 'The Clergy and the Independence of New Spain'. *Hispanic American Historical Review* 34 (1954): 289–312.

Schmitz, Hermann. *Die Bussbücher und die Bussdisciplin der Kirche*. Mainz, 1883; repr., Graz, 1958.

Schumacher, John, S.J. *Revolutionary Clergy. The Filipino Clergy and the Nationalist Movement, 1850-1903*. Quezon City, 1981.

Scott, Tom. 'From Polemic to Sobriety: Thomas Müntzer in Recent Research'. *JEH* 39 (1988): 557–72.

Shattuck, Gardiner, Jr. *A Shield and Hiding Place. The Religious Life of the Civil War Armies*. Macon, Ga., 1987.

Shaw, Christine. *Julius II. The Warrior Pope*. Oxford-Cambridge, Mass., 1993.

Shepard, John, Jr. 'Religion in the Army of Northern Virginia'. *North Carolina Historical Review* 25 (1948): 341–76.

Sherr, Merrill. 'Bishop Edmund Bonner: A Quasi Erasmian'. *HMPEC* 43 (1974): 359–66.

Smith, Katherine Allen. *War and the Making of Medieval Monastic Culture*. Woodbridge, 2011.

Smith, M. G. *Fighting Joshua. A Study of the Career of Sir Jonathan Trelawny, Bart. 1650–1721, Bishop of Bristol, Exeter and Winchester*. Redruth, 1985.

Smith, Waldo. *The Navy and Its Chaplains in the Days of Sail*. Toronto, 1961.

Smet, Joachim, O.Carm. *The Carmelites. A History of the Brothers of Our Lady of Mount Carmel*. 4 vols. Darien, Ill., 1975–85.

Southern, R. W. *Robert Grosseteste. The Growth of an English Mind in Medieval Europe*. 2nd ed. Oxford, 1992.

_____. *Saint Anselm and His Biographer*. Cambridge, 1963.

Spalding, David, C.F.X. 'Martin John Spalding's "Dissertation on the American Civil War"'. *Catholic Historical Review* 52 (1966): 66–85.

Spatz, Wilhelm. *Die Schlacht von Hastings*. 1896; repr., Vaduz, 1965.

Spence, Jonathan. *To Change China*. Boston, 1969.

Stacey, R. W. *Politics, Policy and Finance under Henry III, 1216–1245*. Oxford, 1987.

Stanton, R. L. *The Church and the Rebellion*. New York, 1864.

Stenton, Frank. *Anglo-Saxon England*. 3rd ed. Oxford, 1971.

_____, ed. *The Bayeux Tapestry*. New York, 1956.

Stevick, Daniel B. *Canon Law. A Handbook*. New York, 1965.

Stokes, Durward. 'The Presbyterian Clergy in South Carolina and the American Revolution'. *South Carolina Historical Magazine* 71 (1970): 270–82.

Strickland, Agnes. *Lives of the Seven Bishops Committed to the Tower in 1688 . . .* London, 1866.

Stone, George Cameron. *A Glossary of the Construction, Decoration and Use of Arms and Armor in All Countries and in All Times*. New York, 1934.

Stowe, Walter. 'John Croes (1762–1832), First Bishop of New Jersey (1815–1832)'. *HMPEC* 35 (1966): 221–30.

Sutherland, E. S. S. *Dibdin and the English Establishment*. Durham, N.C., 1995.

Sweet, William Warren. *The Methodist Episcopal Church and the Civil War*. Cincinnati, 1912.

Sykes, Norman. *Church and State in England in the XVIIIth Century*. 1934; repr., Hamden, Conn., 1962.

_____. *Edmund Gibson, Bishop of London 1660–1748*. Oxford, 1926.

Tackett, Timothy. *Priest and Parish in Eighteenth-Century France*. Princeton, 1977.

Tarrant, Jacqueline. 'The Clementine Decrees on the Beguines: Conciliar and Papal Versions'. *Archivum historiae pontificiae* 12 (1974): 300–308.

_____. 'The Manuscripts of the Constitutiones Clementinae. Part I: Admont to München'. *ZRG KA* 70 (1984): 67–133

Tellenbach, Gerd. *Church, State and Christian Society at the Time of the Investiture Contest*. R. F. Bennett, tr. Oxford, 1940.

Thomas, Albert. 'Robert Smith (1732–1801), First Bishop of South Carolina (1795–1801)'. *HMPEC* 15 (1946): 15–29.

Thomas, Hugh. *The Spanish Civil War.* Rev. ed. New York, 1977.

Thomassin, Louis. *Ancienne et nouvelle discipline de l'église.* New ed., rev. M. André. 7 vols. Bar-le-Duc, 1864–67.

Thompson, Augustine, O.P. 'The Afterlife of an Error: Hunting in the Decretalists (1190–1348)'. *SC* 33 (1999): 151–68.

Thompson, E. A. *The Goths in Spain.* Oxford, 1969.

Townsend, George. *The Life and Defence of the Conduct and Principles of the Venerable and Calumniated Edmund Bonner . . .* London, 1842.

Tucker, Phillip. *The Confederacy's Fighting Chaplain. Father John B. Bannon.* Tuscaloosa, 1992.

Tyerman, Christopher. *The Invention of the Crusades.* Toronto-Buffalo, 1998.

Ullman, Walter. *The Origins of the Great Schism.* 1948; repr., New York, 1967.

Valencia, Ambrosio de, O.F.M.Cap. *Los Capuchinos de Andalucia en la guerra de la independencia.* Seville, 1910.

Vanderpol, A. *Le droit de guerre d'après les théologiens et les canonistes du moyen-age.* Paris, 1911.

Van Tyne, Claude. 'Influence of the Clergy, and of Religion and of Sectarian Forces, on the American Revolution'. *American Historical Review* 19 (1913–14): 44–64.

Velde, Lewis Vander. *The Presbyterian Churches and the Federal Union 1861–1869.* Cambridge, Mass., 1932.

Vodola, Elizabeth. *Excommunication in the Middle Ages.* Berkeley-Los Angeles, 1986.

Watters, Mary. *A History of the Church in Venezuela, 1810–1930.* Chapel Hill, 1933.

Wedgwood, C. V. *The Thirty Years War.* Garden City, 1961.

Weigand, Rudolf. 'Magister Rolandus und Papst Alexander III'. *Archiv für Katholisches Kirchenrecht* 149 (1980): 3–44.

Welsby, Paul. *George Abbot. The Unwanted Archbishop 1562–1633.* London, 1962.

Whittow, Mark. 'Ruling the Late Roman and Early Byzantine City: A Continuous History'. *Past and Present* 129 (Nov. 1990): 3–29.

Wigfield, W. McDonald. *The Monmouth Rebellion.* Totowa, N.J., 1980.

Wight, Willard E. 'The Churches and the Confederate Cause'. *Civil War History* 6 (1960): 361–73.

_____.'War Letters of the Bishop of Richmond'.' *Virginia Magazine of History and Biography* 67 (1959): 259–70.

Wilkinson, Alan. *The Church of England and the First World War.* London, 1978.

Williams, George H. 'Stanislas Hosius'. In Jill Rait, ed., *Shapers of Religious Traditions in Germany, Switzerland, and Poland, 1560–1600.* New Haven, 1981.

Wilshire, Leland. 'Boniface of Savoy, Carthusian and Archbishop of Canterbury'. *Analecta Cartusiana* 31 (1977): 1–89.

Winroth, Anders. *The Making of Gratian's Decretum.* Cambridge, 2000.

Workman, Herbert B. *John Wyclif. A Study of the Medieval English Church.* 2 vols. Oxford, 1926.

Young, Charles R. *Hubert Walter, Lord of Canterbury and Lord of England.* Durham, N.C., 1968.

Zagorin, Perez. *Rebels and Rulers, 1500–1660.* 2 vols. Cambridge, 1982.

INDEX

Abbreviations used here: abp=archbishop, bp=bishop, k=king, q=queen

Printed and bound by CPI Group (UK) Ltd, Croydon, CR0 4YY

09/06/2025

14685695-0001